HIGHER 11–14 MATHEMATICS

Revision and Practice

Peter McGuire

Ken Smith

OXFORD

OXFORD
UNIVERSITY PRESS

Great Clarendon Street, Oxford OX2 6DP

Oxford University Press is a department of the University of Oxford. It furthers the University's objective of excellence in research, scholarship, and education by publishing worldwide in

Oxford   New York

Auckland Cape Town Dar es Salaam Hong Kong Karachi
Kuala Lumpur Madrid Melbourne Mexico City Nairobi
New Delhi Shanghai Taipei Toronto

With offices in

Argentina Austria Brazil Chile Czech Republic France
Greece Guatemala Hungary Italy Japan Poland Portugal
Singapore South Korea Switzerland Thailand Turkey
Ukraine Vietnam

Oxford is a registered trade mark of Oxford University Press in the UK and in certain other countries

© Peter McGuire and Ken Smith 2000

The moral rights of the author have been asserted

Database right Oxford University Press (maker)

First published 2000

All rights reserved. No part of this publication may be reproduced, stored in a retrieval system, or transmitted, in any form or by any means, without the prior permission in writing of Oxford University Press, or as expressly permitted by law, or under terms agreed with the appropriate reprographics rights organisation. Enquiries concerning reproduction outside the scope of the above should be sent to the Rights Department, Oxford University Press, at the above address

You must not circulate this book in any other binding or cover and you must impose this same condition on any acquirer

British Library Cataloguing in Publication Data

Data available

ISBN-13: 978-0-19-914782-5
ISBN-10: 0-19-914782-5

10 9 8

Typeset in Great Britain by Tech-Set Ltd
Printed in Great Britain by Ashford Colour Press Ltd, Gosport.

About this book

This book is designed to help you achieve your best result in the National Tests at the end of Key Stage 3. It targets the 5 – 7 tier of entry.

The book also contains some extension material at **Level 8**. This content is clearly marked with an asterisk (*).

How to use this book
The units in this book are arranged in the same order as the National Curriculum so you can be sure it covers everything you need to know.

Use the **contents list** on the next page or the **index** at the end of the book to find the material you want.

The book provides:

Key information highlighted so you can see the important information at a glance, for example:

▶ To **multiply** a number by 10 move all the digits 1 place to the **left**.

Worked examples showing the techniques you need to be able to use.

Plenty of questions so you can practise the techniques. The exercises are differentiated helping you to build up your skills and allowing you to revisit topics. The **A** exercises are more straightforward than the **B** exercises.

Investigations. There are seven investigations in the book to help you practise your Using and Applying Maths skills. They can be found on pages 28, 60, 83, 134, 195, 205 and 256.

Revision exercises at the end of each unit to help you identify areas of weakness so you can see what you need to revise. The **Review** column points you to the relevant material in the chapter.

Practice SATS papers at the end of the book. They mirror the types of question you will be asked in the actual test and so provide practice for the real thing.

Answers to the exercises are provided in a separate answer book: ISBN 0 19 914568 7.

Contents

1	**NUMBERS AND THE NUMBER SYSTEM**	**1 - 28**
1.1	Integers - multiplying and dividing	1
1.2	Rounding to the nearest 10, 100, 1000, . . .	3
1.3	Directed numbers	4
1.4	The four operations with directed numbers	5
1.5	Multiplying and dividing with indices	7
1.6	Standard form	8
1.7	Factors, common factors, multiples and primes	10
1.8	Square and cube numbers	12
1.9	Finding square or cube roots	13
1.10	To simplify a fraction to its lowest terms	14
1.11	Equivalent fractions	15
1.12	Ordering and comparing fractions	16
1.13	Decimals	16
1.14	Converting a fraction to a decimal	18
1.15	Rounding to n decimal places	20
1.16	Ratio	21
1.17	Equivalent ratios and ratios in their lowest terms	23
1.18	Direct proportion	24
	Revision Exercise 1	25

Investigation: In the frame — 28

2	**NUMBER CALCULATIONS**	**29 - 60**
2.1	Non-calculator multiplication of integers	29
2.2	Non-calculator division of integers	30
2.3	Calculating with integers of any size	31
2.4	Using brackets and the order of operations	33
2.5	Finding a fraction of an amount	36
2.6	One number as a fraction of another	37
2.7	Adding fractions	38
2.8	Subtracting fractions	39
2.9	Multiplying fractions	40
2.10	Dividing fractions	41
2.11	Simple percentages of an amount	42
2.12	Finding any percentage of an amount	44
2.13	Converting fractions and percentages	45
2.14	Percentage increase	46
2.15	Percentage decrease	47
2.16	Percentage problems	48
2.17	Simple interest	49
2.18	Compound interest	50
2.19	Working with ratios	51
2.20	Adding and subtracting decimals	53
2.21	Multiplying and dividing decimals	55
2.22	The effect of multiplying or dividing by numbers less than one	57
	Revision Exercise 2	58

Investigation: The stamp machine — 60

3	**EQUATIONS, FORMULAE AND IDENTITIES**	**61 - 83**
3.1	Collecting like terms	61
3.2	Brackets in algebra*	62
3.3	Simple factorising*	64
3.4	Solving an equation by balancing	66
3.5	Equations with unknowns on both sides	67

3.6	Solving equations with fractions	68
3.7	Solving equations with brackets	70
3.8	Solving equations by trial and improvement	71
3.9	Substituting in formulae*	72
3.10	Constructing formulae	74
3.11	Changing the subject of formulae*	76
3.12	Simultaneous equations	78
	Revision Exercise 3	**80**

Investigation: Side totals   **83**

4	**SEQUENCES, FUNCTIONS AND GRAPHS**	**84 - 110**
4.1	Sequences from patterns	84
4.2	Continuing a sequence	85
4.3	Finding a rule for a sequence	86
4.4	Quadratic sequences*	87
4.5	Graphs from sequences*	88
4.6	Coordinates in all four quadrants	90
4.7	Simple line graphs	91
4.8	Drawing linear graphs	92
4.9	Everyday linear graphs*	96
4.10	Graphs of distance, time and speed*	98
4.11	More complex distance/time graphs*	99
4.12	Graphs of vessels filling*	102
4.13	Inequalities	103
4.14	Inequalities with two variables*	105
	Revision Exercise 4	**106**

5	**GEOMETRICAL REASONING**	**110 - 134**
5.1	Facts about angles	110
5.2	Bearings	113
5.3	The angle sum of a triangle	116
5.4	Types of triangle	117
5.5	Congruent triangles	119
5.6	The exterior angles of a triangle	119
5.7	Quadrilaterals	121
5.8	Angles in polygons	123
5.9	Pythagoras' theorem	124
5.10	Faces, edges and vertices	126
5.11	Drawing 3-D shapes	127
5.12	Plans and elevations	130
	Revision Exercise 5	**132**

Investigation: On the surface   **134**

6	**TRANSFORMATIONS AND COORDINATES**	**135 - 161**
6.1	Line symmetry	135
6.2	Rotational symmetry	137
6.3	Plane symmetry	138
6.4	Reflection	139
6.5	Rotation	141
6.6	Translation	143
6.7	Enlargement	144
6.8	Scale and scale drawing	148
6.9	Similar shapes*	150
6.10	Using trigonometry to find sides and angles*	152
	Revision Exercise 6	**157**

7	**MEASURES AND CONSTRUCTION**	**161 - 195**
7.1	Metric and Imperial measure	161
7.2	Compound units/measures	163
7.3	Constructing regular polygons	164
7.4	Constructing triangles and quadrilaterals	165
7.5	Bisecting angles and lines	169
7.6	To construct a perpendicular from a point to a line	171
7.7	Congruent triangles*	171
7.8	The perimeter of 2-D shapes	173
7.9	The area of 2-D shapes	175
7.10	Formulae for length area and volume*	178
7.11	Nets of cuboids and similar solids	179
7.12	Nets of prisms and pyramids	182
7.13	The language of the circle	183
7.14	To calculate the area of a circle	186
7.15	Volume	187
7.16	Surface area	189
7.17	Loci	191
	Revision exercise 7	**193**

Investigation: Aromatic pyramid   **195**

8	**PLANNING AND COLLECTING DATA**	**196 - 205**
8.1	Collecting data	196
8.2	Frequency tables	199
8.3	Questionnaires	202
	Revision Exercise 8	**204**

Investigation: A private sale   **205**

9	**REPRESENTING AND INTERPRETING DATA**	**206 - 241**
9.1	Frequency diagrams	206
9.2	Line graphs	209
9.3	Pie charts	212
9.4	Scatter diagrams	219
9.5	Cumulative frequency graphs*	223
9.6	Stem-and-leaf plots	225
9.7	Average values	227
9.8	Comparing data*	232
9.9	Working with grouped data*	234
	Revision Exercise 9	**239**

10	**EXPERIMENTS AND PROBABILITY**	**242 - 256**
10.1	Simple probability	242
10.2	Experimental probability	245
10.3	Relative frequency	247
10.4	Sample space diagrams	248
10.5	Tree diagrams	250
10.6	Probabilities from two events*	251
10.7	Dependent and independent events*	253
	Revision exercise 10	**254**

Investigation: Dicey money   **256**

SATS Paper 1 – Non-calculator   **257 – 260**
SATS Paper 2 – Calculator allowed   **261 – 264**

Index   **265 – 266**

1 NUMBERS AND THE NUMBER SYSTEM

1.1 Integers – multiplying and dividing

▶ To **multiply** a number by 10 all the digits move 1 place to the **left**.
To multiply by 100 all the digits move 2 places to the left.

Example 1 $745 \times 100 = 74\,500$

▶ To **divide** a number by 10 the digits move 1 place to the **right**.

Example 2 $8650 \div 10 = 865$

To divide by 100 all the digits move 2 places to the right.

▶ To multiply or divide by numbers such as 20, 600 or 5000 break down the multiplier or divisor into smaller parts.

Example 3   Calculate 14×300
This is the same as $14 \times 3 \times 100 = 42 \times 100 = 4200$

Example 4   Calculate $15\,600 \div 40$
This is the same as $15\,600 \div 4 \div 10 = 3900 \div 10 = 390$

Exercise 1.1A

1 What is the value of the bold digit in each of these numbers?
   a **2**453   **b** 1**5**383   **c** 7**3**492   **d** 18**4**623
   e **6**283 465 **f** 2**8**47 345 **g** 1**8**365 426 **h** 1 9**5**4 683

   Hint:
   1 million is 1 000 000

2 **a** Make the largest number you can using all the digits 0, 6, 2, 5, 7, 3.
   b Make the smallest number you can.

3 Calculate:
   a 7×1000 **b** 20×100 **c** 164×10 **d** $5620 \times 100\,000$

4 Divide 43 000 000 by:
   a 100   **b** 1000   **c** 10 000   **d** 1 million

5 Multiply 230 by 1 million.

6 Which is smaller: $784\,000 \div 100$ or $78\,400\,000 \div 100\,000$?

7 Which is larger: 200×100 or $20 \times 10\,000$? Explain why.

8 Divide 450 000 by 100. Give your answer in words.

9 The digit 4 in 1432 is worth 4 hundreds.
   What is the digit 4 worth when 1432 is multiplied by 100?

10 Calculate the answers to each of these:
   a 17×20
   b 3×7000
   c 44×300
   d 12×80
   e 173×50
   f 34×400
   g $140 \div 20$
   h $8000 \div 400$
   i $69\,000 \div 3000$
   j $18\,000 \div 60$
   k $1500 \div 30$
   l $7000 \div 200$

11 Calculate $126\,000 \times 50 \div 400$.

Exercise 1.1B

1 Find the number from these hints:
   It has more than 168 hundreds. It has fewer than 17 thousands. It contains the digits 8, 6, 1, 9, 2, 5 and it has an even number of tens.

2 When a number is multiplied by 10 the answer is two hundred thousand. What is the number?

3 A number becomes 6 million when multiplied by 100. What is the number?

4 A curb stone is 120 cm long. Give the total length of:
   a 100 stones
   b 10 000 stones
   c 1000 stones

5 There are 1000 millimetres in a metre. How many millimetres in:
   a 14 metres
   b 960 metres
   c 6007 metres?

6 Mike multiplies 45 by 10 six times.
   Julie gets the same answer as Mike by multiplying 45 by a number once. What number did Julie multiply by?

7 Multiply one hundred and seventy thousand by ten thousand. Give your answer in digits.

8 Divide 120 000 000 by 10, then the answer by 100 and then by 1000. Give the answer in words.

9 Divide 59 million by one hundred thousand.

10 Dave plans to cycle from Aberdeen to Penzance which is 700 miles. He can average 80 miles a day. How many days should he allow for his trip?

11 The Sun is 93 000 000 miles from us. Manchester to London is 200 miles. How many times further is the Sun from us than Manchester is from London?

12 An old ton was 20 hundredweight.
   How many hundredweight were in 734 tons?

13 I think of a number.
   My number is greater than 83 000 ÷ 200 but less than 14 × 30.
   List any numbers I could be thinking of.

14 Make the largest number you can from the digits
   0, 0, 6, 4, 0, 7, 0.
   Divide it by the largest number you can make from 0, 4, 0.
   Give your answer in words.

1.2 Rounding to the nearest 10, 100, 1000, ...

▶ To round a number to the nearest 10 look at the digit in the units position. If it is 5 or above then round up the tens digit.

Example 1   Round 1647 to the nearest 10.

   1647

So 1647 rounded to the nearest 10 is **1650**.

Yes! 7 is 5 or above. So round **up** the tens digit from 4 to 5.

▶ To round a number to the nearest 100 look at the digit in the tens position.

Example 2   Round 1647 to the nearest 100.

   1647

So round down to **1600**.

No! 4 is not 5 or above. So **do not** round up the hundreds digit from 6 to 7.

Exercise 1.2A

1 Round each number to the nearest 10.
   a 124   **b** 1509   **c** 6358   **d** 547 864   **e** 173 599

2 Round each number to the nearest 100.
   a 7364   **b** 8339   **c** 183 999   **d** 86 909

3 Round each number to the nearest 1000.
   a 1638   **b** 7288   **c** 12 975   **d** 65 995

4 Round 127 484 to:
   a the nearest 10   **b** the nearest 100   **c** the nearest 1000

5 Round 17 384 429 to the nearest million.

6 Round seven million, two hundred and fifty three thousand, four hundred and six to the nearest hundred thousand.

Exercise 1.2B

1. What is 77 rounded to the nearest 100?

2. **a** Round 12 999 to the nearest 10, nearest 100 and nearest 1000.
   b What do you notice?

3. George did a survey of passenger numbers on each of the route N54 buses.
   He rounded each figure to the nearest hundred people.
   Why was his survey not a great success?

4. A number is rounded to the nearest 10 and the answer is 120.
   a What is the largest number it could be?
   b What is the smallest number it could be?

5. Rounded to the nearest thousand the number of trees in a park is 12 000. What is the largest number of trees there could be in the park?

6. Explain why it is not sensible to round the population of each town in Wales to the nearest million.
   What would be a sensible rounding?

1.3 Directed numbers

A number line orders numbers.

For ⁻3:

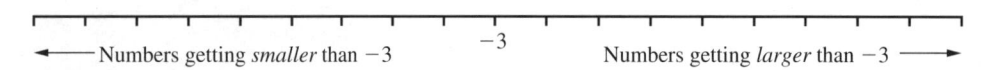

⟵ Numbers getting *smaller* than −3   −3   Numbers getting *larger* than −3 ⟶

Numbers *smaller* than ⁻3 are: ⁻4, ⁻5, ⁻6, ⁻7, ⁻8, … all numbers to the *left*.
Numbers *larger* than ⁻3 are: ⁻2, ⁻1, 0, 1, 2, 3, … all numbers to the *right*.

You can use shifts on a number line to calculate with numbers.

Example
What number is 5 less than 3?

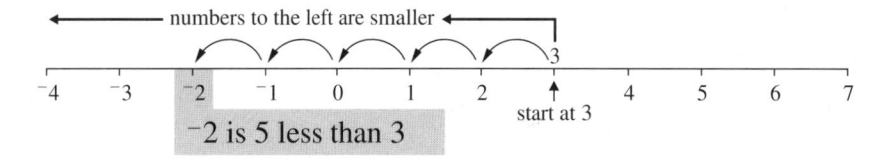

⟵ numbers to the left are smaller ⟵

⁻4　⁻3　⁻2　⁻1　0　1　2　3　4　5　6　7

start at 3

⁻2 is 5 less than 3

Exercise 1.3A

1 Order each set of numbers. Start with the smallest.
  a 5, ⁻3, 1, ⁻2, ⁻1, ⁻4
  b ⁻4, 2, ⁻1, 3, ⁻5, 4
  c 0, 3, ⁻7, 1, ⁻1, ⁻2

2 Which of these is smaller than ⁻3?
  a ⁻2   **b** 0   **c** 3   **d** ⁻5
  e 4   **f** ⁻4   **g** 1   **h** ⁻7

3 For each number give the value that is 7 more.
  a ⁻5   **b** 0   **c** ⁻8   **d** ⁻1   **e** 3   **f** ⁻11

4 For each number give the value that is 5 less.
  a 4   **b** ⁻2   **c** ⁻5   **d** 0   **e** ⁻8   **f** 9

Exercise 1.3B

1 Order each set of numbers. Start with the largest.
  a 3, ⁻4, ⁻1, 0, 5, ⁻6, 1
  b 4, ⁻11, 3, ⁻3, 0, 1, ⁻2
  c 0, ⁻12, 1, ⁻6, ⁻3, ⁻7, ⁻9

2 Which of these is larger than ⁻5?
  a ⁻9   **b** ⁻14   **c** 2   **d** ⁻3
  e 0   **f** ⁻4   **g** 1   **h** ⁻1

3 Copy and complete this table.

8 less than start number	Start number	6 more than start number
	⁻3	
	1	
	⁻8	
	3	

1.4 The four operations with directed numbers

Adding directed numbers

This can be seen as shifts on a number line or as a mental task.
For example:

$$^-4 + 5 = 1$$
$$^-6 + -8 = {^-14}$$

Subtracting directed numbers

You can use similar approaches to addition.
For example:

$$^-8 - 12 = {^-20}$$

6 Numbers and the number system

▶ Subtracting a negative number has the same effect as adding the same positive number.
For example:
$$^-9 - ^-23$$
$$= ^-9 + 23 = 14$$

Multiplying directed numbers

▶ When you multiply two numbers, if the signs are the same then the answer will be positive, but if the signs are different then the answer will be negative.
For example:
$$^-8 \times ^-5 = 40$$
$$^-12 \times 5 = ^-60$$

Dividing directed numbers

The rule for dividing is the same as for multiplying.
For example:
$$^-88 \div 11 = ^-8$$
$$^-45 \div ^-9 = 5$$

Exercise 1.4A

1 Work out:
a $^-8 + ^-15$
b $^-6 + 3 + 22$
c $^-5 + ^-6 + 18$
d $^-16 + ^-8 - 5$
e $^-8 + 15 - 7 + 22$
f $^-4 + ^-8 + ^-12 + 5$
g $^-6 + ^-5 - 17 - ^-8$
h $^-15 - ^-4 + 3 - 21$
i $^-17 + 14 + ^-8 - 5$

2 Work out:
a $^-9 \times ^-4$
b $^-6 \times 7$
c $^-4 \times ^-3 \times 2$
d $^-6 \times ^-5 \times ^-8$
e $^-16 \div 4$
f $^-24 \div ^-3 \times 5$
g $^-21 \div ^-3 \times 8 \times ^-1$
h $^-125 \div 5 \times ^-4$

Exercise 1.4B

1 Work out:
a $^-8 - 4$
b $^-16 + 21$
c $^-34 + 18 - 6$
d $^-56 - 62 + 38 + 7$
e $125 - 188 + 3 - 26$
f $^-67 + 13 - ^-55$
g $34 - 157 - ^-88 - 25$
h $32 - 156 + ^-8 - ^-85$
i $17 - 135 + 22 - ^-67$

2 Work out:
a $^-17 \times 12$
b $13 \times ^-15$
c $23 \times ^-16$
d $^-6 \times ^-5 \times ^-18$
e $56 \div ^-8 \times 3$
f $^-27 \div ^-9 \times 13$
g $^-144 \div ^-16 \div ^-3$
h $^-165 \div 5 \times 32$
i $^-84 \div ^-7 \times 14$
j $63 \div ^-9 \times 25$
k $96 \div ^-16 \div 6$
l $200 \div ^-25 \times ^-3$

1.5 Multiplying and dividing with indices

▶ 3^4 is an index number

3 is the base, 4 is the index

$$3^4 = 3 \times 3 \times 3 \times 3$$

▶ To multiply index numbers with the same **base**, you **add** the indices.

Example 1
Express $8^2 \times 8^3$ as a single index number.

$8^2 = 8 \times 8$ and $8^3 = 8 \times 8 \times 8$
So $8^2 \times 8^3 = 8^5$ $(8 \times 8 \times 8 \times 8 \times 8)$

▶ To divide index numbers with the same base you **subtract** the indices.

Example 2
Express $5^8 \div 5^2$ as a single index number.

$5^8 \div 5^2 = 5^6$ (subtract the indices: $8 - 2 = 6$)

> When you subtract the indices you may get a negative index, e.g. $5^4 \div 5^7 = 5^{-3}$

Exercise 1.5A

1 Express as a single index number:
  a $3^2 \times 3^5$ **b** $4^5 \times 4^4$ **c** $2^5 \times 2^7$ **d** $4^5 \times 4^2$ **e** $4^9 \times 4^5$

2 Express as a single index number:
  a $5^6 \div 5^3$ **b** $6^9 \div 6^3$ **c** $7^{12} \div 7^4$ **d** $3^{15} \div 3^5$ **e** $9^8 \div 9^7$

3 Express as a single index number:
  a $3^5 \div 3^2 \times 3$ **b** $7^3 \div 7 \times 7^5$ **c** $5^4 \div 5^2 \times 5$ **d** $10 \times 10^4 \div 10^3$

> **Hint:**
> 3 is the same as 3^1.

4 Find the missing indices.
  a $3^3 \times 3^\square = 3^{15}$ **b** $2^\square \times 2^2 = 2^6$ **c** $3^4 \times 3^\square = 3^8$ **d** $2^\square \times 2^5 = 2^8$
  e $8^{15} \div 8^\square = 8^3$ **f** $3^\square \div 3^4 = 3^3$ **g** $4^{20} \div 4^\square = 4^4$ **h** $6^\square \div 6^3 = 6^{12}$

Exercise 1.5B

1 Express as a single index number:
  a $3^5 \times 3^2 \times 3^4 \times 3$ **b** $5^2 \times 5^6 \times 5^5 \times 5^3$ **c** $7^{14} \times 7^4 \times 7^2 \times 7^5$
  d $3^2 \times 3^5 \div 3^4$ **e** $4^5 \div 4 \div 4^2$ **f** $2^3 \times 4^2 \times 8$

2 Find the missing indices:
  a $2^6 \times 2^{-3} = 2^\square$ **b** $3^5 \times 3^{-5} \times 3^3 = 3^\square$ **c** $4^{-3} \times 4^{-2} \times 4^5 \times 4 = 4^\square$
  d $3^5 \times 3^4 \div 3^\square = 3^7$ **e** $2^2 \times 2 \div 2^4 \times 2^\square = 2^2$ **f** $5^\square \times 5^2 \times 5 \div 5^5 = 5^0$
  g $3^4 \div 3^\square \times 3^2 = 3^6$ **h** $4^3 \times 4^3 \times 4^\square \div 4 = 4$ **i** $4^3 \times 8^2 \div 2^5 = 2^\square$

1.6 Standard form

You can use standard form to write very large or very small numbers.

▶ A number in standard form is

a number between 1 and 10 × a power of 10

> Standard form may be called:
> standard index form.

Example 1
The distance from the Sun to the Earth is about 150 000 000 km. Write this distance in standard form.

$$150\,000\,000 = 1.5 \times 100\,000\,000$$
$$= 1.5 \times 10^8 \quad [1.5 \text{ is between 1 and 10}]$$

To write very small numbers in standard form, first notice that dividing by a positive index is the same as multiplying by a negative index:

$$10^9 \div 10^6 = 10^3$$
$$10^9 \times 10^{-6} = 10^3$$

These are equivalent operations.

Example 2
Write 0.000 001 25 in standard form.

$$0.000\,001\,25 = 1.25 \times 10^{-6}$$

Example 3
Calculate $(5.4 \times 10^6) \times (6.1 \times 10^5)$ giving your answer in standard form.

$$5.4 \times 10^6 \times 6.1 \times 10^5 = 5.4 \times 6.1 \times 10^{11}$$
$$= 32.94 \times 10^{11}$$
$$= 3.294 \times 10^{12}$$

Exercise 1.6A

1 Write each of these numbers in standard form:
- **a** 25 000
- **b** 265 000
- **c** 25 000 000
- **d** 345 000 000
- **e** 65 650 000 000
- **f** 10 405 000 000

2 Write each of these numbers in standard form:
- **a** 0.0125
- **b** 0.000 026 5
- **c** 0.100 54
- **d** 0.000 000 155
- **e** 0.000 040 5
- **f** 0.000 000 000 122

3 Write each of these as ordinary numbers:
- **a** 3.65×10^4
- **b** 1.725×10^6
- **c** 6.075×10^5
- **d** 8.104×10^9
- **e** 3.565×10^3
- **f** 2.85×10^{12}

4 Write each of these as ordinary numbers:
 a 2.62×10^{-4} b 1.05×10^{-7} c 3×10^{-8}
 d 7.65×10^{-11} e 8.45×10^{-9} f 5.375×10^{-7}

5 Write each of these statements using standard form.
 a The diameter of Mercury is about 5 470 100 yards.
 b The diameter of Mars is about 22 271 000 feet.
 c One second is about 0.0028 hour.

6 Calculate each of these giving your answer in standard form.
 a $(3.5 \times 10^4) \times (7.6 \times 10^8)$ b $(3.7 \times 10^5) \times (6.4 \times 10^{-2})$

Exercise 1.6B

1 Write each of these numbers in standard form:
 a 75 800 000 b 107 500 000 c 878 500 000 000
 d 0.000 000 010 2 e 0.002 07 f 0.000 000 001 055 65

2 Write each of these as an ordinary number:
 a 2.75×10^4 b 3.165×10^8 c 4.075×10^7
 d 7.1065×10^{-3} e 5.1024×10^{-9} f 1.025×10^{-11}

3 Rewrite this replacing each number with a value in standard form.
 The rig was producing 35 million barrels of oil every six months or so. The company itself was making profits of $344.5 million each year employing some 168 500 people worldwide. This all came to an end when a 0.000 12 mm crack appeared in a vital section of pipe.

4 The speed of light is about 3×10^5 km/s. The distance from the Sun to the Earth is about 1.5×10^8 km. About how long does light take to reach the Earth from the Sun?

5 A ream of paper is 500 sheets.
 Each sheet in the ream is 0.000 087 metres thick.
 a Write 500 and 0.000 087 in standard form.
 b Use your answers to part **a** to calculate the height of one ream of this paper.

6 A molecule of carbon dioxide CO_2 has two atoms of oxygen and one of carbon. The mass of an oxygen atom is about 2.66×10^{-23}, and a carbon atom is about 2×10^{-23}. Calculate the mass of one molecule of CO_2.

1.7 Factors, common factors, multiples and primes

▶ The **factors** of a number are whole numbers that divide exactly into it.

For example:
The **factors** of 20 are: 1, 2, 4, 5, 10, 20
The **factors** of 35 are: 1, 5, 7, 35

Some factors of 20 and 35 are the same.
These are known as the **common factors**.
The **common factors** of 20 and 35 are: 1 and 5
The HCF (**highest common factor**) of 20 and 35 is: 5

▶ Factors and multiples are linked:
if 3 is a factor of a number, then that number is a **multiple** of 3.

     3, 6, 9, 12, 15, 18, 21, 24, 27, 30, 33, 36, 39, 42, ..., ... are
all **multiples** of 3.

The 15th multiple of 3 is $15 \times 3 = 45$.
                            3 is a **factor** of 45, so 45 is a **multiple** of 3.

Multiples may be **common**: 12, 24, 36, and 48 are all **common multiples** of 3 and 4.
The LCM (**lowest common multiple**) of 3 and 4 is 12.

> The LCM of two or more numbers is the smallest number into which they will all divide exactly.

▶ Prime numbers are numbers which have only two different factors.
The first four **prime** numbers are: 2   (factors 1 and 2)
                                       3   (factors 1 and 3)
                                       5   (factors 1 and 5)
                                       7   (factors 1 and 7)

For any number you can find its **prime factors** and write it as a product of primes.

> The product of two or more numbers is the answer to multiplying them. The product of 2, 3 and 4 is $2 \times 3 \times 4 = 24$.

Example
a Find the prime factors of 72.
b Write 72 as a product of primes.

a • Break 72 into factors $72 = 12 \times 6$
    • Break down each factor $72 = 3 \times 4 \times 3 \times 2$
       until only prime numbers remain $72 = 3 \times 2 \times 2 \times 3 \times 2$
         The prime factors of 72 are: 2 and 3.

b As a product of primes: $72 = 3 \times 2 \times 2 \times 3 \times 2$
                                     $= 3 \times 3 \times 2 \times 2 \times 2$
                                     $= 3^2 \times 2^3$

> The prime factors are simply the factors that are prime numbers.

> You can use indices as a type of shorthand when you write a product of primes.

Exercise 1.7A

1. List all the factors of: **a** 36   **b** 120

2. **a** List all the factors of 75.
   b List all the factors of 90.
   c Find the HCF of 75 and 90.

3. **a** What is the 6th multiple of 8?
   b Find the 9th multiple of 7.

4. Which of these is a multiple of 9:   19, 24, 27, 45, 56, 63?

5. **a** List the first eight multiples of 6.
   b List the first eleven multiples of 7.
   c Which number less than 45 is a multiple of 6 and 7?

6. Find the LCM of 7 and 12.

7. List the first ten prime numbers.

8. List all the prime numbers between 30 and 70.

9. Which prime number is closest to 150?

10. Find the prime factors of:
    a 42   **b** 36   **c** 50   **d** 90   **e** 65

11. **a** What are the prime factors of 96?
    b Write 96 as a product of primes. Use indices in your answer.

12. Write each of these as a product of primes:
    a 150   **b** 240   **c** 375

Exercise 1.7B

1. List all the factors of 240.

2. **a** List all the factors of 96.
   b List all the factors of 56.
   c Find the HCF of 56 and 96.

3. Add the seventh multiple of 9 to the fifteenth multiple of 5.

4. Subtract the sixth multiple of 9 from the eleventh multiple of 14.

5. **a** What numbers less than 100 are multiples of 3, and 5?
   b What is the LCM of 3 and 5?

6. **a** What numbers less than 150 are multiples of 4, 5, and 6?
   b What is the LCM of 4, 5 and 6?

7. Is it true to say that any multiple of 8 must be a multiple of 4? Explain your answer.

8 Find the sum of all the prime numbers less than 30.

9 Which prime number is closest to 1200?

10 733 is half-way between two prime numbers.
What are the prime numbers?

11 Find the prime factors of:
  a 84   **b** 108   **c** 110   **d** 725   **e** 136

12 Write each of these as a product of primes.
Use indices to give your answers.
  a 108   **b** 200   **c** 450   **d** 1500

13 As a product of primes, a number is given by: $2^5 \times 3^2 \times 5$
What is the number?

1.8 Square and cube numbers

▶ To make a **square** number you multiply a number by itself.
400 is a square number because $20 \times 20 = \mathbf{400}$
You say 'twenty squared' = 400 and write $20^2 = 400$

Note:
1×1 is not equal to 2.

▶ To make a **cube** number you multiply a number by itself three times. **27** is a cube number because $3 \times 3 \times 3 = \mathbf{27}$.

▶ You write 8^3 to mean $8 \times 8 \times 8$. You call it 'eight cubed'.

Example   Find the value of 4^3.

$4^3 = 4 \times 4 \times 4 = \mathbf{64}$

Exercise 1.8A

1 Calculate the value of 6^2.

2 What is the value of the first square number?

3 Calculate the value of 'ten cubed'.

4 Calculate the value of each of these:
  a 7^2 **b** 8^2 **c** 5^3 **d** 1000^2 **e** 10^3
  f 6^3 **g** 17^2 **h** 100^3 **i** 1^3 **j** 40^3

5 What is the value of 'three cubed + four squared'?

6 List the first ten square numbers.

7 List the first seven cube numbers.

8 Calculate $20^3 \div 20^2$.

Exercise 1.8B

1. Which is larger 2^3 or 3^2? Explain your answer.
2. Calculate the value of each of these:
   a 15^2 b 9^3 c 56^2 d 0^3 e 800^3
3. List all the square numbers between 120 and 150.
4. What cube number is greater than 100 but less than 150?
5. Calculate the value of each of these:
   a $4^2 + 5^2 - 2^3$ b $7^2 + 4^3 + 10^2$ c $8^3 - 16^2$
   d $4^2 \times 8^2 \div 2^2$ e $3^3 + 5^3 + 6^3$ f $1000^2 - 10^3$
6. What is the missing number? $5^2 + 12^2 = \square^2$
7. A mystery number is squared to give number A and cubed to give B. When B is divided by A the answer is 14.
   What is the mystery number? Explain how you worked this out.
8. Which is larger and by how much, $7^3 + 8^3$ or $(7 + 8)^3$?

1.9 Finding square or cube roots

▶ Finding a **square root** is the opposite of finding a **square**.

Example 1
Find the square root of 64. $64 = 8 \times 8$ so $\sqrt{64} = 8$

▶ Finding a **cube root** is the opposite of finding a **cube**.

Example 2
Find the cube root of 64. $64 = 4 \times 4 \times 4$ so $\sqrt[3]{64} = 4$

▶ You can find the square or cube root of a number in three different ways:

Example 3: by inspection when you can see the answer.
Find $\sqrt[3]{125}$ Answer = **5**

Hint:
You should remember that $5 \times 5 \times 5 = 125$

Example 4: with a calculator.
Find $\sqrt{3136}$ Press: [3] [1] [3] [6] [√]   Answer = **56**

Example 5: by trial and improvement.
Find $\sqrt[3]{2744}$ Try 10 $10 \times 10 \times 10 = 1000$ – too small
Try 20 $20 \times 20 \times 20 = 8000$ – too large
Try 15 $15 \times 15 \times 15 = 3375$ – a bit too large
Try 14 $14 \times 14 \times 14 = 2744$ – just right
So $\sqrt[3]{2744} = 14$

Exercise 1.9A

1 Find each of these roots by inspection.
   a $\sqrt{25}$ **b** $\sqrt[3]{27}$ **c** $\sqrt{81}$ **d** $\sqrt[3]{1000}$ **e** $\sqrt{169}$

2 Use a calculator to find these roots.
   a $\sqrt{1849}$ **b** $\sqrt{80\,656}$ **c** $\sqrt{15\,129}$
   d $\sqrt[3]{17\,576}$ **e** $\sqrt[3]{5832}$ **f** $\sqrt[3]{29\,791}$

3 Use trial and improvement to find $\sqrt{484}$.

4 Use trial and improvement to find $\sqrt[3]{10\,648}$.

> On some calculators you find $\sqrt[3]{1728}$ like this:
>
> | 1 | 7 | 2 | 8 |
>
> | inv | y^x | 3 | = |
>
> This should give 12.
> Find out your calculator does $\sqrt[3]{1728}$

Exercise 1.9B

1 Use trial and improvement to find $\sqrt{2304}$.

2 Use a calculator to approximate these roots.
   a $\sqrt{66}$ **b** $\sqrt[3]{94}$ **c** $\sqrt{7225}$ **d** $\sqrt[3]{776}$
   e $\sqrt{24\,336}$ **f** $\sqrt[3]{1263}$ **g** $\sqrt{45\,684}$ **h** $\sqrt[3]{88\,888}$

3 a Find $\sqrt{10}$ with your calculator.
   b Square the answer you get. What happens and why is this?

4 Use trial and improvement to find:
   a $\sqrt{1296}$ **b** $\sqrt[3]{1331}$ **c** $\sqrt{1936}$

> The roots of some numbers will have decimal answers.

1.10 To simplify a fraction to its lowest terms

When a fraction is in its lowest terms, the two parts of the fraction have no common factor.

You can simplify a fraction to its lowest terms by dividing top and bottom by their HCF.

> **Remember**
> In the fraction $\frac{3}{4}$
> 3 is the numerator
> 4 is the denominator.

Example

Simplify $\frac{24}{64}$ to its lowest terms.

The factors of 24 are: 1, 2, 3, 4, 6, **8**, 12, 24

The factors of 64 are: 1, 2, 4, **8**, 16, 32, 64   HCF is **8**.

So: $\frac{24 \div 8}{64 \div 8} = \frac{3}{8}$ In its *lowest terms* $\frac{24}{64} = \frac{3}{8}$

Exercise 1.10A

1 Simplify each of these fractions to its lowest terms.

a $\frac{24}{40}$ b $\frac{18}{81}$ c $\frac{12}{32}$ d $\frac{28}{70}$ e $\frac{24}{78}$ f $\frac{30}{70}$ g $\frac{32}{88}$ h $\frac{36}{90}$ i $\frac{20}{72}$ j $\frac{16}{56}$

Exercise 1.10B

1 Simplify each of these fractions to its simplest form.

a $\frac{24}{60}$ b $\frac{32}{72}$ c $\frac{27}{90}$ d $\frac{36}{84}$ e $\frac{45}{60}$ f $\frac{40}{152}$ g $\frac{48}{144}$ h $\frac{56}{105}$ i $\frac{12}{138}$ j $\frac{48}{156}$

1.11 Equivalent fractions

Equivalent fractions use different numbers but have the same value.
For equivalent fractions, multiply both parts of a fraction by the same number.

Example
Find 3 different fractions equivalent to $\frac{3}{5}$.

$\frac{3}{5}$
- multiply both parts by 3 $\frac{3 \times 3}{5 \times 3} = \frac{9}{15}$
- multiply both parts by 4 $\frac{12}{20}$
- multiply both parts by 9 $\frac{27}{45}$

So: $\frac{9}{15}$, $\frac{12}{20}$, and $\frac{27}{45}$ are all equivalent to $\frac{3}{5}$.

Exercise 1.11A

1 Find three different fractions equivalent to:

a $\frac{3}{4}$ b $\frac{2}{5}$ c $\frac{5}{8}$ d $\frac{4}{7}$

2 Show how these fractions are equivalent:

a $\frac{3}{4}$ and $\frac{15}{20}$ b $\frac{5}{12}$ and $\frac{30}{72}$

3 For $\frac{6}{8}$ and $\frac{18}{24}$:
a Give each in its lowest terms.   b Are they equivalent?

Exercise 1.11B

1 Find three different fractions equivalent to:

a $\frac{5}{6}$ b $\frac{7}{10}$ c $\frac{3}{8}$ d $\frac{3}{12}$

2 Show how these fractions are equivalent:

a $\frac{5}{9}$ and $\frac{20}{36}$ b $\frac{7}{12}$ and $\frac{63}{108}$

3 Are equivalent fractions the same in lowest terms?
Explain your answer.

1.12 Ordering and comparing fractions

One way to order fractions is to write them with a common denominator. You can then compare them by looking at the value of the numerator.

> Common denominator means all fractions have the same denominator.

Example
Order these fractions by size, smallest first: $\frac{3}{5}, \frac{2}{3}, \frac{7}{12}, \frac{5}{8}$

The denominators are: 5, 3, 12 and 8 which have an LCM of 120. Write each as an equivalent fraction with a denominator of 120:

$\frac{3}{5} = \frac{72}{120}$ $\frac{2}{3} = \frac{80}{120}$ $\frac{7}{12} = \frac{70}{120}$ and $\frac{5}{8} = \frac{75}{120}$

Compare the numerators. In order of size they are: $\frac{7}{12}, \frac{3}{5}, \frac{5}{8}$ and $\frac{2}{3}$.

> As the denominators are the same the fractions are ordered by their numerators.

Exercise 1.12A

1 Order each set of fractions by size, smallest first.

  a $\frac{3}{4}, \frac{7}{9}, \frac{13}{18}, \frac{7}{12}$ **b** $\frac{5}{6}, \frac{6}{7}, \frac{11}{14}, \frac{19}{21}$ **c** $\frac{13}{15}, \frac{4}{5}, \frac{2}{3}, \frac{7}{9}$

2 Which is smaller $\frac{13}{25}$ or $\frac{11}{20}$? Explain your answer.

Exercise 1.12B

1 Order each set of fractions by size, smallest first.

  a $\frac{7}{8}, \frac{5}{6}, \frac{23}{24}, \frac{11}{12}, \frac{15}{16}$ **b** $\frac{7}{10}, \frac{7}{12}, \frac{5}{6}, \frac{23}{30}$ **c** $\frac{4}{7}, \frac{5}{8}, \frac{11}{14}, \frac{25}{28}$

2 Which is larger $\frac{73}{120}$ or $\frac{29}{40}$? Explain your answer.

1.13 Decimals

▶ You can write the decimal part of a number as a fraction.

Example
Convert 0.225 and 4.32 to fractions in their simplest form.

$0.225 = \frac{225}{1000}$ $4.32 = 4\frac{32}{100}$

$ = \frac{9}{40}$ (dividing by 25) $ = 4\frac{8}{25}$ (dividing by 4)

To order decimals:

- put the decimal points underneath each other.
- arrange the numbers in order. Start with the units, then the tenths, hundredths and so on.

Example
Order these, largest first.

    0.26   1.574   0.045   6   0.58   0.2734

In a table:
```
0 . 2 6 0 0
1 . 5 7 4 0
0 . 0 4 5 0
6 . 0 0 0 0
0 . 5 8 0 0
0 . 2 7 3 4
```

Arranged in order:
```
6 . 0 0 0 0
1 . 5 7 4 0
0 . 5 8 0 0
0 . 2 7 3 4
0 . 2 6 0 0
0 . 0 4 5 0
```

So, in order, the numbers are: 6, 1.574, 0.58, 0.2734, 0.26, 0.045

Exercise 1.13A

1 In 173.296 935 what does the underlined digit mean?

Hint: Simplest form is the same as lowest terms.

2 Convert each decimal to a fraction in its simplest form.
   a 0.6   **b** 0.22   **c** 0.155   **d** 0.45   **e** 0.408

3 Make the smallest decimal number possible from 9, 0, 2, 5, ., 0 and 7.

4 Put these decimals in order, smallest first:
0.6, 0.284, 0.46, 0.5281

5 Put these in order, largest first:
1.062, 0.193 22, 0.02, 0.3, 0.100 04

Exercise 1.13B

1 Convert each decimal to a mixed number in its simplest form.
   a 5.34   **b** 1.8   **c** 9.125
   d 12.306   **e** 17.45   **f** 6.2
   g 6.118   **h** 1.065   **i** 5.256

2 How many times larger is the first underlined digit than the second?
   a 6.46   **b** 24.627   **c** 1.4524

3 Arrange each set of numbers in order, smallest first.
   a 0.039, 8, 0.27, 0.0008, 1.24, 0.0972
   b 0.1, 0.09, 0.28, 0.009 99, 0.0742

18 Numbers and the number system

4 Which widths of letters will pass through a post box slot 0.23 m wide?
0.229 56 m, 0.301 m, 0.209 99 m, 0.291 m, 0.199 935 m, 2.021 m, 0.281 11 m

5 The length of a bolt must lie between 0.0463 m and 0.046 28 m. Which of these lengths fits? 0.0465 m, 0.046 31 m, 0.046 278 m, 0.046 293 m

1.14 Converting a fraction to a decimal

▶ A fraction can be written as a decimal.

To convert a fraction to a decimal divide the numerator by the denominator.

Example 1
Convert $\frac{7}{8}$ to a decimal.

$$\begin{array}{r} 0.875 \\ 8\overline{)7.000} \end{array}$$

So $\frac{7}{8} = 0.875$

▶ You may get a **recurring decimal** as your answer.

Example 2
Convert $\frac{5}{11}$ to a decimal.

$$\begin{array}{r} 0.4\ 5\ 4\ 5\ 4\ 5\ldots \\ 11\overline{)5.\,^50^60^50^60^50^60} \end{array}$$

So $\frac{5}{11} = 0.4545\ldots = 0.\dot{4}\dot{5}$

Remember:
Place dots over the first and last digits that repeat.

▶ To order a mixture of decimals and fractions first write them all as decimals.

Example 3
Order these starting with the smallest.

$\frac{5}{16}$, 0.34, $\frac{7}{24}$, $\frac{1}{3}$, 0.282, $\frac{5}{17}$

Changing them to decimals gives

0.3125, 0.34, 0.291$\dot{6}$, 0.$\dot{3}$, 0.282, 0.2941 ...

So in order, smallest first we have:

0.282, $\frac{7}{24}$, $\frac{5}{17}$, $\frac{5}{16}$, $\frac{1}{3}$, 0.34

Hint:
You should learn the common fractions as decimals e.g. $\frac{3}{4}$, $\frac{1}{2}$, $\frac{1}{10}$, $\frac{2}{10}$, $\frac{3}{10}$ ..., $\frac{1}{100}$, $\frac{2}{100}$, ..., $\frac{1}{5}$, $\frac{2}{5}$, ...

Exercise 1.14A

1 Convert these fractions to decimals.
  a $\frac{5}{8}$ **b** $\frac{3}{4}$ **c** $\frac{3}{20}$
  d $\frac{3}{5}$ **e** $\frac{1}{8}$ **f** $\frac{1}{2}$
  g $\frac{17}{100}$ **h** $\frac{4}{25}$ **i** $\frac{3}{40}$

2 0.13 of a cake went to Sonia, $\frac{3}{8}$ went to Simon and $\frac{7}{20}$ went to Amy. What decimal was left for Andy?

3 Show the full calculator display when you convert these fractions to decimals.
  a $\frac{3}{11}$ **b** $\frac{5}{9}$ **c** $\frac{5}{6}$ **d** $\frac{2}{3}$ **e** $\frac{7}{15}$ **f** $\frac{3}{37}$

4 Write each number in question **3** in shorthand as a recurring decimal.

5 Put these in order, smallest first.
  $\frac{2}{5}$, 0.375, $\frac{17}{45}$, 0.29, $\frac{9}{25}$, $\frac{5}{18}$

6 a By how much in decimals is $\frac{7}{8}$ larger than $\frac{7}{25}$?
  b Write this decimal as a fraction in its simplest form.

Exercise 1.14B

1 Convert each fraction to a decimal, showing any recurring decimals in their shorthand form.
  a $\frac{7}{8}$ **b** $\frac{7}{9}$ **c** $\frac{1}{32}$ **d** $\frac{5}{11}$ **e** $\frac{5}{22}$ **f** $\frac{7}{45}$

2 a Convert $\frac{7}{40}$ to a decimal.
  b Check your answer to part **a** by converting your answer back to a fraction in its simplest form.

3 Put these in order, starting with the smallest.
  $\frac{5}{8}$, 0.6, $\frac{1}{2}$, 0.635, $\frac{2}{3}$, 0.495, $\frac{7}{16}$

4 Put these in order starting with the largest.
  $\frac{3}{4}$, $\frac{57}{79}$, $\frac{189}{250}$, $0.\dot{7}$, $\frac{777}{1000}$, $\frac{31}{40}$

5 Is $\frac{5}{17}$ smaller or larger than $\frac{147}{500}$?

6 a Convert each of these ninths to a recurring decimal.
  $\frac{1}{9}$, $\frac{2}{9}$, $\frac{3}{9}$, $\frac{4}{9}$
  b Use your answers above to help you write $\frac{n}{9}$ as a recurring decimal where n is any digit.

7 a Convert each of these fractions to a recurring decimal.

$\frac{1}{11}, \frac{2}{11}, \frac{3}{11}, \frac{4}{11}$

b Use your answers to predict what $\frac{5}{11}$ will be.

Now check your answer.

c Describe any patterns you see in fractions with 11 as the denominator.

8 The 13ths give recurring decimals but the recurring part is too long to see on most calculators.

a Give the calculator display when each of these is converted to a decimal.

$\frac{1}{13}, \frac{2}{13}, \frac{3}{13}, \frac{4}{13}$

b By using your calculator and looking at your answers to part **a** write $\frac{7}{13}$ as a recurring decimal showing the full recurring part.

1.15 Rounding

Measurements are not exact. They are rounded to a certain degree of accuracy.

▶ To round a number to a certain number of decimal places look at the digit immediately to the right of this number of places.

▶ The first non-zero figure in a number to the first **significant figure** (sf). For example: The first significant figure in each of these numbers is 5:

567 123, 51.05, 0.000 521 6, 5000.001 23

Example 1
Round 146.278 49 correct to: **a** 3 decimal places (3 dp), **b** to 2 sf.

a 146.278 49 rounds **down** to 146.278 because 4 is not 5 or above.

b The first two significant figures are 1 and 4.
The 3rd is 6 so it rounds up. 146.278 9 = 150 (to 2 sf).

Example 2
Round 0.0486 correct to: **a** 1 decimal place, **b** 1 sf.

a 0.0486 rounds **down** to 0.0 (to 1 dp).

b In 0.0486 the first significant figure is 4.
The second significant figure is 8.
So 0.0486 = 0.05 (to 1 sf).

Note:
0.0 is not the same as 0.

Exercise 1.15A

1 Round each of these numbers to 2 decimal places.
   a 3.243   **b** 16.2649   **c** 12.417 32
   d 0.0452   **e** 1.3092   **f** 0.006 24

2 Round each number to 1 sf.
   a 543.75   **b** 0.921   **c** 354.625

3 Round 164.278 357 to:
   a 2 dp   **b** 3 dp   **c** 4 dp   **d** 5 dp

4 Round 24.789 53 correct to 3 dp.

> dp is short for decimal places.
> sf is short for significant figures.

Exercise 1.15B

1 Round each number to the number of
   i decimal places, and **ii** significant figures, in brackets.
   a 34.626 (2)   **b** 17.935 499 (3)   **c** 0.007 29 (2)
   d 176.280 086 (4)   **e** 38.795 (2)   **f** 0.071 999 999 9 (2)

2 Round 3.999 999 correct to 4 decimal places.

3 Round 3.1274 metres to the nearest centimetre.

4 A tank holds 37 646 575 litres of fuel when full.
   Calculate the volume of fuel correct to 1 significant figure.

5 The length of a pencil was given as 12.7 cm correct to 1 dp.
   What is the shortest length the pencil could have?

6 Two lengths A and B are each rounded to 1 dp.
   They are then added. Is the answer accurate to 1 dp?
   Illustrate your answer with an example.

1.16 Ratio

You can use ratio to compare the size of two, or more, quantities.
Ratio may use the term *parts*.
Each of the *parts* must be the same size.

Example
A fruit drink is made up from two parts of juice to seven parts of water.

In a carton of this drink, 2 parts will be juice and 7 parts will be water.

Thinking in fractions, this ratio means that:

$\frac{2}{9}$ of the carton is juice and $\frac{7}{9}$ of the carton is water and, the **ratio** of juice to water is **2:7**.

> Do not confuse ratio and fractions.
>
> The juice is not $\frac{2}{7}$ of the drink!

Exercise 1.16A

1. Colour E44 dye is mixed from red and yellow in the ratio 5:9.
   a What fraction of E44 is yellow?
   b What fraction is red?

2. For biscuits flour and butter are mixed in the ratio 15:7.
   a What fraction of the mix is flour?
   b What fraction is butter?

3. In animal feed, protein and fibre are mixed in the ratio 7:25.
   a What fraction of the mix is fibre?
   b What fraction of the mix is protein?

4. For a furniture polish, wax and spirit are mixed in the ratio 15:4. Jo claims that spirit is over $\frac{1}{4}$ of the mix, but Sam says spirit is about $\frac{1}{5}$ of it.
   a Who do you think is correct? Explain why
   b Explain how you think the mistake was made.

5. To make tiles, powdered clay, water and dye are mixed in the ratio 63:24:6.
   a What fraction of the mix is water?
      Give your answer in its lowest terms.
   b Kim gives the fraction of powdered clay as about $\frac{2}{3}$.
      Do you agree? Explain your answer.

Exercise 1.16B

1. The ratio of silver coins to copper coins in a bag was given as 8:13. What fraction of the coins in the bag was:
   a silver?   b copper?

   Lowest terms see page 14.

2. In a fish shop cod and haddock are sold in the ratio 15:8. What fraction of the fish sold is:
   a cod   b haddock?

3. A recipe to make muffins uses 5 parts of flour to 4 parts of sugar to 3 parts of fat.
   a What fraction of the mix is sugar?
   b What fraction is the sugar and fat together?

4. $\frac{9}{25}$ of the flour used by a bakery in a week is corn flour the rest is wheat flour.
   a Give the fraction for wheat flour.
   b Give the ratio of wheat flour to corn flour.

5. $\frac{11}{30}$ of the flowers sold in a florists are roses.
   a What fraction are not roses?
   b Give the ratio roses:not roses for this florist.

1.17 Equivalent ratios and ratios in their lowest terms

▶ Equivalent ratios show the same comparison.
To make equivalent ratios multiply both parts of a ratio by the same number.

Example 1
Find three different ratios equivalent to $3:5$.

$$3:5 = 12:20 = 21:35 = 30:50$$
$$\times 4 \times 7 \times 10$$

▶ To put a ratio in its lowest terms divide each part of the ratio by the HCF of all parts.

Example 2
Give the ratio $24:40$ in its lowest terms.

$24:40 = 3:5$ (Divide each part by the HCF, 8)

HCF see page 10.

Exercise 1.17A

1 Find three different ratios equivalent to:
   a $4:7$ **b** $7:9$ **c** $13:24$ **d** $17:1$ **e** $5:11$

2 Show how these ratios are equivalent:
   a $5:7$ and $45:63$ **b** $3:8$ and $21:56$ **c** $8:15$ and $72:135$

3 Give each in its lowest terms:
   a $24:42$ **b** $56:84$ **c** $32:44$ **d** $63:18$ **e** $34:22$

Exercise 1.17B

1 Find three different ratios equivalent to:
   a $5:4$ **b** $7:12$ **c** $10:19$ **d** $15:23$ **e** $25:9$

2 Show how these are equivalent:
   a $16:35$ and $32:70$
   b $124:64$ and $31:16$
   c $24:7$ and $120:35$

3 Give each in its lowest terms:
   a $45:30$ **b** $51:17$ **c** $36:90$ **d** $63:28$ **e** $93:63$

1.18 Direct proportion

▶ Quantities are in **direct proportion** if an increase in one quantity matches an increase in the other quantity.

Example
Nine rose trees cost a total of £29.61.
Calculate the cost of five of these rose trees.

$\quad$ 9 rose trees cost a total of $\qquad$ £29.61

$\quad$ 1 tree costs $\qquad$ $\dfrac{£29.61}{9}$

$\quad$ 5 of the rose trees will cost a total of: $\dfrac{£29.61}{9} \times 5 = £16.45$

Exercise 1.18A

1 A group of 8 fans bought match tickets for a total of £78. What would be the total cost of tickets for a group of 11 fans for the same match?

2 A recipe for six uses 450 g of plain flour. If the recipe is used to serve 35 people how many grams of plain flour will be needed?

3 Weedkiller is used at the rate of 240 g to every 15 m² of ground to be treated. How much weedkiller is needed to treat 95.625 m² of ground.

4 In a fizzy drink 125 ml of colouring is added to every 2000 litres. How much colouring is needed for the week's production of half a million litres?

5 It takes 4 machines, $17\frac{1}{2}$ hours to make a set of parts. The firm buys another 5 machines. Using all the machines how long should they allow to make an identical set of parts?

Exercise 1.18B

1 A recipe for 4 people uses 15 ml of vanilla essence. The recipe is being adapted to serve 235 people. How much vanilla essence will be needed?

2 A fuel additive is used at the rate of 140 ml to every 15 litres of fuel. How much additive is needed to treat a quarter of a million litres of fuel?

3 A plant extract is produced at the rate of 0.04 ml from every 12 kg of plant. How much extract can be expected from 7.6 tonnes of plant?

4 A machine can test 135 000 fuses in 90 minutes. At this rate, how long will it take the machine to test 3 million fuses?

5 It takes three pumps $34\frac{1}{2}$ hours to empty a tank. How long do you expect it would take to empty the tank with eight of the same type of pump?

Revision exercise 1 *Review*

1 Give the value of the digit 6 in each of these numbers.
   a 365.08   **b** 458.1762   **c** 0.0657   **d** 164 083.155 *Unit 1.1*

2 Use the digits: 3, 6, 5, 8, 0, 6, 0 to make:
   a the smallest number possible
   b the largest number possible. *Unit 1.1*

3 Calculate:
   a 4565 × 1000   **b** 677 231 × 100 000   **c** 4 × 10 000 000 *Unit 1.1*

4 Calculate:
   a 254.62 ÷ 100   **b** 288 637.175 ÷ 10 000   **c** 35 ÷ 1 000 000 *Unit 1.1*

5 Calculate answers to each of these.
   a 34 × 20 000   **b** 46 × 3000   **c** 122 × 200 000
   d 75 ÷ 500   **e** 386 ÷ 2000   **f** 15 000 ÷ 200 *Unit 1.1*

6 Divide sixteen million by two hundred thousand.
   a Give your answer in digits.
   b Give your answer in words. *Unit 1.1*

7 A web site had 150 000 hits during an advertising campaign. The site owners say they have about two hundred hits each day. Roughly how long, in days, was the advertising campaign? *Unit 1.1*

8 A number is a multiple of ten and:
   • larger than 8 570 000 ÷ 100 000
   • smaller than 840 000 ÷ 7000
   What might be the number? *Unit 1.1*

9 Copy and complete this table.

Number	\multicolumn{4}{c}{Round to nearest:}			
	10	100	1000	10 000
130 456				
96 488				
104 085				
336 792				
757 608				

Unit 1.2

26   Numbers and the number system

10 An integer is rounded to the nearest 10 and the answer is 456 720.
   a What is the smallest the number might be?
   b What is the largest the number might be?

Review

Unit 1.2

11 Give the number that is 9 more than each of these.
   a $^-6$ **b** 3   **c** $^-15$ **d** $^-21$ **e** $^-1$

Unit 1.3

12 Give the number that is 17 less than each of these.
   a 5   **b** 11   **c** $^-6$ **d** $^-18$ **e** $^-125$

Unit 1.3

13 Order this set of numbers. Start with the smallest.
   12, 15, $^-2$, 0, $^-5$, 3, $^-21$, 4, $^-18$

Unit 1.3

14 Calculate each of these.
   a $^-5 + 6 - 8$ **b** $^-11 + 2 - 6 + 1$ **c** $15 - ^-7 + 3$
   d $^-8 + 5 - ^-9$ **e** $15 - 7 - ^-5 + 21$ **f** $12 - 56 + 21 - ^-67$
   g $13 \times ^-8$ **h** $45 \times ^-8 \times 2$ **i** $^-4 \times ^-8 \times ^-9 \times ^-2$
   j $56 \div ^-7$ **k** $24 \div ^-3 \times 5$ **l** $15 \times ^-5 \div ^-9$

Unit 1.4

15 Express each of these as a single index number.
   a $3^5 \times 3^8$ **b** $6^7 \times 6^2$ **c** $5^9 \times 5^4 \times 5^2$ **d** $6^4 \times 6^2 \times 6$
   e $4^8 \div 4^2$ **f** $7^{10} \div 7^2$ **g** $3^9 \div 3^3$ **h** $3^5 \div 3^5$
   i $4^2 \times 4^5 \div 4^4$ **j** $6^6 \times 6 \div 6^8$ **k** $5^3 \div 5^8 \times 5^2$ **l** $8^2 \times 8^{14} \div 8^8 \div 8$

Unit 1.5

16 Write each of these in standard form.
   a 13 563.44   **b** 877 654.2   **c** 10 054.875   **d** 232 004 005 067.0034
   e 0.005 46   **f** 0.000 045   **g** 0.054 365   **h** 0.000 000 051 87

Unit 1.6

17 Write each of these as ordinary numbers.
   a 3.6056×10^7 **b** $2.385\,066\,2 \times 10^9$ **c** $3.466\,560\,27 \times 10^{12}$
   d 2.453×10^{-5} **e** $3.445\,420\,7 \times 10^{-8}$ **f** $0.464\,63 \times 10^{-15}$

Unit 1.6

18 List all the factors of:
   a 36   **b** 60   **c** 100   **d** 144

Unit 1.7

19 Find the HCF of:
   a 65 and 104   **b** 56 and 162   **c** 150 and 20 075

Unit 1.7

20 List the first seven multiples of 12.

Unit 1.7

21 Find the LCM of:
   a 4 and 5   **b** 6 and 8   **c** 6 and 9   **d** 3, 4 and 5

Unit 1.7

22 Find the sum of all the prime numbers between 20 and 60.

Unit 1.7

23 Find the prime factors of:
   a 56   **b** 72   **c** 33   **d** 115   **e** 136

Unit 1.7

24 Write each of these as a product of primes.
Use indices to simplify your answer.
  a 50   b 120   c 156
  d 200   e 450   f 640

25 As a product of primes a number is given as $2^2 \times 3^5 \times 5$
What is the number?

26 What is the value of 9^2?

27 List the first fifteen square numbers.

28 Calculate the value of five cubed.

29 Is four cubed the same as eight squared? Explain your answer.

30 Evaluate each of these.
  a 4^2 b 5^3 c 6^2 d 8^3 e 1000^3 f 600^2

31 List all the square numbers between 200 and 300.

32 What cube number is closest to 1000? Explain your answer.

33 Calculate the value of each of these.
  a $5^2 + 4^2 - 3^2$ b $6^2 + 2^3 + 1^3$ c $5^3 - 4^2 - 2^3$

34 Find the value of:
  a $(2+5)^3$ b $(4+4)^2 + (17-15)^3$ c $(22+1)^2 - (14-9)^3$

35 Find each of these roots by inspection.
  a $\sqrt{81}$ b $\sqrt{36}$ c $\sqrt{144}$ d $\sqrt{361}$

36 Use a calculator to approximate each root.
  a $\sqrt{340}$ b $\sqrt{5630}$ c $\sqrt{1554}$ d $\sqrt{10\,504}$

37 Calculate $\sqrt{576}$ by trial and improvement.

38 For each of these give an approximate root.
  a $\sqrt[3]{275}$ b $\sqrt[3]{4565}$ c $\sqrt[3]{5650}$ d $\sqrt[3]{232\,550}$

39 Write each of these fractions in its lowest terms.
  a $\frac{16}{56}$ b $\frac{35}{75}$ c $\frac{35}{100}$ d $\frac{42}{54}$

40 Find three different fractions equivalent to:
  a $\frac{3}{5}$ b $\frac{7}{12}$ c $\frac{15}{28}$ d $\frac{14}{44}$

41 Order each set of fractions by size. Start with the smallest.
  a $\frac{3}{5}, \frac{3}{4}, \frac{2}{3}, \frac{1}{2}$ b $\frac{5}{8}, \frac{2}{3}, \frac{4}{5}, \frac{3}{4}$

42 Convert each decimal to a fraction in its lowest terms.
  a 0.72   b 0.125   c 0.54   d 0.224

Review

Unit 1.7

Unit 1.7

Unit 1.8

Unit 1.8

Unit 1.8

Unit 1.8

Unit 1.8

Unit 1.8

Unit 1.8

Unit 1.8

Unit 1.8

Unit 1.9

Unit 1.9

Unit 1.9

Unit 1.9

Unit 1.10

Unit 1.11

Unit 1.12

Unit 1.13

43 List these decimals in order, smallest first.   *Review*
0.065   0.055 65   0.0504   0.03   0.0025   0.060 988 5   *Unit 1.13*

44 Convert each of these fractions to a decimal.
a $\frac{1}{8}$ **b** $\frac{3}{5}$ **c** $\frac{15}{20}$ **d** $\frac{34}{100}$ **e** $\frac{7}{9}$ *Unit 1.14*

45 Round each value.
a 3.656 (2 dp)   **b** 4.082 54 (4 dp)
c 0.005 674 (5 dp)   **d** 0.025 263 (4 dp)   *Unit 1.15*

46 A dye is mixed from red, blue and yellow in the ratio 4 : 3 : 8.
Give the fraction of each colour in the mix.   *Unit 1.16*

47 Give three different ratios that are equivalent to 3 : 5 : 9.   *Unit 1.17*

48 Find • if these ratios are equivalent. 3 : 7 : 11 and 21 : • : 77   *Unit 1.17*

49 Eight bags of fuel cost £30.80. Find the cost of five bags of this fuel.   *Unit 1.18*

50 A dye is added to fuel at the rate of 12 ml to every 35 litres of fuel. How much dye is added to half a million litres of fuel?   *Unit 1.18*

Investigation

In the frame

- Make a rectangular grid of numbers starting:

1	2	3	4	5	6	7	8
9	10	11	12	13	14	15	...

  ...
  ...
  89 90

- Cut a square hole in a piece of paper so that when you place the hole over the grid you can see a 3 × 3 grid of numbers.
- Multiply the corner numbers diagonally opposite each other on the grid and subtract the two answers.
  The answer is the 3 × 3 frame value for this position on the grid.

a Investigate frame values for the 3 × 3 frame in different positions.
b Try the 3 × 3 frame on other rectangular number grids. What about frame values now?
c Write a rule that links the frame value to the width of the number grid.
d Try different square frames (2 × 2, 4 × 4, 5 × 5, etc) on the number grids.
Write a report on what you discover.

2 Number calculations

2.1 Non-calculator multiplication of integers

This is a non-calculator method you can use to multiply large numbers.

> This is known as long multiplication.

Example 1
Show your working for this calculation. 373×53

```
        3 7 3
    ×    5 3
    1 8₃6₁5 0
      1 1₂1 9
      1 9 7 6 9
```

Start multiplying by the 50
Now multiply by the 3
Add the results of multiplying

In this method you work out 50×373 and 3×373 then add the two results.

Example 2
Show how you calculate: 438×352

```
          4 3 8
      ×   3 5 2
      1 3₁1₂4 0 0
        2 1₁9 0 0
            8 7₁6
      1 5 4 1 7 6
              ₂
```

Multiply by the 300
Multiply by the 50
Multiply by the 2
Add the results of multiplying

> A whole number multiplied by 300 will end in 00. So put in the 00 before you multiply by the 3.

Exercise 2.1A

1 Show how you calculate each of these:
  a 537×45 **b** 682×537 **c** 636×58 **d** 362×87
  e 675×39 **f** 368×75 **g** 934×52 **h** 744×88

2 Show how you calculate each of these:
  a 254×376 **b** 374×882 **c** 546×773 **d** 684×881
  e 724×538 **f** 845×557 **g** 763×674 **h** 488×495

Exercise 2.1B

1 Copy and complete this multiplication table.
   Show all your working.

×	386	575	94	479	683	86	3049
74				35 446			
659							

2 Calculate the total distance travelled by each bus.

Bus 37B   Route length 72 km,   number of journeys 653
Bus 518Ex   Route length 374 km,   number of journeys 278

2.2 Non-calculator division of integers

This is a non-calculator method you can use to divide large numbers.

Example
Calculate $6372 \div 18$

```
              3 5 4
         18 ) 6 3 7 2
18 into 63 is 3 rem 9 ——  5 4
18 into 97 is 5 rem 7 ——    9 7
                            9 0
18 into 72 is 4 rem 0 ——      7 2
                              7 2
                              0 0
```

This is known as long division.

Exercise 2.2A

1 Show how you calculate each of these:
    a $4599 \div 7$ **b** $3140 \div 4$ **c** $3498 \div 6$
    d $7384 \div 13$ **e** $5264 \div 14$ **f** $2805 \div 17$

2 Show your method for calculating:
    a $27\,336 \div 6$ **b** $28\,406 \div 7$ **c** $5370 \div 15$
    d $88\,488 \div 12$ **e** $94\,992 \div 16$ **f** $3857 \div 19$

3 A tent hire firm buys 15 identical marquees, and a total of 5670 tent pegs. How many pegs are needed for each marquee?

4 A printer prints a total of 8748 pages for 18 copies of a book. How many pages in each book?

Exercise 2.2B

1 Show how you calculate each of these:
    a $4488 \div 12$ **b** $5520 \div 15$ **c** $8874 \div 18$
    d $10\,205 \div 13$ **e** $5744 \div 16$ **f** $4692 \div 23$

2 A drilling platform weighs 68 592 tonnes and 16 legs share the weight equally.
Calculate the weight taken by each leg, showing all your working.

3 An aircraft costs £22 million.
  Lazyjet orders aircraft at a total cost of £39 336 million.
  How many aircraft is this?

4 A company buys 24 lap-top computers at a total cost of £135 768.
  Calculate the price of one of these computers using a non-calculator method.

2.3 Calculating with integers of any size

In calculation questions you will have to decide which mathematical operators to use.

> Mathematical operators are: add, subtract, multiply and divide.

Example
On a car test, 16 cars covered a total of 192 496 kilometres. Each car covered the same distance. How far did each car travel?

$$\text{Distance travelled by each car} = 192\,496 \div 16$$
$$= 12\,031$$

Each car travelled 12 031 kilometres.

Exercise 2.3A

1 Last year Lazyjet made 1653 holiday flights using planes that carry 354 passengers. Lazyjet claim that last year they carried 600 000 passengers with no empty seats.
  a If there were no empty seats exactly how many passengers flew Lazyjet?
  b Is their claim to carry 600 000 passengers justified?
  c How might they have rounded passenger numbers? Explain your answer.

2 A channel ferry can carry 3278 passengers.
  In a year the ferry makes 1456 crossings.
  a Calculate the maximum number of people that might use this ferry in a year.

  In 1996 this ferry carried 3 032 848 passengers.
  b If each crossing had the same number of passengers, how many would this be?

  Each passenger spent £7 on on-board shopping.
  c In total was this more or less than £20 million? Explain your answer.

3 A reservoir holds twenty-three and a quarter million litres of water when full. Water leaves the reservoir at the rate of 50 million litres per day.
   a If no water flows into the reservoir, in how many days will the reservoir be empty?

   At 9 o'clock last Tuesday the reservoir was full. For each of the next three hours one-and-three-quarter million litres flowed out of the reservoir and 920 000 litres flowed in.
   b At 12 o'clock how many litres of water were in the reservoir?

4 This data gives the distances travelled by two aircraft over five days.
   Aircraft 1:   2178 km each day.
   Aircraft 2:   Mon 1977 km,   Tues 2085 km,   Wed 3254 km,
                 Thurs 3565 km,   Fri 1884 km
   a Which aircraft flew furthest over the five days?
   b Find the difference in the distances travelled by the two aircraft.
   c If aircraft 2 had covered the same total distance but that distance was equally spread over the five days, how far would it have flown each day?
   d Between them did the aircraft fly more than 25 000 km in the five days? Explain your answer.

Exercise 2.3B

1 The number of fans that watched the first match of the season was given as 42 675. Ticket sales showed that 15 322 reduced price tickets were sold. A full price ticket cost £9 and a reduced price ticket was £7.
   a How many full price tickets were sold?
   b In total, how much money was taken in ticket sales for the match?

2 A new 9 km road project by-passing Shevington cost £144 million. The work took a total of 648 days to complete.
   a Calculate the cost per kilometre for this road.
   b Does the cost of the road work out as more or less than a quarter of a million pounds per day? Explain your answer.

   This data gives the cost of bridges built for the road.

Bridge	Cost
3745/C	£1 720 000
3745/D	£2 300 650
3745/D/1	£827 575
3745/E	£4 056 750

   c Calculate the total cost of the bridges built for the project.
   d Calculate the cost of the road project excluding bridges.

3 A water pump is used to drain water from a swimming pool. The pump takes 135 litres of water from the pool every minute it is in use.
  a If the pump works for three hours, find how much water is removed from the pool.
  b Estimate the number of gallons of water removed in 12 hours if 9 litres is roughly 2 gallons.
  c The pump took 51 hours to empty the pool. Calculate the amount of water in the pool at the start of pumping.

4 The table gives the number of light bulbs made by Clearlight last year.

Bulb type (Watts)	15W	40W	60W	100W	150W
Number produced	36 580	58 625	135 765	272 500	388 725

  a How many of the bulbs produced were at least 100W?
  b How many of the bulbs were less than 60W?
  c In total did Clearlight produce more or less than three-quarters of a million bulbs? Explain your answer.

This year Clearlight have a target to make one million bulbs.
  d In total, how many more bulbs must they make this year over last year to reach their target?

2.4 Using brackets and the order of operations

You can use brackets to package a calculation so that it can only give one answer.
Without brackets it is often possible to find more than one answer.

Example 1
Calculate the value of: $\quad 4 + 5 \times 3 - 1$

Think of it this way:	$4 + 5 \times 3 - 1 = 9 \times 3 - 1 = 27 - 1 = 26$
Brackets for this answer:	$(4 + 5) \times 3 - 1 = 26$
Or, think of it this way:	$4 + 5 \times 3 - 1 = 4 + 15 - 1 = 19 - 1 = 18$
Brackets for this answer:	$4 + (5 \times 3) - 1 = 18$
Or, think of it this way:	$4 + 5 \times 3 - 1 = 4 + 10 = 14$
Brackets for this answer:	$4 + 5 \times (3 - 1) = 14$

Work out the calculation in the bracket first.

Exercise 2.4A

1 Copy each calculation and put brackets in to give the answer shown.
   a $5 + 9 \times 4 - 2 = 39$
   b $5 + 9 \times 4 - 2 = 23$
   c $5 + 9 \times 4 - 2 = 54$
   d $7 + 12 - 4 \times 3 + 1 = 46$
   e $7 + 12 - 4 \times 3 + 1 = 8$
   f $24 \div 8 - 5 - 8 = 0$
   g $15 \times 5 - 3 + 7 = 37$
   h $15 \times 5 - 3 + 7 = 135$

2 Complete these calculations:
   a $(12 + 4) \times 3 - 18 =$
   b $35 \div (7 - 2) =$
   c $(35 \div 7) - 2 =$
   d $23 - (5 \times 4) =$
   e $(19 + 5 - 22) \times 16 =$
   f $(42 \div 7) + 19 =$
   g $(66 \div 11) - (48 \div 16) =$
   h $12 \times (15 - 7) \div 4 =$

Exercise 2.4B

1 Copy each calculation and put brackets in to give the answer shown.
   a $13 - 5 \times 7 + 2 = {}^-20$
   b $13 - 5 \times 7 + 2 = 72$
   c $12 \times 4 + 5 - 75 = {}^-792$
   d $63 \div 9 - 12 + 15 = {}^-6$

2 Complete these calculations:
   a $15 + (54 \div 3) - 32$
   b $(16 - 5) \times (5 + 7)$
   c $(44 - 8) \div (26 - 17)$
   d $4 \times (5 - 17 + 22) \div 8$

3 Copy and complete each of these.
   a $(16 - \Box) \div (1 + \Box) = 3$ (Find two different answers).
   b $17 \times (15 - \Box) - 36 = 100$
   c $(224 \div \Box) + (3 \times 5) = 31$
   d $7 \times (14 - \Box) + (15 \times 5) = 54$
   e $18 \times (32 - \Box + 6) \div 5 = 72$
   f $(23 + \Box - 55) \times (33 - 15 + 1) = 38$
   g $390 \div (22 - \Box) - (182 \div 7) = 0$

If a calculation has brackets you work out the value of the bracket first.
For the rest of the calculation you do each mathematical operation in order.

The **BODMAS** rule will help you remember the order:

It stands for: **B** rackets
          powers   **O** f
                         D ivision
                         M ultiplication
                         A ddition
                         S ubtraction

The four operations are: **add**, **subtract**, **multiply** and **divide**.

Examples
Use **BODMAS** to evaluate these:

$(9-3)^3 \times (15-6.4)^2 = 6^3 \times 8.6^2 = 216 \times 73.96 = 15\,975.36$

$3 + 14 \times (7-4.2)^2 = 3 + 14 \times 2.8^2 = 3 + 14 \times 7.84 = 112.76$

$\sqrt{(5+3)} \times 5 - 24 \div 8 = \sqrt{8} \times 5 - 24 \div 8 = 2.828\ldots \times 5 - 24 \div 8$

$\qquad\qquad\qquad = 2.828\ldots \times 5 - 3 = 14.142\ldots - 3 = 11.14 \,(\text{to 2 dp})$

Exercise 2.4C

1 Use BODMAS to evaluate each of these:
 a $16 + 5 \times 4 - 42 \div 7$
 b $72 \div 9 - 15 + 7 \cdot 4 \times 3$
 c $54 \div 6 - 15 + 3 \times (17-12)^2$
 d $16 - \sqrt{45} \div 9 + (13-5) \times 3 - 32$
 e $12 \times (25-13) \div 48 + 15$
 f $120 \div (15-7)^2 + 9 \times 3 - \sqrt{35}$

> Most calculators work to BODMAS rules. Try yours.

2 Complete each of these using BODMAS:
 a $\left(\frac{1}{2} + \frac{3}{4}\right) \times 12 - 5 \times \frac{1}{3}$
 b $\frac{1}{2} + \frac{3}{5} \times 15 - \frac{3}{4}$
 c $\frac{5}{8} \div 5 + 4 \times \frac{3}{4} - \frac{1}{8}$
 d $\left(\frac{1}{2}\right)^2 + 5 \times \frac{1}{4} - \frac{1}{2}$

> In decimal calculations give your answers to 2 dp.

3 Write a calculation that uses BODMAS and gives an answer of 56.

Exercise 2.4D

1 Use BODMAS to evaluate each of these:
 a $\sqrt{56} \div 8 - 4 + 4 \times \sqrt{\frac{1}{4}}$
 b $24 - 3 \times 5 + \sqrt{108} \div (12-9)^2$
 c $\sqrt{(19+24)} + 5 - \sqrt{\frac{1}{9}} \times 18$
 d $(35+19) \div (13-11.5)^2 \times \sqrt{55}$
 e $(19+36) \div \sqrt{(8-3)} \div (8-5)^2$
 f $\sqrt{(16 \times 5 + 170)} \div 50 - (4-1)^3$

2 Complete each of these using BODMAS:
 a $\frac{3}{4} \div 3 + \frac{3}{8} \times 16 - \frac{1}{2}$
 b $1.5 \div 3 + \frac{1}{4} \times 7 - \frac{3}{4}$
 c $\frac{1}{2} + \left(\frac{1}{2}\right)^3 \times 8 + \frac{3}{2} \div 3$
 d $\left(\frac{2}{3}\right)^2 \times 18 + \frac{3}{4} \div 3 + 5$

3 Write a BODMAS calculation, with brackets that gives an answer of 148.

2.5 Finding a fraction of an amount

▶ To find a fraction of an amount you can use one of these methods:

- **Method 1**
  Multiply the amount by the numerator then divide by the denominator.

  Example 1   Find $\frac{5}{6}$ of £72
  Multiply £72 by 5 then divide the answer by 6.
  $72 \times 5 = 360$ $360 \div 6 = 60$
  So $\frac{5}{6}$ of £72 = £60

- **Method 2**
  Think of the problem as fraction multiplication.

  Example 2   Find $\frac{3}{8}$ of 60

  $$\frac{3}{8} \times \frac{60}{1} = \frac{3}{\cancel{8}_2} \times \frac{\cancel{60}^{15}}{1}$$

  $$= \frac{45}{2} = 22\frac{1}{2}$$

  So $\frac{3}{8}$ of 60 is $22\frac{1}{2}$

  Remember:
  4 is a common factor of 8 and 60 so you can cancel.

Exercise 2.5A

1 Use Method 1 to calculate $\frac{3}{4}$ of 420.
2 Use Method 2 to calculate $\frac{3}{16}$ of 240.
3 Calculate using any method:
   a $\frac{5}{7}$ of 140
   b $\frac{2}{5}$ of 80
   c $\frac{1}{9}$ of 72
   d $\frac{2}{3}$ of 99
   e $\frac{5}{12}$ of 72
   f $\frac{6}{11}$ of 55
4 Calculate:
   a $\left(\frac{3}{8} \text{ of } 72\right) + \left(\frac{3}{8} \text{ of } 272\right)$
   b $\frac{3}{8}$ of $(72 + 272)$

Exercise 2.5B

1 Use Method 2 to find:
   a $\frac{3}{5}$ of 220
   b $\frac{5}{8}$ of 568
   c $\frac{9}{10}$ of 1550
   d $\frac{5}{18}$ of 270
   e $\frac{6}{7}$ of 329
   f $\frac{3}{4}$ of 5884

2 In a group of 2264 students, $\frac{5}{8}$ were female. How many students were male?

3 Calculate $\frac{3}{7}$ of £253.75.

4 Andy thought Alex spent $\frac{3}{4}$ of the time over a full week in bed. How many hours would this be?

5 What is $\frac{7}{16}$ of £445 to the nearest pound?

6 $\frac{5}{8}$ of the 10 440 people at a fair were male. $\frac{3}{5}$ of the females were under 21. How many females were 21 or over?

2.6 One number as a fraction of another

▶ You can write one number as a fraction of another.

Example A classroom contains 14 girls, 18 boys and 2 adults. What fraction of the people present are girls?

There were 14 girls. There were 34 people present altogether.

So the fraction is $\frac{14}{34} = \frac{7}{17}$ (÷2)

So $\frac{7}{17}$ of the class are girls.

Exercise 2.6A

1 Calculate each number as a fraction of the other number.
   a 120 as a fraction of 200   **b** 28 as a fraction of 700
   c 36 as a fraction of 414   **d** 5 as a fraction of 425

2 In Class 9R there are 30 pupils, 18 of whom are girls.
In Class 9T of the 35 pupils, 28 are girls.
Which class has the larger fraction of girls?
Explain your answer.

3 Sally has £665. She spends £19.
What fraction of her money has she left?

4 Which is the larger fraction in each case?
   a 56 out of 136 or 96 out of 204
   b 112 out of 322 or 245 out of 805

Exercise 2.6B

1 Steve eats 3 meals a day. Over a full week 14 meals contained meat.
What fraction of Steve's meals in a week did not contain meat?

2 Of the nine planets, six are further from the Sun than the Earth.
What fraction of the planets are nearer the Sun than the Earth?

3 In a showroom there are 30 red cars, 90 blue cars and 24 green cars.
   a What fraction of the cars are: **i** red **ii** blue **iii** green?
   b What must these three fractions add up to?

4 In a group of 264 people in a café, $\frac{3}{8}$ of them are younger than 18. Of these, 22 people go to school. What fraction of the whole group are under 18 but do not go to school?

5 This list gives the numbers of trees in a wood.
   Beech: 312, Oak: 708, Elm: 28, Ash: 148, Chestnut: 144, Yew: 4.
   List each tree type as a fraction of the number of trees in the wood.

2.7 Adding fractions

▶ To add fractions the denominators must first be made equal.

Example 1   Calculate $\frac{1}{4} + \frac{3}{8}$

Find the LCM of 4 and 8, which is 8.
Then change the fractions to equivalent ones with 8 as the denominator.

So $\frac{1}{4} + \frac{3}{8} = \frac{2}{8} + \frac{3}{8} = \frac{5}{8}$

Remember:
The LCM of two numbers is the lowest number they will both divide into without remainders.
4 and 8 both go into 8.

Example 2   Calculate $1\frac{2}{3} + 3\frac{3}{4}$

Find the LCM, which is 12
(because 3 and 4 divide exactly into 12).
Then change both fractions to the equivalent 12ths.

So $1\frac{2}{3} + 3\frac{3}{4} = 1\frac{8}{12} + 3\frac{9}{12} = 4\frac{17}{12} = 5\frac{5}{12}$

Remember:
$2 \times 4 = 8$
$3 \times 4 = 12$
$3 \times 3 = 9$
$4 \times 3 = 12$

Exercise 2.7A

1 Add these pairs of fractions.
   a $\frac{1}{4} + \frac{1}{8}$ **b** $\frac{1}{3} + \frac{1}{4}$ **c** $\frac{1}{6} + \frac{2}{3}$ **d** $\frac{3}{8} + \frac{5}{16}$ **e** $\frac{7}{16} + \frac{1}{4}$
   f $\frac{1}{3} + \frac{5}{9}$ **g** $\frac{1}{2} + \frac{1}{3}$ **h** $\frac{1}{8} + \frac{5}{6}$ **i** $\frac{2}{9} + \frac{2}{3}$ **j** $\frac{7}{10} + \frac{3}{5}$

2 Add these pairs of mixed numbers.
   a $1\frac{5}{8} + 7\frac{1}{4}$ **b** $5\frac{7}{10} + 2\frac{1}{5}$ **c** $3\frac{1}{2} + 2\frac{17}{40}$ **d** $3\frac{5}{12} + 1\frac{5}{6}$ **e** $4\frac{2}{5} + 6\frac{19}{20}$ **f** $\frac{7}{8} + 6\frac{57}{68}$

One number as a fraction of another   39

Exercise 2.7B

1 Calculate:

a $\frac{5}{8}+\frac{1}{6}$ b $\frac{2}{7}+\frac{1}{3}$ c $\frac{2}{3}+\frac{3}{8}$ d $\frac{1}{3}+\frac{3}{8}$ e $2\frac{3}{5}+\frac{1}{4}$

f $6\frac{1}{5}+3\frac{1}{6}$ g $\frac{2}{9}+\frac{1}{6}$ h $5\frac{1}{4}+7\frac{1}{7}$ i $3\frac{2}{5}+\frac{17}{20}$ j $2\frac{3}{4}+1\frac{2}{5}$

2 Of the people invited to the party, $\frac{3}{8}$ could not come because of illness and $\frac{2}{5}$ could not come because of transport problems. What fraction of those invited **could** come?

3 Add these fractions.

a $\frac{1}{2}+\frac{5}{7}+\frac{3}{4}$ b $\frac{5}{8}+\frac{7}{10}+\frac{9}{16}$

c $\frac{4}{5}+2\frac{5}{6}+\frac{7}{8}$ d $3\frac{7}{16}+5\frac{4}{5}+4\frac{19}{40}$

> To add three fractions you need to find the LCM of all three denominators.

2.8 Subtracting fractions

▶ To subtract two fractions first make sure they have the same denominators.

Example 1   Calculate $\frac{5}{6}-\frac{3}{4}$

$$\frac{5}{6}-\frac{3}{4}=\frac{10}{12}-\frac{9}{12}=\frac{1}{12}$$

> **Remember:**
> The LCM of 6 and 4 is 12.

▶ You may also need to convert some whole numbers to improper fractions.

Example 2   Calculate $4\frac{3}{7}-1\frac{8}{9}$

$$4\frac{3}{7}-1\frac{8}{9}=4\frac{27}{63}-1\frac{56}{63}=3\frac{63}{63}+\frac{27}{63}-1\frac{56}{63}=2\frac{34}{63}$$

Notice how 1 unit from the 4 units has been converted to $\frac{63}{63}$.

Exercise 2.8A

1 Subtract these fractions.

a $\frac{7}{8}-\frac{1}{4}$ b $\frac{2}{3}-\frac{4}{9}$ c $\frac{7}{16}-\frac{1}{4}$ d $\frac{7}{20}-\frac{1}{15}$ e $\frac{5}{8}-\frac{1}{7}$

f $\frac{7}{10}-\frac{2}{15}$ g $\frac{4}{9}-\frac{1}{13}$ h $\frac{1}{2}-\frac{9}{25}$ i $\frac{3}{4}-\frac{2}{9}$ j $\frac{7}{8}-\frac{6}{7}$

2 Subtract these fractions that include mixed numbers.

a $4\frac{1}{2}-1\frac{3}{11}$ b $6\frac{1}{8}-2\frac{5}{16}$ c $1\frac{1}{7}-\frac{7}{9}$ d $3\frac{1}{4}-1\frac{3}{5}$ e $6\frac{5}{14}-2\frac{2}{3}$ f $2\frac{3}{8}-\frac{4}{5}$

Exercise 2.8B

1 Subtract these fractions.

a $\frac{5}{8} - \frac{1}{6}$ b $\frac{5}{6} - \frac{1}{4}$ c $\frac{5}{7} - \frac{1}{2}$ d $1\frac{2}{3} - \frac{3}{10}$ e $4\frac{1}{2} - 1\frac{3}{7}$ f $\frac{8}{9} - \frac{2}{3}$

g $4\frac{1}{8} - \frac{3}{10}$ h $2\frac{3}{7} - \frac{1}{3}$ i $5\frac{1}{6} - \frac{7}{10}$ j $1\frac{1}{12} - \frac{3}{8}$ k $2\frac{2}{9} - \frac{3}{10}$ l $4\frac{5}{18} - \frac{15}{16}$

2 $\frac{3}{4}$ of refugees were female.
$\frac{2}{5}$ of the refugees were girls of 19 years or younger.
What fraction of the refugees were women over 19?

3 Mike sat looking at his record collection.
$\frac{2}{3}$ of the collection were Blues or Jazz, and $\frac{1}{5}$ were Jazz.
What fraction of his collection were Blues?

4 Sally realised she had been working for $4\frac{3}{8}$ days.
Over that time in total she had spent $1\frac{7}{10}$ days asleep.
How long had she been awake?

2.9 Multiplying fractions

▶ To multiply two fractions multiply the denominators and the numerators.

Example 1 Calculate $\frac{5}{8} \times \frac{3}{7}$

$$\frac{5}{8} \times \frac{3}{7} = \frac{15}{56}$$

$5 \times 3 = 15$
$8 \times 7 = 56$

▶ Sometimes you can cross cancel.

Example 2 Calculate $\frac{6}{7} \times \frac{2}{9}$

Write this as: $\frac{\cancel{6}^2}{7} \times \frac{2}{\cancel{9}_3} = \frac{2}{7} \times \frac{2}{3} = \frac{4}{21}$

Example 3 Calculate $\frac{5}{8} \times \frac{4}{15}$

$$\frac{\cancel{5}^1}{\cancel{8}_2} \times \frac{\cancel{4}^1}{\cancel{15}_3} = \frac{1}{2} \times \frac{1}{3} = \frac{1}{6}$$

▶ Convert mixed numbers to improper fractions first.

Example 4 Calculate $1\frac{5}{6} \times 2\frac{4}{7}$

$$1\frac{5}{6} \times 2\frac{4}{7} = \frac{11}{\cancel{6}} \times \frac{\cancel{18}^3}{7} = \frac{33}{7} = 4\frac{5}{7}$$

Exercise 2.9A

1 Calculate each of these, showing any cancelling:
 a $\frac{3}{4} \times \frac{2}{5}$ b $\frac{5}{9} \times \frac{3}{4}$ c $\frac{2}{3} \times \frac{6}{7}$ d $\frac{3}{5} \times \frac{1}{16}$ e $\frac{7}{8} \times \frac{24}{49}$
 f $\frac{3}{4} \times \frac{8}{21}$ g $\frac{5}{7} \times \frac{35}{48}$ h $\frac{5}{12} \times \frac{7}{8}$ i $\frac{2}{3} \times \frac{15}{16}$ j $\frac{5}{36} \times \frac{18}{25}$

2 Calculate these multiplications which include mixed numbers.
 a $1\frac{3}{4} \times \frac{5}{8}$ b $\frac{6}{7} \times 2\frac{1}{2}$ c $\frac{5}{6} \times 4\frac{3}{4}$
 d $5\frac{1}{2} \times 2\frac{1}{3}$ e $6\frac{2}{7} \times 1\frac{11}{20}$ f $3\frac{2}{3} \times 1\frac{7}{8}$

Exercise 2.9B

1 Calculate:
 a $\frac{6}{11} \times \frac{2}{3}$ b $\frac{5}{6} \times \frac{3}{5}$ c $\frac{5}{8} \times \frac{4}{25}$ d $\frac{15}{34} \times \frac{2}{3}$
 e $\frac{12}{25} \times \frac{5}{9}$ f $1\frac{3}{8} \times \frac{5}{6}$ g $\frac{7}{16} \times \frac{12}{13}$ h $5\frac{1}{6} \times \frac{9}{10}$
 i $2\frac{4}{5} \times \frac{5}{22}$ j $\frac{3}{4} \times 6\frac{4}{9}$ k $1\frac{6}{13} \times 1\frac{2}{5}$ l $2\frac{5}{9} \times 4\frac{6}{35}$

2 $\frac{4}{5}$ of the cars on the road are saloons. Of these saloons $\frac{1}{8}$ are red. What fraction of the cars on the road are red saloons?

3 Kate says $\frac{1}{2}$ of $\frac{1}{5}$ of $\frac{1}{19}$ is larger than $\frac{1}{3}$ of $\frac{1}{7}$ of $\frac{1}{10}$.
 a Is Kate correct?
 b What is the difference between the two answers?

2.10 Dividing fractions

▶ To divide a fraction by 5 you can multiply the fraction by $\frac{1}{5}$.

Example 1 Divide $\frac{5}{6}$ by 4

$\frac{5}{6} \div 4$ is the same as: $\frac{5}{6} \times \frac{1}{4} = \frac{5}{24}$

▶ In the same way. If you divide by $\frac{3}{4}$ it is the same as multiplying by $\frac{4}{3}$.

Example 2 Calculate $\frac{6}{7} \div \frac{3}{8}$

$\frac{6}{7} \div \frac{3}{8}$ is the same as: $\frac{6}{7} \times \frac{8}{3} = \frac{\cancel{6}^2}{7} \times \frac{8}{\cancel{3}_1} = \frac{2}{7} \times \frac{8}{1} = \frac{16}{7} = 2\frac{2}{7}$

Exercise 2.10A

1 Calculate each of these:

a $\frac{3}{4} \div 2$ **b** $\frac{5}{11} \div 4$ **c** $\frac{5}{8} \div 6$

d $\frac{9}{10} \div 3$ **e** $\frac{4}{7} \div 5$ **f** $\frac{3}{8} \div 7$

g $\frac{3}{4} \div 21$ **h** $\frac{16}{17} \div 32$ **i** $\frac{4}{11} \div 12$

2 Use cancelling where necessary to calculate:

a $\frac{7}{15} \div \frac{3}{5}$ **b** $\frac{2}{3} \div \frac{4}{9}$ **c** $\frac{12}{13} \div \frac{2}{3}$

d $\frac{7}{8} \div \frac{5}{7}$ **e** $\frac{7}{9} \div \frac{4}{5}$ **f** $\frac{5}{6} \div \frac{2}{3}$

g $\frac{3}{4} \div \frac{7}{8}$ **h** $\frac{6}{17} \div \frac{8}{9}$ **i** $\frac{5}{12} \div \frac{5}{8}$

j $\frac{8}{9} \div \frac{3}{5}$ **k** $\frac{3}{5} \div \frac{8}{9}$ **l** $\frac{5}{8} \div \frac{5}{32}$

Exercise 2.10B

1 Calculate each of these, showing any cancelling you use.

a $\frac{4}{7} \div \frac{2}{5}$ **b** $\frac{3}{8} \div \frac{3}{7}$ **c** $\frac{9}{10} \div \frac{6}{25}$

d $\frac{14}{15} \div \frac{3}{7}$ **e** $\frac{11}{20} \div \frac{3}{10}$ **f** $\frac{49}{100} \div \frac{7}{18}$

g $\frac{12}{29} \div \frac{3}{4}$ **h** $\frac{15}{19} \div \frac{5}{12}$ **i** $\frac{64}{99} \div \frac{20}{99}$

2 What is a twentieth of $\frac{100}{121}$?

3 Sadie has already driven $\frac{13}{28}$ of the distance between college and home. She wants to split the remaining distance into 5 equal parts. What fraction of the whole journey is each part?

4 a Write the mixed number $2\frac{6}{7}$ as an improper fraction.
  b Use your answer to part **a** to divide $2\frac{6}{7}$ by $\frac{5}{8}$.

5 Calculate:

a $\frac{3}{4} \div 1\frac{1}{2}$ **b** $\frac{7}{8} \div 1\frac{7}{8}$ **c** $2\frac{1}{6} \div 2\frac{5}{8}$ **d** $4\frac{1}{2} \div 2\frac{2}{3}$

> To divide with mixed numbers first convert them to improper fractions.

2.11 Simple percentages of an amount

▶ You need to know some simple fractions as percentages:

$\frac{1}{2} = 50\%$ $\frac{1}{4} = 25\%$ $\frac{1}{10} = 10\%$

$\frac{1}{5} = 20\%$ $\frac{1}{3} = 33\frac{1}{3}\%$

> **Remember:**
> % means out of 100

▶ You can find other percentages by using these fractions.

Example 1 Find $27\frac{1}{2}\%$ of £460

$$27\frac{1}{2}\% = (10\% \times 2) + 5\% + 2\frac{1}{2}\%$$

10% of £460 is $\frac{1}{10} \times £460 = £46$

So $27\frac{1}{2}\%$ of £460 $= (£46 \times 2) + £23 + £11.50 = £126.50$

Example 2 Find 85% of 280

85% is the same as $(25\% \times 3) + 10\%$

25% of 280 is $\frac{1}{4}$ of $280 = 70$

10% of 280 is $\frac{1}{10}$ of $280 = 28$

So 85% of $280 = (70 \times 3) + 28 = 210 + 28 = 238$

Exercise 2.11A

1 Calculate each of these using fractions.
- **a** 20% of £50
- **b** 60% of 600 people
- **c** 40% of 820 boxes
- **d** 80% of £45
- **e** 75% of 80 tins
- **f** $92\frac{1}{2}\%$ of £300

2 Vicky must pay 40% tax on a house she inherits.
The house is worth £120 000. How much tax must she pay?

Remember:
The red cars and the non-red cars must total 100%.

3 Carlo says 15% of the cars he sells are red.
He sells 420 cars a year. How many are **not** red?

Exercise 2.11B

1 Calculate each of these, showing all your working.
- **a** 35% of £700
- **b** 5% of £60
- **c** 45% of $360
- **d** 15% of 80 French francs
- **e** $67\frac{1}{2}\%$ of £513
- **f** $66\frac{2}{3}\%$ of 369 animals

2 VAT in some countries is set at 17.5%.
Calculate the VAT payable on these items which are net of VAT. Give your answers to the nearest penny.
- **a** Video £320
- **b** Computer £1250
- **c** Camera £34.70
- **d** Bike £645
- **e** Car £7840
- **f** Pen £9.45

Net of VAT means shown without VAT.

3 Of the £25 000 collected for charity, 35% went to children's funds, 47.5% went to overseas charities and the rest went to animal funds. How much went to each type of charity?

2.12 Finding any percentage of an amount

▶ To find a percentage of an amount you can use either of these methods.

- **Method 1**
  Multiply the amount by the percentage as a fraction.

  Example 1   Find 34% of £350

  $$\frac{34}{100} \times \frac{350}{1} = \frac{34^{17}}{100_{\cancel{2}\cancel{1}}} \times \frac{^{7}\cancel{350}}{1} = \frac{17}{1} \times \frac{7}{1} = \frac{119}{1}$$

  So 34% of £350 is £119

- **Method 2**
  Multiply the amount by the percentage as a decimal.

  Example 2   Find 34% of £350

  34% as a decimal is 0.34

  Work out $0.34 \times 350 = 119$ (with a calculator)

  So 34% of £350 is £119

Exercise 2.12A

1 Use Method 1 to calculate:
  a 45% of £600
  b 24% of £150
  c 25% of $240
  d 65% of 360 francs

2 Use Method 2 to calculate:
  a 36% of £550
  b 74% of £530
  c 57% of £3652
  d 6% of £78.50

Exercise 2.12B

1 Calculate:
  a 44% of £50
  b 68% of $300
  c 83% of £250
  d 55% of $360
  e 65% of $460
  f 42% of 400 Euros

2 Use Method 2 for these questions.
  Give each answer to the nearest penny.
  a 35% of £630
  b 58% of £56.50
  c 78% of £625
  d 17% of £124.40
  e 32% of £361.80
  f 57% of £93.67

3 a What decimal fraction is the same as $34\frac{1}{2}$%?
  b Calculate $34\frac{1}{2}$% of £784.50

4 a What decimal fraction is the same as $12\frac{3}{4}$%?
  b Calculate $12\frac{3}{4}$% of £48.70

2.13 Converting fractions and percentages

▶ To convert a fraction to a percentage multiply the fraction by $\frac{100}{1}$.

Example 1 Convert $\frac{5}{7}$ to a percentage.

$\frac{5}{7} \times \frac{100}{1} = \frac{500}{7}$

By calculator $500 \div 7 = 71.42857$ which is 71.4 correct to 1 dp.

So $\frac{5}{7}$ is about 71.4%

See rounding to 1 dp on page 20.

▶ To convert a percentage to a fraction
- first write it as a fraction in 100th
- then convert the fraction to its simplest form.

Example 2 Convert 18% to a fraction.

18% is $\frac{18}{100}$ Now simplify: $\frac{18}{100} = \frac{9}{50}$

So 18% is equal to $\frac{9}{50}$

See page 14. Divide the top and bottom by the HCF, 2 in this case.

Exercise 2.13A

1 Convert each fraction to a percentage.

a $\frac{3}{20}$ b $\frac{3}{5}$ c $\frac{3}{10}$ d $\frac{3}{8}$
e $\frac{7}{40}$ f $\frac{7}{10}$ g $\frac{9}{20}$ h $\frac{1}{5}$
i $\frac{27}{50}$ j $\frac{2}{7}$ k $\frac{2}{6}$ l $\frac{5}{13}$

2 Convert each percentage to a fraction in its simplest form.

a 12%   b 24%   c 83%
d 95%   e 6%   f 72%
g 15%   h 36%   i 47%

Exercise 2.13B

1 Convert each fraction to a percentage correct to 1 dp.

a $\frac{6}{13}$ b $\frac{7}{11}$ c $\frac{7}{16}$
d $\frac{5}{8}$ e $\frac{17}{24}$ f $\frac{29}{70}$
g $\frac{6}{11}$ h $\frac{7}{15}$ i $\frac{12}{23}$

2 Convert each percentage to a fraction in its simplest form.

a 8%   b 35%   c 19%   d 55%

3 By converting either to fractions or percentages decide which of each pair is the smaller.

a 16% or $\frac{7}{50}$ b 36% or $\frac{8}{25}$ c 84% or $\frac{22}{25}$

2.14 Percentage increase

▶ To increase an amount by a percentage you can use fractions or decimals. You do not need to find the increase and add it on.

- **Method 1 Using fractions**

  Example 1 Increase £650 by 35%
  An increase from 100% by 35% is equal to 135% of the amount.

  $$\frac{135}{100} \times \frac{650}{1} = \frac{\overset{27}{\cancel{135}}}{\underset{20_4}{\cancel{100}}} \times \frac{\overset{130}{\cancel{650}}}{1} = \frac{27}{4} \times 130 = \frac{3510}{4} = £877.50$$

- **Method 2 Using decimals**

  Example 2 Increase £243 by 27%
  An increase from 100% by 27% is equal to multiplying the amount by 1.27

  By calculator, £243 × 1.27 = £308.61

Exercise 2.14A

1 Use the fraction method to increase:
   a £450 by 20%   **b** £84 by 25%   **c** £560 by 10%
   d £520 by 45%   **e** £6 by 60%   **f** £568 by 15%

2 Use the decimal method to increase:
   a £48 by 19%   **b** £80 by 47%   **c** £123 by 28%
   d £7.50 by 34% **e** £7845 by 11% **f** £455 by 83%

3 What decimal would you multiply an amount by to find an increase of $17\frac{1}{2}\%$?

Exercise 2.14B

1 Use the most convenient method to increase:
   a £56 by 40%   **b** £2000 by 25% **c** £8.50 by 13%
   d £465 by 27%   **e** £84 by 46%   **f** £754 by 33%

2 Increase these amounts giving your answer to the nearest penny.
   a £124.62 by 12%   **b** £8.45 by 29%   **c** £56.30 by 55%

3 a By what decimal would you multiply to find an increase of $23\frac{1}{2}\%$?
   b Find £462 increased by $23\frac{1}{2}\%$ to the nearest penny.

4 Increase these amounts giving your answer to the nearest penny.
   a £14.63 by $8\frac{1}{2}\%$ **b** £156 by $34\frac{1}{4}\%$ **c** £186 by $6\frac{3}{4}\%$

2.15 Percentage decrease

▶ To decrease an amount by a percentage you can use fractions or decimals. You do not need to find the decrease and subtract it.

- **Method 1 Using fractions**

  Example 1 Decrease £650 by 35%
  A decrease from 100% by 35% is equal to 65% of the amount.

  $$\frac{65}{100} \times \frac{650}{1} = \frac{\cancel{65}^{13}}{\cancel{100}_{20_4}} \times \frac{\cancel{650}^{130}}{1} = \frac{13}{4} \times 130 = \frac{1690}{4} = £422.50$$

- **Method 2 Using decimals**

  Example 2 Decrease £243 by 27%
  A decrease of 100% by 27% is equal to multiplying the amount by 0.73

  > 0.73 is 1.00 − 0.27

  By calculator, £243 × 0.73 = £177.39

Exercise 2.15A

1 Use the fraction method to decrease:
   a £450 by 20%   b £84 by 25%   c £560 by 10%
   d £520 by 45%   e £6 by 60%   f £568 by 15%

2 Use the decimal method to decrease:
   a £48 by 19%   b £80 by 47%   c £123 by 28%
   d £7.50 by 34%   e £7845 by 11%   f £455 by 83%

3 What decimal would you multiply an amount by to find a decrease of $17\frac{1}{2}\%$?

Exercise 2.15B

1 Use the most convenient method to decrease:
   a £56 by 40%   b £2000 by 25%   c £8.50 by 13%
   d £465 by 27%   e £84 by 46%   f £754 by 33%

2 Decrease these amounts giving your answer to the nearest penny.
   a £124.62 by 12% b £8.45 by 29%   c £56.30 by 55%

3 a By what decimal would you multiply to find a decrease of $23\frac{1}{2}\%$?
   b Find £462 decreased by $23\frac{1}{2}\%$ to the nearest penny.

4 Decrease these amounts giving your answer to the nearest penny.
   a £14.63 by $8\frac{1}{2}\%$ b £156 by $34\frac{1}{4}\%$ c £186 by $6\frac{3}{4}\%$

2.16 Percentage problems

Exercise 2.16A

1 Of the 21 000 seats in a stadium, 45% are for season ticket holders.
How many seats are for non-season ticket holders?

2 A fashion jacket is usually sold for £160.
A sale has signs saying '15% off'.
What is the price of the jacket in the sale?

3 A shop sold 360 bikes in June 2000.
Of these 10% were classic touring bikes, 25% were childrens'
bikes, 40% were ATBs and 5% were for women.
  a List the number of bikes of each type that were sold.
  b In 2001 sales were expected to increase by about 8%.
  Roughly how many of each type were expected to be sold in 2001?

4 After a sales drive a company expects a 3.5% increase in sales.
They sell 134 000 items per month now.
  a How many do they hope to sell after their sales drive?
  b How many more items per month do they hope to sell?

Exercise 2.16B

1 A car park has 4700 cars in it. 21% are red, 17% are blue, 33%
are diesels, 2% are left-hand drive, 52% have 4 doors.
  a Add up all the percentages.
  Explain why this does not come to 100%?
  b Rewrite the passage above with numbers (i.e. not with percentages).

2 12.5% of the accidents in Bantron involve cars turning right.
There are 17 000 accidents in Bantron each year.
  a How many accidents last year **did not** involve cars turning right?

After road changes the number of accidents for cars turning
right was reduced by 16% but the overall number of accidents
stayed the same.
  b How many accidents now involved cars turning right?
  c What percentage of the total number of accidents was this?

3 28% of a mystery number is 742.
By using trial-and-improvement find the mystery number.

4 A mystery number was increased by 24% and became 193.44.
By using trial-and-improvement find this mystery number.

5 A mystery number was reduced by 12% and became 315.04.
By using trial-and-improvement find this mystery number.

2.17 Simple interest

▶ When you take out a loan you have to pay **interest** at a fixed percent. Occasionally **simple interest** is used.

Example 1 Calculate the total you must pay on £120 borrowed for 3 years at 4% pa. ('per annum' or 'each year')

After 1 year you owe £120 + 4% of £120
After 2 years you owe £120 + (2 × 4% of £120)
After 3 years you owe £120 + (3 × 4% of £120) = £120 + (3 × £4.80)
= £134.40

Simple interest – you only pay interest on the original loan and not on any interest you also owe.

▶ You can find the simple interest on any amount using:

$$\text{Interest} = \frac{\text{Principal} \times \text{Rate} \times \text{Time}}{100} \quad \text{or} \quad I = \frac{PRT}{100}$$

Principal – the amount you borrow.
Rate – the percentage rate per annum as a decimal.
Time – in years.

Example 2 Calculate the interest charged on a loan of £460 for 5 years at 7% pa.

$$I = \frac{P \times R \times T}{100} = \frac{460 \times 7 \times 5}{100} = £161$$

Exercise 2.17A

1 Calculate the simple interest on:
   a £420 for 5 years at 8% pa
   b £850 for 3 years at 10% pa
   c £62 for 8 years at 12% pa
   d £4280 for 7 years at 2% pa

2 Calculate the total amount to repay after borrowing:
   a £200 for 2 years at 7% pa
   b £782 for 3 years at 6% pa
   c £6843 for 7 years at 13% pa
   d £856 for 8 years at 3% pa

3 Rita borrows £600 at $5\frac{1}{3}$% pa simple interest from a friend and intends to repay the loan after $3\frac{1}{2}$ years.
How much will she have to repay in total?

Exercise 2.17B

1 Calculate the simple interest on:
   a £657 for 5 years at 11% pa
   b £340 for 6 years at 14% pa
   c £82 for 5 years at $12\frac{1}{2}$% pa
   d £1584 for 7 years at $2\frac{1}{2}$% pa

2 Calculate the total capital to repay after borrowing:
   a £240 for 2 years at 7.5% pa
   b £862 for $3\frac{1}{2}$ years at 6% pa
   c £640 for 8 years at 12.5% pa
   d £45 for 8 years at 3.5% pa

3 Calculate the simple interest payable on:
   a £480 for 4 months at 6% pa
   b £300 for 9 months at 11% pa
   c £40 for 2 months at 4.5% pa
   d £2600 for 18 months at $2\frac{1}{2}$% pa

2.18 Compound interest

▶ Most often with commercial loans **compound interest** is used. Look at how the interest builds up and is rounded in this example.

> **Compound interest** – you pay interest on the original loan **and** on any interest you also owe.

Example 1 Calculate the total you must pay on £120 borrowed for 3 years at 4% pa compound interest.

After 1 year you owe £120 + 4% of £120 = £120 + £4.80 = £124.80
After 2 years you owe £124.80 + 4% of £124.80 = £124.80 + £4.99 = £129.79
After 3 years you owe £129.79 + 4% of £129.79 = £129.79 + £5.19 = £134.98

▶ You can also find the compound interest using this formula:

$$\text{Interest} = \{\text{Principal} \times (1 + \text{Rate})^{\text{Time}}\} - \text{Principal}$$

> Rounding has been done in these examples just to show what is happening. Leave your rounding to the end.

Example 2 Calculate the interest charged on a loan of £460 for 5 years at 7% pa.

$$I = \{P \times (1 + R)^T\} - P = \{460 \times (1 + 0.07)^5\} - 460$$
$$= \{460 \times 1.07^5\} - 460$$
$$= \{460 \times 1.4026\} - 460$$

So the compound interest = 645.17 − 460 = £185.17

Exercise 2.18A

1 Calculate the total amount to repay after borrowing:
   a £200 at 3% pa compound interest for 2 years.
   b £600 at 10% pa compound interest for 3 years.
   c £70 at 5% pa compound interest for 3 years.
   d £2400 at 9% pa compound interest for 2 years.

2 Use the formula above to calculate the compound interest on
   a £100 invested for 2 years at 4% pa.
   b £500 borrowed for 3 years at 10% pa.

Exercise 2.18B

1 Calculate the total amount to repay after borrowing:
   a £1000 at 8% pa compound interest for 5 years.
   b £230 at 6% pa compound interest for 4 years.

2 Use the formula above to calculate the compound interest on:
   a £250 invested for 6 years at 2% pa.
   b £640 borrowed for 3 years at 9% pa.
   c £720 invested for 5 years at 17% pa.
   d £482 borrowed for 4 years at 12% pa.

2.19 Working with ratios

With ratio you can compare different parts of a whole.
You can use ratio to divide a quantity into unequal parts.

Example 1
Divide £2130 in the ratio 2:5:8.

The ratio is   2 parts : 5 parts : 8 parts   which is 15 parts in total.

So the £2130 must be divided into 15 equal parts which are then put in the ratio 2:5:8

To find 1 part	$2130 \div 15 = 142$
For 2 parts	$2 \times 142 = 284$
For 5 parts	$5 \times 142 = 710$
For 8 parts	$8 \times 142 = 1136$

So, £2130 divided in the ratio 2:5:8 is   £284 : £710 : £1136

> To check a ratio division the total of the parts will be the same as the quantity that you divided. Here the check is:
> $284 + 710 + 1136 = 2130$

Example 2
A paint colour is made by mixing red and blue dyes in the ratio 5:9. In the mix 315 litres of blue dye is used, how much red dye is used?

The ratio red : blue is 5:9   so the 315 litres of blue dye is 9 parts of the mix.

1 part is $315 \div 9 = 35$
for 5 parts $35 \times 5 = 175$

So, 175 litres of red dye are used in this mix.

> Check this gives the same ratio:
> $175 : 315$
> $= 5 : 9$

Exercise 2.19A

1 Divide each of these amounts in the ratio stated.
  a £56.24   in the ratio   3:5   **b** £63.36   in the ratio   4:5
  c £108.60   in the ratio   5:7   **d** £418.24   in the ratio   9:7
  e £963.24   in the ratio   15:8   **f** £248.27   in the ratio   13:24

2 Divide each of these amounts in the ratio stated.
  a 5005 km   in the ratio   4:5:2   **b** 930 km   in the ratio   7:3:5
  c 1743 km   in the ratio   5:3:7   **d** 6516 km   in the ratio   9:4:5
  e 16 000 km in the ratio   9:4:7   **f** 43 173 km in the ratio   7:12:22

3 The players in a hockey club are in the ratio 13:8 male to female. The club has 52 male players. How many of the players are female?

4 Sunfresh is a mix of water and fruit juice in the ratio 19:12. A mix uses 1054 litres of juice. How much water is in the mix?

5 A recipe for a sauce to serve four people uses:

200 g of butter, 320 g of flour and 200 ml of stock.

How much of each item is needed if you change the recipe to serve ten people?

6 A paint colour is made by mixing red, blue and yellow paint in the ratio 5 : 2 : 11. In the final mix 2257.5 litres of yellow paint are used.
  a For each of the other colours how much paint is used in the mix?
  b In total, how many litres of paint are in the mix?

7 Last year BJ Hols sold holidays to Spain, Portugal, Tenerife, Majorca, Ibiza and Minorca in the ratio 5 : 4 : 3 : 7 : 11 : 10.
The value of the holidays sold to Tenerife was £412 872.
  a Calculate the value of the holidays sold to Ibiza.
  b Calculate the total value of the holidays sold by BJ Hols last year.

> Check your answers.

Exercise 2.19B

1 Divide £5877.24 in the ratio 9 : 8.

2 Divide 141 048 km in the ratio 8 : 13 : 3.

3 A street collection makes a total of £120 066.60 for charity.
The money is shared between these charities:

Treescape, Shelter at Night, Infant Line and Animal Rescue

in the ratio 2 : 9 : 6 : 4. How much is given to each charity?

4 A team of five cyclists take part in a race.
The cyclists Jan, Kim, Ryan, Rob and Jo do the distance in the ratio 7 : 3 : 4 : 9 : 11. Kim cycles 177 km.
  a How far does Ryan cycle? **b** How far is the race?

5 A farmer sells four types of potato: Cara, Wilja, Desiree and Esteema. Last month the sales of Cara, Wilja, Desiree and Esteema were in the ratio 15 : 9 : 11 : 8, and records show that 1947 tonnes of Desiree were sold.
  a How many tonnes of Cara were sold?
  b In total, how many tonnes of potatoes did this farmer sell in the month?

6 The length and width of a rectangle are in the ratio 13 : 5.
The length of the rectangle is 45.5 cm.
  a Calculate the perimeter of the rectangle.
  b Calculate the area of the rectangle.

7 A recipe for 12 biscuits uses:

   300 g of butter, 600 g of flour and 200 g of sugar

   How much of each ingredient is needed to make 27 biscuits?

8 A group of friends shared £16 037 in prize winnings.
   Liam had 5 shares of the total which gave him £2765.
   Cara had 9 shares of the total.
   Karl had £3871 but couldn't remember how many shares he was given.
   Sasha had 8 shares of the total.
   a How much of the winnings did each of the friends receive?
   b Give the ratio in which the winnings were shared between them.

2.20 Adding and subtracting decimals

You can add or subtract decimals by keeping place values matched.
Very often you can do the calculation mentally.
Before you calculate an exact answer you should estimate the answer.

Example 1

Calculate the value of: $16.44 + 3.8 + 1.08$

Estimate the answer: $16 + 4 + 1 = 21$

To calculate the answer:

- write the numbers under each other
  to match the place values
- add the columns

```
  16.44
   3.8
   1.08
  -----
  21.32      (Estimate 21)
```

You can do a decimal calculation mentally by adding the two parts of the number separately.

Example 2

Calculate the value of: $44.86 + 13.5 + 7.16$

Estimate the answer: $45 + 14 + 7 = 66$

To calculate the answer mentally:

- add the decimal part $.86 + .5 + .16$ gives 1.52
- Add the whole number part $44 + 13 + 7$ gives 64

So, $44.86 + 13.5 + 7.16 = 65.52$ (Estimate 66)

Example 3

Calculate the value of: 78.62 − 24.76

Estimate the answer: 80 − 25 = 55

To calculate the answer:
- write the numbers under each other
  to match the place values
- subtract the columns

$$\begin{array}{r} 78.62 \\ 24.76 \\ \hline 53.86 \end{array}$$ (Estimate 55)

You can do the calculation mentally by counting on.

Example 4

Calculate the value of: 66.24 − 27.46

Estimate the answer: 66 − 28 = 38

To calculate the answer mentally:
- count on from 27.46 to 28   this gives   0.54
- count on from 28 to 66   this gives   38.54
- count on from 66 to 66.24   this gives   38.78

So, 66.24 − 27.46 = 38.78   (Estimate 38)

Exercise 2.20A

1 Use a mental method to calculate:
   a 12.46 + 17.5   **b** 34.21 + 16.82   **c** 15.66 + 43.08
   d 14.5 + 6.38 + 1.6 **e** 2.5 + 6.16 + 7.4   **f** 6.62 + 3.05 + 1.4

2 Use a written method to calculate each of these.
   You must show your working.
   a 45.62 + 73.9 + 122.07   **b** 123.4 + 58.05 + 8.4   **c** 188.06 + 2562.7
   d 12.17 + 245.6 + 39.75   **e** 162.88 + 53.76 + 14.09   **f** 1.61 + 12.6 + 66.08

3 Use a mental method to calculate:
   a 12.4 − 8.56   **b** 7.56 − 3.82   **c** 24.6 − 13.75   **d** 18.04 − 7.57
   e 34.2 − 17.65   **f** 19.2 − 15.78   **g** 38.07 − 17.4   **h** 20.6 − 13.75

4 Use a written method to calculate each of these.
   You must show your working.
   a 145.6 − 57.88   **b** 560.4 − 165.57   **c** 675.3 − 496.58   **d** 45.06 − 29.7
   e 2.07 − 0.85   **f** 0.8 − 0.09   **g** 0.7 − 0.07   **h** 157.08 − 0.7

Exercise 2.20B

1 Use a mental method to calculate:
   a 15.88 + 23.6   **b** 44.6 + 14.07   **c** 67.3 + 54.18   **d** 45.7 + 54.57
   e 123.8 + 43.87   **f** 56.8 + 25.75   **g** 56.08 + 167.6   **h** 107.15 + 74.65

2 Use a written method to calculate each of these.
You must show your working.
  a $23.16 + 7.04 + 25.3$
  b $108.75 + 56.8 + 39.97$
  c $56.62 + 76.86$
  d $125.4 + 3.07 + 76.86$
  e $345.83 + 57.07 + 45.3$
  f $1040.67 + 3.5$

3 Use a mental method to calculate:
  a $34.6 - 25.76$
  b $67.8 - 45.45$
  c $165.85 - 156.8$
  d $204.15 - 67.5$
  e $565.14 - 456.8$
  f $404.04 - 294.4$
  g $600.07 - 517.17$
  h $800.01 - 408.8$

4 Use a written method to calculate each of these.
You must show your working.
  a $200.5 - 156.78$
  b $450.3 - 375.28$
  c $460.08 - 367.72$
  d $565.55 - 348.88$
  e $2006.06 - 867.59$
  f $1004.04 - 444.44$
  g $3.08 - 0.19$
  h $0.4 - 0.75$

2.21 Multiplying and dividing decimals

You can use mental and written calculations to multiply or divide decimals. Remember to estimate answers, no matter which method you choose.

Example 1

Calculate the value of: 36.6×6.8

Estimate the answer: $40 \times 7 = 280$

To calculate the answer:

- write the calculation as numbers with no decimal points
- multiply in the normal way

$$\begin{array}{r} 366 \\ \times\ \ 68 \\ \hline 21960 \\ 2928 \\ \hline 24888 \end{array}$$

The estimate is 280 so you have to place the decimal point between the digits of the answer to make a number close to the estimate.

As a simple guide you could say:

  the answer must be between 200 and 300

With the digits 24888 you can make 248.88 between 200 and 300.

So $36.6 \times 6.8 = 248.88$ (Estimate 280)

> Notice that:
> $36.6 \times 6.8 = 248.88$
> ...   .
> 1 dp + 1 dp = 2 dp

Example 2

Calculate the value of $33.6 \div 1.2$

You can think of this as $336 \div 12$

Estimate the answer: $300 \div 10 = 30$

Calculate the answer

$$12 \overline{)33^96}^{028}$$

So $33.6 \div 1.2 = 28$ (Estimate 30)

You can now answer a family of decimal calculations:

As	$336 \div 12$	$= 28$
You can say that:	$33.6 \div 1.2$	$= 28$
and	$3.36 \div 0.12$	$= 28$
and	$0.336 \div 0.012$	$= 28$ and so on.

Exercise 2.21A

1 Use a written method to calculate each of these.
You must show your working.
- **a** 27.6×5.7
- **b** 38.5×8.6
- **c** 67.8×8.3
- **d** 48.7×5.9
- **e** 67.8×5.4
- **f** 6.7×14.8
- **g** 56.8×4.7
- **h** 75.4×5.9

2 Show how you calculate:
- **a** 342.6×1.8
- **b** 565.4×7.6
- **c** 643.8×5.7
- **d** 226.4×5.8
- **e** 207.6×7.6
- **f** 707.9×4.3
- **g** 885.4×6.2
- **h** 3004.7×7.6

3 Use a written method to calculate:
- **a** $47.6 \div 1.4$
- **b** $75.4 \div 1.3$
- **c** $118.4 \div 1.6$
- **d** $110.4 \div 1.2$
- **e** $185.6 \div 1.6$
- **f** $244.8 \div 1.8$
- **g** $362.1 \div 1.7$
- **h** $613.7 \div 1.9$

Exercise 2.21B

1 Use a written method to calculate each of these.
You must show your working.
- **a** 38.4×1.8
- **b** 37.5×9.4
- **c** 69.8×6.5
- **d** 68.7×7.8
- **e** 97.8×7.2
- **f** 3.8×16.6
- **g** 36.8×5.4
- **h** 95.4×3.7

2 Show how you calculate:
- **a** 432.6×2.4
- **b** 656.4×8.1
- **c** 436.8×7.4
- **d** 626.4×6.7
- **e** 720.6×5.3
- **f** 636.9×5.8
- **g** 585.4×8.3
- **h** 4006.7×2.8

3 Use a written method to calculate:
- **a** $109.2 \div 1.4$
- **b** $315.9 \div 1.3$
- **c** $571.2 \div 1.6$
- **d** $899.2 \div 1.6$
- **e** $70.2 \div 2.6$
- **f** $355.6 \div 2.8$
- **g** $1021.2 \div 3.7$
- **h** $1635.6 \div 2.9$

2.22 The effect of multiplying or dividing by numbers less than one

▶ When you multiply a decimal value by a number that is less than one, the answer will be less than the decimal value you started with.

Example 1
Calculate 15.6×0.4

Estimate the answer: $\quad 16 \times \frac{1}{2} = 8$

Think of the calculation as 156×4, this gives the digits 624
(You could use long multiplication for this.)

So $\quad 15.6 \times 0.4 = 6.24 \quad$ (Estimate 8)

Note, working in this way you must be sure that your answer is of the right size.

Similarly you can calculate the value of 6.7×0.8

$\quad 6.7 \times 0.8 = 5.36 \quad (67 \times 8 = 536)$
$\quad$ 1 dp + 1 dp = 2 dp

▶ When you divide a value by a number less than one, the answer will be **greater** than the value you started with.

Example 2
Calculate $7.56 \div 0.6$

Estimate the answer: $\quad 8 \div \frac{1}{2} = 16$

Think of the calculation as $756 \div 6$, this gives the digits 126
(You could use long division for this.)

So $\quad 7.56 \div 0.6 = 12.6 \quad$ (Estimate 16)

You can check your answer:

If $\quad 7.56 \div 0.6 = 12.6 \quad$ then $\quad 12.6 \times 0.6$ should be 7.56

(As $12.6 \times 0.6 = 7.56$ the calculation is correct.)

Exercise 2.22A

1 Calculate:
- a $\;4.88 \times 0.7$
- b $\;5.6 \times 0.3$
- c $\;18.7 \times 0.2$
- d $\;29.7 \times 0.8$
- e $\;6.7 \times 0.2$
- f $\;18.9 \times 0.6$
- g $\;27.4 \times 0.9$
- h $\;36.5 \times 0.7$
- i $\;45.68 \times 1.3$
- j $\;18.64 \times 1.7$
- k $\;22.75 \times 2.6$
- l $\;3.67 \times 3.5$
- m $\;16.7 \times 2.8$
- n $\;25.6 \times 4.8$
- o $\;63.4 \times 6.7$
- p $\;47.3 \times 1.2$

2 Calculate:
   a $27.6 \div 0.4$
   b $38.5 \div 0.5$
   c $22.5 \div 0.3$
   d $46.9 \div 0.7$
   e $138.6 \div 0.6$
   f $569.6 \div 0.8$
   g $463.5 \div 0.5$
   h $304.2 \div 0.3$
   i $366.1 \div 0.7$
   j $5073.5 \div 0.5$
   k $283.4 \div 0.2$
   l $146.7 \div 0.9$
   m $5062.6 \div 0.2$
   n $357.6 \div 0.8$
   o $4226.5 \div 0.3$
   p $1337.6 \div 0.4$

Exercise 2.22B

1 Calculate:
   a 38.6×0.8
   b 132.4×0.7
   c 204.8×0.3
   d 166.5×0.4
   e 304.6×1.2
   f 223.6×1.4
   g 15.8×6.2
   h 131.4×4.5
   i 24.6×3.8
   j 18.4×3.7
   k 37.8×5.4
   l 65.2×7.2

2 Calculate:
   a $45.6 \div 0.4$
   b $157.8 \div 0.6$
   c $487.5 \div 0.5$
   d $743.4 \div 0.7$
   e $46.2 \div 1.2$
   f $400.8 \div 1.5$
   g $65.7 \div 1.8$
   h $140.64 \div 2.4$
   i $354.2 \div 1.4$
   j $471.25 \div 2.5$
   k $90.24 \div 1.6$
   l $846.12 \div 2.2$

3 A calculation was answered in this way:
   $$333.84 \div 2.6 = 100.2$$
   Show how a check will tell you that the answer is wrong.

Revision exercise 2   *Review*

1 Show how you calculate each of these.
   a 345×68 b 673×84 c 125×654 d 764×835 *Unit 2.1*

2 Show how you calculate each of these.
   a $3\,309\,345 \div 9$ b $8218 \div 14$ c $9525 \div 15$ d $25\,024 \div 16$ *Unit 2.2*

3 A metalworking machine costs £365 485.
   A firm buys 17 of these machines.
   How much will they pay in total?   *Unit 2.3*

4 The total ticket sales for a concert was £1 012 572.
   Tickets were £18 each. How many tickets were sold?   *Unit 2.3*

5 In 28 days an aircraft flew a total of 14 896 km.
   How many km per day is this?   *Unit 2.3*

6 Water is pumped from a river at a rate of 11 100 litres per hour.
   a How many litres per minute is this?
   b How many litres per day is this?
   c How much water is pumped over 3 years? (1 year = 52 weeks)   *Unit 2.3*

7 Copy each calculation and put in brackets to give the answer.
   a $6 + 7 \times 5 - 3 = 26$ b $5 \times 9 - 5 \div 8 + 2 = 2$ *Unit 2.4*

8 Use **BODMAS** to evaluate each of these. *Review*
  a $4 + 5 \times 16 + 8 \div 2 =$ **b** $24 - 16 \times 4 + 20 \div 4 \div 12 =$
  c $\sqrt{81} + 5 \times 12 - 10 \div 2 =$ **d** $(12.4 + 3.6) \div 8 - 55 \times 4 =$ *Unit 2.4*

9 Write a BODMAS calculation that gives an answer of 120. *Unit 2.4*

10 Calculate each of these.
  a $\frac{2}{3}$ of £36 000 **b** $\frac{3}{5}$ of £455 000 **c** $\frac{3}{8}$ of 4224 km
  d $\frac{7}{12}$ of 8328 kg **e** $\frac{11}{15}$ of 10 425 ml **f** $\frac{17}{20}$ of 642 800 tons *Unit 2.5*

11 Write each number as a fraction of the other.
  a 12 as a fraction of 20 **b** 15 as a fraction of 50 *Unit 2.6*

12 A club has 72 players and 42 of them are female.
  What fraction of the players are male? *Unit 2.6*

13 On a flight a total of 264 meals were served. Of these 36 meals were vegetarian.
  What fraction of the meals served were not vegetarian? *Unit 2.6*

14 Calculate each of these.
  a $\frac{2}{3} + \frac{3}{4}$ **b** $\frac{3}{5} + \frac{5}{8}$ **c** $\frac{3}{4} + \frac{7}{10}$ **d** $\frac{1}{3} + \frac{7}{8}$
  e $1\frac{1}{2} + 1\frac{3}{5}$ **f** $2\frac{3}{4} + 1\frac{3}{5}$ **g** $2\frac{1}{8} + 3\frac{5}{9}$ **h** $\frac{5}{8} + 3\frac{7}{10}$ *Unit 2.7*

15 Calculate each of these.
  a $\frac{3}{4} - \frac{2}{5}$ **b** $\frac{5}{8} - \frac{1}{6}$ **c** $\frac{7}{10} - \frac{1}{8}$ **d** $\frac{4}{7} - \frac{1}{2}$
  e $1\frac{1}{2} - \frac{7}{12}$ **f** $2\frac{1}{4} - 1\frac{2}{3}$ **g** $2\frac{1}{2} - 1\frac{5}{6}$ **h** $1\frac{3}{4} - 1\frac{2}{5}$ *Unit 2.8*

16 Calculate each of these.
  a $\frac{3}{5} \times \frac{2}{3}$ **b** $\frac{5}{8} \times \frac{2}{7}$ **c** $\frac{5}{6} \times \frac{5}{8}$ **d** $\frac{3}{8} \times \frac{7}{9}$ *Unit 2.9*

17 Calculate:
  a $1\frac{1}{2} \times \frac{3}{5}$ **b** $1\frac{2}{3} \times 3\frac{1}{2}$ **c** $2\frac{1}{4} \times 1\frac{5}{8}$ **d** $3\frac{2}{3} \times 2\frac{3}{7}$ *Unit 2.9*

18 Calculate each of these.
  a $\frac{5}{8} \div 2$ **b** $\frac{3}{4} \div 5$ **c** $\frac{2}{3} \div 4$ **d** $\frac{4}{9} \div 6$
  e $\frac{3}{7} \div \frac{1}{2}$ **f** $\frac{4}{5} \div \frac{3}{8}$ **g** $\frac{3}{5} \div \frac{5}{8}$ **h** $\frac{4}{7} \div \frac{5}{12}$ *Unit 2.10*

19 Evaluate:
  a $1\frac{1}{2} \div \frac{3}{4}$ **b** $2\frac{1}{3} \div 3\frac{1}{2}$ **c** $1\frac{3}{5} \div 1\frac{1}{4}$ **d** $3\frac{1}{4} \div 2\frac{2}{7}$ *Unit 2.10*

20 Calculate each of these showing all your working.
  a 35% of £1650 **b** 54% of £2040 **c** 71% of £328 851 *Unit 2.11*

21 What decimal fraction is equivalent to each of these?
  a 57% **b** 39% **c** 16% **d** 7% **e** $12\frac{1}{2}$% **f** 27.4% *Unit 2.12*

22 Show how you calculate each of these.
  a 18% of £344 566 **b** 82% of £34.50 **c** 44% of £74 560.50 *Unit 2.12*

Review
Unit 2.13

23 Convert each of these to a percentage correct to 1 dp.
   a $\frac{5}{8}$ b $\frac{3}{13}$ c $\frac{5}{18}$ d $\frac{7}{20}$ e $\frac{9}{24}$ f $\frac{11}{30}$

24 Convert each of these to a fraction in its lowest terms.
   a 35%   b 42%   c 65%   d 94%   e 85%   f 12%

Unit 2.13

25 Increase these amounts, giving your answer to the nearest penny.
   a £245.60 by 16%   b £34 482.50 by 37%   c £855.24 by 61%

Unit 2.14

26 Decrease each of these amounts, giving your answer correct to 2 dp.
   a 356 kg by 28%   b 48 858 km by 38%   c 5675 tonnes by 74%

Unit 2.15

27 Calculate the simple interest on:
   a £380 for 4 years at 5%   b £4765 for 6 years at 7.5%

Unit 2.17

28 Calculate the compound interest on:
   a £1455 for 9 years at 6%   b £35 688 for 15 years at 4.5%

Unit 2.18

29 Divide each of these in the ratio given.
   a £9656 in the ratio 3 : 5   b £67 704 in the ratio 2 : 3 : 7

Unit 2.19

30 Calculate each of these and show your working.
   a $125.68 + 34.07 + 0.4 + 205$ b $34.9 + 1258.04 + 19 - 0.6 + 34.0052$

Unit 2.20

31 Calculate each of these showing all your working.
   a $300 - 197.0855$ b $245.06 - 87.86581$ c $10\,004.01 - 588.5925$

Unit 2.20

32 Use a written method to calculate each of these.
   a 34.6×1.2 b 35.4×3.8 c 56.5×7.5 d 78.2×8.3

Unit 2.21

33 Calculate each of these using a written method.
   a $789.6 \div 1.4$ b $12\,113.6 \div 2.6$ c $19\,288.8 \div 34.2$

Unit 2.21

34 Calculate each of these using a written method.
   a 5.75×0.6 b 6.84×0.9 c 2.55×0.88 d 3.61×0.56

Unit 2.22

35 Calculate each of these using a written method.
   a $3604.565 \div 0.2$ b $324.884 \div 0.5$ c $1827.36 \div 0.4$

Unit 2.22

Investigation

The stamp machine

A stamp machine is to be built to dispense two different books of postage stamps.

The type of book dispensed will depend on the amount of money put into the machine.

What do you think these books of stamps should sell for and what value stamps should they contain?

Should the machine give change?

What other things need to be taken into account?

Write a report giving your suggestions and reasons.

3 Equations, Formulae and Identities

▶ In an **equation** a letter stands for an unknown number:
$$3x + 1 = 7, \quad x^2 - 7 = 42.$$

▶ In an **identity**, both sides of the equation are exactly the same whatever the value of the letter:
$$x + x = 2x, \quad t^2 = t \times t.$$

> An identity is a special kind of equation.

▶ In a **formula** a letter stands for a quantity that can vary:
$$s = \frac{D}{T}, \quad a^2 = b^2 + c^2.$$

> The plural of formula is formulae.

3.1 Collecting like terms

$3x + 4y - 6z$ is an algebraic expression.
Each part of the expression is a term.
So $3x$, $4y$ and $6z$ are terms in the expression.
Like terms use exactly the same variable (letter).

$4y$ and $6y$ are **like terms**, $4y$ and $6ay$ are **not like terms**.

You can simplify an algebraic expression by collecting like terms.

Example 1
Collect like terms to simplify: $\quad 6ab + 5y + 2ab - y$

$6ab + 5y + 2ab - y = 8ab + 4y$ (You treat ab as one variable.)

> **Remember:**
> y is the same as $1y$.

Example 2
Collect like terms to simplify: $9bx + k - 8 + 3k - 2bx$

$9bx + k - 8 + 3k - 2bx = 7bx + 4k - 8$ (The 8 is a number with no variable.)

Exercise 3.1A

1 Collect like terms to simplify:
  a $5y + 3x + y + 3x$
  b $3c + 7a + c - 4a$
  c $12 + 4y - 5a + 3y + 9a$
  d $5bc + 4 - 3x - 3bc + 2x$
  e $ax + ay + 4x + 2ay + ax$
  f $4v + 5 - v + 2ab + 3v - ab$

2 Collect like terms and simplify:
  a $5ay - 3ax + ay - ax$
  b $17c + 3ax + c - 4ax + 3$
  c $5 - 6h + 3xy + h - xy + 1$
  d $8k + 4 - 5v + 2ay + k - 9v$

Exercise 3.1B

1 Collect like terms in each of these expressions.
  a $7x + 5xy + 3 - xy + 5x$
  b $8t + 5bc + y - bc - 13t + 6$
  c $12y - 4cv - 7 + cv - y + 1$
  d $5 - 3ac + x + ac - 6x - 1$

2 Copy and complete each of these.
  a $5y + 6x + \square + 5x = 11x + 7y$
  b $3cx + 5y - cx + \square + 3 = 2cx + 6y + 3$
  c $8 - \square + 2bc + 8x - bc - 1 = 2x + bc + 7$
  d $5k + 3 - \square + 3k - 9av - 15 = 8k - 15av - 12$
  e $gh - 7 + gh + \square - 8h + gh - 12g = 3gh - 8h - 7g - 7$
  f $\square + 12xy - 15x - 15y - 70 + 35x = 20x + 12xy - 15y - 15$

3.2 Brackets in algebra*

You can multiply out a bracket in algebra.
You must multiply each term *inside* the bracket by the term *outside* the bracket.

> Multiply out the bracket means the same as:
> - remove the bracket
>   or
> - expand the bracket.

Example 1
Multiply out: $4(5y + 3x - 2xy - 7)$

$$4(5y + 3x - 2xy - 7) = 20y + 12x - 8xy - 28$$

Exercise 3.2A

1 Multiply out each of these brackets.
  a $5(6x + 3y - 4)$
  b $2(3ax + 5ay - 5 - k)$
  c $7(3vt - k + 4 + 3xy)$
  d $5(kt + 3x - 2y + 5 - xy)$
  e $12(4gx - 1 + 2gh - 3xy + 8h)$
  f $2(gx + 3gy - xt + 5)$

2 Remove the brackets from each of these.
  a $6(5ak - ay + 7k - 19)$
  b $25(6x - 2xy + 3y - 4)$
  c $9(12gh - hk - 23 - 4ah)$
  d $15(cky + 7y - 3ax + 4x - 9c + 1)$
  e $22(4hy - 5pk + 3h - 7y - p)$
  f $\frac{1}{2}(2x - 4y + 3z)$

Exercise 3.2B

1 Remove the brackets from each of these.
  a $3(5ay - 4x + 7cy - 3 + 5ax)$
  b $7(6xy + 7py - 4y + 2p - 18)$
  c $14(3y + 5p - 7py + x - 12)$
  d $9(15ax + xy + ay - 3x + cx + 1)$
  e $3(15k - 31ak + by + 5ax - bk)$
  f $21(3hk - 4ay + 8gh - 7k - 4y + 1)$

2 Copy and complete each of these.

  a $4(3ay + \square - \square) = 12ay + 20x - 28$
  b $8(\square - 7a - \square + 6x - 2) = 40xy - \square - 8bc + \square - \square$
  c $5(5ac - \square + 5y - \square + 9x - \square) = \square - 10ay + \square - 5xy + \square - 60$
  d $154 \div 11 - 6 \times \square + 2 \times 9 = 2$

3 This wrong answer was given by a student.

$$4(3ay + 5ax - xy + 4) = 12ay + 20ax + 16$$

  a Explain the mistake the student made.
  b Give the correct answer.

4 These two brackets, when expanded give the same expression

$\quad\quad\quad 5(8ax + 4y + 12xy - 4)$
and $\quad 4(10ax + 3y + 20xy + 2y - 5xy - 5)$

Explain how this can be.

You can multiply two brackets.
You must multiply each term in the second bracket by each term in the first.

Example 2
Multiply out and simplify: $(3y + 4)(2y - 3)$

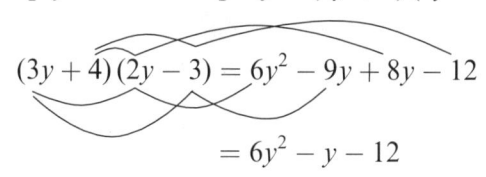

$(3y + 4)(2y - 3) = 6y^2 - 9y + 8y - 12$

$\quad\quad\quad\quad\quad\quad\quad = 6y^2 - y - 12$

> Multiplying out brackets may be called expanding brackets.

> Here you collect like terms to simplify the expression.

Exercise 3.2C

1 Multiply out the brackets in each of these.
  a $(4y + 2)(3y + b - 2)$ **b** $(2x - 3)(3a + 2x - 5)$
  c $(3x - 5)(5 - 3x)$ **d** $(3y + 5)(6y - 8)$
  e $(7k + 3)(3k + 7)$ **f** $(3b - 9)(4b + 7)$
  g $(3x + 1)(x - 1)$ **h** $(y + 4)(7 - 5y)$
  i $(3x + 4)(4 - x)$ **j** $(5 - y)(y - 5)$

2 In each of these, expand the brackets.
  a $(2k + 3x - 4)(5 + 2x)$ **b** $(3x - 4)(2y + 3x - 5)$
  c $(6 - 7y)(5 + y - 2c)$ **d** $(a + b - c)(3y + 4x)$
  e $(5 + 2y - k)(3k - 4)$ **f** $(3k - 4)(3k + 4)$
  g $(4x - 3)(4x + 3)$ **h** $(a + h)(a - h)$

Exercise 3.2D

1 Expand the brackets and simplify each of these.
  a $(x+4)(3x-5)$
  b $(2y-3)(3y-7)$
  c $(5y-4)(3y+5x-2)$
  d $(6k+8)(9-5k)$
  e $(5-8y)(2c+y-7)$
  f $(x-5)(x^2+3x-8)$
  g $(x^2-4x-3)(x+2)$
  h $(h^3+40)(3h-5)$
  i $(5y^2-4)(7-2y^2)$
  j $(p^2+1)(5-4p+p^2)$

2 a $(8-3c)(5+4c-c^2)$
  b $(c^2-4)(3c^2+5c-8)$
  c $(5+4y)(5-4y)$
  d $(y^2+5)(y^2-5)$
  e $(x^2+5x-3)(x^2+6x-4)$
  f $(x^3+x^2-5x)(7-4x)$

3 Write and simplify an expression for the area of each of these shapes.

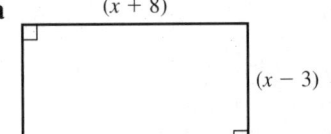

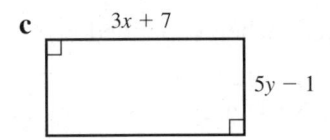

  a rectangle with sides $(x+8)$ and $(x-3)$
  b square with sides $x+y$ and $3x-y$
  c rectangle with sides $3x+7$ and $5y-1$

> There is more about area on page 177.

3.3 Simple factorising*

You can think of factorising as the reverse of multiplying out a bracket. You can factorise an expression to end up with a bracket and a term outside.

Example 1
Factorise $12ax - 15y$

- There are no letters common in every term.
- There is a factor of 3 in every term.

$$12ax - 15y = 3 \times 4ax - 3 \times 5y$$

You can take the common 3 outside a bracket.

So, $12ax - 15y = 3(4ax - 5y)$

> A common factor can be a number or a letter. Common means the number or letter can be found in every term of the expression.

Example 2
Factorise $6ay + 5ab - 4ax$

- There is a letter a common in every term.
- There is no number that is a common factor in every term.

You can take the common a outside a bracket.

So, $6ay + 5ab - 4ax = a(6y + 5b - 4x)$

Exercise 3.3A

1 Factorise each of these expressions.
- **a** $16ab + 20xy$
- **b** $24kx - 3bc$
- **c** $27ay + 36bx$
- **d** $56xy + 32kp$
- **e** $72bc - 108gh$
- **f** $32ty + 120k$

2 Factorise each expression.
- **a** $12xy - 19ax + 17bx$
- **b** $11ac + 20ck - 8cy$
- **c** $25kp - 5ap + 12px$
- **d** $9kx + 3ak - 5ky$
- **e** $7abc + 9bx - 11aby$
- **f** $7c + 3bc - 5acy + 2cx$

Exercise 3.3B

1 Factorise each of these expressions.
- **a** $12ax + 6kx - 9ak$
- **b** $30xy - 5ay + 15ax$
- **c** $28kp - 21px + 35kx$
- **d** $8bc + 14x - 4y$
- **e** $144gh + 60xy - 36$
- **f** $32ty + 56km - 8 + 16xy$

2 Factorise each expression.
- **a** $3ax + 5axy - 2xy$
- **b** $15kxy + 9kx - 2ak$
- **c** $24bc + 16ab - 12b$
- **d** $4xy + 16ax - 8bx$
- **e** $27abc - 24axy + 9a$
- **f** $axy + abx - acy$

You can sometimes factorise expressions like: $x^2 + 5x - 24$
The x^2 term shows there will be two factors, usually brackets.

Example 3
Factorise $x^2 + 5x - 24$
$+8$ and -3 are factors of -24, also $+8$ and -3 added give $+5$
$$x^2 + 5x - 24 = (x + 8)(x - 3)$$

Exercise 3.3C

1 Factorise each of these expressions.
- **a** $x^2 + 4x - 5$
- **b** $x^2 + 7x - 18$
- **c** $x^2 - 5x - 24$
- **d** $x^2 - 9x + 14$
- **e** $x^2 + 8x - 20$
- **f** $x^2 - 11x + 24$
- **g** $x^2 + 3x - 108$
- **h** $x^2 - 9x - 22$
- **i** $x^2 - 10x + 24$
- **j** $x^2 + 8x - 48$
- **k** $x^2 - 11x + 28$
- **l** $x^2 - 14x + 24$

> You can check each of your answers by expanding the brackets you have found and simplifying. You should get the expression you factorised.

Exercise 3.3D

1 Factorise each of these expressions.
- **a** $x^2 + x - 56$
- **b** $x^2 - x - 56$
- **c** $x^2 - 23x - 24$
- **d** $14 + 9x + x^2$
- **e** $x^2 - 5x - 36$
- **f** $x^2 - 25x + 24$
- **g** $x^2 - 23x + 132$
- **h** $x^2 + x - 72$
- **i** $x^2 - 2x - 24$
- **j** $x^2 - 19x - 20$
- **k** $x^2 + 10x - 75$
- **l** $x^2 + 2x - 24$

66 Equations, formulae and identities

An expression like $x^2 - 36$ is known as a difference of two squares.
(Each term is a square and the terms are subtracted.)
A difference of two squares can be factorised.

Example 4
Factorise $x^2 - 36$

$$x^2 - 36 = (x+6)(x-6) \quad [(\sqrt{x^2} + \sqrt{36})(\sqrt{x^2} - \sqrt{36})]$$

Exercise 3.3E

1 Factorise each of these:
  a $x^2 - 49$ **b** $x^2 - 64$ **c** $x^2 - 625$ **d** $4x^2 - 144$ **e** $x^6 - 81$

Exercise 3.3F

1 Factorise each of these:
  a $x^4 - 121$ **b** $4x^2 - 100$ **c** $16x^2 - 169$ **d** $a^2 - b^2$ **e** $x^4 - 4y^2$

3.4 Solving an equation by balancing

▶ You can think of an equation like a balance.
  The = sign is the balance point.

Example 1
Solve $3x + 5 = 11$

You need to isolate the unknown term.

Stage 1: Take 5 **from both sides**.

$$3x + 5 - 5 = 11 - 5$$

So $3x = 6$

Stage 2: Divide **both sides** by 3.

$$3x \div 3 = 6 \div 3$$

So $x = 2$

Example 2
Solve the equation $3d - 6 = 18$.

Add 6 to both sides $\quad 3d - 6 + 6 = 18 + 6$

So $\quad 3d = 24$

Divide both sides by 3 $\quad 3d \div 3 = 24 \div 3$

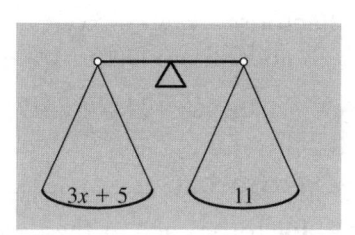

So $\quad d = 8$

> You add 6 because you want the −6 to cancel out.

Exercise 3.4A

1 Solve these equations. Show all the stages.
   a $h + 3 = 12$ **b** $v + 6 = 9$ **c** $f + 4 = 10$
   d $d + 7 = 22$ **e** $s + 21 = 40$ **f** $10 + t = 28$
   g $2x + 5 = 11$ **h** $3z + 1 = 16$ **i** $4s + 7 = 23$
   j $2h + 6 = 16$ **k** $7k + 7 = 42$ **l** $4f + 4 = 40$

> Check each answer by putting its value back in the equation to make sure it balances.

2 Solve each of these equations.
   a $f - 24 = 56$ **b** $w - 53 = 173$ **c** $g - 9 = 14$ **d** $2d - 2 = 8$
   e $5f - 3 = 12$ **f** $4e - 10 = 26$ **g** $5s - 10 = 0$ **h** $6w - 2 = 58$
   i $7x - 6 = 43$ **j** $5q - 3 = 52$ **k** $3e - 8 = 25$ **l** $20y - 4 = 96$

Exercise 3.4B

1 Solve each of these equations.
   a $5s + 4 = 39$ **b** $5a - 20 = 80$ **c** $17 = x - 5$
   d $6d - 17 = 67$ **e** $5r + 6 = 6$ **f** $6p + 54 = 120$

> **Remember:**
> $17 = x - 5$ is the same as $x - 5 = 17$

2 Solve each of these equations showing each stage.
   a $5s + 4 = 19$ **b** $45 = y - 8$ **c** $4x - 13 = 27$ **d** $6d - 14 = 58$
   e $19 = 2s + 3$ **f** $48 = 4g - 4$ **g** $12t + 7 = 103$ **h** $7v - 27 = 29$
   i $0 = 6r - 48$ **j** $93 = 6t + 9$ **k** $5t + 34 = 124$ **l** $56 = 7r - 7$

3.5 Equations with unknowns on both sides

▶ To solve an equation with unknown letters on both sides first change it so all the unknowns are on one side.

Example 1   Solve $5t - 4 = 2t + 8$

Subtract $2t$ from both sides $5t - 2t - 4 = 2t - 2t + 8$
So $3t - 4 = 8$
Add 4 to both sides $3t - 4 + 4 = 8 + 4$
So $3t = 12$
Divide both sides by 3 $3t \div 3 = 12 \div 3$
So $t = 4$

> **Hint:**
> Collect the ts on the side with the higher number of them.

> **Check:**
> $5 \times 4 - 4 = 20 - 4 = 16$
> $2 \times 4 + 8 = 8 + 8 = 16$
>
> Both answers are the same so the answer is correct.

Example 2   Solve $2s - 7 = 6s - 27$

Subtract $2s$ from both sides $2s - 2s - 7 = 6s - 2s - 27$
So $^-7 = 4s - 27$
Add 27 to both sides $-7 + 27 = 4s - 27 + 27$
So $20 = 4s$
Divide both sides by 4 $20 \div 4 = 4s \div 4$
So $5 = s$ or $s = 5$

Hint:
Here the ss are collected on the right-hand side because $6s$ is larger than $2s$.

Check:
$2 \times 5 - 7 = 10 - 7 = 3$
$6 \times 5 - 27 = 30 - 27 = 3$
Both sides are the same so the answer is correct.

Exercise 3.5A

1 Solve these equations.
   a $6f = 4f + 14$
   b $8d = 3d + 15$
   c $12 + 3g = 7g$
   d $6w + 7 = 7w$
   e $7z + 1 = 48$
   f $4q - 8 = 2q$

2 Solve these equations.
   a $5x + 1 = 3x + 13$
   b $7d - 4 = 2d + 16$
   c $6x + 3 = 2x - 5$
   d $5p - 3 = 3p - 15$

Remember:
$^-5 - 3 = {}^-8$ and
$^-15 + 3 = {}^-12$
See page 4.

Exercise 3.5B

1 Solve these equations.
   a $3a + 2 = 2a + 7$
   b $7h - 2 = 3h + 2$
   c $7g - 15 = g - 3$
   d $6p + 3 = 3p + 12$
   e $3u + 20 = 8u$
   f $5h - 7 = h + 9$
   g $17q - 5 = 2q + 10$
   h $7s + 94 = 23s + 14$

2 Solve these equations.
   a $5a + 6 = 2a - 3$
   b $8h - 4 = 2h - 20$
   c $9t - 3 = 8t - 18$
   d $7y + 3 = 12y + 8$
   e $6h - 5 = 4h - 17$
   f $3c - 2 = 7c + 6$
   g $5x - 2 = x - 14$
   h $y + 2 = 5y + 18$

3.6 Solving equations with fractions

▶ To solve an equation including fractions:
  - rearrange the equation if necessary
  - multiply all the terms in the equation by the denominator.

Example 1 Solve $\frac{3t}{4} + 5 = 59$

So $\quad \frac{3t}{4} = 54 \quad$ (Subtract 5 from both sides.)

$\quad\quad 3t = 54 \times 4 \quad$ (Multiply every term by 4.)

$\quad\quad 3t = 216$

So, $\quad t = 72 \quad$ (Divide both sides by 3.)

Check: $(3 \times 72 \div 4) + 5 = 59$ ✓

▶ When the unknown is the denominator you multiply through by the unknown.

Example 2 Solve $\frac{54}{k} - 12 = 6$

$\quad \frac{54}{k} = 18 \quad$ (Add 12 to both sides.)

$\quad 54 = 18 \times k \quad$ (Multiply every term by k.)

$\quad \frac{54}{18} = k \quad$ (Divide both sides by 18.)

$\quad k = 3 \quad$ (Calculate and reverse.)

Check: $(54 \div 3) - 12 = 6$ ✓

Exercise 3.6A

1 Solve these equations.

  a $\frac{p}{4} = 86$ **b** $\frac{t}{2} + 7 = 19$ **c** $\frac{h}{8} - 14 = 24$

2 Solve these equations.

  a $\frac{40}{y} = 10$ **b** $\frac{15}{t} - 3 = 2$ **c** $\frac{148}{x} + 8 = 32$

Exercise 3.6B

1 Solve these equations.

  a $\frac{w}{4} + 7 = 14$ **b** $\frac{40}{y} + 7 = 2$ **c** $\frac{225}{h} - 8 = 7$

  d $\frac{c}{6} + \frac{2}{3} = 6$ **e** $8 + \frac{62}{n} = 12$ **f** $4 = 7 - \frac{12}{h}$

For part **d** multiply through by 6 first.

3.7 Solving equations with brackets

▶ To solve an equation with brackets you can do two things, *either*

- expand the brackets

or

- remove the need for brackets by multiplying or dividing through.

Example 1 Solve $4(3x + 2) = 2(x - 6)$

So $\quad 12x + 8 = 2x - 12 \quad$ (Expand the brackets.)
$\quad\quad\quad 10x + 8 = {}^-12 \quad$ (Subtract $2x$ from both sides.)
$\quad\quad\quad 10x = {}^-12 - 8 = {}^-20 \quad$ (Subtract 8 from both sides.)

So $\quad\quad\quad x = {}^-2 \quad$ (Divide both sides by 10.)

Check: $\quad 4({}^-6 + 2) = {}^-16$
$\quad\quad\quad 2({}^-2 - 6) = {}^-16 \quad$ ✓

Example 2 Solve $\frac{2}{3}(7x - 4) = 3x + 6$

So $\quad 2(7x - 4) = 3(3x + 6) \quad$ (Multiply both sides by 3.)
$\quad\quad 14x - 8 = 9x + 18 \quad$ (Expand the brackets.)
$\quad\quad 5x - 8 = 18 \quad$ (Subtract $9x$ from both sides.)
$\quad\quad 5x = 26 \quad$ (Add 8 to both sides.)
$\quad\quad x = \frac{26}{5} = 5\frac{1}{5} \quad$ (Divide both sides by 5.)

Omit the check here because it is much more difficult than the problem.

Exercise 3.7A

1 Solve these equations.

a $4(2x + 7) = 60$
b $3(3x - 3) = 6x + 15$
c $2(5c - 3) = 3(2c + 6)$
d $5p - 1 = 2(4p - 8)$
e $3(4p - 5) = 9$
f $28 = 7(3r - 5)$
g $5(4w + 2) = 3(2w - 6)$
h $7(d + 3) = 12(d - 7)$
i $3(4p - 2) = 5(2p + 6)$
j $6(2x - 4) = 2(5x + 4) + x$
k $2(3x + 3) = 9(5x - 8)$
l $5(3x + 1) = 2(2x - 4) + 2$

Exercise 3.7B

1 Solve these equations.

a $2(3k - 5) + 5k = 6k + 12$
b $\frac{3}{5}(3f - 4) = 12$
c $8(2 - 3q) = 4(2q + 1)$
d $\frac{5}{8}(2h + 4) = 15$
e $3(4x - 1) = 5(x + 3)$
f $3(2x + 1) = \frac{3}{4}(x - 5)$
g $5(3s + 4) = 2(s + 12)$
h $6(2z - 6) = 3(z - 3)$
i $4(2a - 7) = 5(4a + 8)$
j $2(3x + 4) = 5(x + 5)$
k $\frac{3}{5}(2d - 1) = \frac{1}{3}(3d - 6)$
l $\frac{2}{3}(g + 1) = \frac{3}{4}(2g - 3)$

3.8 Solving equations by trial and improvement

▶ An equation with a squared term is called a **quadratic equation**.
Examples are $3y^2 = 15$, $6p^2 + 2p = 12$, $4x(x+2) = 12$
One with a cubed term is called a **cubic equation**.
Examples are $2y^3 + 5y = 20$, $2p(p+4)(p-4) = 165$

> $4x(x+2) = 12$ is quadratic because it is also $4x^2 + 8x = 12$

▶ Trial and improvement can be used to solve a quadratic or cubic equation.

Example
Find a solution to the equation $2x^2 + 3x - 4 = 32$
Try a value for x, let's say $x = 2$
$2x^2 + 3x - 4 = 2 \times 2^2 + (3 \times 2) - 4 = 8 + 6 - 4 = 10$ much too small
Try $x = 3$
$2x^2 + 3x - 4 = 2 \times 3^2 + (3 \times 3) - 4 = 18 + 9 - 4 = 23$ still too small
Try $x = 4$
$2x^2 + 3x - 4 = 2 \times 4^2 + (3 \times 4) - 4 = 32 + 12 - 4 = 40$ too large
Try $x = 3.5$
$2x^2 + 3x - 4 = 2 \times 3.5^2 + (3 \times 3.5) - 4 = 24.5 + 10.5 - 4 = 31$ almost there
Try $x = 3.55$
$2x^2 + 3x - 4 = (2 \times 12.6025) + 10.65 - 4 = 31.855$ just too small
Try $x = 3.56$
$2x^2 + 3x - 4 = (2 \times 12.6736) + 10.68 - 4 = 32.0272$ almost right
So a solution is $x = 3.56$ (to 2 dp).

Exercise 3.8A

1 Find a solution to the equation $x^2 + 2x = 24$ by trial and improvement. Use $x = 2$ as your first estimate.

2 Find a solution to $4p^3 = 158$ by trial and improvement.

3 Find a solution to $3p^2 - 4p + 12 = 912$ by trial and improvement. Use $p = 10$ as your first estimate.

4 Find a solution to $4w(2w + 3) = 3780$ by trial and improvement.

Exercise 3.8B

1 Find a solution to $x^2 - 8x - 12 = 248$ by trial and improvement. Give your value of x correct to 2 dp.

2 Find a solution to $3g^2 + 6g - 28 = 1648$ by trial and improvement. Give your value of g correct to 2 dp.

3 Find a solution to $2x^2 - x + 7 = 840$ by trial and improvement.
Give your value of x correct to 2 dp.

4 Find a solution to $2x^3 + x^2 = 1000$ by trial and improvement.

3.9 Substituting in formulae*

A formula links variables so you can use it for different values.
A formula can be given in words or in symbols.

> A variable is a quantity that can change.

Example
The volume V of a cuboid is given by the formula

$$V = l \times w \times h$$

Calculate the volume of a cuboid where:
$l = 18\,cm$, $h = 12\,cm$ and $w = 9\,cm$

$$\begin{aligned} V &= l \times w \times h \\ &= 18 \times 9 \times 12 \\ V &= 1944 \end{aligned}$$

So, the volume of the cuboid is $1944\,cm^3$.

Exercise 3.9A

1 The formula for the area A of a rectangle is: $A = l \times w$
Calculate the area of a rectangle with:
a length l of 12.4 cm and a width w of 8 cm.

2 The formula for the area of a triangle is: $A = 0.5 \times b \times h$
Calculate the area of a triangle with:
a base b of 185 mm and a height h of 228 mm.

3 The formula for the perimeter P of a rectangle is:
$P = 2(l + w)$ where l is the length and w is the width.
Use the formula to complete this table

Rectangle	l (cm)	w (cm)	P (cm)
a	15	12	
b	8.5	6.5	
c	57	22.8	

4 A formula for velocity V is: $V = u + ft$
Use the formula to calculate:
a a value for V when: $u = 35$, $f = 15$ and $t = 8$
b a value for V when: $u = 245$, $f = 32$ and $t = 12$
c a value for V when: $u = 0$, $f = 122$ and $t = 94$

Exercise 3.9B

1 A decorator uses this formula to calculate charges:

£175 plus £35 for each window and £17.50 for each door.

Calculate the charge for painting these properties:

a a house with 15 windows and 3 doors
b a bungalow with 9 windows and 4 doors
c a block of flats with 52 windows and 16 doors.

2 The formula for the area A of a trapezium is:
$A = 0.5h(a + b)$
Use the formula to complete this table:

Trapezium	h cm	a cm	b cm	A cm²
ABCD	9	17	25	
KLMN	17	21	33	
RSTV	15	15.5	18.5	

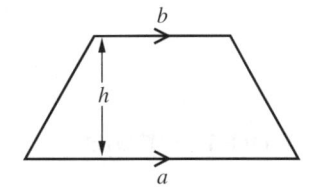

3 A formula for the area of card A needed to make a tube is $A = \pi dl$.
In the formula, d is the diameter of the tube and l is the length of the tube. Use the formula to copy and complete this table.

Tube	Length (cm)	Diameter (cm)	Area of card (cm²)
a	48	16	
b	125	9	
c	85.5	20.4	

For π use the value given by the key on your calculator or $\pi = 3.142$

4 The formula for the surface area of a cylinder is $2\pi r(r + h)$
In for formula, r is the radius and h is the height of the cylinder.
Copy and complete this table.

Cylinder	Surface area	Radius (r cm)	Height (h cm)
a		3.8	10.6
b		5.4	8.3
c		12.3	1.8

5 A different formula for velocity is: $v^2 = u^2 + 2as$
Calculate the value of:
  a v when $u = 8$, $a = 12$ and $s = 22$
  b v when $u = 0$, $a = 44$ and $s = 135.4$
  c v when $u = 6.5$, $a = 0.8$ and $s = 11$
  d v when $u = 2.4$, $a = 12.5$ and $s = 355.8$

6 A formula that links p, v and w is $p = 3v^2 + 4kw$.
Calculate the value of:
  a p when $v = 2$, $k = {}^-6$ and $w = 3$
  b p when $v = 6.5$, $k = 8$ and $w = {}^-5$
  c p when $v = 4.8$, $k = {}^-6$ and $w = {}^-2$

7 A formula that links g, h, x and y is: $g = 2(h^3 + 4x)$.
Calculate the value of g
  a when $h = {}^-5$ and $x = 9$
  b when $h = 4$ and $x = {}^-17$
  c when $h = {}^-1$ and $x = {}^-3.5$
  d when $h = 0$ and $x = {}^-2.8$

3.10 Constructing formulae

You can construct algebraic formulas from word formulae.
You use letters to stand for the amounts that can vary.

Example
Write this formula using algebra.
Time taken to check the squad kit:
  Allow 3 minutes per player and 15 minutes for general items.

The time depends on the number of players in the squad.

The time and the number of players can vary, they are both **variables**.

To write the formula:
  Let t stand for the number of minutes
  and p stand for the number of players in the squad.
The formula is $t = 3p + 15$

Remember:
a formula is a rule that you can use to work something out.

Exercise 3.10A

1 Asa buys cards to send to players in his hockey club.
He uses this rule to work out the number of cards to buy:
  Twelve for each player and 85 for the club staff.
Write this rule as a formula using letters.
(Let c stand for the number of cards and p for the number of players.)

2 To work out how many passengers to expect on a car ferry this rule is used:

   The number of passengers is 3 per car plus 165 extra.

   Write this as an algebraic formula. (Use p for passengers and c for cars.)

3 For the amount of cable needed to fix telephones in an office, fitters use this rule:

   The cable needed is 12 metres for each phone and 50 metres extra.

   Write this as an algebraic formula. Choose your own variables.

4 Anya makes jeans.
   She uses this rule to work out how many rivets to buy for each order.

   The number of rivets is 11 for each pair of jeans plus 120 extra.

   a What are the two variables in this rule?
   b Write an algebraic formula for the number of rivets to order. (Choose the variables.)

5 Write an algebraic formula for the perimeter P of rectangles with length l and width w.

Exercise 3.10B

1 A supermarket uses this rule for the number of plastic bags it uses in a day:

   The number of bags is 5 for each customer plus 350 extra.

   a What are the variables in this rule?
   b Write the rule as a formula with letters.
   Explain the letters you use for variables.

2 A milkman uses this rule for the number of bottles to load on his van:

   The number of bottles is 4 for each house plus 35 for other sales.

   a Write this as an algebraic formula. Explain the variables you use.
   b Use your rule to work out the number of bottles to load for a round of 365 houses.

3 Hi-Way Markings uses this rule for the number of litres of white line paint it needs for each job:

   The amount of paint is 14.5 litres per mile of road plus 15 litres.

   a Write this as an algebraic formula. Explain the variables you use.
   b Use your formula to calculate the amount of paint needed to white-line 56 miles of road.
   For one job Hi-Way ordered 1291 litres of paint.
   c How many miles of road did they plan to white-line?

4 A firm that makes greenhouses uses this rule to calculate the number of clips to pack in a kit:

   The number of clips is 5 per pane of glass plus 12 clips per kit.

   a Write this rule as an algebraic formula. Explain the variables you use.
   b Use your formula to calculate the number of clips in a Yeoman kit.

   The Yeoman greenhouse has 18 panes of glass.
   The Grower model has 152 clips in the kit.
   c How many panes of glass does the Grower model have?

5 A carpet fitter uses this rule to calculate his charge in £s for grippers.

   Add the length and width of the room in metres, multiply the answer by £1.15 then add £6.50.

   a Write this rule as an algebraic formula.

   A room 4.6 metres long and 3.8 metres wide is to be carpeted.

   b Use your formula to calculate the charge in £s for grippers.

6 Three straight lines on a plan meet at a point.
   The angles between the lines are w, p and y.
   a Write an algebraic formula that links w, p and y.
   b Use your formula to calculate the value of p when $w = 156°$ and $y = 48°$.

7 The three angles of a triangle are give as k, r and t.
   a Write an algebraic formula that links k, r and t.
   b Use your formula to calculate t when $k = 72.6°$ and $r = 51.8°$.

3.11 Changing the subject of formulae*

In the formula $P = 2(l + w)$ the subject is P, the unknown value to be found.
You can change the subject of any formula, but you must use the rules of algebra.

Example 1
Make w the subject of the formula $P = 2(l + w)$

- **Step 1** Deal with any fractions or brackets. $P = 2l + 2w$
- **Step 2** Get the term with the new subject
              on its own on one side of the formula. $P - 2l = 2w$
- **Step 3** Divide both sides by 2 to get the subject $\dfrac{P - 2l}{2} = w$

              w is now the subject of the formula.

Example 2
Make g the subject of the formula $\quad t = 2\pi \sqrt{\dfrac{l}{g}}$

- **Step 1** Deal with the $\sqrt{}$ by squaring both sides. $\qquad t^2 = \dfrac{4\pi^2 l}{g}$
- **Step 2** Deal with the fraction by × both sides by g. $\quad gt^2 = 4\pi^2 l$
- **Step 3** Divide both sides by t^2 to get the subject. $\qquad g = \dfrac{4\pi^2 l}{t^2}$

g is now the subject of the equation.

(The subject of the formula can be written on the LHS or the RHS.)

Exercise 3.11A

1 Make y the subject of each of these formulas.
- **a** $3(x - 4) = y - 5$
- **b** $2(4 + 3y) = 5(3x - 2)$
- **c** $2(4 - 5y) = 3x + y$
- **d** $6(2x - 3y) = 5 - 4x$
- **e** $2x(3x - 4) = 5(3 + 2y)$
- **f** $2a(3x + a) = b(2y + 1)$
- **g** $3(4y - 5) = 5(2y - 3x)$
- **h** $k(3x + 2) = 4(y - 3k)$
- **i** $3x(2 - 3x) = 4(5y - 2x)$

2 In each formula make k the subject.
- **a** $3x = \dfrac{2(k - 5)}{3}$
- **b** $\dfrac{3(2k - 5)}{4} = 8x$
- **c** $5(ax + 2k) = \dfrac{ax + 1}{2}$
- **d** $2x(x^2 + k) = \dfrac{kx - 3}{3}$
- **e** $\dfrac{3y(2k - y)}{4} = 5yk - 1$
- **f** $2a(3k + 1) = b^2 + \dfrac{4ak}{5}$

3 Make w the subject of each of these.
- **a** $\sqrt{w} = 4x$
- **b** $5 = \sqrt{(2a + w)}$
- **c** $9 = \sqrt{(3w + ax^2)}$
- **d** $\sqrt{\dfrac{2w}{3}} = 5$
- **e** $8 = \sqrt{\dfrac{5w}{k}}$
- **f** $7 = \sqrt{\dfrac{3w}{2x} + 1}$
- **g** $\sqrt{\dfrac{w}{4}} = \sqrt{(3y - 5)}$
- **h** $\sqrt{(3w - 4x + 1)} = 3$
- **i** $\sqrt{2(3x^2 + 2w)} = \dfrac{3x}{2}$

4 This formula is used to convert °C to °F:

$F = \tfrac{9}{5} C + 32$.

Rearrange the formula so you can convert °F to °C.

Exercise 3.11B

1 Make v the subject of each formula.
- **a** $2y(3v - 5) = 4y - 3$
- **b** $3y + 5 = y(3a + 2v - 4)$
- **c** $3(x + 4) = y(ax + 3bv)$

2 Make n the subject of each formula.
- **a** $\dfrac{3n - 4x}{5} = 2y - n$
- **b** $3n + 5x^2 = \dfrac{2(x^2 + n - 3)}{3}$
- **c** $\dfrac{ax - 3n}{2} = \dfrac{5 + a^2 x}{3}$
- **d** $\dfrac{4n^2 - 3x}{3} = 4x - 5y + 1$

3 Make k the subject in each case.

   a $\sqrt{(kx - 3)} = ay$ **b** $5 = \sqrt{(3x^2 + 5kx - 4)}$

   c $\sqrt{\dfrac{5ak + y}{2}} = x^2$ **d** $a^2 x = \sqrt{(xy + 3k + 2)}$

4 A formula used to calculate velocity is:

   $v = u + ft$

   a Make t the subject of the formula.
   b Find a value for t when $v = 34.5$, $u = 6.75$ and $f = 2.62$
   c Calculate a value for u when $v = 175.4$, $f = 28.6$ and $t = 4.5$

> Give all decimal answers correct to 2 dp.

5 Velocity can be calculated with this formula:

   $v^2 = u^2 + 2fs$

   a Make s the subject of the formula.
   b Calculate a value for s when: $v = 11.6$, $u = 0.8$ and $f = 4.65$
   c Make v the subject of the formula.
   d Calculate a value for v when: $u = 0.88$, $f = 16.5$ and $s = 100.8$
   e Make u the subject of the formula.
   f Calculate a value for u when: $v = 15.65$, $f = 3.4$ and $s = 7.3$

3.12 Simultaneous equations

When you have 2 unknowns you need 2 equations to find them.
The process is called **solving simultaneously**.

Example 1
Solve these equations to find value for a and b. $2a - 3b = 1$
$$4a + 2b = 26$$

- Label the equations 1 and 2. $2a - 3b = 1$ [1]
                                         $4a + 2b = 26$ [2]
- Multiply both sides of [1] by 2 $4a - 6b = 2$ [3]
  to give two equations with $4a$. $4a + 2b = 26$ [2]
- Subtract [3] − [2] $-8b = -24$
- Find the value of b $b = 3$
- Substitute the value of b in [1]: $2a - 3b = 1$
  to find the value of a: $2a - 3(3) = 1$
                                          $2a = 10$
                                          $a = 5$

So, the solution is $a = 5$ and $b = 3$

> **Check:**
> $2a - 3b$
> $= 2 \times 5 - 3 \times 3 = 1$
> $4a + 2b$
> $= 4 \times 5 + 2 \times 3 = 26$

Example 2

Solve these equations to find value for a and b. $5a - 2b = 12$
$2a + 6b = {}^-2$

- Label the equations 1 and 2. $5a - 2b = 12$ [1]
  $2a + 6b = {}^-2$ [2]
- Multiply both sides of [1] by 3 $15a - 6b = 36$ [3]
  to give two equations with $6b$. $2a + 6b = {}^-2$ [2]
- Add [3] + [2]. $17a = 34$
- Find the value of a. $a = 2$
- Substitute the value of a in [1]: $5a - 2b = 12$
  to find the value of b: $5(2) - 2b = 12$
  $-2b = 2$
  $b = -1$

Check:
$5a - 2b$
$= 5 \times 2 - 2 \times {}^-1 = 12$
$2a + 6b$
$= 2 \times 2 + 6 \times {}^-1 = -2$

So, the solution is $a = 2$ and $b = {}^-1$

Exercise 3.12A

1 Solve each of these simultaneous equations.

Remember to check your answers.

a $2a + 3b = 7$
   $4a + 2b = 10$

b $3a - 5b = 11$
   $9a + 2b = 16$

c $4a + 3b = 9$
   $3a - 6b = 3$

d $8a - 3b = 5$
   $4a + 5b = 13$

e $5a + 2b = 7$
   $10a - 3b = 42$

f $6a + 3b = 30$
   $18a - 5b = 62$

g $2a + 5b = 5$
   $4a - 3b = 23$

h $4a - 3b = 14$
   $2a + 6b = {}^-8$

i $6a - b = 19$
   $3a + 4b = 5$

j $6a + 7b = 5$
   $3a - 5b = 11$

k $5a + 3b = 12$
   $4a - 6b = 18$

l $4a + 6b = 4$
   $3a - 3b = 18$

m $7a + 5b = 4$
   $3a - 10b = 26$

n $8a - 6b = 36$
   $24a + b = 70$

o $3a + 7b = 1$
   $2a - 21b = {}^-25$

2 Two groups of people bought tickets for a pantomime. A group of 4 adults and 5 children paid a total of £35 for their tickets. Two adults and three children paid a total of £19 for their tickets.
   a Form two equations that represent the tickets bought by the groups.
   b Solve the equations to find the cost of an adult and a child ticket.

Exercise 3.12B

1 Solve each of these simultaneous equations.

a $6a + b = 15$
   $5a - 3b = 1$

b $7a - 3b = {}^-17$
   $5a + 9b = {}^-1$

c $5a + 4b = 11$
   $10a - 3b = 33$

d $8a - 7b = 10$
   $5a + 14b = 43$

e $3a + 5b = 7$
   $2a - 15b = 23$

f $7a + 4b = 3$
   $35a - b = 36$

g $12a + 5b = 2$
   $2a - b = 4$

h $24a + 7b = 3$
   $4a - b = 7$

i $35a - 6b = 52$
   $7a + 5b = 29$

2 In a supermarket Jo paid £1.78 for 3 cartons of milk and 2 cartons of orange juice. Ed bought 4 cartons of milk and 5 of orange juice and paid a total of £3.33.

> You will find it easier to work in pence for the price of each carton.

  a Form two equations that represent the cartons bought by Jo and Ed.
  b Solve the equations for the price of a carton of milk and a carton of orange juice.

3 Two adults and three children paid a total of £26 for their match tickets.
Four adults and five children paid a total of £47.50 for their tickets.
Form and solve two equations to find the cost of an adult and a child match ticket.

Revision exercise 3   *Review*

1 Collect like terms and simplify:
  a $5x + 3c - 3x + c$
  b $9k + y + 5k - 8y$
  c $3x - 5y + x + 9y$
  d $ax + 9y + 5ax - 23y$
  e $ax + ay + 5x - 4ay$
  f $3xy + kx + y + 4kx - 7ay$
  g $k + 3ax + y + ky - ax$
  h $9ax + y - 5ax - 12y$
  i $3axy + 5k - 7axy - 11k$
  j $15xy - 12kx + xy - kx + 3x - 5y$ *Unit 3.1*

2 Multiply out each of these brackets.
  a $3(5x - 3y + kx + 8)$
  b $15(4ax + 5xy - 3ab + 9)$
  c $4(3ax + 2ab - 5y + x - 3)$
  d $8(axy - 5k + 3kx - 7y + 1)$
  e $8(5ay + 6ax - 12y - x + 2)$
  f $12(6x - 5axy + 5y - k + 3kx - 22)$ *Unit 3.2*

3 Remove the brackets from each of these.
  a $9(12ay + 7x - 15ay - 3)$
  b $21(3x - 8ay + 9k - y + 1)$
  c $18(3x + 5ay + kx - xy + 1)$
  d $32(5x - ay + 8kx + 2k - 15)$ *Unit 3.2*

4 In each of these expand the brackets.
  a $(2x + 1)(3x + a - 4)$
  b $(3x - 2)(2a - 5x + 3)$
  c $(4 + 3x)(2a - x + 1)$
  d $(a + b - c)(3ax + b)$
  e $(2a + x)(3a + b - 4c)$
  f $(2y + 3a - 4x)(a - b)$ *Unit 3.2*

5 Expand the brackets and simplify each of these.
  a $(x + 5)(x + 3)$
  b $(x - 3)(x + 6)$
  c $(x + 5)(x + 8)$
  d $(x - 4)(x - 7)$
  e $(x + 1)(2x - 5)$
  f $(3x - 4)(x - 12)$ *Unit 3.2*

6 Multiply out the brackets and simplify:
  a $(x + 3)(x^2 + 5x - 9)$
  b $(x - 8)(x^2 + x - 9)$
  c $(x^2 + 7x - 11)(x + 3)$
  d $(x^2 - 8x + 15)(3 - x)$
  e $(x^2 + 5x - 1)(x^2 - 3x + 2)$
  f $(x^2 + 4x - 8)(x^2 - 5x - 2)$ *Unit 3.2*

Review

Unit 3.3

7 Factorise each of these expressions.
   a $12ax + 16y$
   b $9x - 3ay$
   c $35xy + 14k$
   d $45ky - 27x + 18$
   e $32ax + 56y - 24k$
   f $105ax - 75ky + 60bc$

8 Factorise each expression.
   a $3ax + 7ay - 5ak$
   b $4xy - 7kx + 11wx$
   c $5kx - 9xy + x - ax$
   d $9ax - 15ay + 3ak$
   e $8ay + 12xy - 20aby$
   f $18axy + 15axk - 24ax$

Unit 3.3

9 Factorise each of these.
   a $x^2 + 7x + 12$
   b $x^2 + 3x - 28$
   c $x^2 - 4x + 21$
   d $x^2 - 9x + 14$
   e $x^2 - 11x + 18$
   f $x^2 - 4x - 45$
   g $x^2 + 16x + 55$
   h $x^2 - 3x - 180$
   i $x^2 - 23x + 120$

Unit 3.3

10 Factorise each of these expressions.
   a $x^2 - 49$
   b $y^2 - 100$
   c $9x^2 - 25$
   d $16y^2 - 81$
   e $36k^2 - 196$
   f $100x^2 - 324$

Unit 3.3

11 What name do we give to an expression like: $x^2 - 36$?

Unit 3.3

12 Solve each equation showing all your working.
   a $k - 9 = 15$
   b $y + 4 = 21$
   c $x + 18 = 5$
   d $3x = 24$
   e $0.5y = 16$
   f $0.2w = 21$
   g $2x + 3 = 27$
   h $5x - 25 = 40$
   i $7x + 3 = 24$
   j $9x - 35 = 28$
   k $23 = 7 + 4x$
   l $105 = 7x - 14$

Unit 3.4

13 Solve each of these equations.
   a $7x - 3 = 5x + 11$
   b $9x + 3 = 6x - 9$
   c $15x - 8 = 5x + 72$
   d $14y + 8 = 7y - 27$
   e $23k + 1 = 15k - 7$
   f $12w + 24 = 7w + 49$
   g $8x + 3 = x - 18$
   h $19k - 8 = k + 10$
   i $17x + 1 = 5x - 95$

Unit 3.5

14 Solve these equations.
   a $\dfrac{x}{4} = 8$
   b $\dfrac{y}{3} = 1$
   c $\dfrac{k}{5} = 18$
   d $\dfrac{x}{12} = {}^-8$
   d $\dfrac{w}{4} + 1 = 5$
   e $\dfrac{x}{2} - 3 = 8$
   f $\dfrac{h}{8} + 1 = 15$
   h $\dfrac{n}{6} - 8 = 21$

Unit 3.6

15 Solve these equations.
   a $3(2x + 5) = 57$
   b $4(2x + 1) = 60$
   c $5(3x + 8) = 70$
   d $9(2x - 3) = 27$
   e $5(6x - 8) = 80$
   f $7(3x - 8) = 28$
   g $2(3x + 1) = 4(x + 5)$
   h $9(3x - 5) = 5(5x - 7)$
   i $3(7x + 2) = 5(4x - 8)$
   j $6(3x + 1) = 7(2x - 4)$

Unit 3.7

16 Solve these equations.
   a $\tfrac{2}{3}(x + 1) = 6$
   b $\tfrac{3}{4}(x - 2) = 8$
   c $\tfrac{3}{5}(2x + 4) = 12$

Unit 3.7

17 Find a solution to the equation $x^2 + 3x = 5$ by trial and improvement.

Unit 3.8

18 Find a solution to the equation $x^3 + x^2 = 500$ by trial and improvement.

Unit 3.8

19 A formula for velocity is: $v = u + ft$
Calculate a value for v when $u = 55$, $f = 18$, and $t = 3.5$.

Review
Unit 3.9

20 A formula that links k, w and h is: $k = 2w^2 - 5h$
Calculate a value for k when $w = 7.5$, and $h = 9.5$.

Unit 3.9

21 A formula that links x, y, p and w is: $y = 2x(3p - w)^2$
Calculate a value for y when $x = 3$, $p = 5$, and $w = 12$.

Unit 3.9

22 In the orders department of a manufacturer this rule is used to calculate the length of banding needed to pack a batch of widgets.

        58 cm per widget plus an extra 3 metres per batch

a Write this as an algebraic formula.
b Use your formula to calculate the length of banding to pack 15 000 widgets.

Unit 3.10

23 A decorator uses this rule to calculate the time needed to paint a house.

        3.25 hours per window, 1.5 hours per door
        plus an extra 5 hours per house

a Write this rule as an algebraic formula.
b Use the rule to calculate the time for a house with 11 windows and 5 doors.

Unit 3.10

24 Make w the subject of each of these formulas.
a $x = 3(k + w)$
b $3k + 1 = 2(3x - 2w)$
c $\frac{1}{2}(w + 1) = k + x$
d $3(k + 2x) = 5k(k + w)$
e $2x(w - 3) = 3k(x - 4)$
f $2(w - 5) = 3(k - w + 1)$
g $\dfrac{2(w - 3)}{5} = w + y - 2x$
h $2x(w + 3x) = \dfrac{3(x - 4)}{4}$
i $\dfrac{3(aw + ax)}{5} = \dfrac{2(3k - 4)}{3}$
j $3w^2 + 2k - 5x = \dfrac{2k(x - 3)}{2}$
k $\sqrt{(2w - 3)} = 8$
l $\sqrt{(kw + 3x - 2)} = 2$
m $\sqrt{(3wx + 2kx + 5)} = \sqrt{(wx - kx - 3y - 1)}$
n $ax^2 = \sqrt{(2xy + 3kw + y - 5)}$

Unit 3.11

25 A formula for velocity is: $v^2 = u^2 + 2fs$
a Make s the subject of the formula.
b Find a value for s when $v = 9.5$, $u = 2.5$ and $f = 26$
c Make u the subject of the formula.
d Find a value for u when $v = 5.2$, $f = 3.6$ and $s = 2.25$

Unit 3.11

26 A formula that links k, w, x and y is: $k = \sqrt{(3wx - 5y^2)}$
a Make x the subject of the formula.
b Find a value for x when $k = 5$, $w = 4$ and $y = 1$
c Make y the subject of the formula.
d Find a value for y when $k = 2$, $w = 8$ and $x = 6.5$

Unit 3.11

27 Solve each pair of simultaneous equations.   *Review*

   a $3a + 5b = 11$ **b** $5a - 4b = 23$ **c** $9a - 6b = {}^-21$
      $3a + 2b = 8$ $3a + 4b = 1$ $5a - 6b = {}^-17$
   d $4a + 3b = 2$ **e** $7a - 5b = 26$ **f** $11a - 9b = 7$
      $5a - 6b = 22$ $3a - 10b = 19$ $4a + 3b = {}^-14$
   g $4a + 6b = 14$ **h** $8a - 5b = {}^-13$ **i** $6a + 11b = 2$
      $7a - 5b = {}^-22$ $6a - 3b = {}^-15$ $5a + 3b = 14$ *Unit 3.12*

28 A group of three adults and four children paid £48 for tickets to a theme park. Another group of two adults and five children paid £46 for their tickets.
   a Form two equations that represent the tickets bought.
   b Solve the equations to find the cost of an adult and a child ticket.   *Unit 3.12*

29 Three cartons of orange juice and two bottles of cola cost £3.85.
Four cartons of orange juice and three bottles of cola cost £5.35.
Calculate the cost of one carton of orange juice and one bottle of cola.   *Unit 3.12*

30 Five cups and six saucers cost a total of £33.95.
Six cups and four saucers cost a total of £32.90.
Calculate the cost of a cup and of a saucer at these prices.   *Unit 3.12*

Investigation

Side totals

Place a number in each of the circles so that each side adds up to the same total.

Use the numbers:
1, 2, 3, 4, 5 and 6
once only

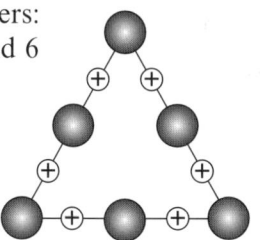

Say you numbered one side like this ...

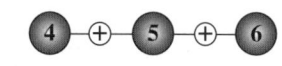

... all sides must total 15 $(4 + 5 + 6) = 15$

a Solve the puzzle.

b • Try other sets of consecutive numbers.
    • For any set of 6 consecutive numbers can you predict:
      – the largest side total
      – the smallest side total?
   Write a rule that will help you make this prediction.

c • What about other shapes and their side totals?
    • Can you still predict?
    • What rules can you find to make predictions?

4 Sequences, Functions and Graphs

4.1 Sequences from patterns

▶ A **sequence** is a set of numbers that are usually linked by a rule.

▶ A **term** is a number in the sequence.

An example of a sequence is 1, 4, 16, 25, …
A rule for this sequence is:
'square the term number of the sequence'.

Exercise 4.1A

1 This is the sequence of triangle numbers.

1   3   6   10   and so on …

> The fourth triangle number is 10.

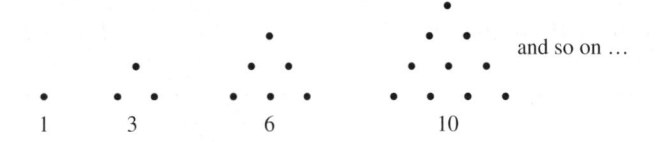

a Describe any link you can see in the number of dots each time.
b Predict the 12th triangle number. Now test it out by drawing.

2

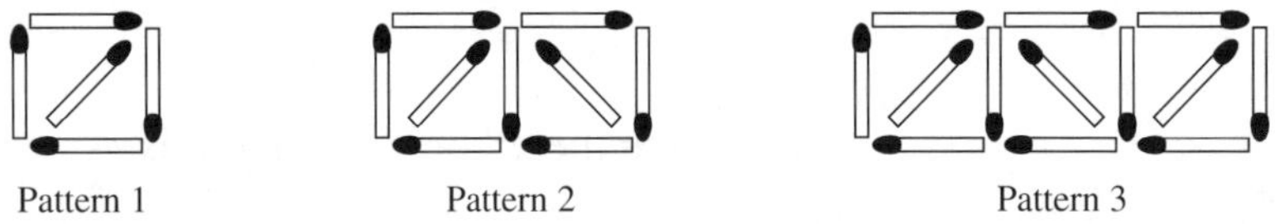

Pattern 1   Pattern 2   Pattern 3

a Draw Pattern 7 in the sequence of match patterns.
b How many matches will there be in Pattern 14?

Exercise 4.1B

1 This shows a sequence of paving stones.

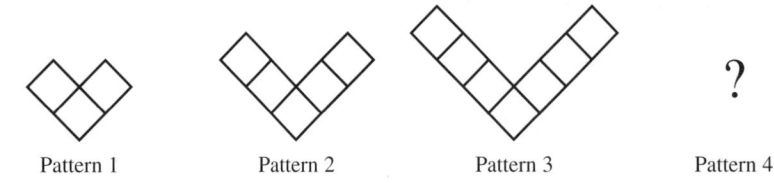

Pattern 1   Pattern 2   Pattern 3   Pattern 4

a What is happening to the number of stones each time?
b Calculate the number of stones in Pattern 10.

2 Paving stones are fixed around tree beds in a sequence.

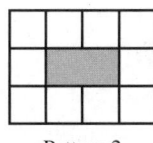

Pattern 1　Pattern 2　Pattern 3　Pattern 4

a Draw patterns 4 and 8.
b Explain how many stones you think would be in Pattern 20.

4.2 Continuing a sequence

▶ To continue a sequence you need to know a rule.
▶ The rule may be based on the previous term.

Example 1
$4 \to 10 \to 28 \to 82 \to 244 \to 730 \to \ldots$
'Multiply the previous term by 3 then subtract 2'.

$10 \times 3 = 30$
$30 - 2 = 28$
So $10 \to 28$

▶ The rule may be based on the term number.

Example 2
2, 5, 8, 11, **14**, … uses this rule
'Multiply the term number by 3, then subtract 1'.

Term 5 will be:
$(5 \times 3) - 1 = 14$

This rule can be written as $3n - 1$ where n is the term number.

Exercise 4.2A

1 Give both types of rule to describe this sequence: 2, 4, 6, 8, 10, …

2 Continue each sequence by three more terms with the rule given.

Sequence	Rule from previous term
a ⁻6, …, …, …	Add 18.
b 2, …, …, …	Square.
c 19, …, …, …	Subtract 9.
d 5, …, …, …	Double and add 6.

3 Continue each sequence by three more terms with the rule given.

a 1, …, …, …　　Multiply the term number by 4 then subtract 3.
b 3, …, …, …　　Double the term number and add 1.
c 7, …, …, …　　Multiply the term number by 3 then add 4.
d 3, …, …, …　　Multiply the term number by 5 then subtract 2.

86 Sequences, functions and graphs

Exercise 4.2B

1 Continue each sequence by three more terms with the rule given.
   a 2, ..., ..., ...   Multiply previous term by 4 and subtract 5.
   b 65 536, ..., ..., ...   Square root the previous term.

2 Write the first seven terms in sequences given by these rules, where n is the term number.
   a $4n + 16$ **b** $5n - 1$ **c** $3(n + 2)$
   d $2(n - 1)$ **e** n^2 **f** $n^2 - 1$

3 A sequence starts 1, 5, ... Give three different rules it could be using.

4 The sequence 7, 11, 15, 19, 23, ... uses the rule
'Multiply the term number by ■ then add ▼'
where ■ and ▼ are whole numbers.
By trying different numbers find the values of ■ and ▼.

4.3 Finding a rule for a sequence

▶ To find a rule from a sequence first find the differences between terms.

Example
Find a rule in words for sequence A: 5, 9, 13, 17, 21, ...

Find the differences: 5   9   13   17   21   ...
                         \ / \ / \ / \ /
                          4   4   4   4

Remember:
The difference between two numbers means subtract one from the other.

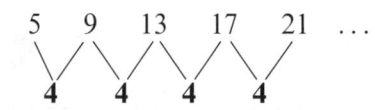

The differences in sequence A are all **4** so compare the sequence with Sequence B that has the rule:
'Multiply the term number by 4'.

Term number (n)	1	2	3	4	5	...
Sequence B ($4n$)	4	8	12	16	20	...
Sequence A	5	9	13	17	21	...

You can see that each term in Sequence A is 2 more than the same term in the $4n$ sequence.

So a rule for Sequence A is 'Multiply the term number by 4 then add 1' or we say its **general term** is $4n + 1$ in symbols.

n stands for any term number in the sequence.

Exercise 4.3A

1. Compare this sequence with Sequence B above: 6, 10, 14, 18, 22, …
   What is a rule for the sequence:
   a in words
   b in symbols?

2. a What are the differences in the sequence 4, 7, 10, 13, 16, …?
   b Find the rule in words for the sequence.

3. Find the differences and a rule for the sequence 5, 8, 11, 14, 17, …

4. Find the differences and general terms for each of these sequences.
   a 2, 4, 6, 8, 10, …
   b 4, 6, 8, 10, 12, …

Exercise 4.3B

1. Use differences to find a general term for each sequence.
   a 6, 11, 16, 21, 26, …
   b 4, 9, 14, 19, 24, …
   c 9, 11, 13, 15, 17, …
   d 9, 15, 21, 27, 33, …
   e 12, 18, 24, 30, 36, …
   f 5, 15, 25, 35, 45, …
   g 7, 19, 31, 43, 55, …
   h 106, 113, 120, 127, 134, …
   i 8, 20, 32, 44, …
   j 44, 45, 46, 47, …
   k 18, 68, 118, 168, …
   l 122, 222, 322, 422, …

2. Find a general term for the sequence ⁻5, ⁻1, 3, 7, 11, …

3. a Write three different sequences that each have a first term of 3.
   b Write the general term for each sequence.

4.4 Quadratic sequences*

▶ A sequence with a square in its general term is a **quadratic sequence**.
For example n^2, $5n^2 + 4$, $n(2n + 3)$, $(n + 1)(n - 1)$

▶ To find the general term for a quadratic sequence you find the **second differences** and compare them with a sequence with a general term of n^2.
n^2 sequence is 1 4 9 16 25
First difference   3 5 7 9
Second difference   2 2 2 ——— All the second differences are 2.

Example

What is the general term for the sequence 5, 11, 21, 35, 53, ...?

```
                5   11   21   35   53
First difference    6   10   14   18
Second difference     4    4    4
```
— All the second differences are 4.

The 2nd differences are 2 times as large as those for the n^2 sequence.
So the first part of the general term is $2n^2$ ...

Now look at the sequence with general term $2n^2$.
This is 2, 8, 18, 32, 50, ...
Each term in the sequence 5, 11, 21, 35, 53, is 3 larger than that for $2n^2$.
So the general term for this sequence is $2n^2 + 3$.

Exercise 4.4A

1 a Copy and complete the differences for this quadratic sequence.

```
                    5   14   29   50   77
First differences      9   15   21   .
Second differences       .    .
```

> The coefficient of n^2 is the number that comes in front of n^2. For $5n^2$ the coefficient of n^2 is 5.

b What number ☐ is the coefficient of n^2 in the general term?

c Write out the first 5 terms in the sequence with ☐n^2.

d What is the general term for the sequence 5, 14, 29, 50, 71?

2 By using differences find the general term for the quadratic sequence 0, 3, 8, 15, 24, ...

Exercise 4.4B

1 Use differences to help you find the general term for each sequence.
  a 7, 16, 31, 52, 79 ...
  b 2, 17, 42, 77, 122, ...
  c 3, 15, 35, 63, 99, ...
  d 11, 14, 19, 26, 35, ...
  e 0, 6, 16, 30, 48, ...
  f ⁻3, 3, 13, 27, 45, ...

4.5 Graphs from sequences*

▶ Sequences of the type 4, 7, 10, 13, ... with equal first differences produce linear graphs.
Quadratic sequences such as 5, 11, 21, 35, ... with equal second differences produce curves.

Example

Plot a graph for the sequence 5, 11, 21, 35, ...

- Find an expression for the nth term of the sequence.

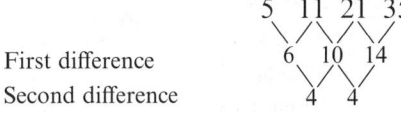

```
                   5    11    21    35
First difference      6    10    14
Second difference        4    4
```

So this sequence is based on $2n^2 + \square$

$\square$ is 3

See page 86 for finding a general term.

- Use the general term $2n^2 + 3$ to make a table of values.

Term number	1	2	3	4	5	6	7
Term	5	11	21	35	53	75	101

- Draw the graph by plotting points
  (1, 5), (2, 11), (3, 21), ...

Exercise 4.5A

1 On the same axes draw graphs to show the linear sequences:
  a 4, 6, 8, ...   **b** 5, 7, 9, ...
  c How do the two graphs compare?

For Question 1 use axes from 0 to 35 for the term, against 1 to 7 for the term number.

2 For the quadratic sequence 1, 10, 25, 46, ...:
  a Find an expression for the nth term (general term).
  b Plot the graph for the first 7 terms and describe its shape.

For Question 2 use axes from 0 to 150 for the term, against 1 to 7 for the term number.

Exercise 4.5B

1 For the quadratic sequence 7, 13, 23, 37, ...:
  a Find its general term.
  b Plot a graph of term against term number for the first 7 terms.

For Question 1 use axes from 0 to 110 for the term, against 1 to 10 for the term number.

2 The fraction sequence $\frac{1}{2}, \frac{2}{3}, \frac{3}{4}, \frac{4}{5}, \ldots$ is increasing in size.
  a By comparing the numerator and denominator with the term number write an expression for the nth term.
  b By converting to decimals, draw a graph for the first 10 terms.
  c What is happening to the values of the terms in the sequence?

For Question 2 use axes from 0 to 1.5 for the term, against 1 to 10 for the term number.

4.6 Coordinates in all four quadrants

You can fix the position of any point on a grid using two numbers called coordinates. Coordinates are written as (x, y).

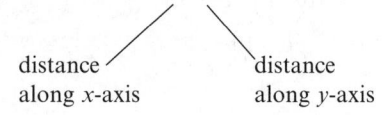

(x, y) — distance along x-axis, distance along y-axis

Example
Give the coordinates of each vertex of the shape ABCDEF.
(A vertex is a corner.)

Vertex	Coordinate
A	(2, 3)
B	(1, 1)
C	(3, ⁻1)
D	(2, ⁻3)
E	(⁻3, ⁻2)
F	(⁻2, 1)

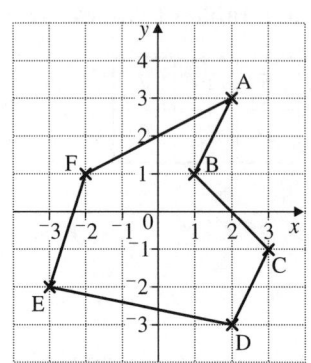

Exercise 4.6A

1 a Plot each of these points on a pair of axes and join them in order.
A(0, 5), B(3, 2), C(2, 2), D(2, ⁻4), E(0, ⁻3), F(⁻2, ⁻4), G(⁻2, 2), H(⁻3, 2)
b Join C to F and G to D.
Give the coordinates where CF and GD cross.

2 a Plot each of these points on a pair of axes and join them in order.
A(⁻4, ⁻3), B(⁻4, ⁻1), C(⁻1.5, 2), D(1, ⁻1), E(1, ⁻3)
b Join A to D and B to E.
Give the coordinates where AD and BE cross.
c Join A to C. Give the coordinates where AC and BD cross.
d Give the coordinates of the midpoint of AE.

3 a Plot each of these points on a pair of axes and join them in order.
A(⁻4, 0), B(⁻2, 0), C(⁻1, ⁻1), D(2, ⁻1), E(3, ⁻2), F(2, ⁻4), G(1, ⁻3), H(⁻2, ⁻3), I(⁻3, ⁻2), J(⁻5, ⁻2)
b Join D to H and C to D.
Give the coordinates where DH and CD cross.
c Join A to I and, B to J.
Give the coordinates where AI and BJ cross.

Exercise 4.6B

1 ABCD is a square with coordinates:
A($^-$1, 3), B(3, 3), C($\square$, $\square$), D($^-$1, $^-$1)
 a Give the coordinates of C.
 WXYZ are the midpoints of AB, BC, CD, and DA.
 b Give the coordinates of W, X, Y, and Z.

2 a Plot each of these points on a pair of axes and join them in order.
 A($^-$4, 2), B($^-$3, 6), C(2, 5), D(4, 2), E(3, $^-$2), F($^-$4, $^-$4)
 b Join B to E and A to D. Give the coordinates where BE and AD cross.
 c Which other diagonal of the shape goes through the point (0, 2)?
 d Give the coordinates of the midpoint of DF.
 e Join A to C. Give the coordinates where BE and AC cross.

3 a Plot each of these points on a pair of axes and join them in order.
 A($^-$2, 4), B(2, 1), C(5, 0), D(2, $^-$1), E($^-$2, $^-$4), F($^-$4, $^-$2), G($^-$4, 2)
 Join A to E, G to D, and B to F.
 b Give the coordinates where, GD and FB cross.
 c Give the coordinates where AE crosses GD, and where it crosses FB.
 d Give the coordinates of the midpoint of AG.

4.7 Simple line graphs

You can give an equation to a line graph.

Example
Give an equation for Line A and for Line B in the diagram.

Line A
 Every point has an x-coordinate of 2.
 The equation of line A is: $x = 2$

Line B
 Every point has a y-coordinate of $^-$2.
 The equation of line B is: $y = ^-2$

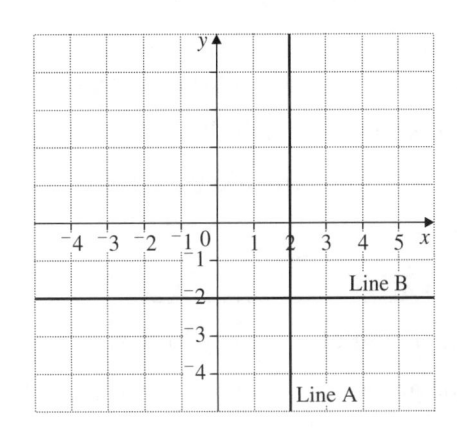

Exercise 4.7A

1 a Draw a pair of axes with values of x from $^-4$ to 4 and y from $^-5$ to 5.
  b On your axes draw and label each of these lines:
   $x = 4 \quad y = 4 \quad x = {^-3} \quad y = {^-5} \quad x = 1 \quad y = 2.5$

2 Give the equation of the x-axis.

Exercise 4.7B

1 Show each pair of lines on a pair of axes and give the coordinates where they cross.
  a $x = 3$ **b** $y = {^-2}$ **c** $x = {^-1}$ **d** $y = 4$ **e** $x = 1.5$
     $y = {^-1}$ $x = 5$ $y = 3$ $x = {^-3}$ $y = 3.5$

2 What is the equation of the y-axis?

4.8 Drawing linear graphs

You can draw a linear graph of an equation by using a table of values.

Example 1
Draw the graph of $y = 2x + 1$ for values of x from $^-3$ to 3.

Make a table of values:

x	$^-3$	$^-2$	$^-1$	0	1	2	3
$2x + 1$	$^-5$	$^-3$	$^-1$	1	3	5	7

The table of values shows the coordinates.

Values of x are from $^-3$ to 3 and values of y are from $^-5$ to 7.

Plot the points:
$(^-3, {^-5}), ({^-2}, {^-3}), ({^-1}, {^-1}), (0, 1), (1, 3), (2, 5), (3, 7)$

Join the plots with a straight line.

Label the line with its equation:
  $y = 2x + 1$

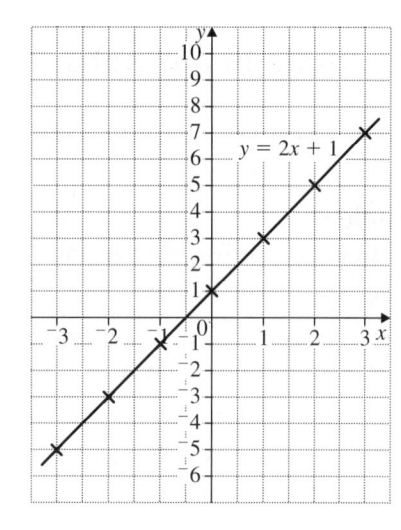

Exercise 4.8A

1 Draw the graph of $y = 3x + 2$ for values of x from $^-3$ to 3.

2 Draw the graph of $y = 2x - 3$ for values of x from $^-2$ to 4.

3 Draw a pair of axes with values of x from $^-3$ to 4 and y from $^-7$ to 7.
   a On the axes draw and label the graph of $y = 2x - 1$
   b On the axes draw and label the graph of $y = x + 2$
   c Give the coordinates of the point where the two graphs cross.

4 Draw a pair of axes with values of x from $^-3$ to 2 and y from $^-5$ to 10.
   a On the axes draw and label each of these graphs.
   $$y = 3x + 4 \quad y = 3x + 1 \quad y = 3x \quad y = {}^-3x - 2$$
   b Explain how the graphs you have drawn are the same.
   c Explain how the graphs are different.
   d How would the graph of $y = 3x + 12$ be different from the graphs you drew?

Exercise 4.8B

1 Draw a pair of axes with values of x from $^-2$ to 4 and y from $^-10$ to 8.
   a On the axes draw and label a graph of $y = 2x - 4$
   b On the axes draw and label a graph of $y = x - 3$
   c Give the coordinates of the point where $y = 2x - 4$ crosses $y = x - 3$

2 a On the same axes draw and label graphs of:
   $$y = x + 1 \quad y = x - 2 \quad y = 1 + x \quad y = 2 - x$$
   b Which of the equations are the same? Explain your answer.

3 Copy the axes and graphs shown in the diagram.
   a What is the equation of Line A?
   b What is the equation of Line B?
   c What is the equation of Line C?
   d What do you think is the equation of Line D?
   e On your axes draw a graph of $y = 3x + 2$
   f Give the coordinates where Line C and the graph of $y = 3x + 2$ cross.

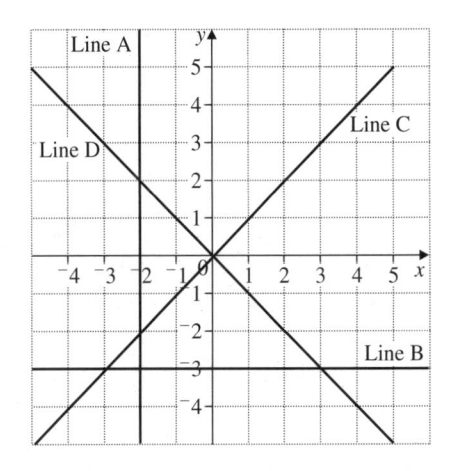

▶ The equation of a straight line graph holds all the information you need to draw its graph. The equation tells you how steep the graph is and where the line crosses the y-axis.

All linear equations look like this: $y = mx + c$
The value of **m** gives you the gradient or slope of the graph.
The value of **c** gives you the intercept of the graph and the y-axis.

> An intercept is the point where two or more lines cross.

Example 2
Give the gradient and the y-intercept for the graph of $y = 5x - 4$

Compare $y = 5x - 4$
with $y = mx + c$
So, the graph of $y = 5x - 4$ has a gradient of 5 and a y-intercept at $^-4$

A gradient of 5 is:

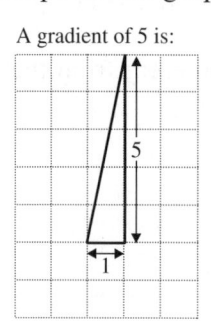

A y-intercept at $^-4$:

Gradient is:
$$\frac{\text{Change along the } y\text{-axis}}{\text{Change along the } x\text{-axis}}$$

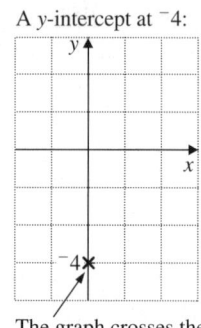

The graph crosses the y-axis here.

> Remember the gradient of a linear graph is the same for any part of the line.

Note:
- any graph with a gradient of 5 will be **parallel** to the graph of $y = 5x - 4$
- a graph with a gradient of $\frac{-1}{5}$ will be **perpendicular** to $y = 5x - 4$
  i.e. the line slopes in the other direction and its gradient is the inverse.

Example 3
Draw the graph of $y = 3x - 1$

The graph has a gradient of 3 and the y-intercept is $^-1$.

Step 1

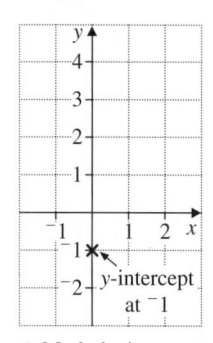

- Mark the intercept.

y-intercept at $^-1$

Step 2

Gradient takes you to this point

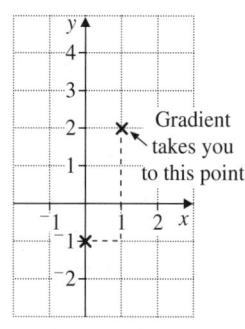

- From the y-intercept draw the gradient 3.

Step 3

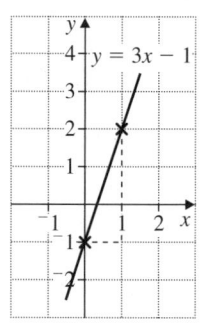

$y = 3x - 1$

- Join the points with a line and label.

Exercise 4.8C

1 Copy and complete this table.

	Equation of line	Gradient	y-intercept
a	$y = 2x + 3$		
b	$y = 3x - 5$		
c	$y = 5x - 8$		
d		2	$^-8$
e		4	7
f		1	$^-1$
g		3.5	7.5

2 Which of the graphs below will be parallel to $y = 2x - 5$?
 a $y = 5x - 2$ b $y = 2x + 5$
 c $y = 2x - 3$ d $y = 5x + 2$
 e Give the gradient of a line perpendicular to $y = 2x - 5$

3 For the graph of $y = 2x + 3$
 a Give the y-intercept.
 b On a pair of axes draw the graph of $y = 2x + 3$

4 On one pair of axes draw and label these graphs.
 a $y = 3x + 1$ b $y = 2x - 3$ c $y = 4x - 1$
 d For each of the lines, give the gradient of a line that is perpendicular to it.

Exercise 4.8D

1 On a pair of axes draw a graph of $y = 2x - 5$

2 a On the same pair of axes draw graphs of $y = 3x + 2$ and $y = x - 2$
 b Give the coordinates of the point where the two graphs cross.

3 Think about the graph of $y = 6x - 5$
 a Give the equation of a graph parallel to $y = 6x - 5$ which has a y-intercept at 7.
 b Give the gradient of a line perpendicular to $y = 6x - 5$

4 Graph A and graph B are parallel.
 Graph A has a gradient of 3 and a y-intercept of 1.
 Graph B has a y-intercept at $^-2$.
 On a pair of axes draw Graph A and Graph B.

5 a On a pair of axes draw the graph of $y = 4 - 3x$
 b Give the gradient of a line perpendicular to $y = 4 - 3x$

You can draw a graph for any linear equation even when it does not start with $y = \ldots$
You may have to rearrange the equation before drawing the graph.

Example 4
Draw the graph of $3y + 6 = 4x$

Rearrange the equation:

$3y + 6 = 4x$
$3y = 4x - 6$ (Subtract 6 from both sides.)
$y = \frac{4}{3}x - 2$

So, the graph of $3y + 6 = 4x$ has

a gradient of $\frac{4}{3}$
a y-intercept at $^-2$

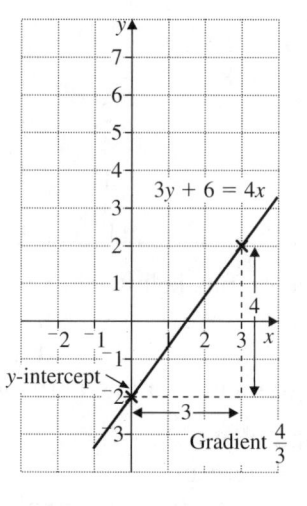

Exercise 4.8E

1 Rearrange the equation and draw the graph for each of these.
- **a** $4y + 12 = 3x$
- **b** $2y - 4 = 3x$
- **c** $5y - 2x = 15$
- **d** $3y - 4x = 9$
- **e** $9 - 3x = 1 - 4y$
- **f** $^-12 = 5x - 6y$
- **g** $3y - 6 = x$
- **h** $5 = x - 5y$

Exercise 4.8F

1 Rearrange the equation and draw the graph for each of these.
- **a** $3y - 12 = x$
- **b** $2y - 8 = 5x$
- **c** $5y - 3x = 10$
- **d** $2y - x = 6$
- **e** $4y + 8 = x$
- **f** $2y - x = 5$
- **g** $4y + 8 = 5x$
- **h** $7y - x = 14$

4.9 Everyday linear graphs*

▶ Graphs are used to show a link between two variables.

Example
The linear graph shows what Carloan charge for rental over a number of days.
What is their fixed cost and their daily rate?

The fixed cost is where the graph intercepts the y-axis, in this case £30.

The daily rate is the gradient (slope) of the graph. The charge goes up £320 over 8 days, so the daily rate is £40 per day.

Carloan Rental Charges

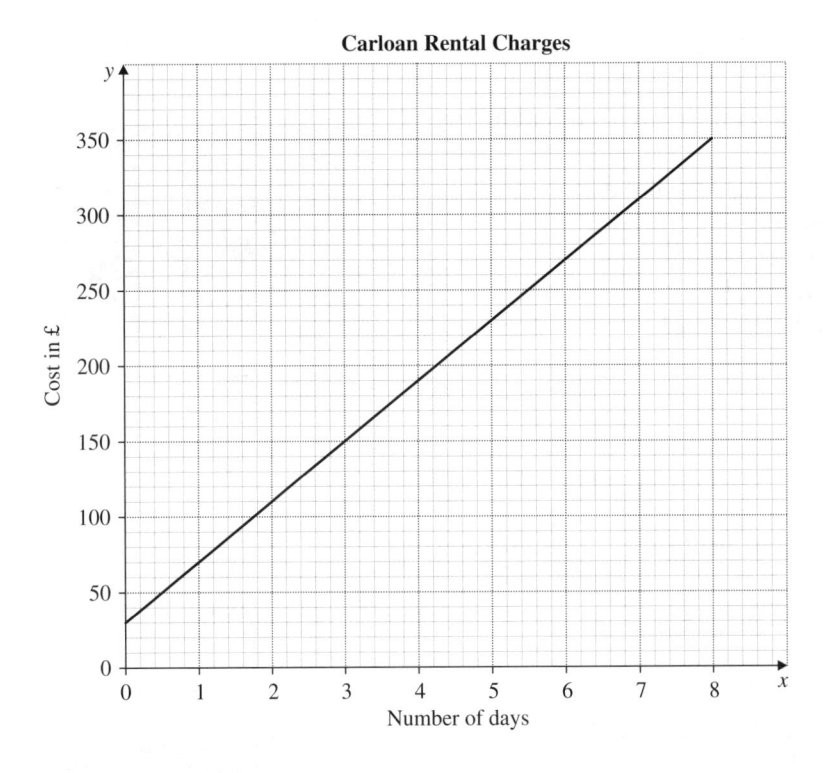

Exercise 4.9A

1 From the graph above:
  a How much does it cost to rent a car for 4 days?
  b For how long could you rent a car if you had £250?
  c This formula calculates the cost in pounds, P, to rent a car for d days. $P = \blacktriangle d + \blacksquare$ What are the values of $\blacktriangle$ and $\blacksquare$?

> The cost is called the **dependent variable**. It depends on the number of days.

2 Simon uses the rule $R = 2P + 4$ to find how many rolls to fill for a buffet. R is the number of rolls and P the number of people.
  a For 8 people how many rolls will he fill?
  b Draw a graph of the number of rolls he fills for up to 15 people.
  c Last time he had rolls left over so Simon changes his rule to: $R = 2P + 2$.   How is this graph different from the one you have drawn?

Exercise 4.9B

1 a Draw a linear conversion graph to change between French Francs and Euros given that €1 = 6.5 FF.
      Scale the horizontal axis from €0 to €20.
  b Use your graph to find the amount in Euros equivalent to 16 FF.

2 At Electroplete, cable is sold at £2.50 per metre plus a cutting charge of £2.
 a Draw a graph to show the cost against length of cable for up to 20 metres.
 b From your graph find the cost of 15 m of cable.
 c A bill for cable came to £24.50.
 How many metres were bought?
 d If T is the total cost in pounds and M is the number of metres, write a formula to link T and M.

> When you are asked to plot a graph of:
> **P against Q**
> then P goes on the vertical axis because it is the dependent variable.

4.10 Graphs of distance, time and speed*

▶ To calculate average speed, time or distance use these formulas.

$$\text{Speed} = \frac{\text{Distance}}{\text{Time}} \qquad \text{Time} = \frac{\text{Distance}}{\text{Speed}} \qquad \text{Distance} = \text{Speed} \times \text{Time}$$

Example 1
Calculate the time taken to travel 154 miles at 40 mph.
Time = Distance ÷ Speed = 154 ÷ 40 = 3.85 hours
  = 3 h 51 minutes

> 0.85 hours
> = 0.85 × 60 minutes
> = 51 minutes

▶ To show speed on a graph plot Distance against Time.
The steeper the slope of the graph, the faster the speed.

Example 2
Anna cycles at 15 kph for 4 h 30 min.
Mike goes 80 km from the same point in 6 hours.
Show these journeys on a distance/time graph.

Anna's distance = 15 × 4.5 = 67.5 km

The graphs show that Anna cycled faster than Mike because her graph is steeper.

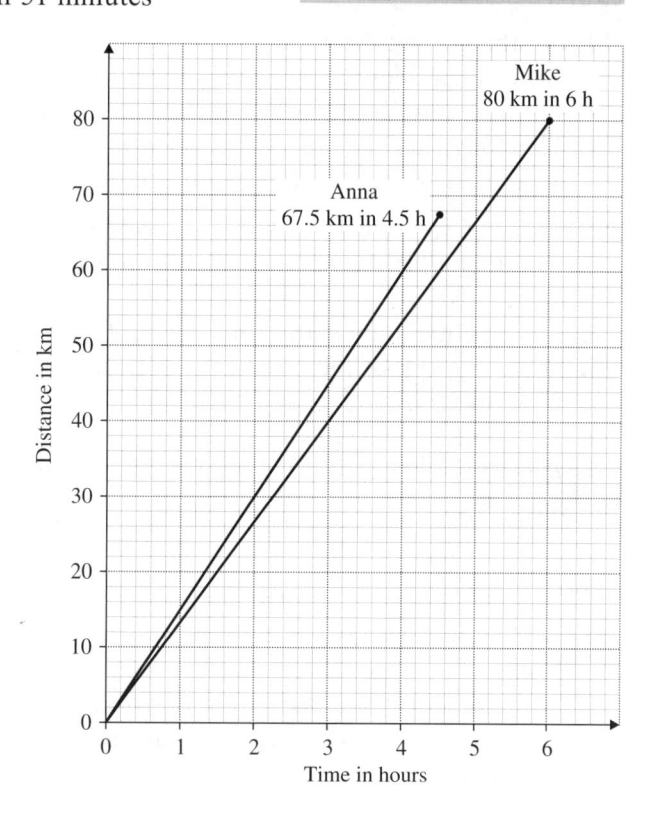

Exercise 4.10A

1. Calculate each of these:
   a. Distance (in miles) if speed is 40 mph and time is 5 h 30 min.
   b. Speed (in kph) if distance is 207 km and time is 4 h 30 min.
   c. Time (in seconds) if distance is 500 metres and speed is 26 metres per second.

2. Copy axes like the ones on page 100 and draw each of these journeys.
   a. Sonia: 40 km in 5 hours
   b. Steve: 15 km in 4 h 30 min
   c. Clare: 30 kph for 2 hours
   d. Evan: 8 kph for 3 hours

Exercise 4.10B

1. Sadie travels 3 hours to York from Carlisle at a speed of 42 mph. Mel averages 30 mph for the same journey.
   a. Show the two journeys on a distance/time graph.
   b. How far apart were the two women after 2 hours?

   > Use axes from 0 to 130 for the distance in km against 0 to 5 for the time in hours.

2. Two cars on a motorway pass a speed camera at the same instant. A Peugeot is travelling at 40 metres/s and a Jaguar at 15 metres/s.
   a. Draw a distance time graph for the cars over the next eight seconds.
   b. How far apart are the cars after 6 seconds?

4.11 More complex distance/time graphs*

▶ Several stages of a journey can be shown on the same graph.
This graph shows Ali as she cycles to her gym, then on to the market, later to return home. Fiona sets off later than Ali from the same house to cycle to work.

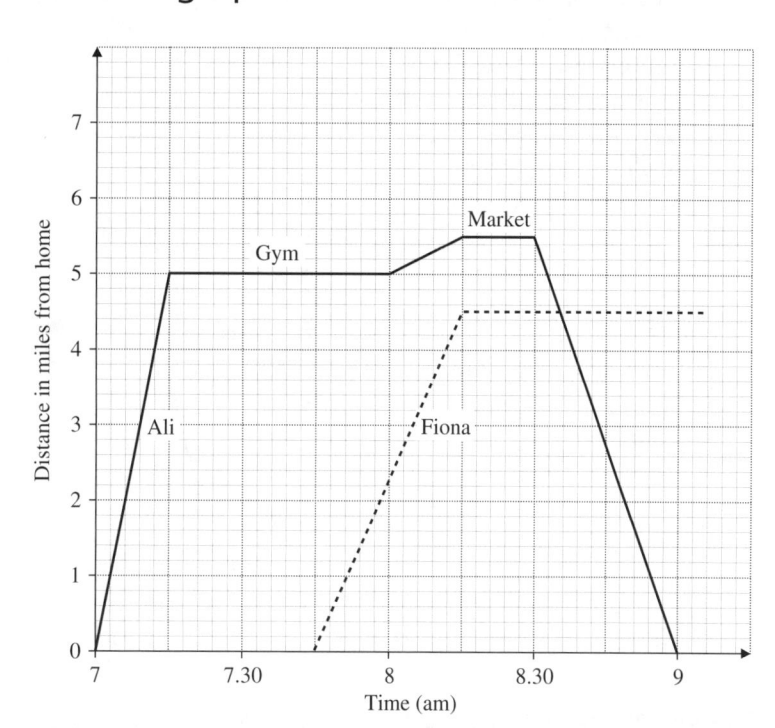

Exercise 4.11A

Use the graph on page 99 for Questions 1–10.

1. At what time did Fiona start off?

2. Why is it shown as a horizontal line while Ali was at the gym?

3. How long did Ali spend at the gym?

4. How far is Fiona's work from her home?

5. **a** How far is Ali's gym from her house?
   b How long did it take her to cycle there?
   c What was Ali's average speed while cycling to the gym?

6. At what time did Ali start cycling home?

7. How long did Ali spend at the market?

8. Who was cycling faster when they left home, Ali or Fiona? How can you tell?

9. At what point in the journey was Ali travelling most slowly?

10. **a** How far was the market from the girls' house?
    b How long did it take Ali to cycle back from the market?
    c At what average speed did Ali cycle home?

11. This distance/time graph shows Sean's journey to a job interview. Describe Sean's day as fully as you can saying what he might be doing at any point. Give speeds if possible.

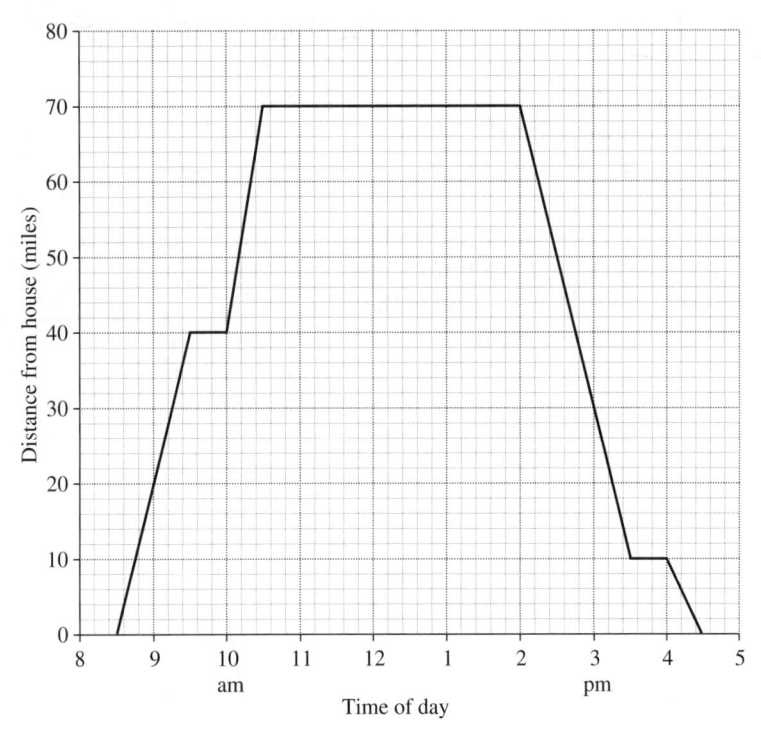

13. Plan a journey for Julie where she visits two friends by car. Draw a distance/time graph to illustrate her journey.

Exercise 4.11B

1 This distance/time graph shows the journeys of a motorbike and a car between Leeds and Doncaster.
  a How far is Leeds from Doncaster?
  b At what time did the car stop?
  c For how long in minutes did the car stop?
  d At what time did the motorbike arrive back in Leeds?
  e Describe the different speeds of the motorbike on its journey back to Leeds.
  f What speed was the car doing at 13:55?
  g Describe what happened at 14:10?
  h What speed was the motorbike doing between 2:04 pm and 2:20 pm?
  i Between what times was the motorbike travelling at its slowest speed?
  j What was the car's average speed over the whole journey?

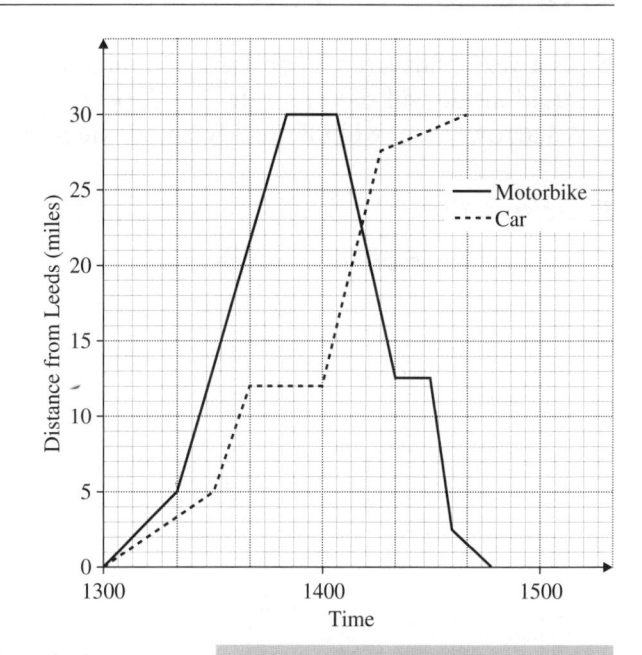

To calculate **average speed** you can use this formula.

$$\text{Average speed} = \frac{\text{Total distance}}{\text{Total time}}$$

2 A mountain cyclist is racing over these hills as shown. Which distance/time graph best approximates to the journey? Explain your decision fully.

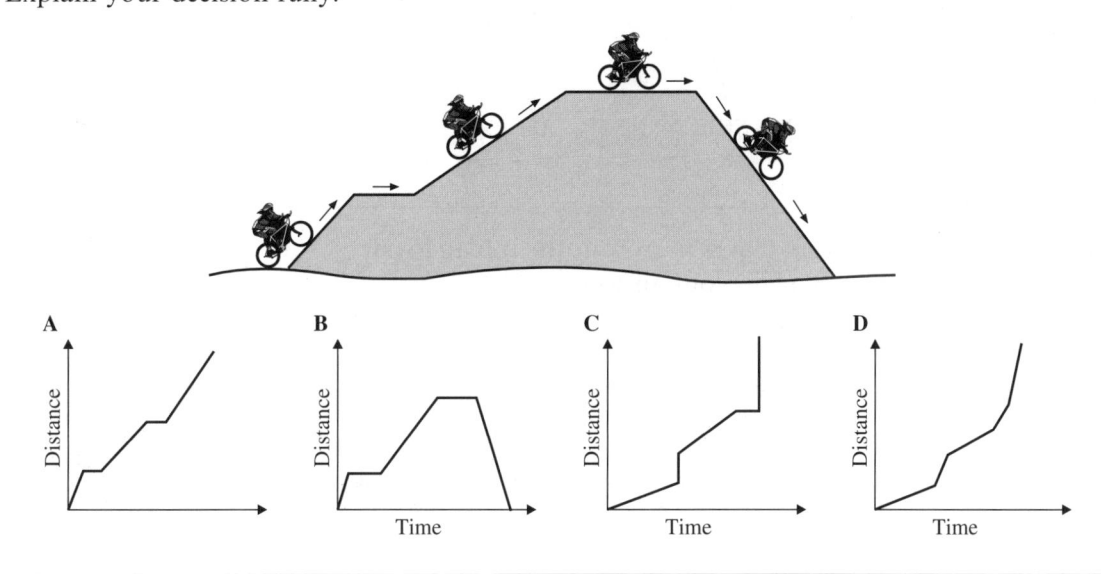

4.12 Graphs of vessels filling*

▶ As a vessel fills from a constantly running tap the height of liquid inside will rise at a rate that depends on the vessel width. A narrow vessel will fill quickly and a wide one slowly.

Exercise 4.12A

1 Match each vessel to its sketch graph.

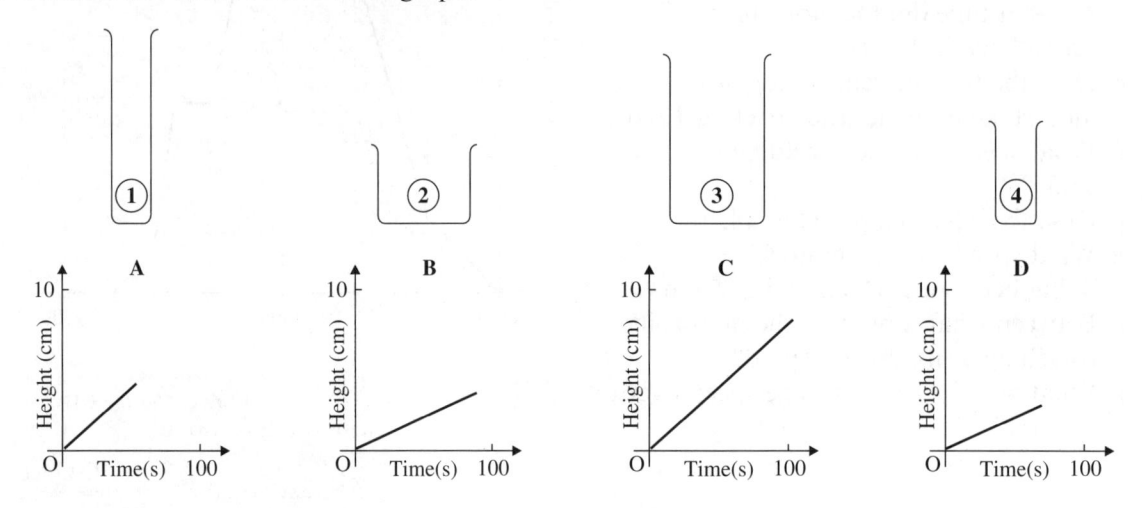

2 Which graph shows how this vessel fills? Explain your answer.

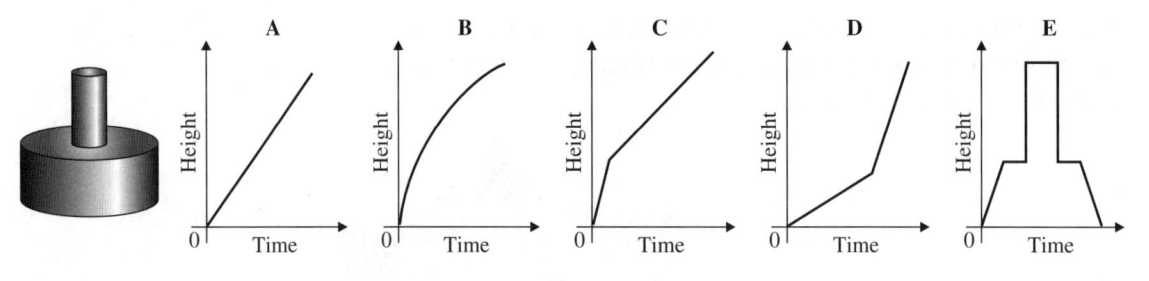

Exercise 4.12B

1 Which graph shows a flask that is narrow at the top and wide at the bottom, **E** or **F**? Explain your answer.

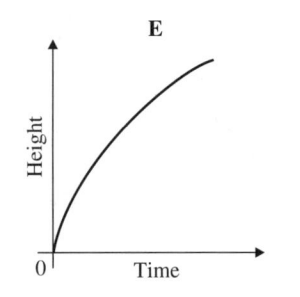

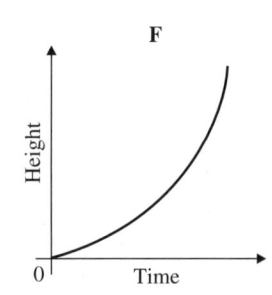

2 Match each vessel with a sketch graph.

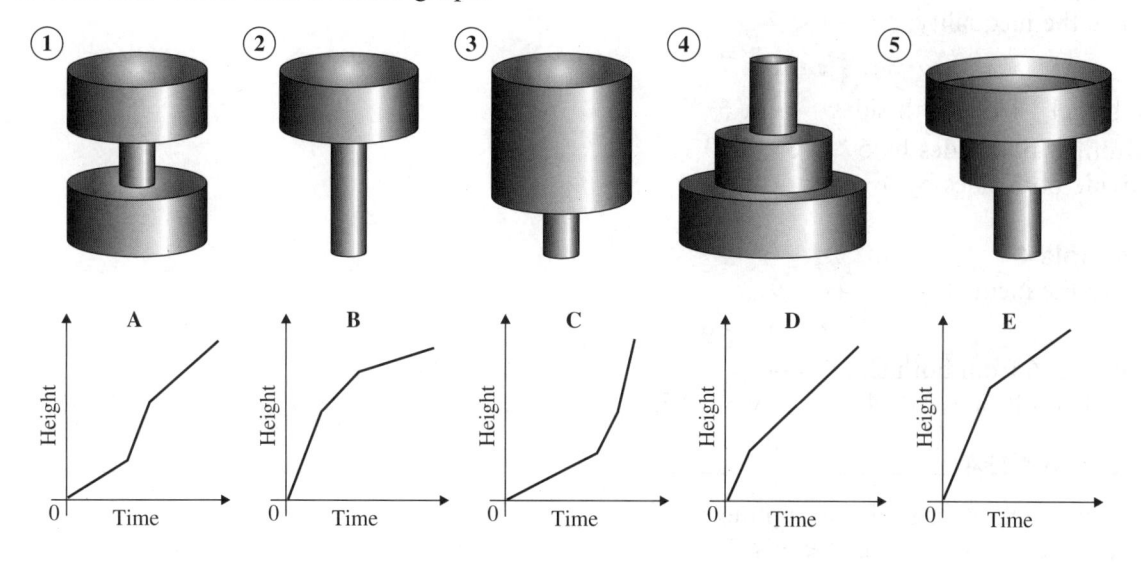

4.13 Inequalities

An inequality states that one value is greater or less than another value. For example we can write: $5 < x$ which means that 5 is less than x, or we might say that x is greater than 5.

Example 1
What values of x satisfy $^-4 < x \leqslant 3$ (x is an integer.)

x can be $^-3, ^-2, ^-1, 0, 1, 2, 3$

Inequalities can be manipulated in a similar way to equations but there are some rules that must be followed.

- A number or variable can be added to or subtracted from both sides of an inequality.
- You can multiply or divide both sides of an inequality by a positive value.
- If you multiply or divide both sides of an inequality by a negative value you must reverse the inequality sign.

Example 2
Solve the inequality $x - 9 < 17$

$$x - 9 < 17$$
Add 9 to both sides $\quad x - 9 + 9 < 17 + 9$
$$x < 26$$

Example 3
Solve the inequality: $\frac{3}{5}x + 1 < 7$

$$\frac{3}{5}x + 1 < 7$$

Subtract 1 from both sides $\quad \frac{3}{5}x < 6$
Multiply both sides by 5 $\quad 3x < 30$
Divide both sides by 3 $\quad\quad x < 10$

Example 4
Solve the inequality: $6 - 4x < 9$

$$6 - 4x < 9$$

Subtract 6 from both sides $\quad -4x < 3$
Divide both sides by $^-4$ $\quad\quad x >^- 0.75$ (Note the sign is reversed.)

Exercise 4.13A

1 Solve each of these if x is an integer.
 a $^-3 < x < 4$ **b** $3 < x \leqslant 7$ **c** $^-1 \leqslant x \leqslant 8$
 d $0 \leqslant x < 5$ **e** $^-2 \leqslant x \leqslant 1$ **f** $2 < x \leqslant 7$

2 Solve each of these if x is an integer.
 a $^-4 \leqslant 2x \leqslant 5$ **b** $^-6 \leqslant 4x < 5$ **c** $^-4 < 5x \leqslant 3$

3 Solve each of these inequalities.
 a $3x + 5 < 23$ **b** $4x - 8 < 36$ **c** $11x + 9 < 130$
 d $14 + 7x < 63$ **e** $12 + 14x < 82$ **f** $23x - 19 < 50$

4 Solve each of these inequalities.
 a $4 - 9x < 31$ **b** $21 - 6x < 93$ **c** $14 - 7x < 98$

5 Solve each of these inequalities.
 a $3 + 8x < 15 + 5x$ **b** $4(3 + 2x) < 68$ **c** $6(3 + 2x) < 5(2x - 6)$

Exercise 4.13B

1 Solve each of these if x is an integer.
 a $^-5 < x \leqslant 4$ **b** $0 < x \leqslant 2$ **c** $^-1 \leqslant x \leqslant 1$
 d $0 \leqslant x < 1$ **e** $^-2 \leqslant x < 1$ **f** $2 < x \leqslant 3$

2 Solve each of these where x is an integer.
 a $^-4 \leqslant 2x \leqslant 6$ **b** $^-8 \leqslant 4x < 12$ **c** $^-10 < 5x \leqslant 30$

3 Solve each of these inequalities.
 a $9x + 15 < 96$ **b** $6x - 25 < 65$ **c** $15x + 95 < 140$
 d $104 + 27x < 158$ **e** $27 - 4x < 15$ **f** $27 - 19x < 141$

4 Solve each of these inequalities.
 a $15 > 5(3x - 6)$ **b** $4(x + 8) > 120$ **c** $9(2x + 1) > 99$

5 Solve each of these inequalities.
 a $3 + 8x < 15 + 5x$ **b** $5x - 4 > 3x + 22$ **c** $3(5 + 4x) < 5(2x + 1)$

4.14 Inequalities with two variables*

Inequalities can be shown on a graph by drawing a line and then shading a region.

Example
Show by shading on a graph, the inequalities $x > 2$ and $y < {}^-x + 3$
Find values of x and y that satisfy both inequalities.

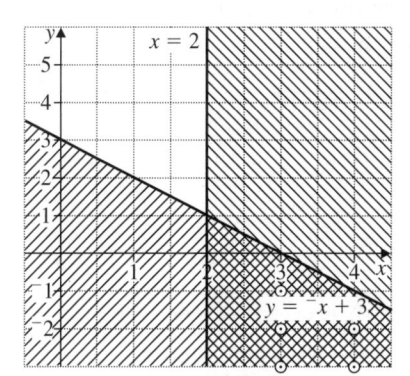

From the shading the values of x and y that satisfy both inequalities are:

$x = 3$ and $y = {}^-1$ $x = 4$ and $y = {}^-2$ and so on.
$x = 3$ and $y = {}^-2$ $x = 4$ and $y = {}^-3$
and so on.   and so on

Exercise 4.14A

1 a Draw graphs and by shading show the regions where
$y < x + 2$ and $x > 1$
 b Find values of x and y that satisfy both inequalities.

2 a On a pair of axes show by shading the region where $y < 2x$ and $x > {}^-1$
 b Find values of x and y that satisfy both inequalities.

3 a On a pair of axes draw graphs of $y = 2x + 1$ and $x = {}^-2$
 b Show by shading an area where values of x and y satisfy the inequalities: $y \leqslant 2x + 1$ and $x > {}^-2$.

Exercise 4.14B

1 a On a pair of axes draw graphs of $y > 2x - 1$ and $x \leqslant 1$.
  b Show by shading an area where values of x and y satisfy both inequalities.

2 By drawing graphs with shading show an area where the following inequalities are satisfied.

$y > 3x + 1$ and $x > {}^-1$

3 On a pair of axes show by shading an area where the values of x and y satisfy the inequalities: $y \leqslant 2x - 4$ and $y > x + 1$

Revision exercise 4 *Review*

1 This is a sequence of match patterns.

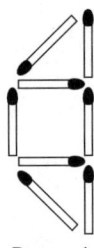

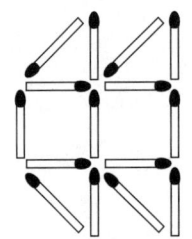

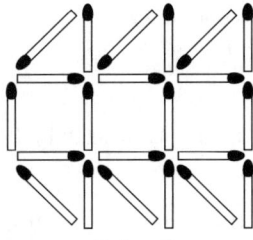

Pattern 1   Pattern 2   Pattern 3

a Draw Pattern 9 in the sequence.
b How many matches will be in Pattern 25?

Unit 4.1

2 This is a sequence of patterns.

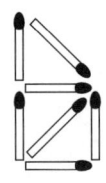

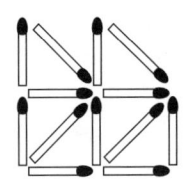

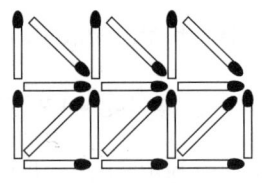

Pattern 1   Pattern 2   Pattern 3

a Describe what is happening as the patterns grow.
b Calculate the number of squares in pattern 150.

Unit 4.1

3 Find the next four terms of each sequence using the rule from the previous term.
  a 2, 17, ...   Add 15.
  b 3, 10, ...   Square and add 1.
  c ⁻7, ⁻15, ...   Double and subtract 1.

Unit 4.2

4 Give the next five terms of each sequence using the rule.
  a 1, ...   Multiply the term number by 5 and subtract 4.
  b 2, ...   Square the term number and add 1.
  c 6, ...   Add 1 to the term number and multiply by 3.

Unit 4.2

5 Write the first six terms in sequences given by these rules.
  a $3n - 5$ **b** $4(2n - 3)$
  c $n^2 - 2$ **d** $(3n + 1)^2$

Unit 4.2

6 Use differences to find a general term for each sequence.
  a 5, 7, 9, 11, ..., ..., ...   **b** 1, 5, 9, 13, ..., ..., ...
  c 6, 11, 16, 21, ..., ..., ...   **d** 1, 7, 13, 19, ..., ..., ...
  e ⁻1, ⁻5, ⁻9, ⁻13, ..., ..., ... **f** 3, 1, ⁻1, ⁻3, ..., ..., ...

Unit 4.3

7 a Write three different sequences that have a first term of 4.
  b Give the general term for each of your sequences.

Unit 4.3

8 Use differences to find a general term for each sequence.
  a 5, 8, 13, 20, 29, ..., ..., ...   **b** ⁻4, ⁻1, 4, 11, 20, 31, ..., ..., ...
  c 2, 5, 10, 17, 26, ..., ..., ...   **d** ⁻1, 5, 15, 29, 47, ..., ..., ...
  e 4, 13, 28, 49, 76, ..., ..., ...   **f** 6.5, 21.5, 46.5, 81.5, 126.5, ..., ..., ...

Unit 4.4

9 For each sequence:
  find its general term, then draw a graph of the sequence.
  a 3, 5, 7, 9, ..., ..., ...   **b** 1, 4, 7, 10, ..., ..., ...
  c 6, 7, 8, 9, ..., ..., ...   **d** 1, 4, 9, 16, ..., ..., ...
  e 2, 5, 10, 17, 26, ..., ..., ... **f** ⁻1, 2, 7, 14, 23, 34, ..., ..., ...

Unit 4.5

10 Create a quadratic sequence, give its general term and draw its graph.

Unit 4.5

11 ABCD is a square. The coordinates of A, B and C are (1, ⁻1), (1, 3), (⁻3, 3).
  a Give the coordinates of D.
  b Give the coordinates of the point where the diagonals of the square intersect.

Unit 4.6

12 Draw a pair of axes with values of x and y from ⁻5 to ⁺5.
  On the axes draw and label these graphs.
  $$y = ⁻4 \qquad x = 3 \qquad y = 5 \qquad x = ⁻4 \qquad y = 1$$

Unit 4.7

13 Draw the graph of $y = 3x + 1$ for values of x from $^-4$ to $^+4$.
Show your table of values.

Review
Unit 4.8

14 a On the same pair of axes draw graphs of $y = 2x + 1$ and
$y = 4x - 1$ for values of x from $^-1$ to $^+4$.
b Give the coordinates of the point where the two lines cross.

Unit 4.8

15 On the same axes draw and label these graphs.
a $y = 2x - 1$ **b** $y = 3 - 2x$
c $y = x$ **d** $y = {}^-x$

Unit 4.8

16 For each graph give its gradient and its y-intercept.
a $y = 3x - 4$ **b** $y = 5 - 2x$
c $y = x + 2$ **d** $y = 4 - 3x$
e $2y = 3x + 4$ **f** $5y = 6x - 18$

Unit 4.8

17 Which of these graphs will be parallel to $y = 3x - 5$?
a $y = 3x + 1$ **b** $y = 2 - 3x$ **c** $2y = 6x - 15$

Unit 4.8

18 For each line give the gradient of a line perpendicular to it.
a $y = 2x + 5$ **b** $y = 4x - 3$ **c** $y = 5 - 6x$

Unit 4.8

19 On a pair of axes draw and label the graph of $3y = 2x - 6$

Unit 4.8

20 A car hire firm uses this scale of charges.
A fixed charge of £35 and £25 per day.
a Draw a linear graph to show charges for up to
ten days hire.
b Show on your graph the charge for 7 days hire.
c What is the gradient of your graph?

21 Copy and complete the following table.

Unit 4.9

Average Speed	Distance	Time
55 kph	■	2.5 hours
45 kph	360 km	■
64 kph	■	2 h 45 min
■	450 km	6 h 15 min

Unit 4.10

22 A train leaves London at 14:46 to travel to Bristol, a distance
of 280 km. The train arrives in Bristol at 17:16.
Calculate the average speed of the train for the journey.

Unit 4.10

23 An aircraft flies at an average speed of 540 mph.
How far will the plane fly in four hours and forty five
minutes?

Unit 4.10

24 This distance time graph shows the journey of two friends. One is travelling from home to the station and the other from the station home.

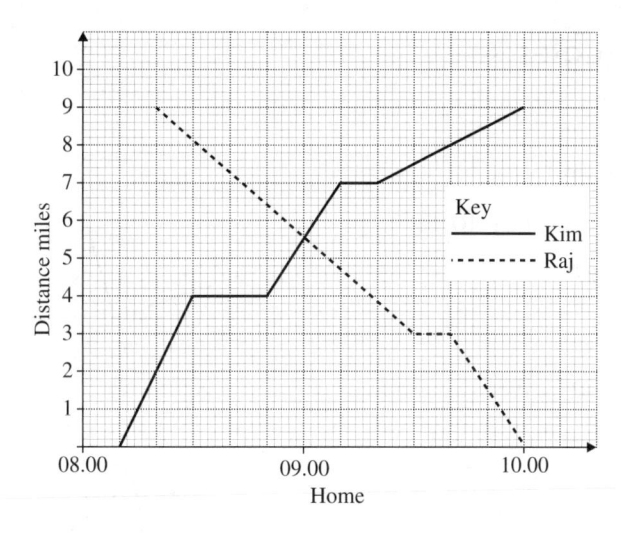

Review

For each of them:
a how long was their journey
b calculate their average speed for the journey
c the speed for the fastest part of their journey.

d At what time and how far from the station did they pass each other?

Unit 4.11

Unit 4.11

25 Four vessels are filled from the same tap at the same rate. Sketch a graph of height of water against time to show how they each fill.

a   b    c 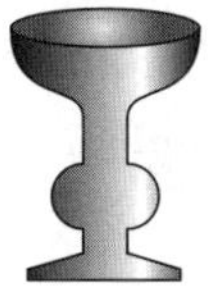   d

Unit 4.12

26 Solve each of these if x is an integer.
a $^-5 < x \leqslant 4$ **b** $0 < 2x < 8$
c $^-5 \leqslant x \leqslant ^-1$ **d** $^-8 \leqslant 3x + 1 \leqslant 14$

Unit 4.13

27 On a pair of axes shade the region where $x < 3$ and $y > 3x$

Unit 4.14

28 Draw graphs of $y > 2x - 1$ and $x < 3$. Shade the area that satisfies both inequalities.

Unit 4.14

29 Show the area that satisfies both $y < 2x - 5$ and $x > ^-2$.

Unit 4.14

30 Show the area that satisfies both $y > 2x + 3$ and $y < 4 - 3x$.

Unit 4.14

5 Geometrical Reasoning

5.1 Facts about angles

▶ A full turn is 360°.
   So, for example, $\frac{5}{8}$ of a turn is $\frac{5}{8} \times 360° = 225°$

▶ Angles on a straight line add up to 180°.
   $$x + 90° + 72° = 180°$$
   So $\quad x = 18°$

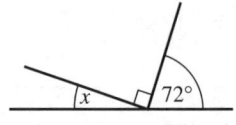

▶ Angles at a point add up to 360°.
   $$y + 90° + 75° + 60° + 62° = 360°$$
   So $\quad y = 73°$

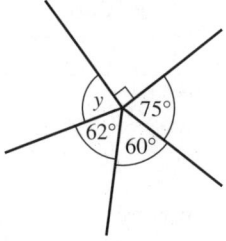

▶ When two straight lines cross the opposite angles are equal. These are called **vertically opposite angles**.
   $p = 56°$ (p and 56° are vertically opposite)
   $q = 124°$

▶ When a straight line crosses two parallel straight lines some angles are equal:
   $a = b, c = d, e = f, g = h$ (Vertically opposite angles)
   $a = c, e = g, b = d, f = h$ (**Corresponding angles**)
   $b = c, f = g$ (**Alternate angles**)

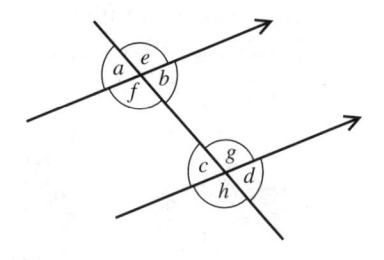

▶ Angles are grouped into three types:

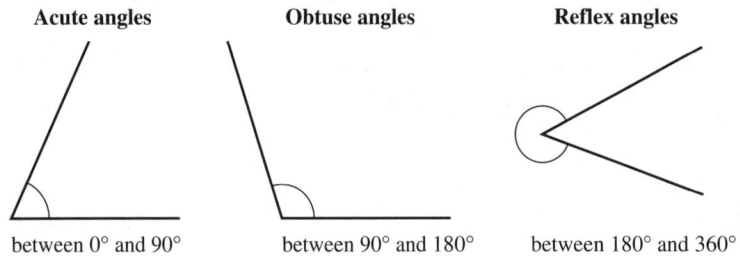

   Acute angles　　　**Obtuse angles**　　　**Reflex angles**

   between 0° and 90°　between 90° and 180°　between 180° and 360°

▶ To measure an angle accurately use a protractor or angle measurer. Decide whether to use the clockwise or the anticlockwise scale.

▶ Estimate the size of an angle before you measure it.
To estimate an angle:
- Compare it with a right angle (90°) – is it smaller or larger?
- Compare it with a straight line (180°)
- Compare it with an angle of 270°

Exercise 5.1A

1 Give each of these turns in degrees.
  a $\frac{3}{5}$ of a full turn   b $\frac{5}{16}$ of a full turn

2 You face North and turn clockwise to the South West.
What fraction of a full turn have you made?

3 Calculate the angles shown by letters.

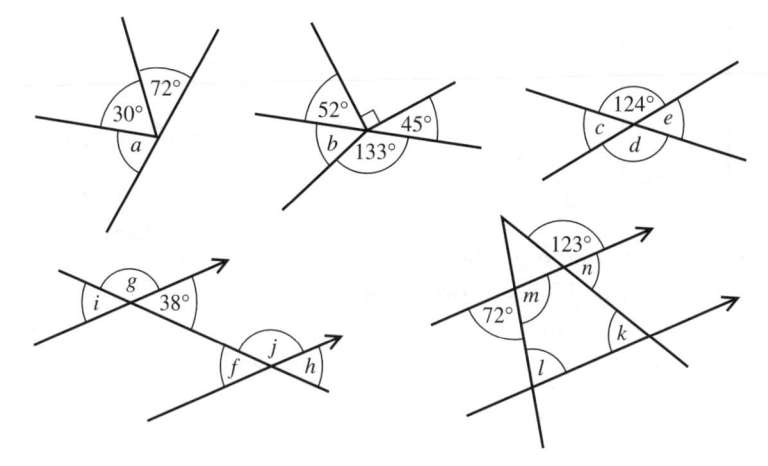

4 Measure each angle and state if it is acute, obtuse or reflex.

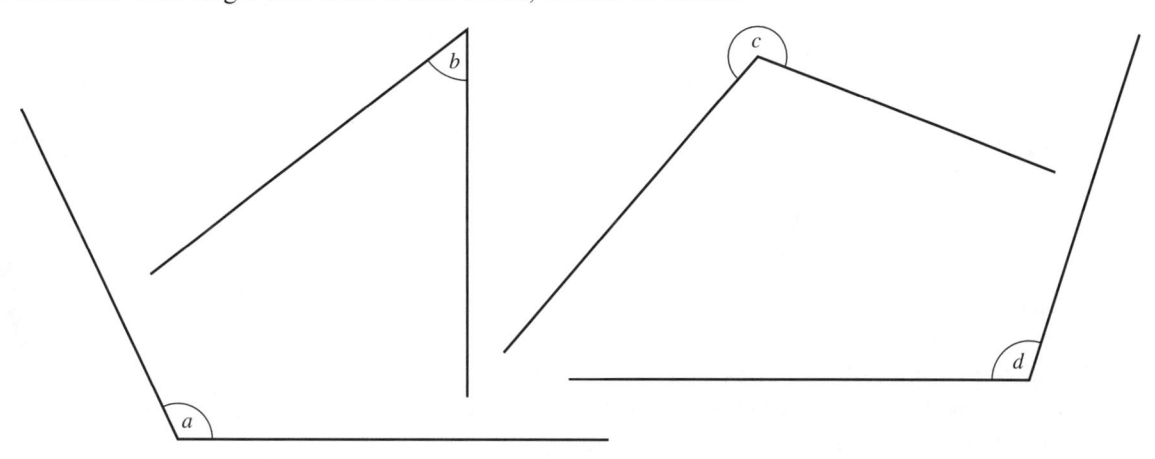

5 Accurately draw angles of:
  a 158°   b 338°   c 264°

Exercise 5.1B

1 Give each of these turns in degrees.

  a $\frac{5}{6}$ of a full turn **b** $\frac{8}{15}$ of a full turn

2 Give two alternative answers to describe each turn in degrees.
  a Face W. Turn towards S. **b** Face S. Turn towards NW.

3 Calculate the size of the unknown letter in each diagram.
Give reasons for your answers.

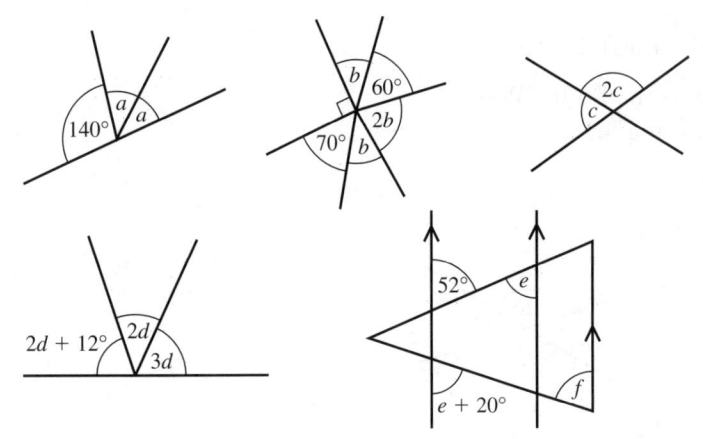

4 The diagram shows a parallelogram. Use the diagram and the information about equal angles between parallel lines to prove that:
  a The opposite angles of a parallelogram are equal.
  b The sum of the interior angles of a parallelogram is 360°.

5 Calculate the missing angles in the diagram below.

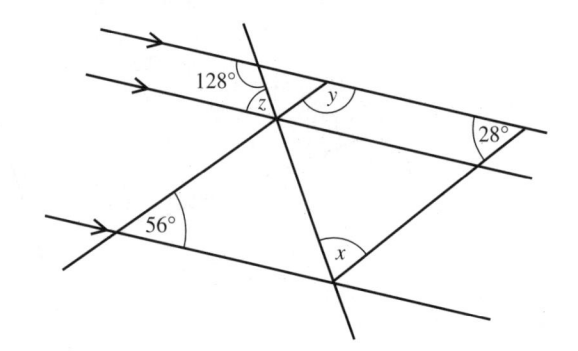

6 Say if each of these is possible or impossible.
  a A triangle with an obtuse interior angle.
  b A triangle with a reflex interior angle.
  c A triangle with two obtuse interior angles.
  d A quadrilateral with a reflex interior angle.
  e A quadrilateral with two obtuse interior angles.

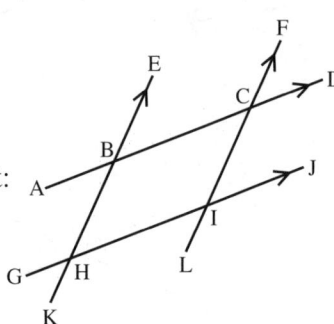

5.2 Bearings

You can fix a position using a bearing and a distance from the centre.
A bearing is a direction measured from North in a clockwise direction.

Example

From a boat the following objects can be seen.

Lighthouse	bearing 085°	distance 2 km
Wreck	bearing 135°	distance 1 km
Rocks	bearing 310°	distance 3 km

Show the boat and the objects on a diagram.

The boat B is at the centre.
Draw in a North line at B.

Measure each bearing in turn.

Use the scale to mark the position of each object.

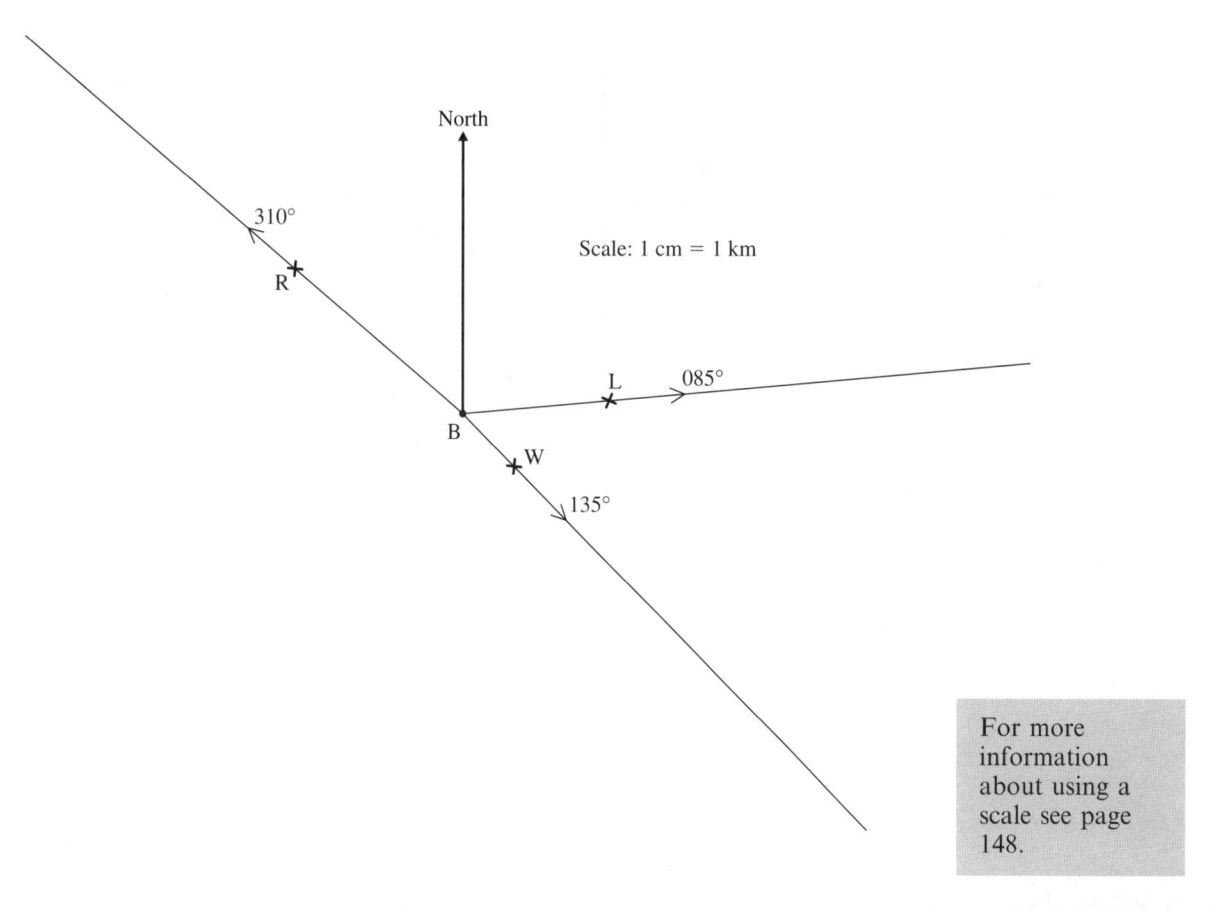

Scale: 1 cm = 1 km

For more information about using a scale see page 148.

Exercise 5.2A

1 Copy and complete this table.
   All bearings and distances are from P.

Location	Bearing	Distance
A	☐	☐
B	☐	☐
C	☐	☐
D	☐	☐
E	☐	☐
F	☐	☐
G	☐	☐
H	☐	☐

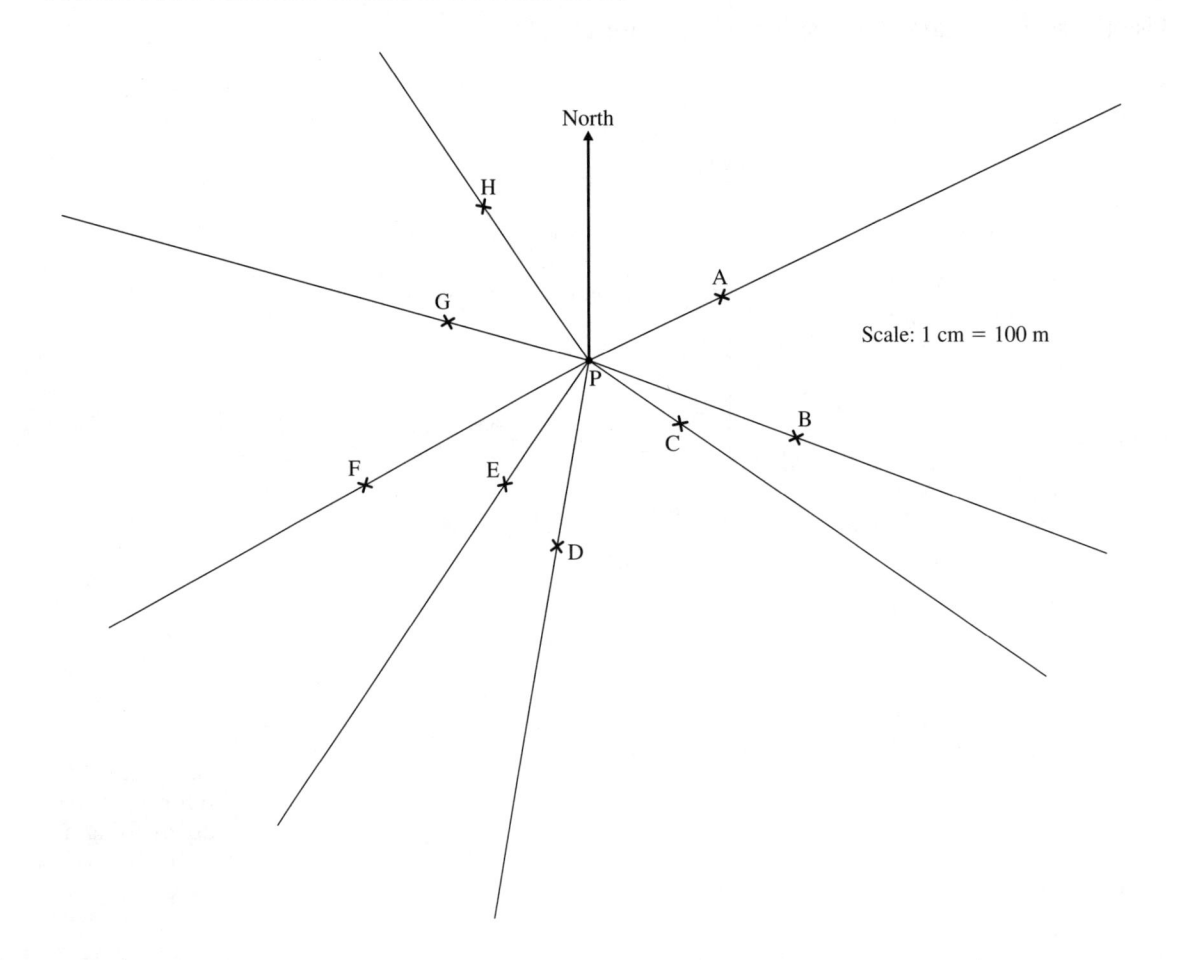

Scale: 1 cm = 100 m

2 Give the bearing of each of these directions.
  a East
  b South West
  c North East
  d West
  e South East
  f North West
  g South South East
  h West North West

3 An aircraft starts a journey on a bearing of 135°, then alters course to fly on 180°. On what bearing is it now travelling?

Exercise 5.2B

1 The diagram shows the journey of an aircraft flying from A to B. The diagram uses a scale of 1 cm = 10 km.

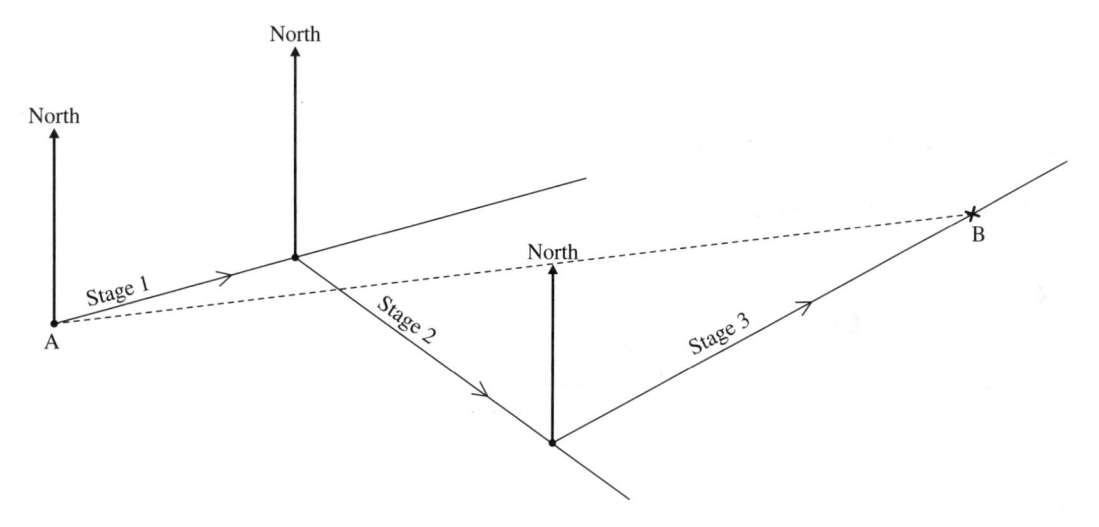

  a What is the bearing and distance for Stage 1?
  b Stage 2 was 43 km long. What was its bearing?
  c For Stage 3, was the bearing greater than or less than 045°?
  d Give the bearing and distance for Stage 3 of the flight.

Imagine the aircraft flew from A to B in a straight line.
  e How far is it from A to B? Give your answer to the nearest 10 km.
  f What is the bearing from A to B?

2 The diagram shows the position of four fishing boats.

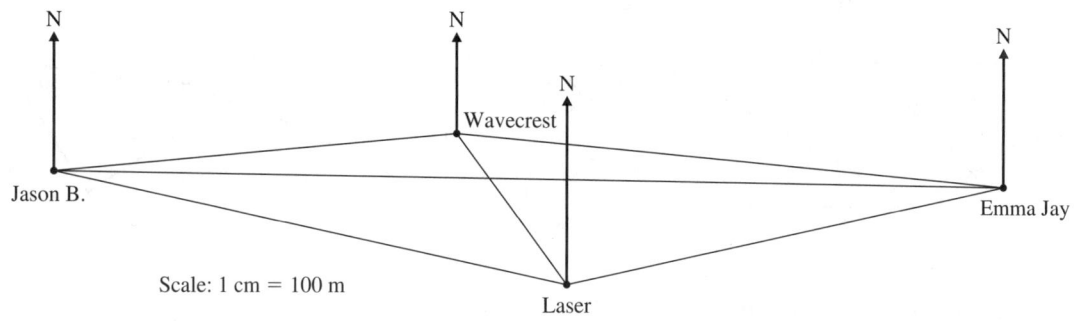

From each boat, give the bearing and distance of the other three boats.

3 Plot this course from A to B on a diagram.
Use a scale of 1 cm = 100 m.

Stage 1:	bearing 080°	distance 250 m
Stage 2:	bearing 130°	distance 100 m
Stage 3:	bearing 105°	distance 200 m
Stage 4:	bearing 350°	distance 300 m

5.3 The angle sum of a triangle

The sum of the angles of a triangle is 180°.

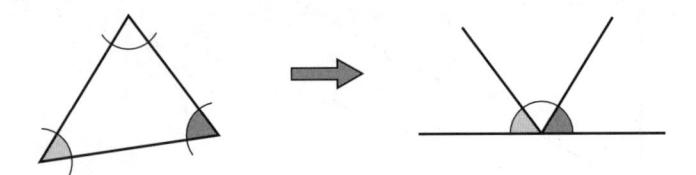

Example
Find the angle marked x in triangle RST.

The three angles must total 180°.

So: $x + 73 + 54 = 180$
$x + 127 = 180$
$x = 53°$

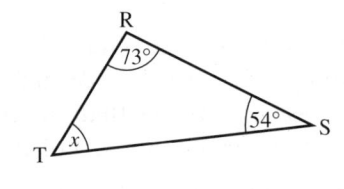

Exercise 5.3A

1 Find the angle marked x in each triangle.

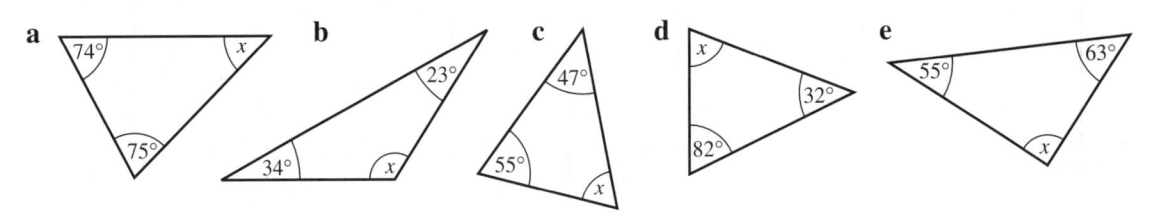

a 74°, 75°, x

b 23°, 34°, x

c 47°, 55°, x

d x, 82°, 32°

e 55°, 63°, x

2 Two of the angles in a triangle are 33° and 51°.
Calculate the size of the third angle.

Exercise 5.3B

1 Calculate the unknown angles in these triangles.

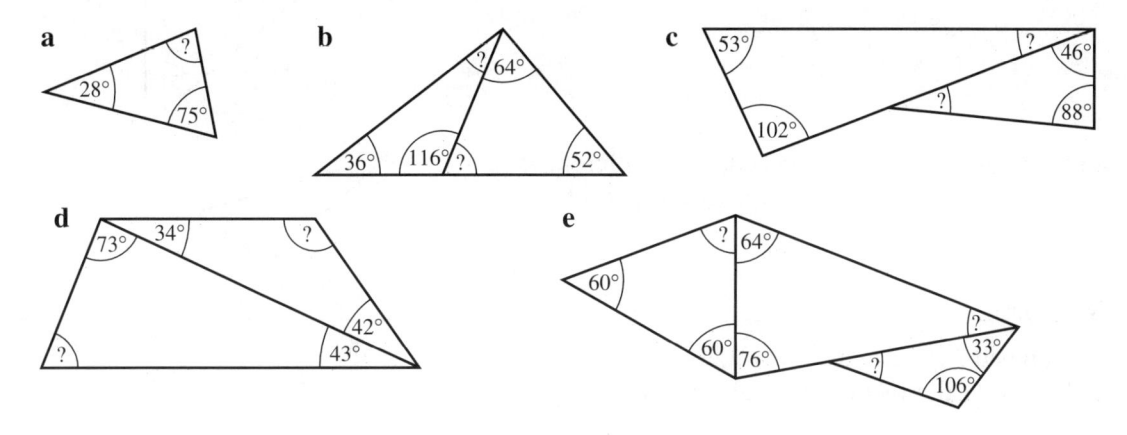

a, b, c, d, e

5.4 Types of triangle

All triangles have three straight edges and an angle sum of 180°.
Here are some special triangles:

- **Equilateral triangle**   has 3 edges the same length
                              3 equal angles – all 60°.

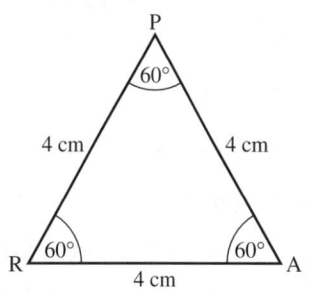

- **Isosceles triangle**   has 2 edges the same length
                              2 angles equal in size.

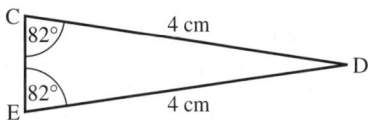

- **Acute-angled triangle**   has no angle greater than 90°.

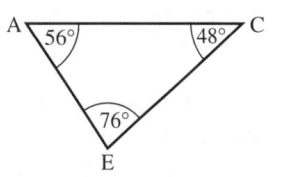

- **Obtuse-angled triangle** has one angle greater than 90°.

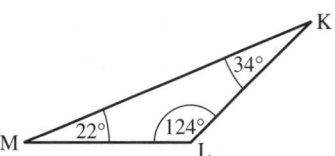

- **Right-angled triangle** one angle is 90°.

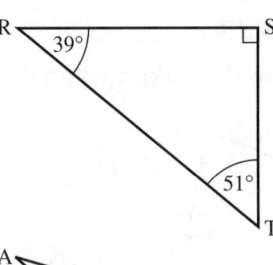

- **Scalene triangle** has edges of different lengths and angles different in size.

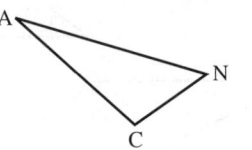

Exercise 5.4A

1. A right-angled triangle has one angle of 58°.
   Give the size of the two other angles in the triangle.

2. Triangle THF has angles of 38° and 44°.
   Is THF an obtuse-angled triangle? Explain your answer.

3. ABC is a right-angled isosceles triangle.
   Give the size of each angle of ABC.

4. Can you draw a triangle that is right angled and equilateral?
   Explain your answer.

5. Triangle ABC is isosceles.
   What is the size of each angle marked x?

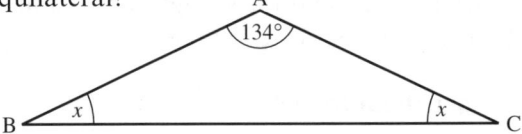

Exercise 5.4B

1. Can a triangle be isosceles and scalene? Explain your answer.

2. Can you draw an obtuse right-angled triangle? Explain your answer.

3. Triangle ARN is equilateral. The length of AR is 6.2 cm. Sketch ARN, label the length of each edge and the size of each angle.

4. Triangle ABC is right angled. The angle at C is 41°.
   What might be the angles at A and B?

5. Triangle TAW is acute and scalene.
   Sketch an example of TAW.
   Label the length of each edge and the size of each angle.

6. Two students make copies of triangle PRC and join two together along one edge.
   One makes a shape with an angle sum of 180°.
   One makes a shape with an angle sum of 360°.
   Sketch what might be the two shapes.

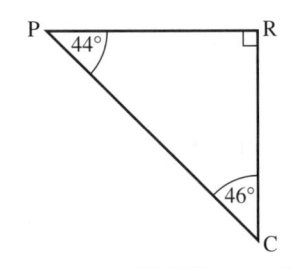

5.5 Congruent triangles

Triangles are congruent if they are exactly the same in shape and size.
If one triangle can be fitted exactly over the other they are congruent.

You can use tracing paper to test for an exact fit.

> Any two shapes are congruent if they are exactly the same shape and size.

Exercise 5.5A

1 Which triangles are congruent to A?

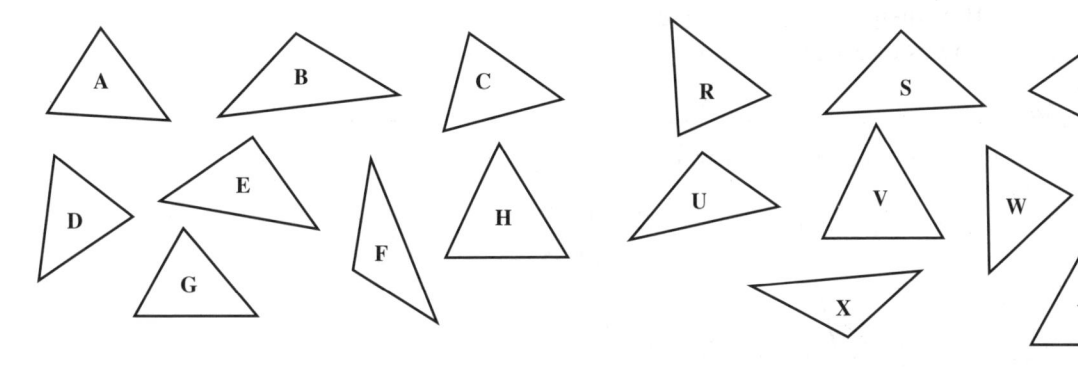

Exercise 5.5B

1 Find all the triangles congruent to R.

5.6 The exterior angles of a triangle

A triangle has three exterior angles, one at each vertex.

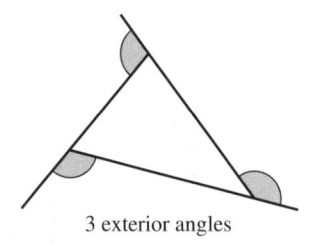

3 exterior angles

> The sum of the exterior angles of any polygon is 360°.

You can calculate the size of an exterior angle in two ways.

1 When you know the size of the corresponding interior angle.

   Exterior angle $y + 48° = 180°$
   (Angles on a straight line add up to 180°.)
   So, the exterior angle $y = 132°$

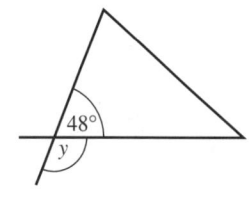

2 When you know the size of the two opposite interior angles.

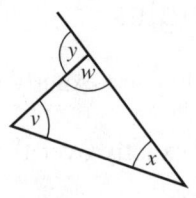

Interior angle $w = 180°$ – Exterior angle y (Angles on a straight line)
Interior angle $w = 180°$ – (Interior angle v + Interior angle x)

So, Exterior angle y = Interior angle v + Interior angle x

Note:
If you add all 3 exterior angles you have: $v + x + x + w + w + v = 2v + 2w + 2x$
as $v + w + x = 180°$ then $2v + 2w + 2x = 360°$
So the external angles of a triangle add up to 360°.

Exercise 5.6A

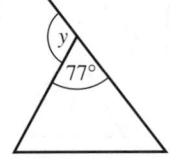

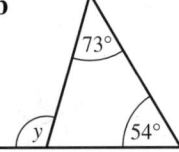

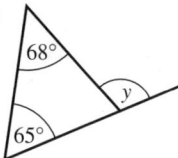

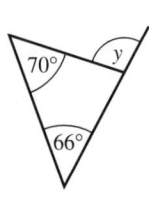

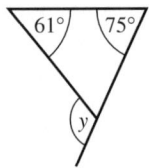

1 Calculate the angle marked y in each triangle.

a 77°

b 73°, 54°

c 68°, 65°

d 70°, 66°

e 61°, 75°

f 86°

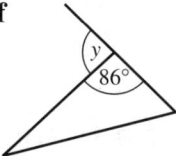

Exercise 5.6B

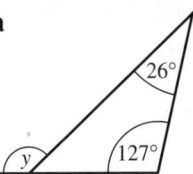

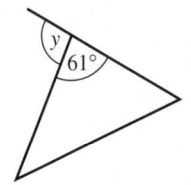

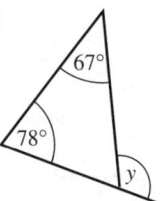

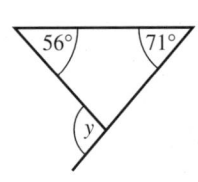

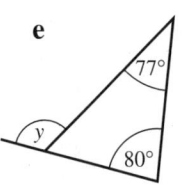

1 Calculate the angle marked y in each triangle.

a 26°, 127°

b 61°

c 67°, 78°

d 56°, 71°

e 77°, 80°

f 56°, 47°

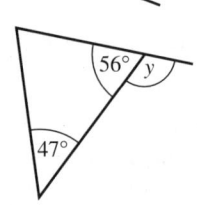

5.7 Quadrilaterals

A quadrilateral is a closed shape with four straight edges.
The four angles of a quadrilateral add up to 360°.

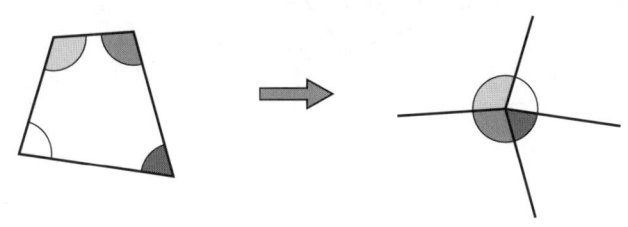

Remember:
To **bisect** a line you divide it into two equal parts.

You need to know these special quadrilaterals.

- **Rectangle**, also known as an oblong.
  All the angles are 90°.
  Opposite edges are equal in length.
  Diagonals are the same length and bisect each other.

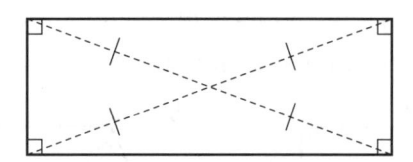

- **Square**
  All the angles are 90°.
  All edges are equal in length.
  Diagonals are equal, and bisect each other at right angles.

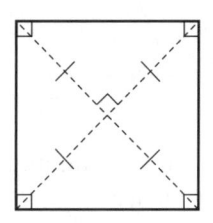

- **Parallelogram**
  Opposite angles are equal.
  Opposite edges are parallel.
  Opposite edges are equal in length.
  Diagonals bisect each other.

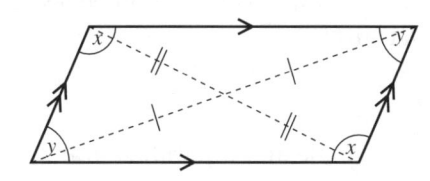

- **Rhombus**
  Opposite angles are equal.
  Opposite edges are parallel.
  All edges are equal in length.
  Diagonals bisect each other at right angles.

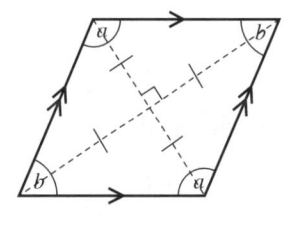

- **Trapezium**
  One pair of opposite sides are parallel.

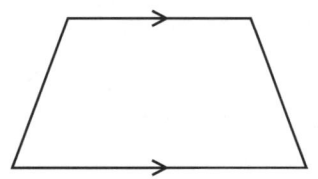

Geometrical reasoning

- **Kite**
  Two pairs of adjacent edges equal in length.
  Diagonals cross each other at right angles.

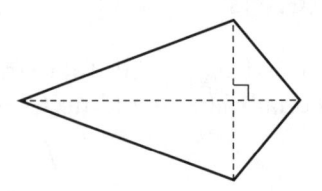

Exercise 5.7A

1. Think about a square and a rhombus.
   a. What is the same about the two shapes?
   b. How do the two shapes differ?

2. Think about a parallelogram and a rhombus.
   a. What are the differences?
   b. What do the shapes have in common?

3. Copy each diagram and fill in the missing angles or lengths.

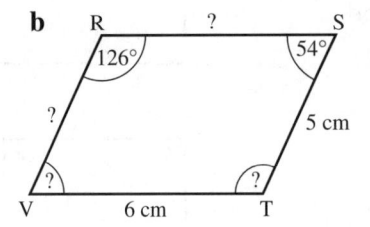

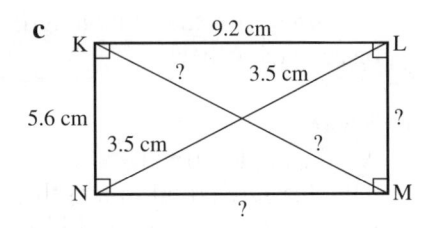

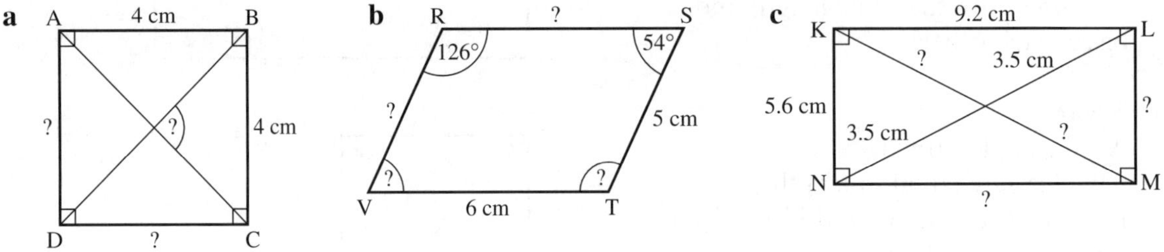

4. Can you draw a parallelogram with an angle of 48° and an angle of 122°? Explain your answer.

5. Is it possible to draw a kite with all edges equal? Explain your answer.

Exercise 5.7B

1. Think of a rectangle and a parallelogram.
   a. How do the two shapes differ?
   b. In what ways are the shapes the same?

2. Think of a trapezium and a rhombus.
   What do they have in common?

3. Copy each diagram and fill in the missing angles or lengths.

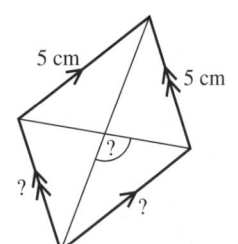

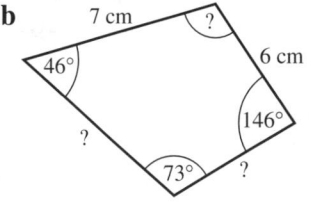

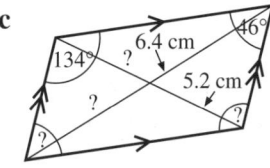

4 Think about the diagonals of an oblong and of a square.
  a What features do they have in common?
  b How do they differ?
  Use diagrams to explain your answers.

5 Classify these quadrilaterals.

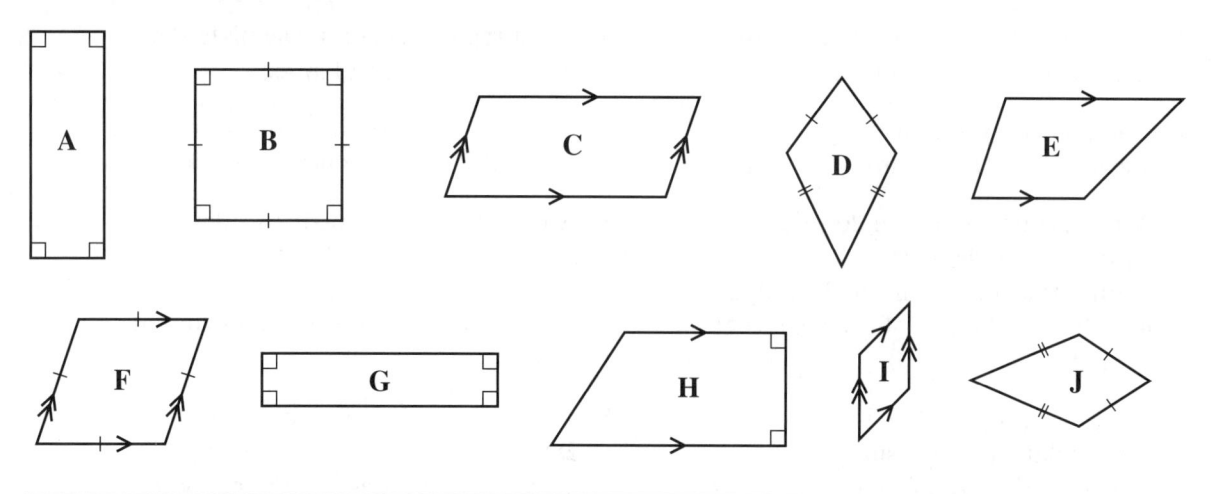

5.8 Angles in polygons

At each vertex of a polygon there are two types of angle.

The interior angle
This is the angle between two edges where they meet at a vertex.

▶ In a regular polygon all interior angles are equal.

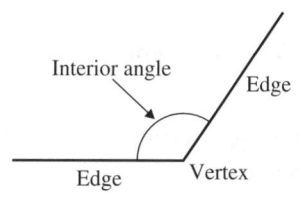

The sum S of the interior angles of a polygon is given by the formula:

$$S = (180° \times \text{number of edges}) - 360°$$

The angle sum of a pentagon is: $S = (180° \times 5) - 360° = 540°$

The external angle
This is the angle between one edge the extended second edge at a vertex.

▶ In a regular polygon all exterior angles are equal.
▶ For any polygon the sum of all the exterior angles is 360°.
▶ An exterior angle at a vertex is:
  180° − the size of the interior angle.

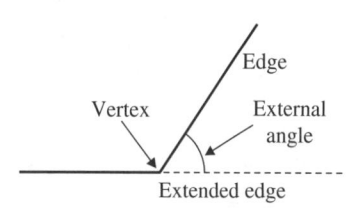

Exercise 5.8A

1. Find the angle sum of a hexagon.

2. A regular nonagon has an angle sum of 1250°. True or false? Explain.

3. For a regular hexagon calculate the size of each external angle.

4. A regular polygon has an external angle of 72°. How many sides has it?

5. A regular polygon with 20 sides has an interior angle of 162°.
   a Find the angle sum for the polygon.
   b Calculate the size of each external angle.

6. A regular polygon has 14 sides.
   a Calculate its angle sum.
   Calculate the size of each:
   b interior angle
   c exterior angle.

Exercise 5.8B

1. Find the angle sum of an octagon.

2. A regular dodecagon has an angle sum of 1500°. True or false? Why?

3. For a regular octagon calculate the size of each external angle.

4. A regular polygon has an external angle of 36°. How many sides has it?

5. A regular polygon with 16 sides has an interior angle of 157.5°.
   a Find the angle sum of the polygon.
   b Calculate the size of each external angle.

6. The angle sum of a regular polygon is 2880°.
   a How many sides has the polygon?
   Calculate the size of each:
   b interior angle   c exterior angle.

5.9 Pythagoras' theorem

Pythagoras's theorem works in any right-angled triangle. The theorem states that:

▶ The square on the hypotenuse is equal to the sum of the squares on the other two sides.

Theorem is another word for rule.

On the diagram for this triangle:
   Area C = Area A + Area B
   Area A = Area C − Area B
   Area B = Area C − Area A

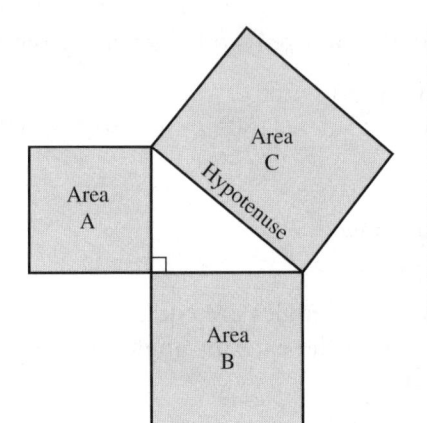

Remember it like this. For triangle ABC

$$c^2 = a^2 + b^2$$

Example 1
In triangle RST find the length of RT.

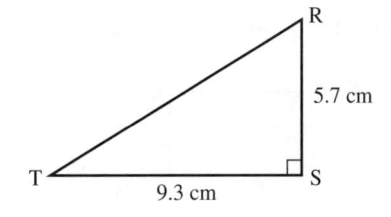

$RT^2 = RS^2 + ST^2$
$= 5.7^2 + 9.3^2$
$= 32.49 + 86.49$
$= 118.98$
$RT = \sqrt{118.98}$
$RT = 10.907\ldots\ldots$

So, the length of RT is 10.91 cm (to 2 dp).

Example 2
In triangle CPR calculate the length of CR.

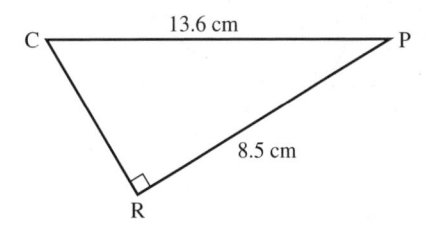

$CR^2 = CP^2 + RP^2$
$= 13.6^2 - 8.5^2$
$= 185.5044 - 72.25$
$= 113.2544$
$CR = \sqrt{113.2544}$
$CR = 10.642\ldots\ldots$

So, the length of CR is 10.64 cm (to 2 dp).

Exercise 5.9A

1 In each of the diagrams calculate the length marked with x or y.

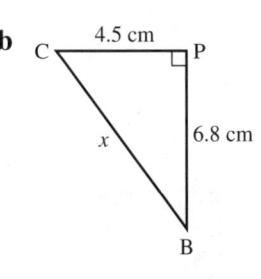

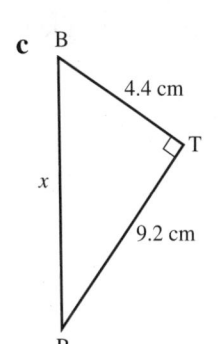

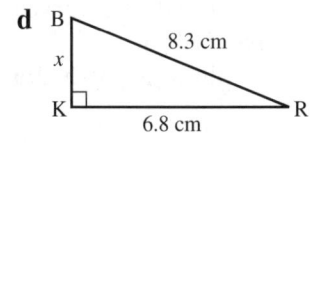

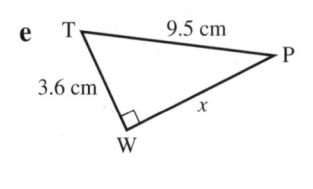

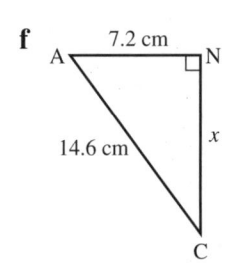

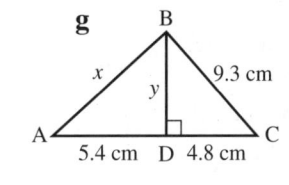

a Triangle with x (AC), AB = 6.2 cm, CB = 7.7 cm

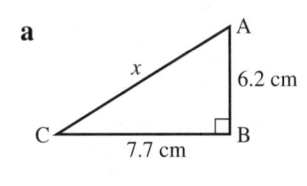

b Triangle with CP = 4.5 cm, PB = 6.8 cm, x (CB)

c Triangle with BT = 4.4 cm, TP = 9.2 cm, x (BP)

d Triangle with x (AB), AR = 8.3 cm, KR = 6.8 cm

e Triangle with TP = 9.5 cm, TW = 3.6 cm, x (WP)

f Triangle with AN = 7.2 cm, AC = 14.6 cm, x (NC)

g Triangle with AB = x, BC = 9.3 cm, AD = 5.4 cm, DC = 4.8 cm, BD = y

h Rectangle with AR = 15.8 cm, RT = 6.7 cm, x (AT)

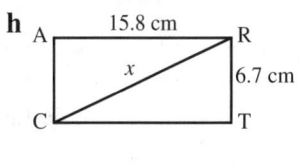

Exercise 5.9B

1 In each diagram calculate the length marked with x, y or z.

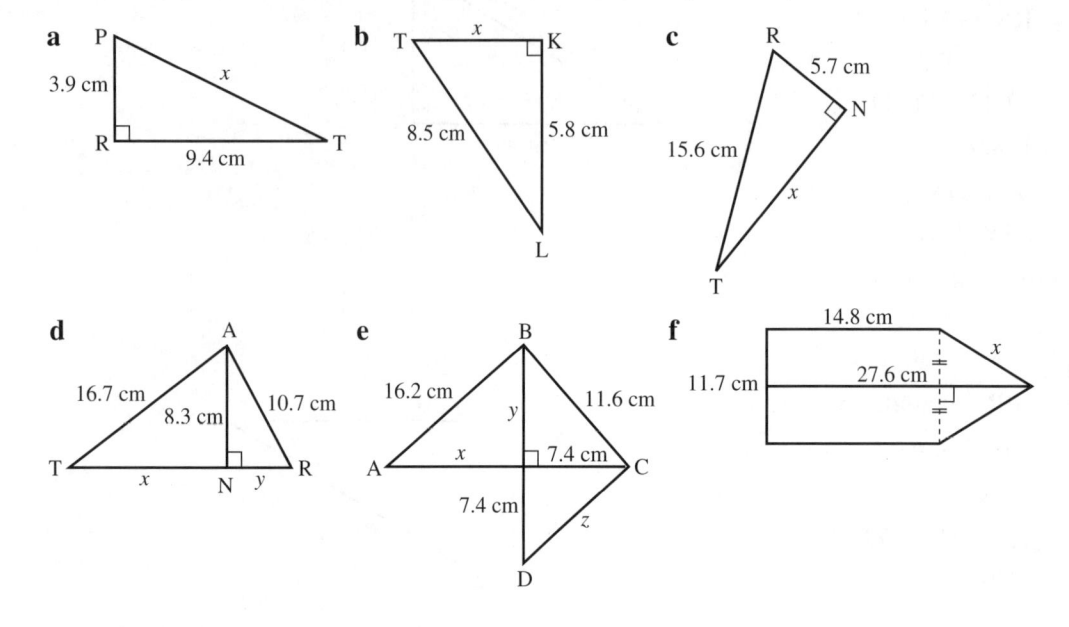

a Triangle PRT with PR = 3.9 cm, RT = 9.4 cm, PT = x

b Triangle TKL with TK = x, KL = 5.8 cm, TL = 8.5 cm

c Triangle RNT with RN = 5.7 cm, RT = 15.6 cm, NT = x

d Triangle TAR with TA = 16.7 cm, AR = 10.7 cm, AN = 8.3 cm, TN = x, NR = y

e Quadrilateral with AB = 16.2 cm, BC = 11.6 cm, diagonal with sides 7.4 cm and 7.4 cm, x, y, z marked

f Shape with 14.8 cm, 11.7 cm, 27.6 cm, x marked

5.10 Faces, edges and vertices

▶ This diagram shows the terms you can use when describing a 3-D shape.
▶ A solid with no curved surfaces is called a **polyhedron**.
The plural is **polyhedra**.

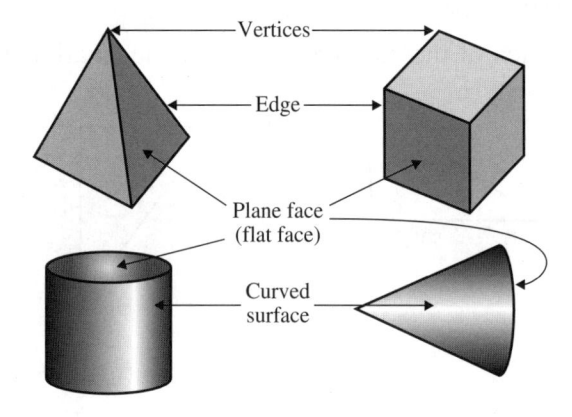

Vertices — Edge — Plane face (flat face) — Curved surface

Exercise 5.10A

1 a How many edges has a cube?
  b How many vertices has it?
  c How many plane faces has it?

2 For a cone list the number of:
  a plane faces
  b edges
  c vertices
  d curved surfaces.

3 For a square-based pyramid, list the number of:
  a edges **b** faces **c** vertices
  d plane faces **e** curved surfaces

4 Which of the 3-D shapes on page 126 are polyhedra?

Exercise 5.10B

1 A square-based pyramid fits exactly on top of a cube.
  How many:
  a faces **b** edges **c** vertices does the solid have?

2 Copy and complete this table.

Solid	Curved surfaces	Plane faces	Vertices	Edges
Sphere	1			
Cone				
Cube				
Cuboid		6		
Square-based pyramid				
Triangular prism				

3 What shape is this?
  It has 1 curved surface, 2 plane faces, 0 vertices and 2 edges.

4 Look at the shaded part of your table.
  Write a formula to link:
  • the number of edges e
  • the number of vertices v
  • the number of plane faces f.

Note:
A formula was discovered by Leonhard Euler in about 1735.

5.11 Drawing 3-D shapes

▶ To draw a 3-D shape you can use isometric dotty paper.

Example Draw this shape on isometric paper.
Make each centimetre one space between the dots.
This type of drawing is called **isometric drawing**.

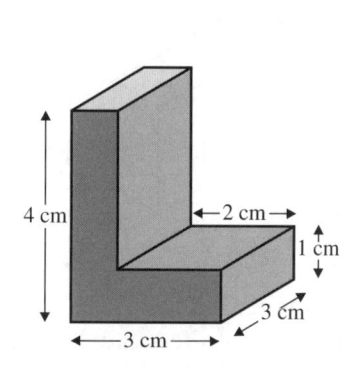

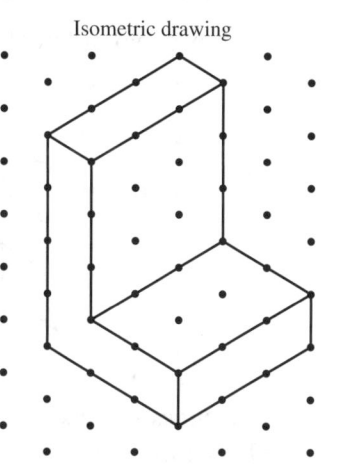

Isometric drawing

Exercise 5.11A

1 Make isometric drawings of each of these solids.

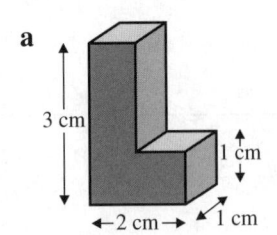

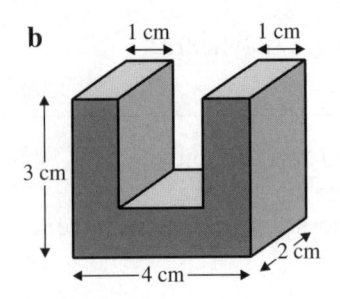

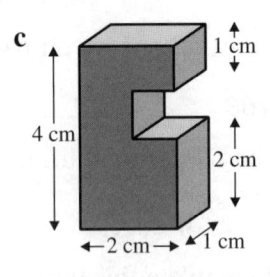

a 3 cm, 1 cm, ←2 cm→, 1 cm

b 1 cm, 1 cm, 3 cm, ←4 cm—, 2 cm

c 1 cm, 4 cm, 2 cm, ←2 cm→, 1 cm

2 This is an isometric drawing of a solid made of centimetre cubes.
You cannot see all the cubes.
  a What is the maximum number of cubes that could be in the bottom layer?
  b What is the minimum number of cubes?
  c The solid is reflected in a mirror on its right. Make an isometric drawing of what the image will look like.

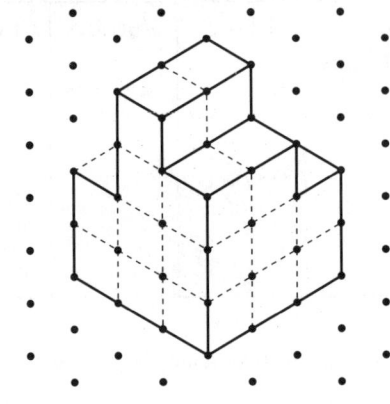

Hint:
Make sure that your paper is the correct way round with the lines of dots vertical.

3 Draw each of these solids on isometric dotty paper.
  a A cuboid with dimensions of 3 cm, 6 cm and 4 cm.
  b A 3 cm cube with a 1 cm cube centrally on top.
  c A 5 cm cube with a 2 cm by 2 cm hole through it.

Exercise 5.11B

1 This shows two different isometric views of the same 3-D shape.

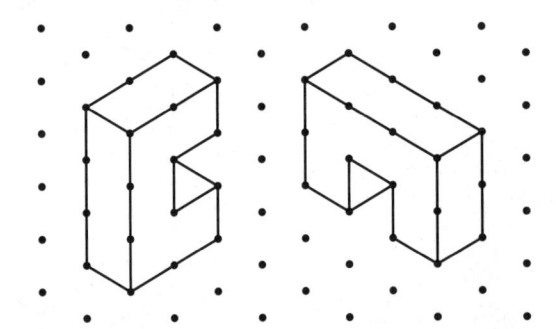

  a Use cubes to make the 3-D shape.
  b Draw three other isometric views of the same 3-D shape.

2 This shows an isometric view of a dolls house table made from plastic cubes.

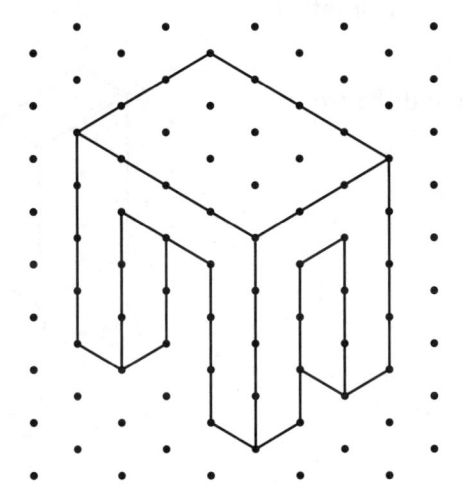

    a How many cubes is it made from?
    b Draw an isometric view of how the table will look when it is turned upside-down.

3 Make as many different 3-D shapes as you can from 5 cubes.
    a How many **different** 3-D shapes can you find?
    b Make an isometric drawing of each one.

4 Each of the 3-D shapes A to C below is made from:
- an L-shape of 4 cubes and
- a Z-shape of 5 cubes.

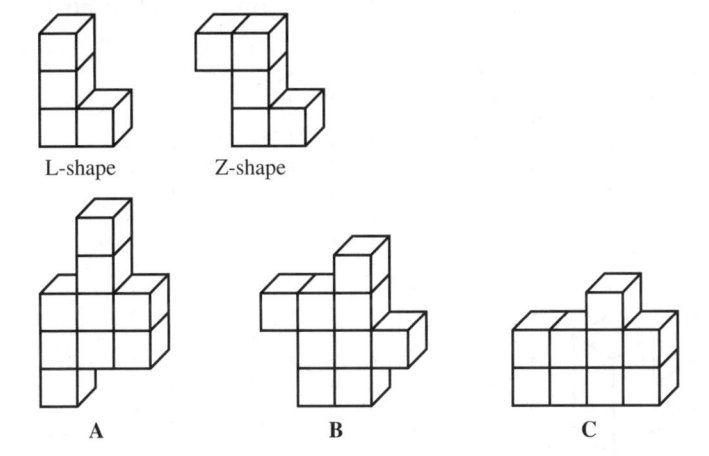

L-shape   Z-shape

A   B   C

    a Make a different isometric drawing of each 3-D shape.
    b On each drawing, show where the boundary is between the L and the Z.

5.12 Plans and elevations

▶ The view of a 3-D shape from a side is called an **elevation**. From above the view is called a **plan**.

Example Draw the plan, a side elevation and the front elevation of this 3-D shape.

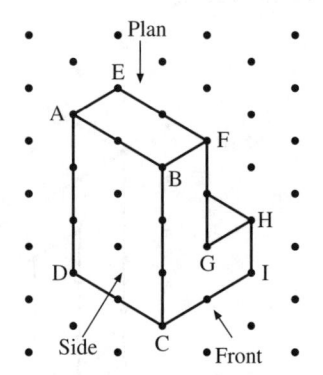

The edge EF will appear as the line EF on the plan. Note how the line AB must be the same length on both the plan and the side elevation.

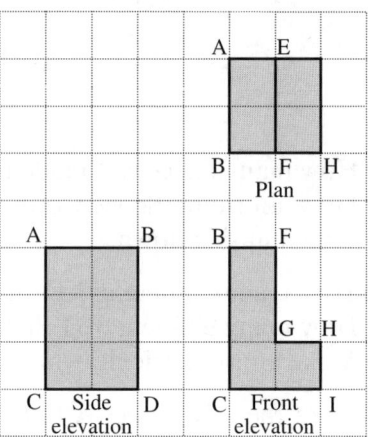

Exercise 5.12A

Use squared paper to draw a plan, a front elevation and a side elevation for each solid.

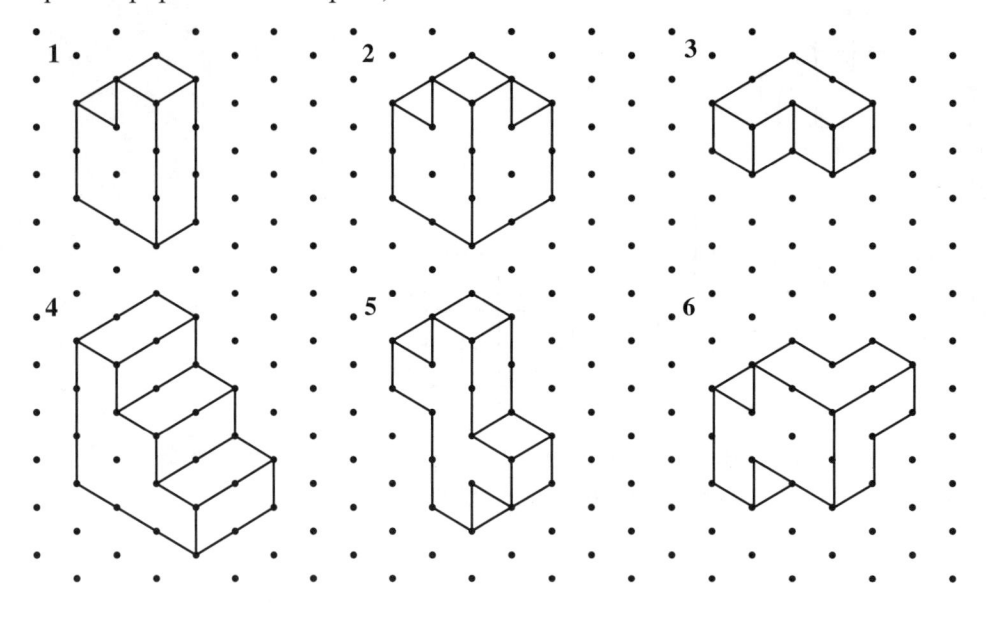

1.
2.
3.
4.
5.
6.

Exercise 5.12B

1. Here are some solids made of cubes.
   a. On squared paper draw plans, front elevations and side elevations for each of these solids.
   b. How many cubes make up solid **A**?
   c. Solid **D** is symmetrical. How many cubes is it made from?

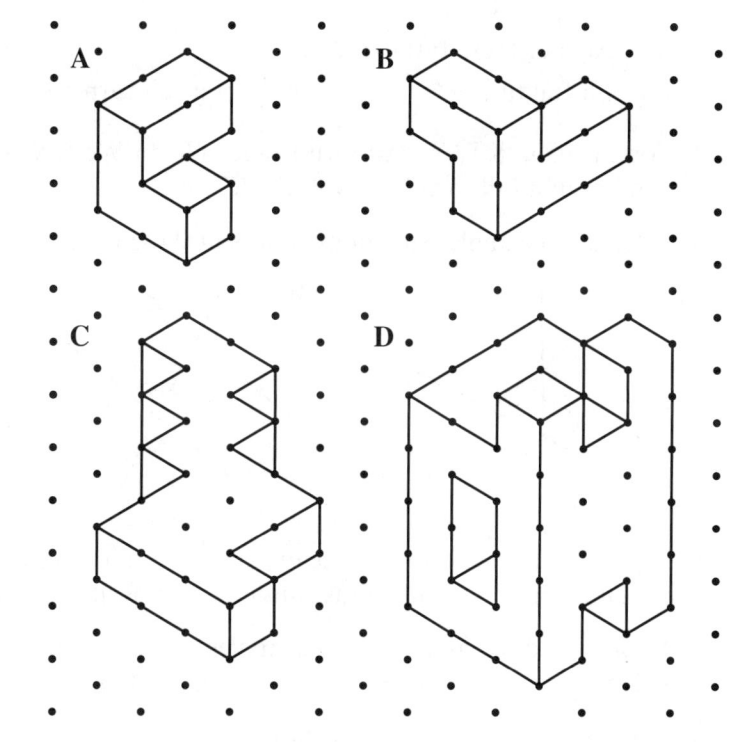

2. This shows the plan, side elevation and front elevation of a solid made from cubes.
   a. Make the solid from cubes.
   b. How many cubes did you use?
   c. Make an isometric drawing of the solid.

3. a. Take turns with a friend to make a solid from cubes.
   b. Draw the plan, side elevation and front elevation.
   c. Pass your drawings to the friend.
      Can your friend make the same solid just by following your drawings?

4. Mark draws three correct views of a solid. He passes his drawings to Becky who makes a different solid that also fits the drawings. Make two different solids that have the same plan, side elevation and front elevation.

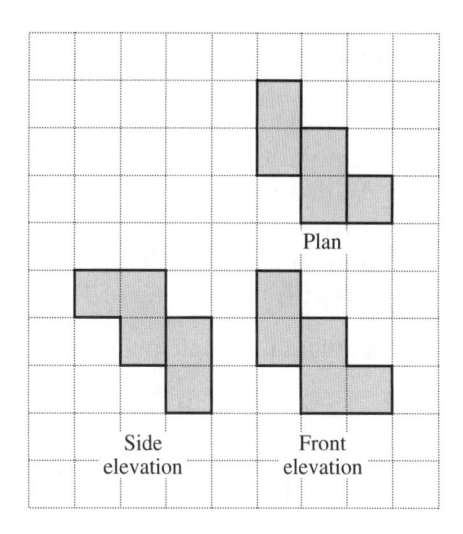

Revision exercise 5 — Review

1 Give each of these turns in degrees.
  a $\frac{3}{8}$ of a full turn **b** $\frac{17}{30}$ of a full turn. *Unit 5.1*

2 You face South West and turn to face North West. What fraction of a full turn have you made? *Unit 5.1*

3 Calculate the angles shown by letters in these diagrams.

  a   **b**   **c**

  Unit 5.1

4 Explain what each of these means and give an example.
  a Acute angle **b** Obtuse angle **c** Reflex angle *Unit 5.1*

5 Accurately draw and label these angles.
  a 255° **b** 65° **c** 125° *Unit 5.1*

6 Give the bearing of each direction.
  a North East **b** South South West **c** East *Unit 5.2*

7 A boat sails from P on a bearing of 120° for a distance of 4 km.
  It then changes course and sails on a bearing of 070° for 5 km to a point Q.
  a With a scale of 1 cm = 1 km make a scale drawing of this trip.
  b In straight line, what is the distance PQ?
  c What is the bearing of P from Q? *Unit 5.2*

8 Calculate the angle marked x in each diagram.

  a **b** **c** **d**

  Unit 5.3

9 Explain the differences between an equilateral triangle and an isosceles triangle. *Unit 5.4*

10 Are all scalene triangles acute-angled triangles? Explain your answer with diagrams. *Unit 5.4*

11 One angle in a right-angled triangle can be obtuse.
True or false? Explain your answer with diagrams. *Unit 5.4*

12 When we say two triangles are congruent, what does this mean? *Unit 5.5*

13 Explain why the external angles of any triangle total 360°. *Unit 5.6*

14 List as many features of a parallelogram as you can. *Unit 5.7*

15 What do a rhombus and a trapezium have in common? *Unit 5.7*

16 One angle in a parallelogram is 131°.
List the other angles in the shape and make a sketch of it. *Unit 5.7*

17 How do a rhombus and a parallelogram differ? *Unit 5.7*

18 a What is the formula for the angle sum of a polygon?
b What is the sum of the interior angles of a regular nonagon? *Unit 5.8*

19 What can you say about the sum of the external angles in a square and a regular pentagon? *Unit 5.8*

20 Add the interior angle of a regular heptagon to the interior angle of a regular decagon. Subtract this total from the sum of the external angles of a dodecagon. *Unit 5.8*

21 In each of the diagrams calculate the length marked x.

a C, 5.6 cm, P, x, 7.2 cm, T

b K, 7.2 cm, L, x, 9.8 cm, M

c A, 14.6 cm, 5.8 cm, P, x, C

Unit 5.9

22 How many vertices, faces and edges has a square-based pyramid? *Unit 5.10*

23 Describe a cylinder in terms of vertices, faces and curved surfaces. *Unit 5.10*

24 Make an isometric drawing of each solid.

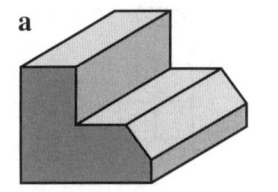

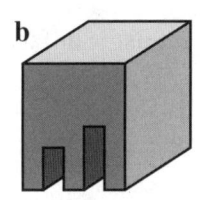

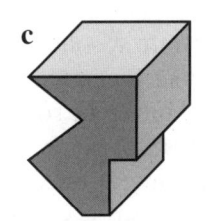

a   b   c

Unit 5.11

25 Draw a plan, a front elevation and a side elevation for each solid.   *Review*

a

b

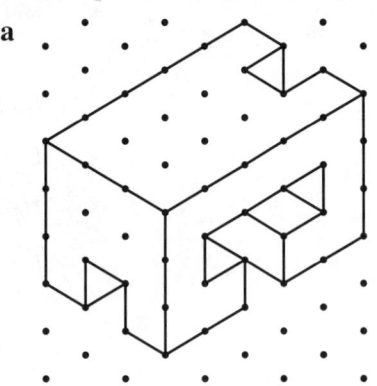

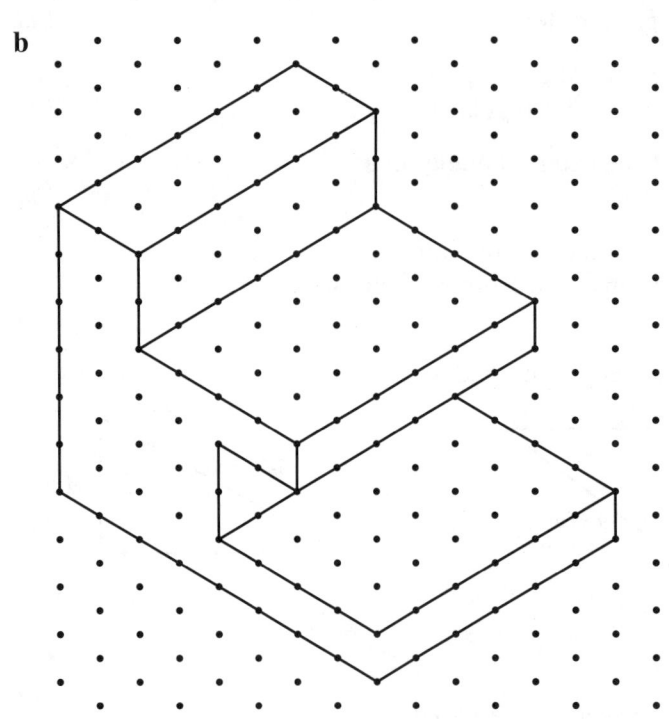

Unit 5.12

Investigation

On the surface

You have five 2 cm cubes.
The five cubes can be built into a solid, but cubes must join face to face.
Investigate solids and their surface area when all
five cubes are used to make different solids.
What about eight 2 cm cubes?
In each case present and comment on your results.

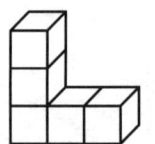

6 Transformations

A transformation is a change carried out under specific rules.
There are 4 different transformations:

- reflection
- rotation
- translation
- enlargement

In this unit you will study each of the transformations in turn.
First you need to be able to describe symmetries.

6.1 Line symmetry

▶ A shape has a **line of symmetry** if one side of a shape is a reflection of the other.
It can have more than one line of symmetry.

You can use a mirror to help you decide if a shape has line symmetry.

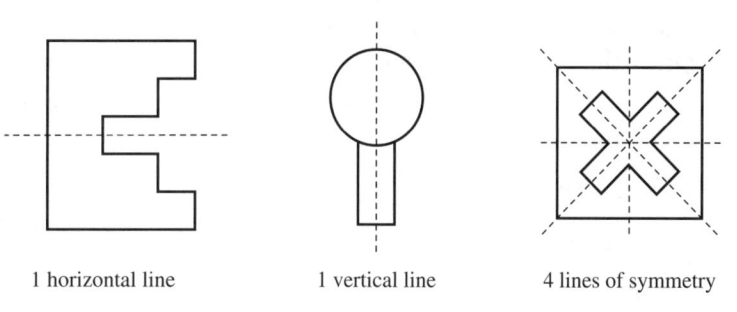

1 horizontal line   1 vertical line   4 lines of symmetry

These shapes have **line symmetry**.

Exercise 6.1A

1 a Decide if each of these European road signs has line symmetry.
 b If it has, copy it and draw in all its lines of symmetry.

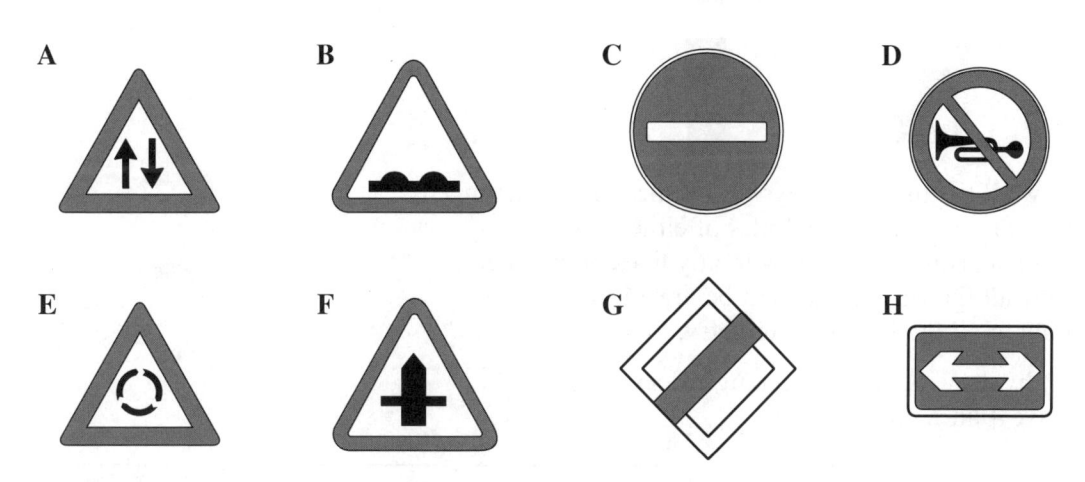

A   B   C   D

E   F   G   H

2 Draw each of these shapes and show all their lines of symmetry.
   a square   **b** rectangle   **c** rhombus   **d** parallelogram   **e** kite

Exercise 6.1B

1 This design is not complete.
Each dotted line is a line of symmetry.
Draw the complete design.

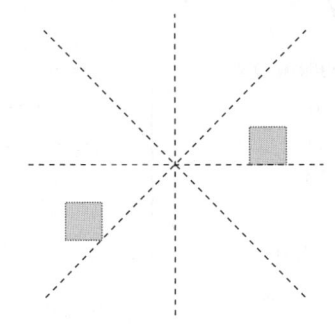

2 In a tile arrangement, black and white square tiles must join along a complete edge.

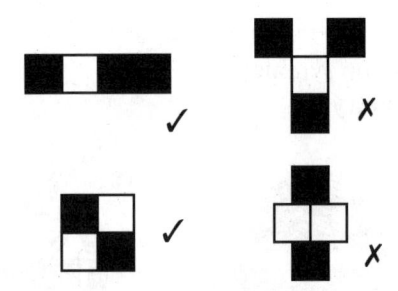

   a Draw all the different ways that 4 tiles can be arranged.
   (You can use from 0 to 4 tiles of either colour)
   b On each arrangement draw in any lines of symmetry.
   c Draw all the ways 5 tiles can be arranged.
   d Draw in all the lines of symmetry.

3 Show, by drawing, that a rectangle does not have 4 lines of symmetry.

6.2 Rotational symmetry

▶ Another type of symmetry is **rotational symmetry**.

▶ A shape has rotational symmetry if it can fit on itself more than once as it is turned through one full turn.

▶ The number of times a shape fits in one turn is called its **order of rotational symmetry** (ORS).

▶ A shape with an order of rotational symmetry of 1 does not have rotational symmetry.

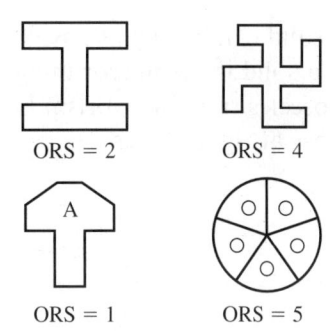

ORS = 2   ORS = 4
ORS = 1   ORS = 5

All these shapes have rotational symmetry except Shape A.

Exercise 6.2A

1 What is the order of rotational symmetry of these shapes?

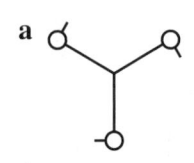

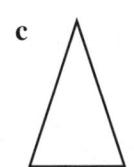

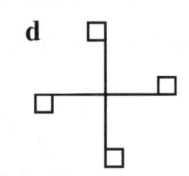

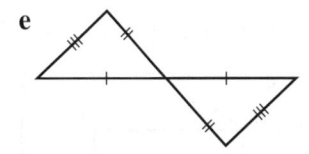

a   b   c   d   e

2 Look at the road signs in Exercise 6.1A on page 135. Give the order of rotational symmetry of each one.

3 A shape has one line of symmetry. What is its order of rotational symmetry?

> You can use tracing paper to help you decide on a shape's order of rotational symmetry.

Exercise 6.2B

1 Draw two different shapes with an order of rotational symmetry of:
   a 1   **b** 2   **c** 3   **d** 4

2 Draw a shape with an order of rotational symmetry of 2 but no lines of symmetry.

3 Draw a hexagon with an order of rotational symmetry of:
   a 6   **b** 2   **c** 1

4 A shape has an order of rotational symmetry of 1. How many lines of symmetry could it possibly have?

5 A shape has an order of rotational symmetry of 5. Does this mean it has 5 lines of symmetry? Explain with an example.

6.3 Plane symmetry

▶ A 3-D solid can have **plane symmetry**. This is where one half of a solid is the mirror image of the other half.
This isosceles triangular prism has two planes of symmetry that cross at right angles.

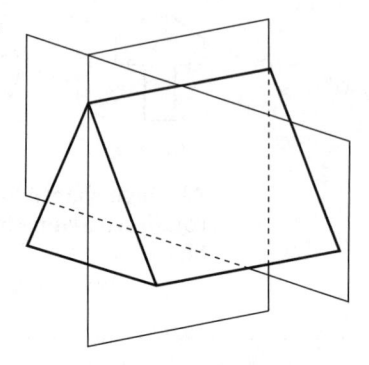

Exercise 6.3A

1 How many planes of symmetry has each of these cuboids?

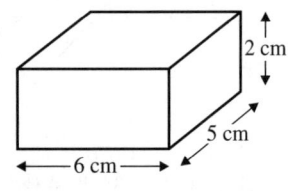

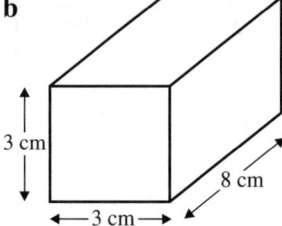

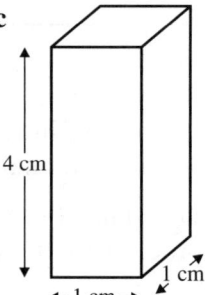

a 6 cm × 5 cm × 2 cm

b 3 cm × 3 cm × 8 cm

c 4 cm × 1 cm × 1 cm

2 **a** List some common household items that have a vertical plane of symmetry.
   b Give a household item that usually has a horizontal plane of symmetry – not such an easy task!

3 Darren says his bike has a vertical plane of symmetry. Explain why he is wrong.

Exercise 6.3B

1 Sketch objects found at school that have:
   a 1 plane **b** 2 planes
   c more than 2 planes of symmetry.

2 A wine bottle with no label has an infinite number of planes of symmetry. List six other objects with an infinite number of planes of symmetry.

3 Give the number of planes of symmetry for each object.

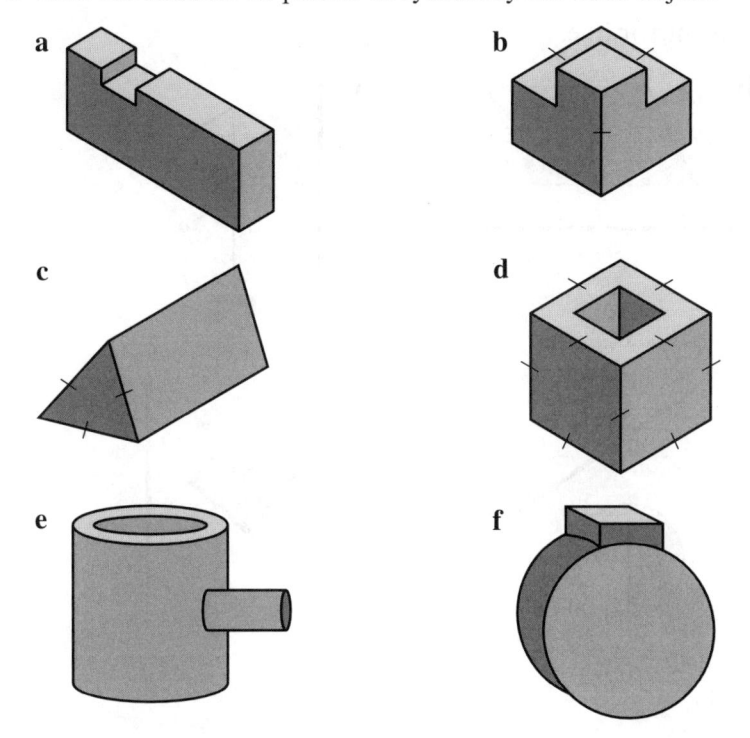

a

b

c

d

e

f

6.4 Reflection

▶ A reflected image is always the same distance from the mirror line as the object.

▶ A line joining corresponding points on the object and the image cuts the mirror at an angle of 90°.

▶ To describe a reflection you must state where the mirror line is or give its equation.

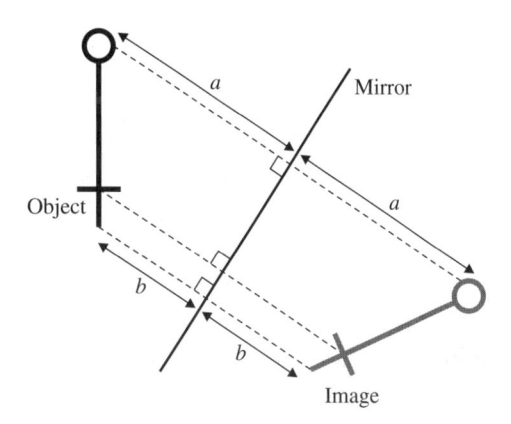

Exercise 6.4A

1 Copy each shape and reflect it in its mirror line.

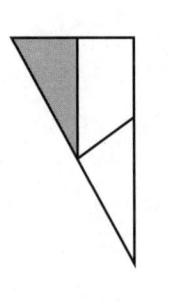

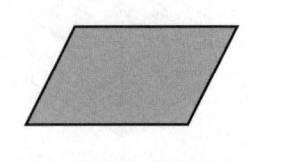

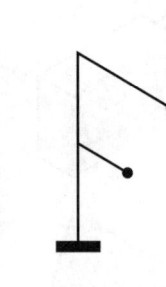

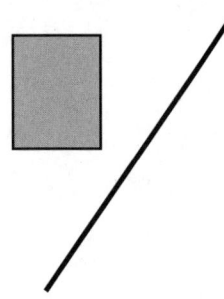

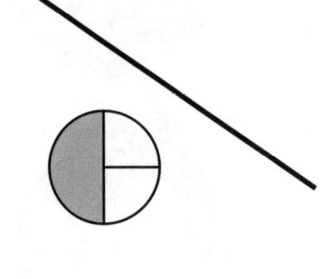

a   b   c

d   e   f

2 Make a copy of the axes and Shape A.

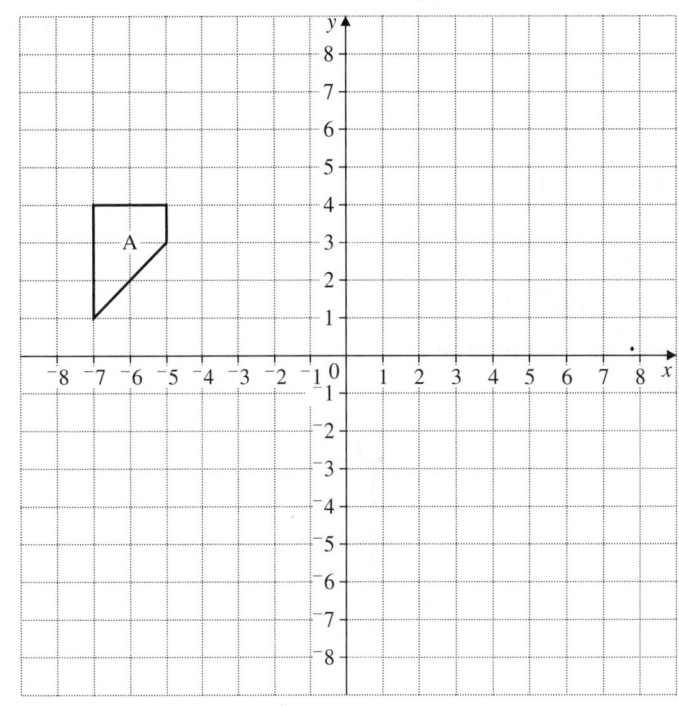

Draw the image of A after reflection in:
a the line $x = {}^-2$ (Call the image D) **b** the line $x = {}^-5$ (Image E)
c the line $y = {}^-1$ (Image F) **d** the line $y = 3$ (Image G)

Exercise 6.4B

1 On a copy of axes above show the reflection of Shape A in:
   a the line $y = x$ (Image H)
   b the line $y = {}^-x$ (Image I)

   Now reflect H in the x-axis to give image J, then reflect J in the y-axis to give K.
   c Compare images I and K. What do you notice?

2 An irregular quadrilateral is reflected in a mirror line.
   For the object and the image:
   a what remains the same in both?
   b what differs in both?

3 What is the inverse of a reflection in the line $y = x$?

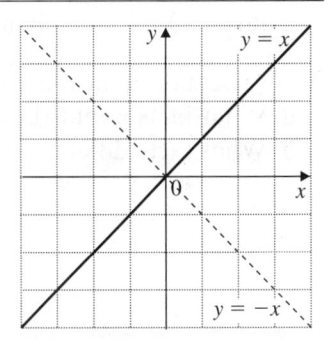

> The **inverse** of an action reverses the action.

6.5 Rotation

▶ To describe a rotation you must give this information:
  - The angle through which the object turns.
  - The direction (clockwise or anticlockwise).
  - The centre of rotation (sometimes given by a pair of coordinates).

▶ A 30° clockwise rotation is said to be a rotation of $^-30°$.
  A 30° anticlockwise rotation is said to be a rotation of $^+30°$.

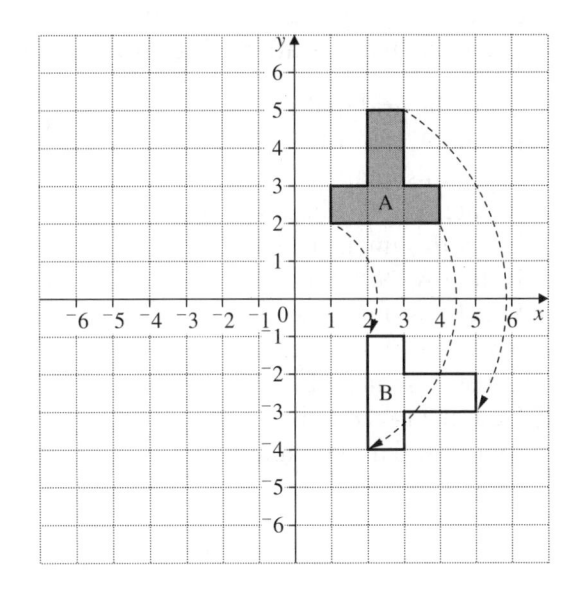

Exercise 6.5A

1 a Copy the grid and the object A.
   b Rotate A 90° anticlockwise about (0, 0) and label the image C.
   c Rotate A 90° clockwise about (0, 2) to make image D.
   d Rotate A 180° clockwise about ($^-1$, 1) to make image E.
   e What is the same about images D and E?
   f What is different about D and E?

> **Hint:**
> By tracing the axes as well as object A you can easily see when the paper has made a turn of 90°, 180° or 270°.

2 Describe a rotation that will take object P onto:
  a image Q **b** image R **c** image S

3 An irregular quadrilateral is rotated by $^+74°$.
  a What facts about the shape remain the same?
  b What facts differ?

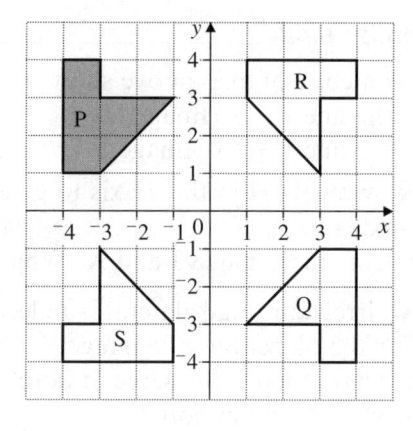

Exercise 6.5B

1 a Draw x and y-axes from $^-5$ to 5.
  b Draw an object of your choice, R, in the bottom right quadrant.
  c Show the image, S, after a rotation of 270° clockwise about the point (0, 0).
  d Show the image T after a 180° rotation about (0, 0).

2 a Copy the grid and object A.
  b Rotate A 180° (3, 3). Label this image B.
  c Rotate A $^+90°$ about (0, 1). Label this image C.
  d Rotate A $^+90°$ about (3, $^-1$). Label this image D.
  e Rotate A $^-90°$ about (1, 2). Label this image E.
  f Describe two different rotations that will take E back to A.

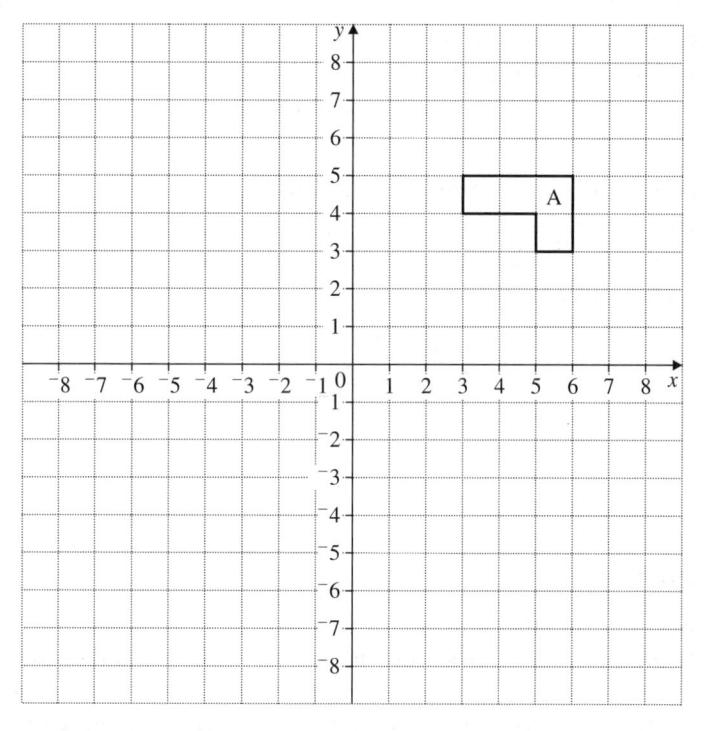

3 Give two different rotations that are both the inverse of a 90° clockwise rotation about (2, $^-3$).

6.6 Translation

▶ A translation is a sliding movement without turns. You describe a translation using a vector like this:

$\begin{pmatrix} 3 \\ 2 \end{pmatrix}$ — move 3 units parallel to the x-axis then
— move 2 units parallel to the y-axis.

Note:
A negative move right is a move left.
A negative move up is a move down.

Example
Draw Triangle A after a translation of $\begin{pmatrix} 4 \\ -2 \end{pmatrix}$.

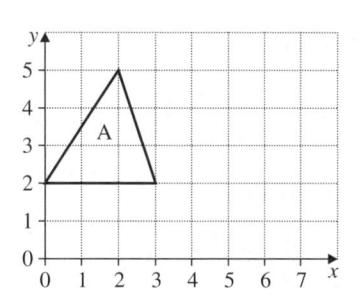

Each vertex of the triangle move:

    4 units to the right along x-axis
    2 units down along the y-axis:

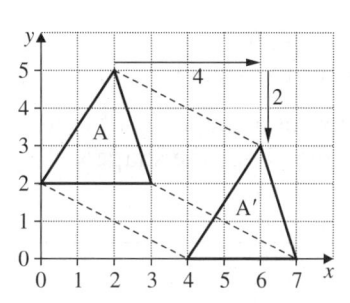

Exercise 6.6A

1 Draw a triangle like A above on a square grid.
Translate it by each of the vectors given and label each image with the letter given.

  a $\begin{pmatrix} 2 \\ 3 \end{pmatrix}$; B   **b** $\begin{pmatrix} -4 \\ 2 \end{pmatrix}$; C   **c** $\begin{pmatrix} -6 \\ -4 \end{pmatrix}$; D

  d $\begin{pmatrix} 2 \\ -5 \end{pmatrix}$; E   **e** $\begin{pmatrix} 4 \\ 0 \end{pmatrix}$; F   **f** $\begin{pmatrix} 0 \\ -6 \end{pmatrix}$; G

Exercise 6.6B

1 Draw some x and y-axes from ⁻6 to 6 and mark the point (2, ⁻3).
In each case, translate the point by the vector and give the coordinates of its final position.

  a $\begin{pmatrix} -6 \\ 0 \end{pmatrix}$ **b** $\begin{pmatrix} -2 \\ 3 \end{pmatrix}$ **c** $\begin{pmatrix} 2 \\ 5 \end{pmatrix}$

  d $\begin{pmatrix} -5 \\ -2 \end{pmatrix}$ **e** $\begin{pmatrix} -4 \\ 8 \end{pmatrix}$ **f** $\begin{pmatrix} 0 \\ 9 \end{pmatrix}$

Do not confuse the vector $\begin{pmatrix} 2 \\ 3 \end{pmatrix}$ with the coordinate (2, 3).

$\begin{pmatrix} 2 \\ 3 \end{pmatrix}$ is a movement.

(2, 3) is a position.

2 Copy the grid and the T shape.

a Translate the T by the vector $\begin{pmatrix} ^-1 \\ 3 \end{pmatrix}$.

b Translate this image by $\begin{pmatrix} ^-5 \\ 0 \end{pmatrix}$.

c Translate this image by $\begin{pmatrix} ^-2 \\ ^-5 \end{pmatrix}$.

d Translate this image by $\begin{pmatrix} 4 \\ ^-4 \end{pmatrix}$.

e Translate this image by $\begin{pmatrix} 4 \\ 6 \end{pmatrix}$.

f What do you discover?

g Add the top vector numbers,
 i.e. ⁻1, ⁻5, ⁻2, 4, 4
 and the bottom numbers,
 i.e.   3, 0, ⁻5, ⁻4, 6
 Use your answer to explain part **f** above.

3 After a translation of a shape, what factors:
 a remains the same about the shape
 b change?

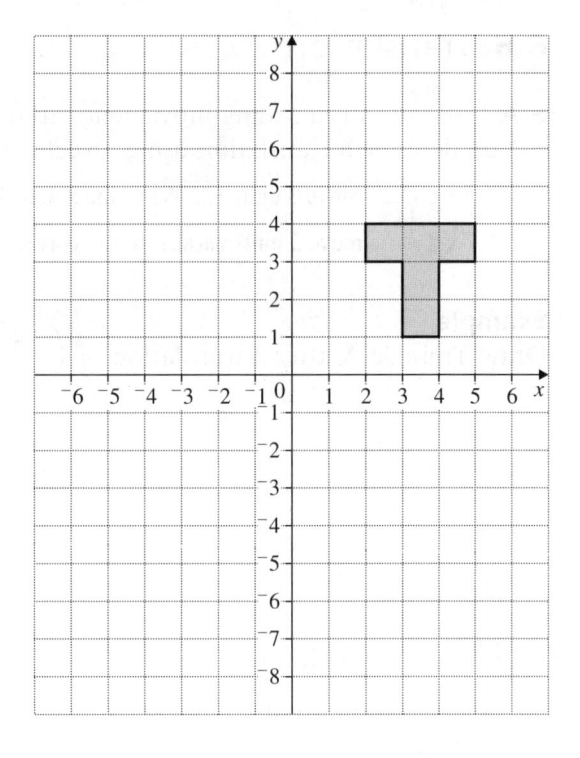

6.7 Enlargement

An enlargement is a transformation which changes the size of an object. The scale factor of an enlargement tells you by how much the size changes.
For a scale factor of 2, all lengths will be twice as long.

You can enlarge a shape on a grid.

Example 1
Enlarge Shape A by a scale factor of 2.
All lengths will be multiplied by 2.
    AB = 2 squares
After the enlargement A′B′ = 4.

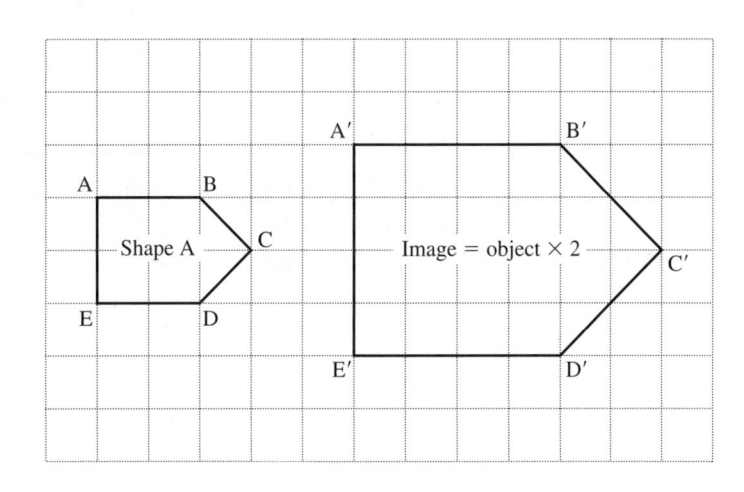

Exercise 6.7A

1 On a grid, enlarge these shapes by the scale factor shown.

a — Scale factor 2
b — Scale factor 3
c — Scale factor 2
d — Scale factor 4

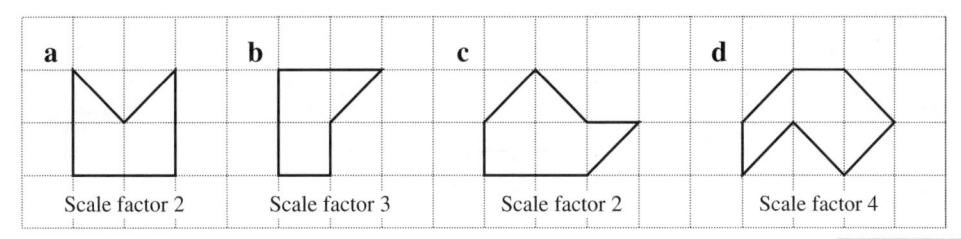

> You will need squared paper for these exercises.

Exercise 6.7B

1 On a grid, enlarge these shapes by the scale factor shown.

a — Scale factor 2
b — Scale factor 4
c — Scale factor 2
d — Scale factor 3

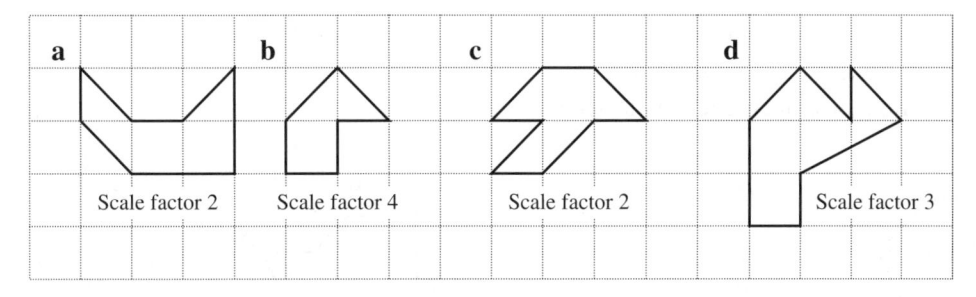

You need to be able to enlarge a shape from a given centre.

Example 2

Enlarge ABCD by a scale factor of 2 with centre P.

Draw a line from P through each vertex.

Measure the distance of each vertex on the line from P and multiply this length by 2.

$$PA = 16 \, mm$$

So, $PA' = 16 \times 2 = 32 \, mm$

$PB' = 29 \times 2 = 58 \, mm$
$PC' = 28 \times 2 = 56 \, mm$
$PD' = 16 \times 2 = 32 \, mm$

Draw the image A'B'C'D'.

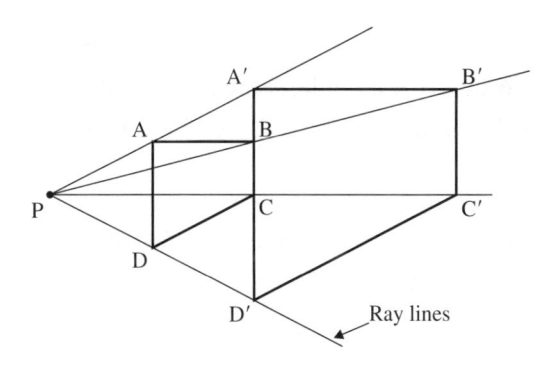

> You need to measure accurately to enlarge a shape using the line method.

Exercise 6.7C

1 Enlarge each shape by the scale factor shown.
In each case the centre of enlargement is labelled P.

a — Scale factor 2
b — Scale factor 2
c — Scale factor 3

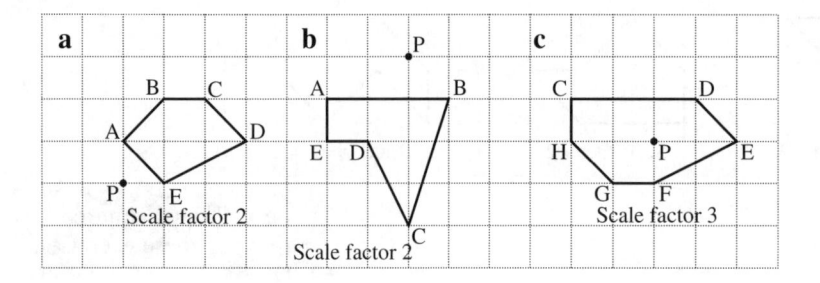

Exercise 6.7D

1 Enlarge each shape by the scale factor shown.
In each case the centre of enlargement is labelled P.

a — Scale factor 2
b — Scale factor 3
c — Scale factor 2

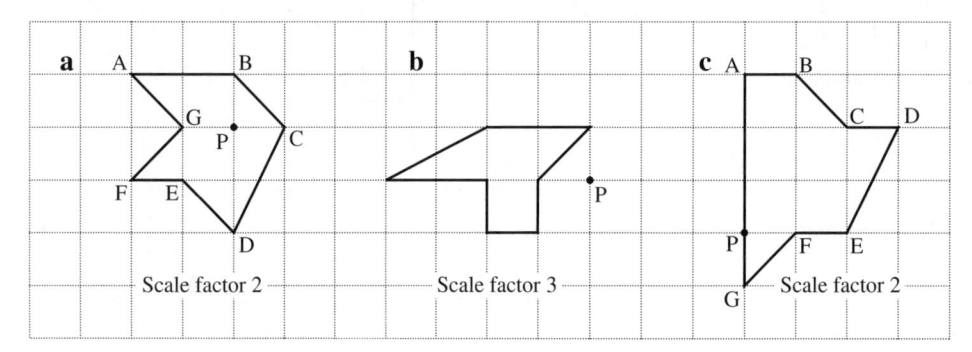

To describe an enlargement you must give:
- the scale factor
- the centre of enlargement.

Example 3
Find the centre and the scale factor of this enlargement.

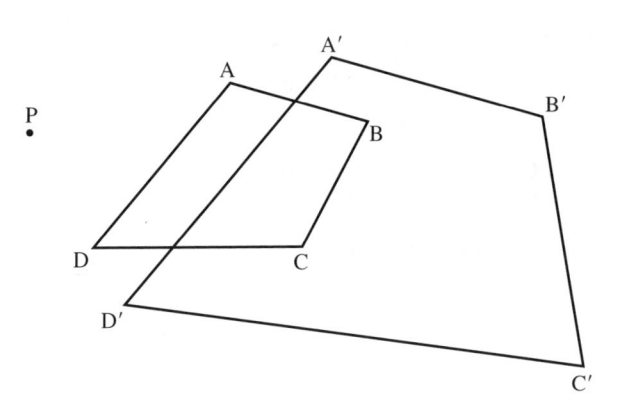

- Draw extended lines:

    from   A′ through A
                C′ through C
                D′ through D

Where the lines cross is the centre of enlargement P.

Scale factor = $\dfrac{\text{length of image}}{\text{length of original shape}}$

$= \dfrac{PA'}{PA} = \dfrac{42}{28} = 1.5$

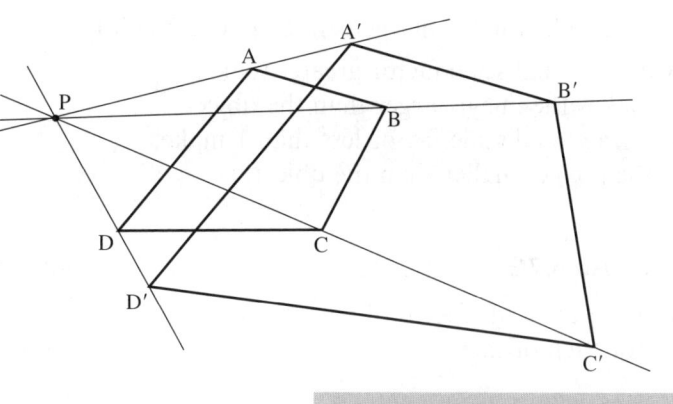

You only need to draw two lines, the third is a check.

Exercise 6.7E

1 Find the centre of enlargement P, and the scale factor of each enlargement.

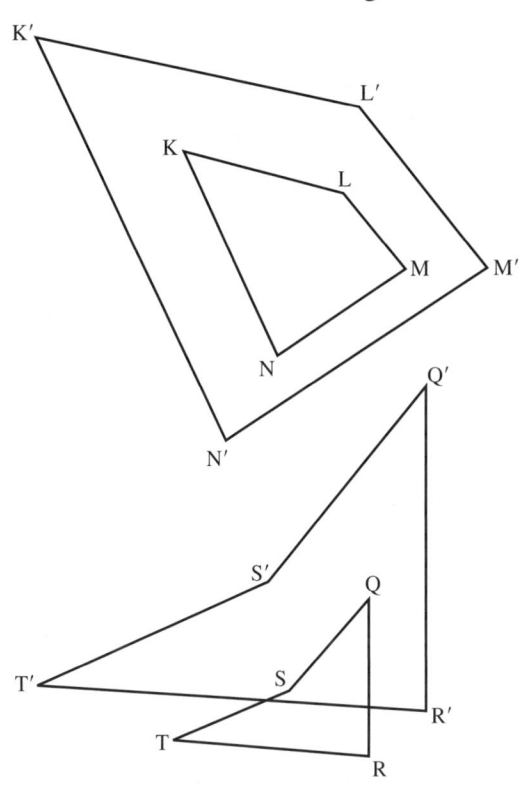

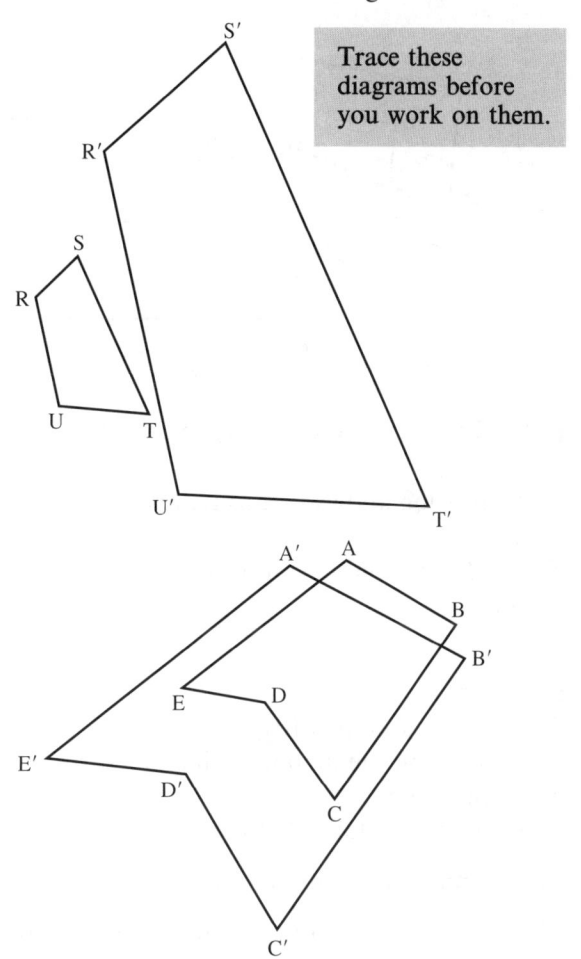

Exercise 6.7F

1 Find the centre of enlargement P, and the scale factor of each enlargement.

Trace these diagrams before you work on them.

148 Transformations

The scale factor of enlargement can be a fraction.
- a fractional scale factor greater than 1 makes the image larger than the object
- a fractional scale factor less than 1 makes the image smaller than the object.

Exercise 6.7G

1 Find the scale factor of enlargement for each of these.

  a

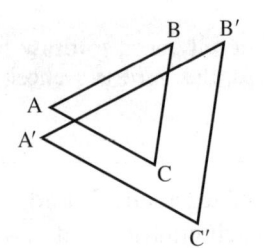

  b

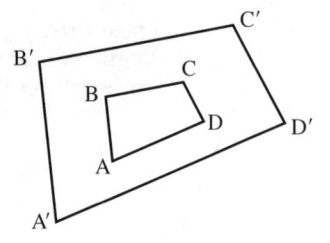

Exercise 6.7H

1 Find the scale factor of enlargement for each of these.

  a

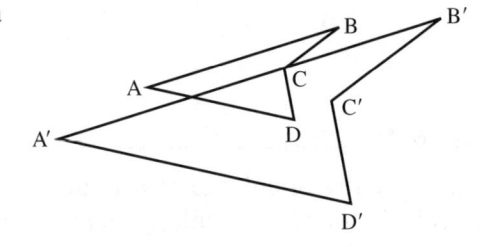

  b

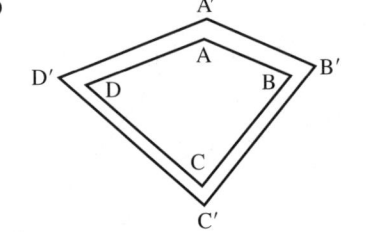

6.8 Scale and scale drawing

Scale drawing allows you to represent large objects with smaller images.
The scale will enable you to link the image and the original object.

Example
The scale of a map is 10 mm = 2.5 km.
Two towns on the map are joined by a road which measures 28 mm.
Calculate the distance between the towns in kilometres.

The distance between the towns is: 2.8×2.5 km = 7 km

The distance between the towns is 7 kilometres.

Exercise 6.8A

1 The scale of a diagram is 12 mm = 3.5 metres. Copy and complete this table.

Length on diagram (mm)	Actual length (metres)
30	8.75
54	
69	
72	
91	
45	
	29.4

2 A beam in a roof is 2.6 metres long. On a scale diagram the beam is 39 mm long. What scale is used for the drawing?

3 On an old map a scale of 1 inch = 4.5 miles was used. On the map a road was measured as 3.25 inches.
   a How long was the road in miles?

   A road 17.2 miles long was shown on the map.
   b On the map, how long was the line representing the road?

4 On the plans for a sports hall a climbing wall is shown with a rectangle measuring 4.2 cm by 6.4 cm.
   The scale of the map was 1 : 1500.
   a Give the dimensions of the climbing wall in the sports hall.
   b Compare the area of the actual climbing wall and the wall on the plan. How many times larger is the real thing?

Exercise 6.8B

1 A scale of 1 : 150 is used for a plan. On the plan a window is shown as a rectangle 4 cm wide and 2.5 cm high.
   a Give the dimensions of the actual window.

   The window frame will have one diagonal metal bar.
   b Make a scale drawing of the window and the bar.
   c Use your diagram to find the actual length of the diagonal bar.

2 A model of a yacht is made to a scale of 1 : 32.
   a The model is 16 inches long. How long, in feet, is the yacht?
   b The mast of the yacht is 6.8 metres high.
     How long is the mast on the model?

3 With a scale of 1 : 12 all lengths on a plan are $\frac{1}{12}$ the length on the object. By what fraction are areas reduced on the plan?

Transformations

4. A map is drawn to a scale of 1 : 250 000.
   Jim says this scale is the same as 1 cm = 2.5 kilometres.
   Do you agree? Explain your answer.

5. An old map was drawn to a scale of 1 inch = 10 miles.
   a Write this scale in the form 1 : n, where n is in inches.
   b Write the scale approximately in the form 1 : n where n is in centimetres.

6.9 Similar shapes*

▶ Shapes are similar when:
- all the corresponding angles are equal
and
- corresponding sides are all in the same ratio.

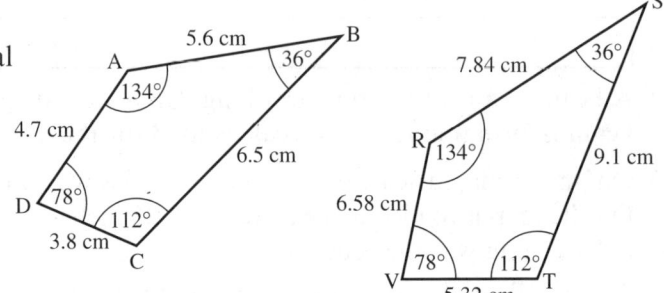

Example
Are ABCD and RSTV similar shapes?

For ABCD and RSTV

$\widehat{A} = \widehat{R}$
$\widehat{B} = \widehat{S}$
$\widehat{C} = \widehat{T}$
$\widehat{D} = \widehat{V}$ So, all corresponding angles are equal.

Ratio of corresponding sides:

$\dfrac{RV}{AD} = \dfrac{6.58}{4.7} = 1.4$ $\dfrac{SR}{BA} = \dfrac{7.84}{5.6} = 1.4$

$\dfrac{ST}{BC} = \dfrac{9.1}{6.5} = 1.4$ $\dfrac{TV}{CD} = \dfrac{5.32}{3.8} = 1.4$

So, all corresponding sides are in the same ratio.
This means that ABCD and RSTV are similar shapes.

Note
We can also say that RSTV is an enlargement of ABCD with scale factor 1.4.
So, similar shapes are enlargements of each other.

> The ratio for corresponding sides can be either:
>
> $\dfrac{\text{larger shape}}{\text{smaller shape}}$
>
> or
>
> $\dfrac{\text{smaller shape}}{\text{larger shape}}$
>
> but it is important that you use the same ratio for all your calculations in a question.

Exercise 6.9A

1

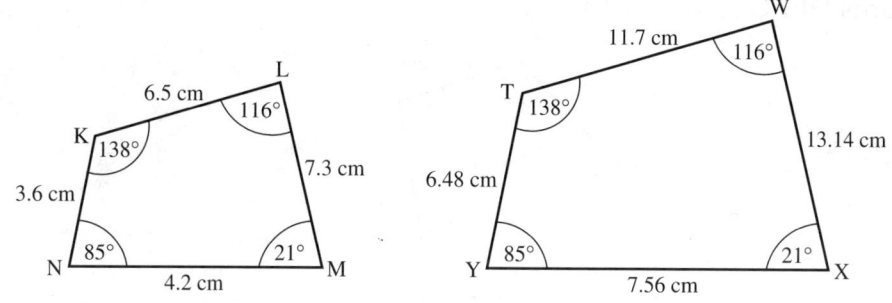

For the shapes KLMN and TWXY calculate:

a the value for each of these ratios $\dfrac{TW}{KL}, \dfrac{WX}{LM}, \dfrac{XY}{MN}, \dfrac{YT}{KN}$.

b What can you say about corresponding angles in KLMN and TWXY?

c Are KLMN and TWXY similar?
Give reasons for your answer.

2 Are FGHJ and TVWY similar shapes? Give reasons for your answer.

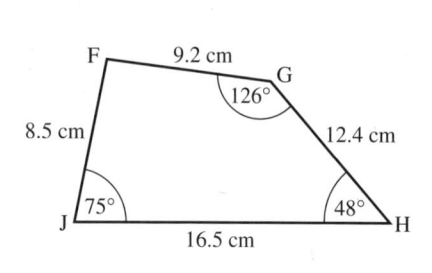

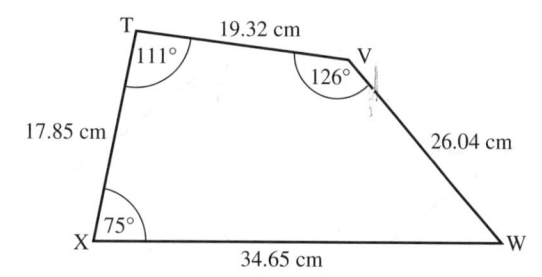

3 Are CBT, STR and GHK similar shapes? Explain your answer.

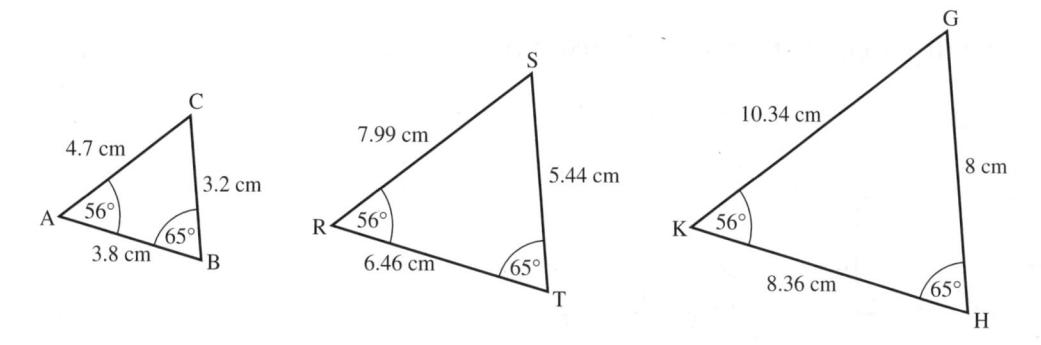

Exercise 6.9B

1 Explain why the shapes DEFG and NRCP are similar.

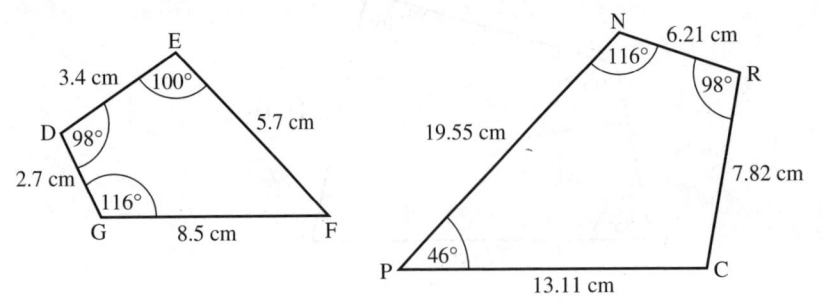

Left shape DEFG: DE = 3.4 cm, angle E = 100°, EF = 5.7 cm, angle D = 98°, DG = 2.7 cm, angle G = 116°, GF = 8.5 cm.

Right shape NRCP: NR = 6.21 cm, angle N = 116°, angle R = 98°, RC = 7.82 cm, NP = 19.55 cm, angle P = 46°, PC = 13.11 cm.

2 Explain why these two shapes are not similar.

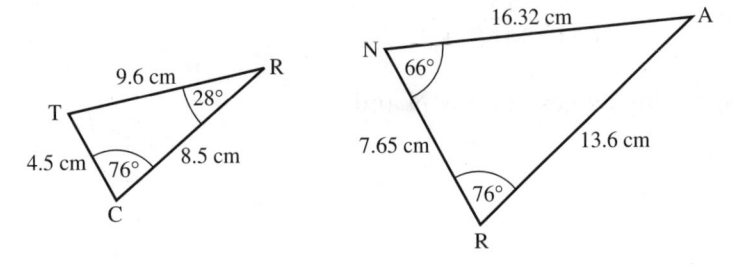

Left triangle TRC: TR = 9.6 cm, angle R = 28°, RC = 8.5 cm, TC = 4.5 cm, angle C = 76°.

Right triangle NAR: NA = 16.32 cm, angle N = 66°, AR = 13.6 cm, NR = 7.65 cm, angle R = 76°.

3 These two shapes are similar. Calculate all the unknown measurements marked with w, x, y or z.

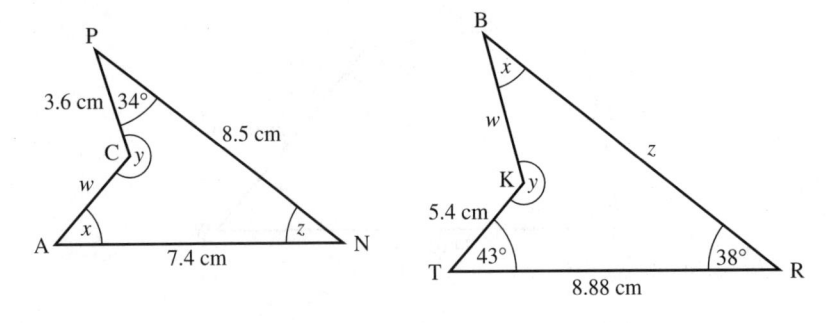

Left triangle PAN: AP = 3.6 cm, angle P = 34°, PN = 8.5 cm, AN = 7.4 cm, angle C = y, angle A = x, side w, angle at N = z.

Right triangle BTR: angle B = x, side z, BK = 5.4 cm, angle K = y, angle T = 43°, angle R = 38°, TR = 8.88 cm, side w.

6.10 Using trigonometry to find sides and angles*

These right angled triangles are similar, so the sides are in the same ratio.

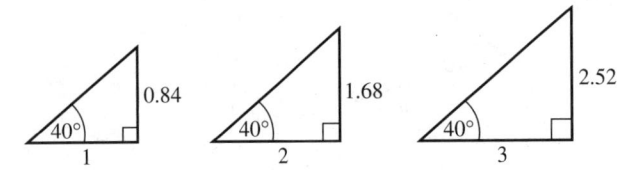

Triangle 1: 40°, opposite = 0.84
Triangle 2: 40°, opposite = 1.68
Triangle 3: 40°, opposite = 2.52

Using trigonometry to find an angle* 153

For any right angled triangle with an angle of 40° you can say that the length of the opposite side will be 0.84 times the length of the adjacent side.

This value 0.84 links the angle 40° and the lengths of the opposite and adjacent sides.

This is the tangent relationship and you write $\tan 40° = 0.84$ (2 dp).

Or, you can think of it this way: $\tan 40° = \dfrac{\text{length of opposite}}{\text{length of adjacent}} = 0.84$ (2 dp).

Exercise 6.10A

1 Calculate the length of the opposite side in each triangle.

a — 40°, 4, ?
b — 40°, 6, ?
c — 40°, 2.5, ?
d — 40°, 5.5, ?

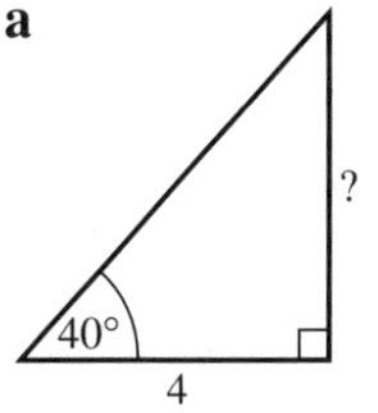

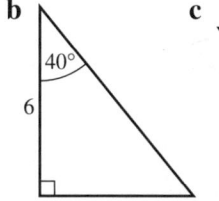

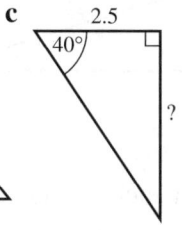

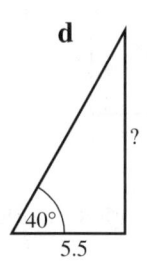

2 Calculate the length of the opposite side in each triangle.

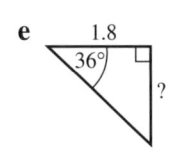

a — 44°, 6, ?
b — 54°, 5.5, ?
c — 47°, 7.4, ?
d — 62°, 8.6, ?
e — 36°, 1.8, ?
f — 15°, 11.6, ?
g — 61°, 3.8, ?
h — 41°, 5.2, ?

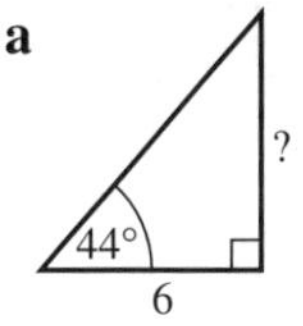

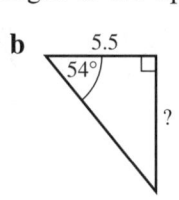

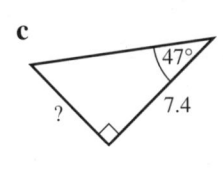

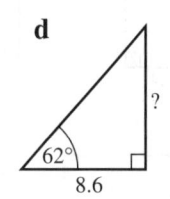

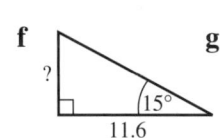

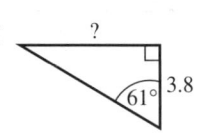

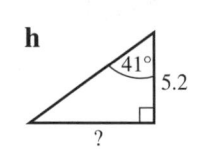

Sine

There is a link between the angle 40°, the length of the opposite and the length of the hypotenuse.

In a right angled triangle, for an angle of 40° the length of the opposite will be 0.64 times the length of the hypotenuse.

This is the sine relationship and you write $\sin 40° = 0.64$ (2 dp).

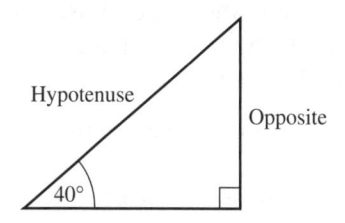

Or, you can think of it this way: $\sin 40° = \dfrac{\text{length of opposite}}{\text{length of hypotenuse}} = 0.64$.

Exercise 6.10B

1. Calculate the length of the opposite side in each triangle.
   All lengths are in cm.

   a. (hypotenuse 8, angle 35°, opposite ?)
   b. (hypotenuse 11, angle 52°, opposite ?)
   c. (adjacent 6.5, angle 21°, opposite ?)
   d. (hypotenuse 8.2, angle 58°, opposite ?)
   e. (angle 62°, adjacent 5.8, opposite ?)
   f. (hypotenuse 7.8, angle 61°, opposite ?)
   g. (hypotenuse 10.2, angle 24°, opposite ?)
   h. (hypotenuse 21.8, angle 12°, opposite ?)

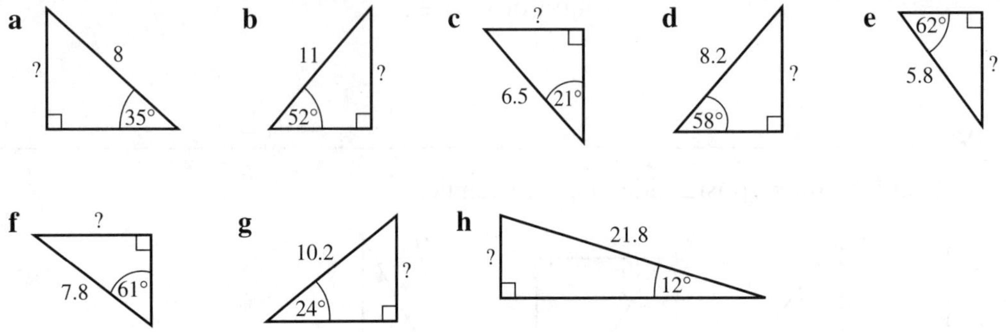

2. Calculate the length of the opposite side in each triangle.
   All lengths are in cm.

   a. (angle 31°, adjacent 3.4, opposite ?)
   b. (hypotenuse 9.8, angle 47°, opposite ?)
   c. (angle 71°, hypotenuse 11.6, opposite ?)
   d. (angle 64°, adjacent 4.3, opposite ?)
   e. (hypotenuse 7.6, angle 72°, opposite ?)
   f. (angle 33°, hypotenuse 14.3, opposite ?)
   g. (angle 14°, 15.2, opposite ?)
   h. (16.3, 56°, 44°, 9.4, opposite ? ?)

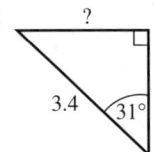

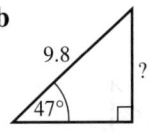

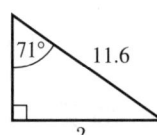

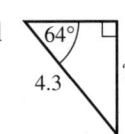

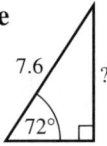

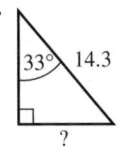

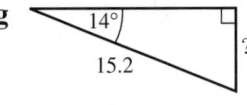

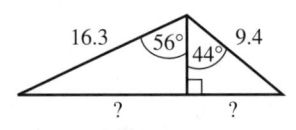

Cosine

There is a link between the angle 40° and the lengths of the adjacent and hypotenuse. In a right angled triangle, for an angle of 40° the length of the adjacent will be 0.77 times the length of the hypotenuse.

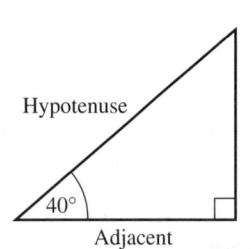

This is the cosine relationship and you write $\cos 40° = 0.77$ (2 dp).

Or, you can think of it this way: $\cos 40° = \dfrac{\text{length of adjacent}}{\text{length of hypotenuse}} = 0.77$.

Exercise 6.10C

1 Calculate the length of the adjacent side in each triangle.

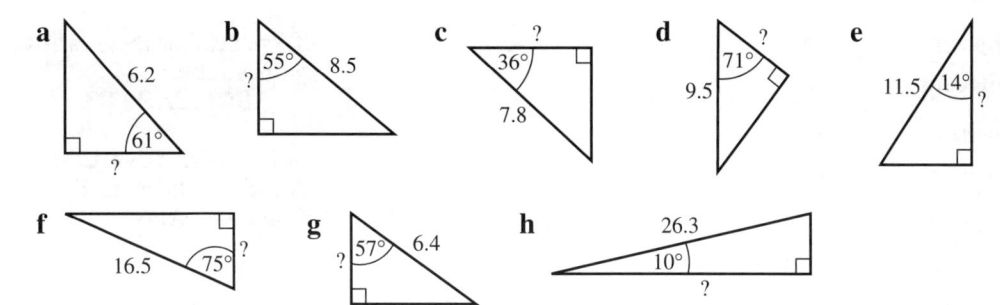

a) 6.2, 61°, ?
b) 55°, 8.5, ?
c) 36°, 7.8, ?
d) 71°, 9.5, ?
e) 11.5, 14°, ?
f) 16.5, 75°, ?
g) 57°, 6.4, ?
h) 26.3, 10°, ?

2 Calculate the length of the adjacent side in each triangle.

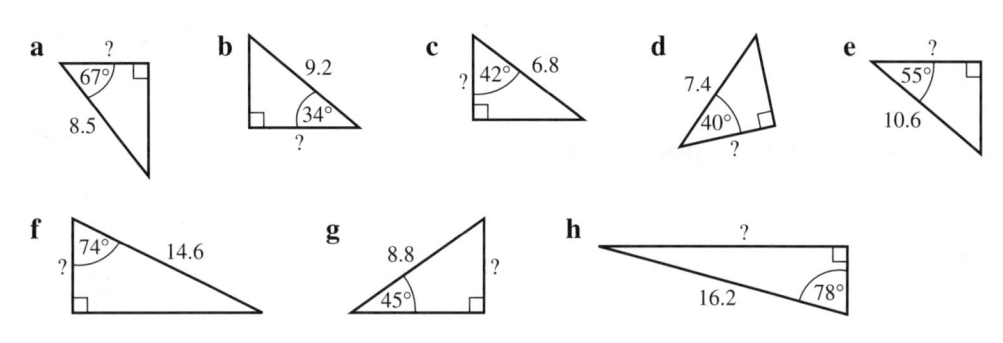

a) 67°, 8.5, ?
b) 9.2, 34°, ?
c) 42°, 6.8, ?
d) 7.4, 40°, ?
e) 55°, 10.6, ?
f) 74°, 14.6, ?
g) 8.8, 45°, ?
h) 16.2, 78°, ?

Exercise 6.10D

1 These are mixed questions. Label the sides first then calculate the length of the sides marked ?

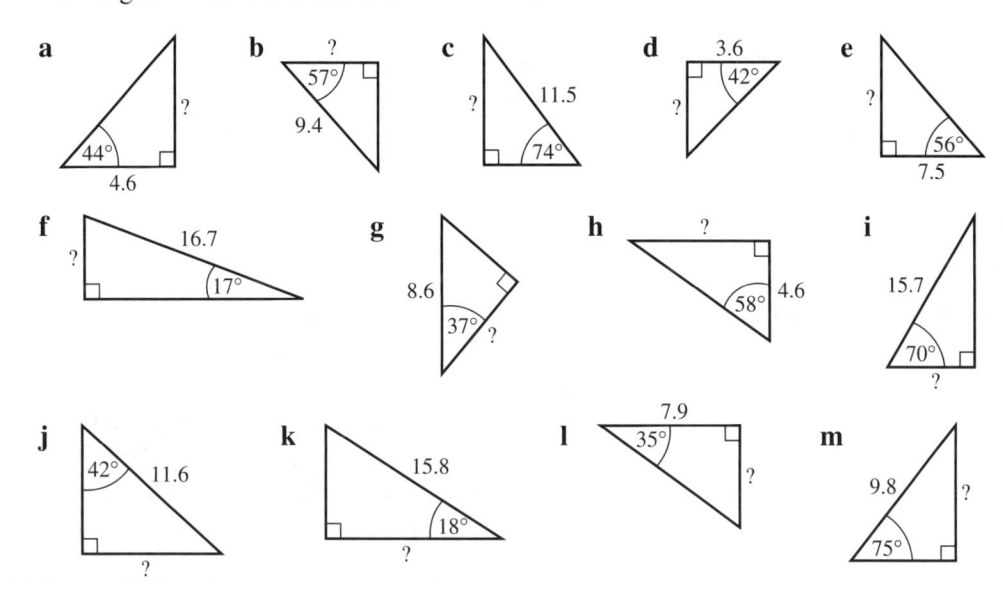

a) 44°, 4.6, ?
b) 57°, 9.4, ?
c) 11.5, 74°, ?
d) 3.6, 42°, ?
e) 7.5, 56°, ?
f) 16.7, 17°, ?
g) 8.6, 37°, ?
h) 4.6, 58°, ?
i) 15.7, 70°, ?
j) 42°, 11.6, ?
k) 15.8, 18°, ?
l) 7.9, 35°, ?
m) 9.8, 75°, ?

You can use the sine, cosine and tangent links to find the size of angles in right angled triangles. If you know the lengths of any two sides then you can calculate an angle. You need to know these ratios:

$$\text{tangent} = \frac{\text{opposite}}{\text{adjacent}} \quad \text{or} \quad t = \frac{o}{a}$$

$$\text{sine} = \frac{\text{opposite}}{\text{hypotenuse}} \quad \text{or} \quad s = \frac{o}{h}$$

$$\text{cosine} = \frac{\text{adjacent}}{\text{hypotenuse}} \quad \text{or} \quad c = \frac{a}{h}$$

To remember these ratios you can use:
SOHCAHTOA
or
Soldiers On High Castles Attack Hedgehogs To Overcome Ants

Example
Find α in this triangle.

You are given the adjacent and hypotenuse so use **cos**.

$$\cos = \frac{\text{adjacent}}{\text{hypotenuse}} = \frac{6.5}{8.6} = 0.7558\ldots$$

With a calculator if $\cos \alpha = 0.7558\ldots$ then $\alpha = 40.9°$.

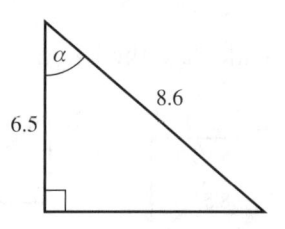

Exercise 6.10E

1 In each triangle calculate a value for either $\sin \alpha$, $\cos \alpha$ or $\tan \alpha$.
Then give α in degrees.

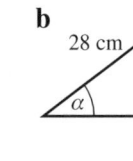

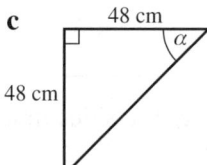

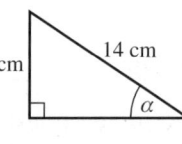

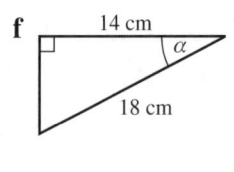

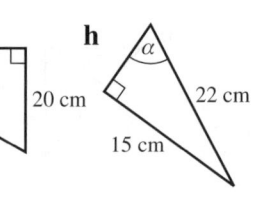

2 A roof structure is shown.

Use trigonometry to calculate the size of:

a angle ACB
b angle BAE
c angle CED
d angle CAE
e angle ABE
f angle AED

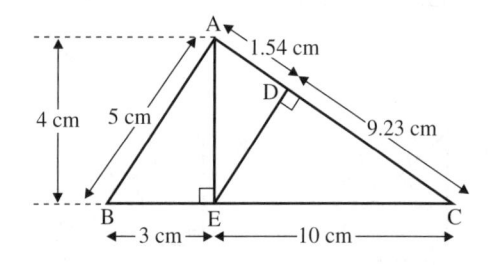

Revision exercise 6

Review

1 Copy each shape and draw in all its lines of symmetry.

   a   b   c   d

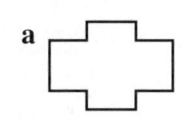

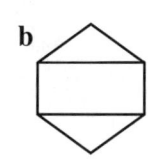

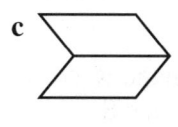

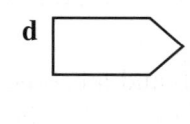

Unit 6.1

2 a How many lines of symmetry has a square?
Show this with a diagram.
  b Do a square and rectangle have the same lines of symmetry?
Explain your answer with a diagram.

Unit 6.1

3 Give the order of rotational symmetry of each shape.

   a   b   c   d

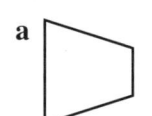

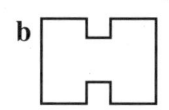

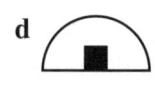

Unit 6.2

4 How many planes of symmetry has each shape?
Make a sketch and show the planes of symmetry.

   a   b   c

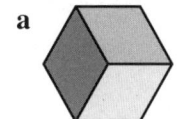

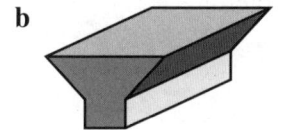

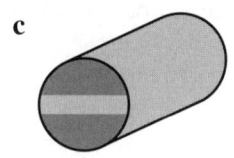

Unit 6.3

5 Copy each shape and reflect it in the mirror line shown.

   a   b   c

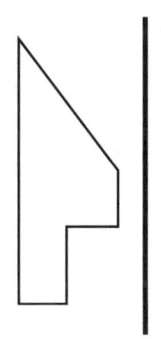

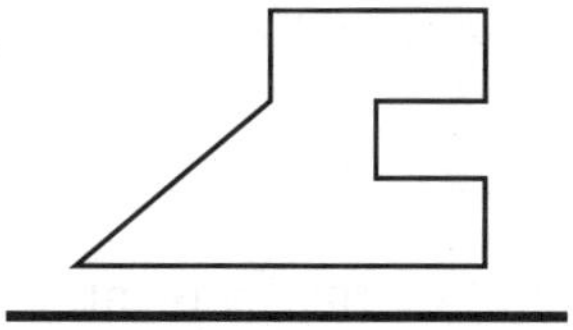

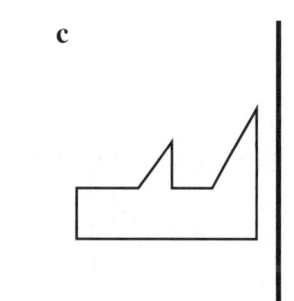

Unit 6.4

6 Draw a pair of axes with values of x and y from $^-8$ to $^+8$.
  a Draw the shape with vertices
A($^-$2, 6), B($^-$2, 3), C($^-$3, 4), D($^-$4, 3), E($^-$4, 6)
  b Reflect ABCDE in the line $x = {^-5}$ and label the image K.
  c Reflect ABCDE in the line $y = 1$ and label the image L.
  d Reflect ABCDE in the line $x = 2$ and label the image M.

Unit 6.4

7 Draw a pair of axes as you did for question 6.
   a Plot the shape with these vertices:

   (2, 5), (3, 5), (3, 4), (4, 4), (4, 3), (3, 3), (3, 2), (2, 2)

   Label the shape P.
   b Rotate P ⁻90° about (0, 0) and label the image R.
   c Rotate P 180° about (1, 2) and label the image S.

Unit 6.5

8 ABC is a triangle with these vertices.

   A(⁻2, 3), B(⁻3, 5), C(1, 4)

   Give the coordinates of the image if ABC is translated by:

   a $\begin{pmatrix} 3 \\ 5 \end{pmatrix}$ **b** $\begin{pmatrix} -4 \\ 0 \end{pmatrix}$ **c** $\begin{pmatrix} 0 \\ -7 \end{pmatrix}$ **d** $\begin{pmatrix} 2 \\ -5 \end{pmatrix}$ **e** $\begin{pmatrix} -6 \\ 1 \end{pmatrix}$

Unit 6.6

9 ABCDE is translated by the vector **V**.
   A is the point (5, ⁻2) and A' is the point (1, 1).
   a What is the vector **V**?
   b If B' is (6, 0) find the coordinates of B.
   c D' is (0, 0) what are the coordinates of D?

Unit 6.6

10 On a grid enlarge each of these shapes by the scale factor given.

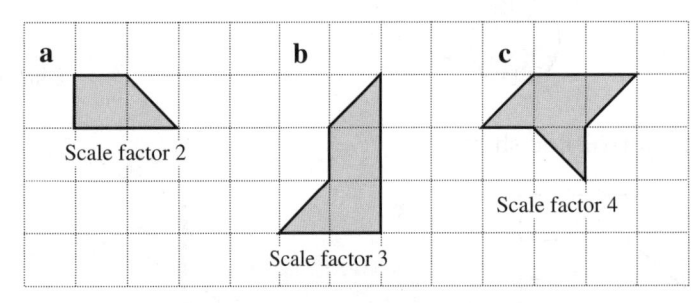

   a Scale factor 2
   b Scale factor 3
   c Scale factor 4

Unit 6.7

11 Copy this enlargement and find the centre of enlargement.

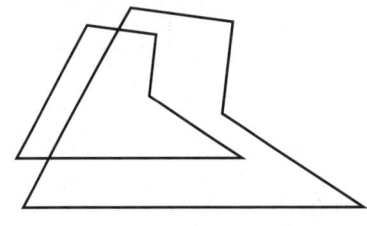

Unit 6.7

12 An old map has a scale of 1 inch = 7.5 miles.
   a On the map a road is measured as 4.75 inches.
      How long is the road in miles?
   b A road between two towns was 35.8 miles long.
      On the map, how long was the line showing this road?

Unit 6.8

13 A model of a steam engine is made to a scale of 1 : 45
 a The model is 42.6 cm long. How long is the steam engine?
 The diameter of a wheel on the engine is 88 cm.
 b What is the diameter of the corresponding wheel on the model?

Unit 6.8

14 What conditions must be true if two shapes are similar?

Unit 6.9

15 Are these two shapes similar? Give reasons for your answer.

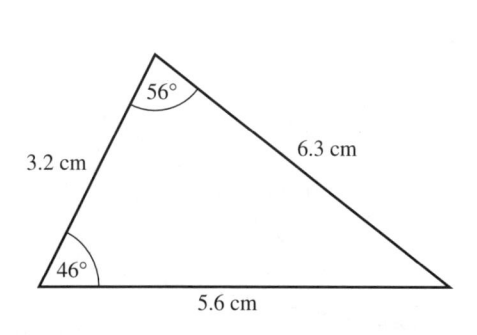

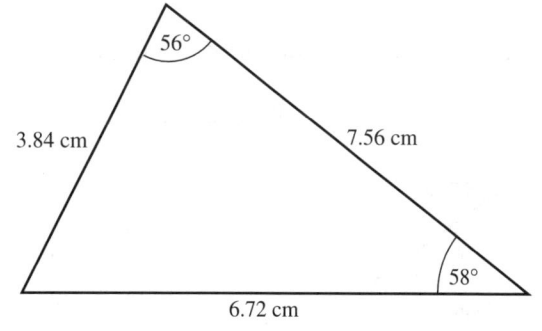

Unit 6.9

16 These two shapes are similar.
Calculate the unknown measurements.

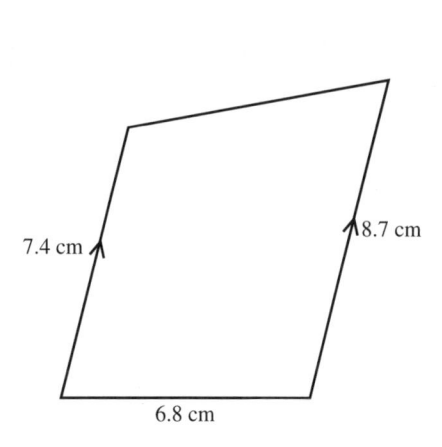

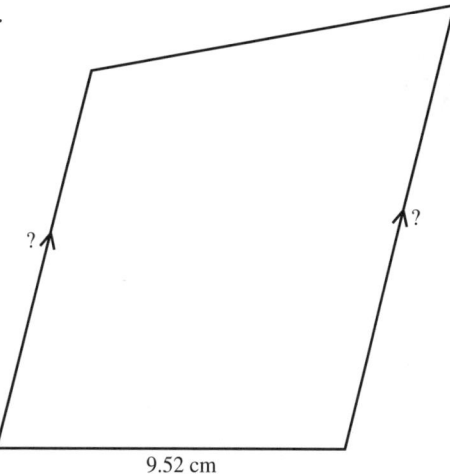

Unit 6.9

17 Use trigonometry to find the marked angle in each triangle.

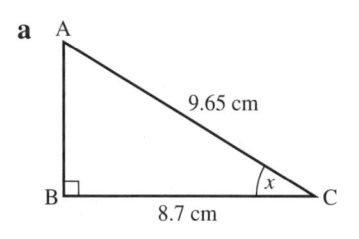

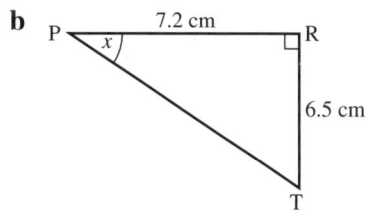

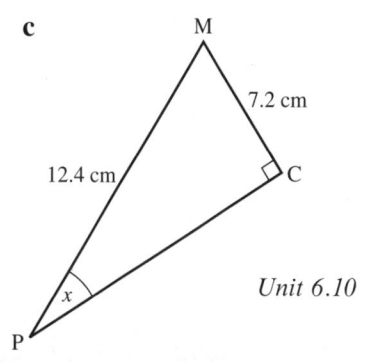

Unit 6.10

18 Use trigonometry to find the marked side in each triangle. *Review*

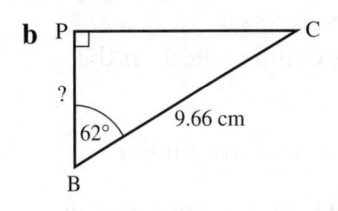

a Triangle with A at top right, C bottom left, N bottom right. Angle C = 34°, CA = 5.8 cm, AN = ?, right angle at N.

b Triangle with P top left (right angle), C top right, B bottom. Angle B = 62°, BC = 9.66 cm, PB = ?.

c Triangle with N top right, K bottom left, R bottom right (right angle). Angle K = 38°, NR = 7.62 cm, KR = ?.

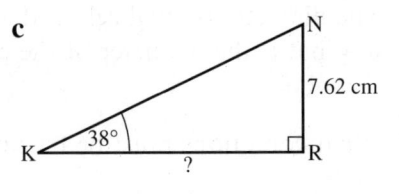

Unit 6.11

19 Use Pythagoras to find the marked side in each triangle.

a Triangle with P top, A bottom left (right angle), R bottom right. PR = 8.7 cm, AR = 6.5 cm, PA = ?.

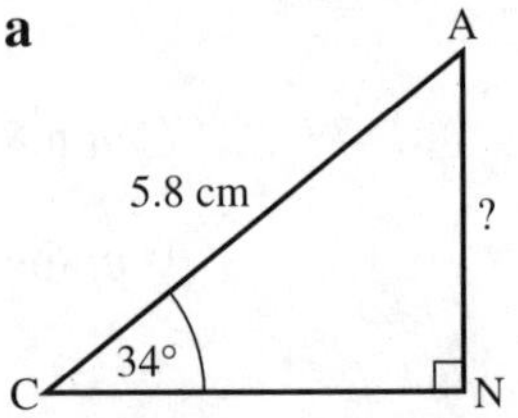

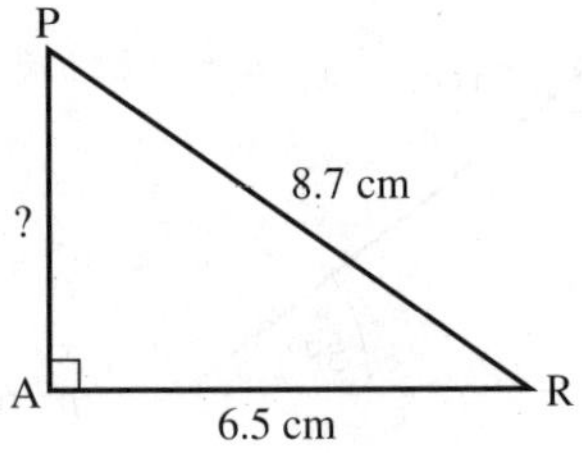

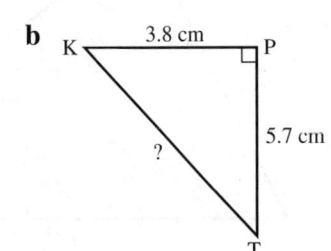

b Triangle with K top left, P top right (right angle), T bottom. KP = 3.8 cm, PT = 5.7 cm, KT = ?.

c Triangle with N top, P bottom left, R right (right angle). PN = 14.6 cm, NR = 5.67 cm, PR = ?.

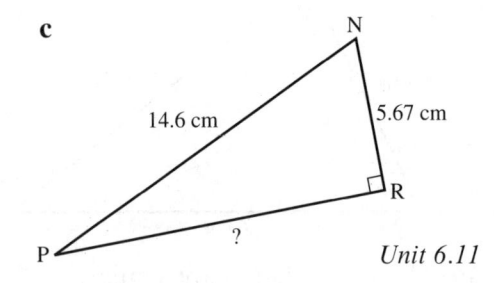

Unit 6.11

7 Measures and Construction

7.1 Metric and Imperial measure

You can use a table like this to help convert between units of measurement. You need to **remember** the facts given in **bold** in the table.

	Metric	Imperial	Some approximate conversions
Length	millimetres (mm) centimetres (cm) metres (m) kilometres (km) **1 cm = 10 mm** **1 m = 100 cm** **1 km = 1000 m**	inches (in) feet (ft) yards (yd) miles 1 ft = 12 in 1 yd = 3 ft 1 mile = 1760 yd	**1 inch = 2.54 cm** 1 foot ≈ 30.5 cm 1 metre ≈ 39.4 in **1 mile ≈ 1.61 km**
Mass	grams (g) kilograms (kg) tonnes **1 kg = 1000 g** **1 tonne = 1000 kg**	ounces (oz) pounds (lb) stones 1 lb = 16 oz 1 stone = 14 lb	**1 pound ≈ 454 g** **1 kilogram ≈ 2.21 lb**

Capacity	millilitres (ml)
	centilitres (cl)
	litres
	
	1 cl = 10 ml
	1 litre = 100 cl
	         = 1000 ml
		pints (pt)
		gallons
		
		1 gallon = 8 pt
			1 gallon ≈ 4.55 litres
			1 litre ≈ 1.76 pints
			        ≈ 0.22 gallons

The symbol ≈ stands for is approximately equal to. The measurement given is a good working estimate.

Exercise 7.1A

1. Give each of these lengths in millimetres (mm).
   a 12 cm   b 3 m   c 35 cm   d 0.7 cm   e 1.2 m

2. Give each of these lengths in centimetres (cm)
   a 5 m   b 1.2 m   c 3.35 m   d 0.7 m   e 0.12 m

3. The width of two pieces of board is measured.
   Board A is 26.3 cm wide and board B is 265 mm wide.
   Which board is the widest and by how much?

4. Give each of these weights in grams (g).
   a 3 kg   b 2.5 kg   c 1.25 kg   d 0.62 kg   e 0.058 kg

5 Write 2652 g as a weight in kg.

6 A watering can holds 3 imperial gallons.
Approximately how many litres is this?

7 A plant produces 14 240 pint bottles of milk in a shift.
How many gallons is this?

8 Wine is sold by the case. A case holds 12 bottles and each bottle holds 75 cl.
How many litres of wine are there in a case?

9 A jam making plant uses 420 lb of sugar an hour.
Roughly how many kg is this?

10 From John O'Groats to Lands End is 868 miles.
Roughly how many km is this?

11 Convert each of these to m^2.
   a $475 \, cm^2$ **b** $1068 \, cm^2$
   c $33\,454 \, cm^2$ **d** $1\,667\,850 \, mm^2$

12 Convert each of these to cm^3.
   a $14 \, m^3$ **b** $8.625 \, m^3$
   c $1.0875 \, m^3$ **d** $106.5 \, m^3$

Exercise 7.1B

1 Give each of these weights in kilograms.
   a 3 tonnes   **b** 6.5 tonnes   **c** 4.2 tonnes
   d 0.6 tonnes   **e** 0.14 tonnes

2 Give each of these in ounces (oz).
   a 4 lb   **b** 0.5 lb   **c** 0.75 lb
   d $2\frac{1}{4}$ lb   **e** $\frac{3}{8}$ lb

3 The length of a carpet is measured as 4 feet 8 inches.
   a Roughly what is this in centimetres?
   b Roughly how long is the carpet in metres?

4 The distance between two towns is 4 miles.
   a How many yards is this?
   b How many feet is this?
   c Is 4 miles more or less than half a million centimetres?
      Explain your answer.

5 For a flight an aircraft has 3850 litres of fuel.
   a Roughly how many gallons is this?
   b Jim estimates that the aircraft has about 2200 pints of fuel.
      Is this a good estimate? Explain your answer.

6 A man gives his weight as 168 lb.
What is his weight in kilograms?

7 A 50 metre length of pipe has to be cut into these lengths:

    3 pieces   2.6 m long
    4 pieces   6 feet 4 inches long
    5 pieces   88 cm long
    2 pieces   4 yards long

Roughly how much pipe will be left? Show all your working.

8 An assault course is 1540 yards long.
People doing the course are told that it is about one and a half km long. Is this a good estimate for the length of the course?
Explain your answer by showing all your calculations.

9 A rectangle of glass measures 95 cm by 66 cm.
Calculate the area of the sheet of glass in m^2.

10 A cuboid measures 85 cm by 35 cm by 58 cm.
Calculate the volume of the cuboid. Give your answer in m^3.

7.2 Compound units/measures

A compound unit or measure needs more than one unit to give its value.
For example, mph (miles per hour) and mpg (miles per gallon).

Example
Calculate the fuel consumption if a car uses 3.8 gallons of fuel to travel 171 miles.

    3.8 gallons are used to travel 171 miles

The distance travelled on one gallon will be: $171 \div 3.8 = 45$

So, the fuel consumption is 45 mpg.

Exercise 7.2A

1 A truck travelled 795.4 miles on 48 gallons of diesel fuel.
Calculate the fuel consumption of the truck.

2 In Milton Close there are 158 households. These households own a total of 538 cars. How many cars per household is this?

3 A motorway is 1288 kilometres long. In total the motorway has 17 service areas. Calculate the number of kilometres per service area for this motorway.

4 An irrigation pump delivers 13 078 litres of water per hour.
Give the amount of water delivered by this pump in litres per minute.

5 A cyclist travels 4.5 miles in 2 hours.
How many feet per minute is this?

6 A generator uses 1.6 litres of fuel every ten seconds.
Calculate this fuel consumption in:
a Litres per hour   **b** Gallons per hour

7 A company employs 12 672 employees and has 188 computer terminals. How many employees per computer terminal is this?

Exercise 7.2B

1 Between 0915 and 1745 a chairlift was used by 5284 people.
How many people per hour is this?

2 An aircraft covered 4624 km in 4 hours and 15 minutes.
How many kilometres per hour is this?

3 A book has 355 pages and 188 photographs. How many photographs per page is this?

4 Last year an airline flew 3.5 million passengers a total of 2410 million miles.
a How many miles per passenger is this?
b How many passengers per million miles is this?

5 A swimming pool holds 358 672 gallons of water. It takes 34.5 hours to empty it. Calculate the rate at which the pool is emptied in litres per minute.

6 A computer firm has 388 customer centres.
Last year the customer centres dealt with four and a quarter million enquiries.
How many enquiries per centre is this?

7.3 Constructing regular polygons

You can construct any regular polygon starting with a circle.
To use this method you must measure angles accurately.

Example
Construct a regular pentagon.

At the centre of the circle the 360° will have to be divided into 5 equal parts i.e.

$360° \div 5 = 72°$

Draw any straight line from the centre to the edge of the circle.

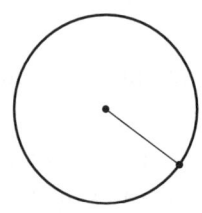

Use this line and:
from the centre measure 72° and mark a point on the edge of the circle.
Join the point to the centre of the circle.

Use the new line and:
from the centre measure 72° and mark a point on the edge of the circle.
Join the point to the centre of the circle.

Repeat this process until you have marked five points on the edge of the circle.
Join the points on the edge to make the regular pentagon.

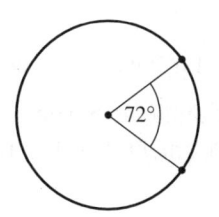

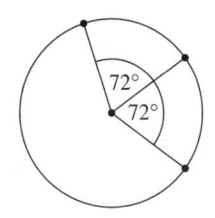

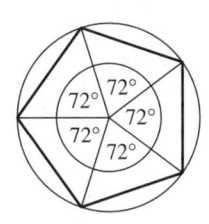

Exercise 7.3A

1 a Construct a regular polygon with six sides.
   b What is the mathematical name for this shape?

2 a Construct a regular polygon with ten sides.
   b What is the mathematical name for this shape?

3 Construct a regular octagon.

Exercise 7.3B

1 a Construct a regular polygon which has 12 sides.
   b What is the mathematical name for this shape?

2 Construct a regular polygon with 20 sides.

3 A polygon is constructed and each angle at the centre is measured as 20°.
   How many sides has the polygon? Explain how you decided on your answer.

4 Construct a regular polygon with fifteen sides.

7.4 Constructing triangles and quadrilaterals

You can construct a triangle as long as:

- you can draw and measure lines and angles accurately
- you have enough data
- you have a ruler and an angle measurer or protractor.

Construct is another way of saying make an accurate drawing.

Example 1
Construct a triangle with a base of 5.5 cm and base angles of 64° and 50°.

Draw the base of the triangle as 5.5 cm. Draw an angle of 64° at one end of the base.

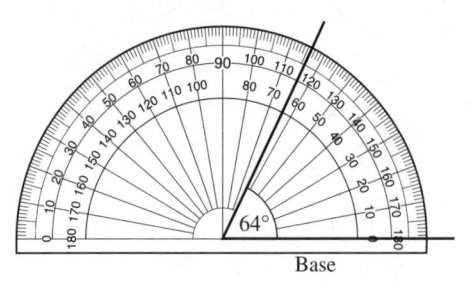

Draw an angle of 50° at the other end of the base. The base and the lines for the angles make the triangle.

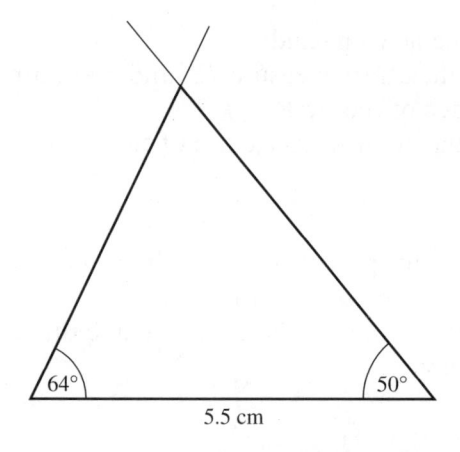

> You can check your drawing as the angle sum of a triangle is 180°. Here the third angle must be 66°.

Example 2
Construct a triangle with a base of 4.8 cm, one side 3.7 cm and the angle between these sides of 55°.

1 Draw the base of 4.8 cm and an angle of 55° at one end.

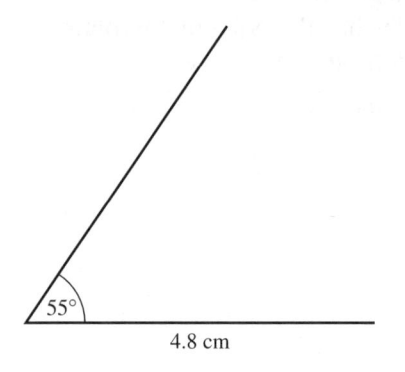

2 Measure 3.7 cm along the line for the angle of 55° and mark a point.

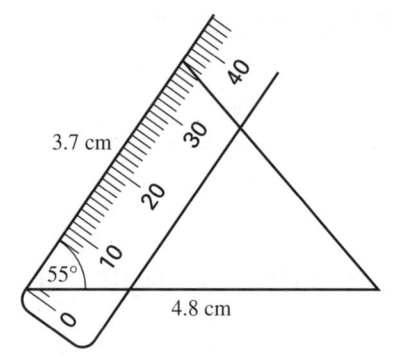

3 Join the point to the other end of the base making the triangle.

Exercise 7.4A

1 Draw each of these triangles accurately.

Triangle	Base	Base angles
A	4.5 cm	55° and 65°
B	5.2 cm	48° and 68°
C	6 cm	38° and 57°

Remember:
Check each triangle you draw.

2 Draw each of these triangles accurately.

Triangle	Base	Side	Angle between base and side
A	5 cm	3.5 cm	58°
B	5.6 cm	4.2 cm	66°
C	6.4 cm	5.2 cm	36°

Exercise 7.4B

1 **a** Construct a triangle with a base of 5.7 cm and base angles of 56° and 47°.
  b Give the lengths of the other two sides of the triangle.

2 **a** Construct a triangle with a base of 6.2 cm, a side of 4.5 cm and the angle between base and side of 52°.
  b What is the length of the third side of the triangle?
  c What is the size of the other angles in the triangle?

3 **a** Construct an equilateral triangle with sides of 5.8 cm.
  b Construct an isosceles triangle with base 6.4 cm and base angles of 38°.

Example 3

Construct a triangle with sides 4.2 cm, 5.2 cm and 4.8 cm.

Choose one side for the base and draw this accurately.

Open a pair of compasses to 5.2 cm, put the point at one end of the base and draw an arc.

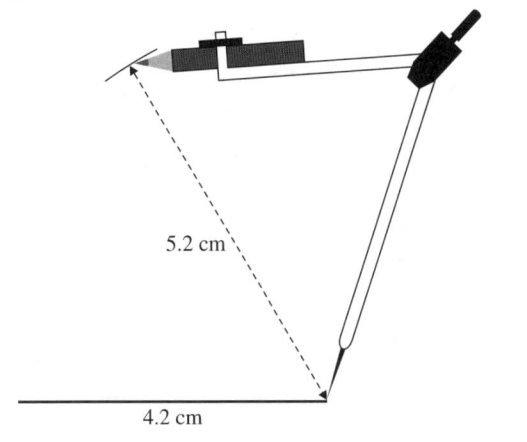

Open the compasses to 4.8 cm, with the point at the other end of the base draw a second arc. Join each end of the base to the point where the arcs cross.

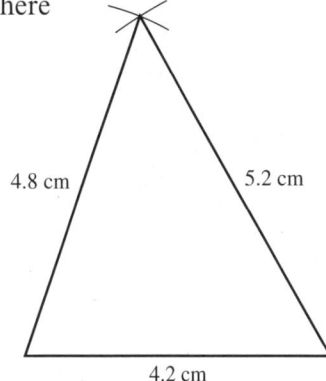

168 Measures and construction

Exercise 7.4C

1 Construct a triangle with sides of 5.4 cm, 5.6 cm and 4.5 cm.

2 Construct an equilateral triangle with sides of 4.4 cm.

3 **a** Construct an isosceles triangle with a base of 5 cm and sides of 6.2 cm.
  b Measure the size of each angle in the triangle.

4 This is a sketch of a triangle.
  Construct the triangle and give the size of each angle.

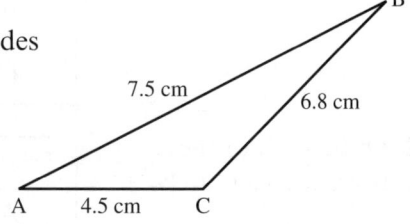

Exercise 7.4D

1 Construct a triangle with sides of 5.5 cm, 4.5 cm and 6.2 cm.

2 This is the sketch of a shape.
  Construct the shape and give the size of each angle.

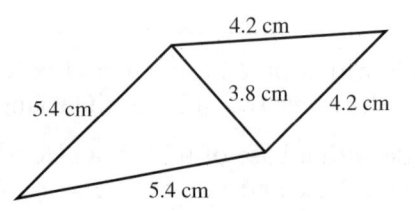

3 Is it possible to construct a triangle with sides of 5 cm, 2.5 cm and 2.5 cm? Explain your answer with a diagram.

4 **a** Construct a triangle with sides of 3 cm, 4 cm and 5 cm.
  b Measure each angle in the triangle. What do you notice?

You can use these skills to construct other 2-D shapes. You need enough data about the shape and to measure lengths and angles accurately.

Example 4
This is a sketch of a quadrilateral.
Construct the quadrilateral.

- Draw the base line.
- Draw a line at 54° to one end of the base.
  Mark a point 3.8 cm along this line.
- Draw a line at 60° to the other end of the base.
  Mark a point 4 cm along this line.
- Join the two marked points to make the quadrilateral.

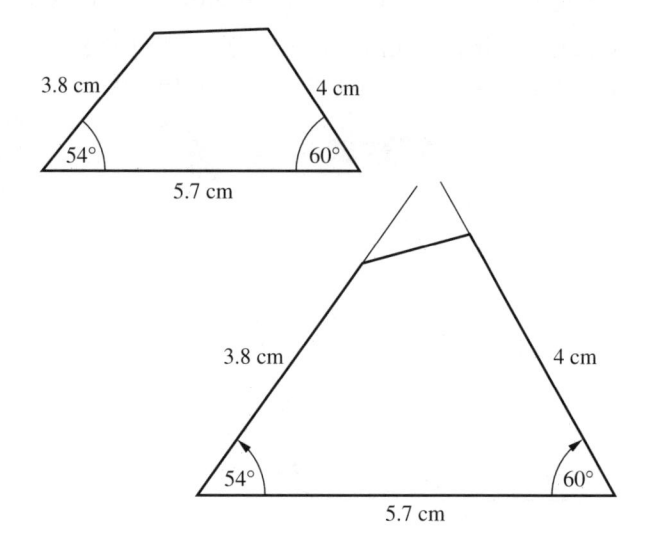

Exercise 7.4E

1 The diagrams show polygons. Construct each polygon from the data given.

a 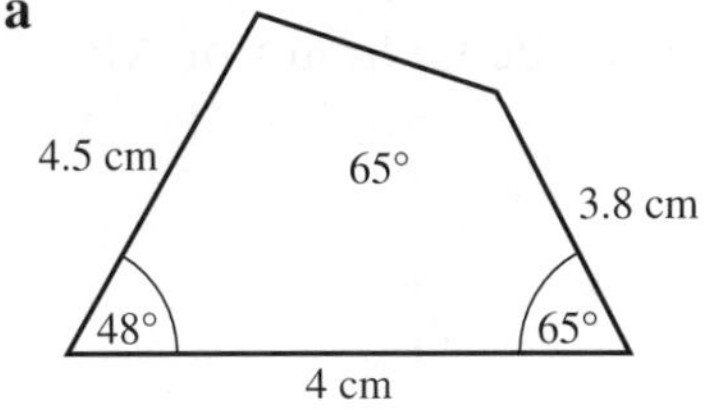 **b** 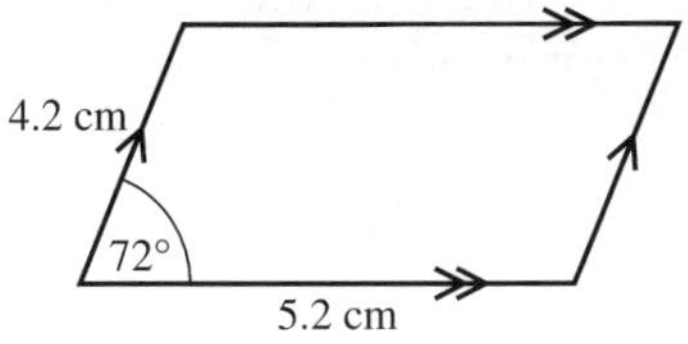 **c**

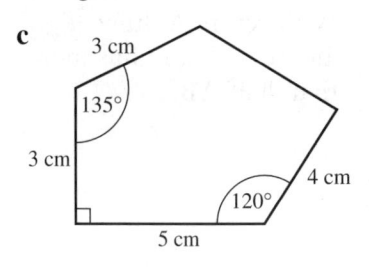

Exercise 7.4F

1 The diagrams show polygons. Construct each polygon from the data given.

a 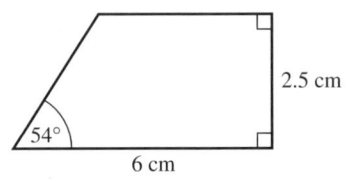 **b** 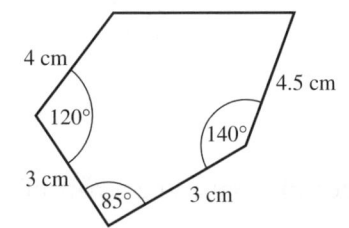 **c**

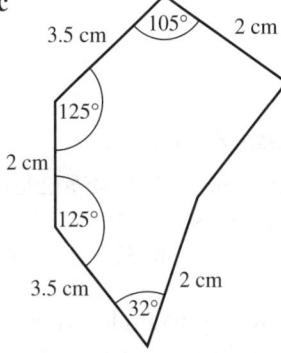

7.5 Bisecting angles and lines

▶ To **bisect an angle** using a pair of compasses:

> When you bisect an angle you divide it into two equal parts.

Step 1
With centre A draw an arc that cuts AB at D and AC at E.

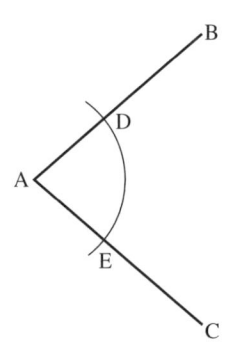

Step 2
With centre D draw an arc, with centre E draw an arc.

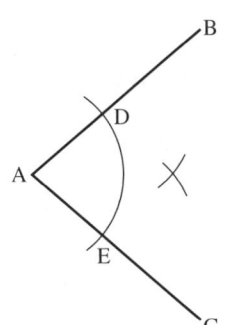

Step 3
Draw the bisector AF.

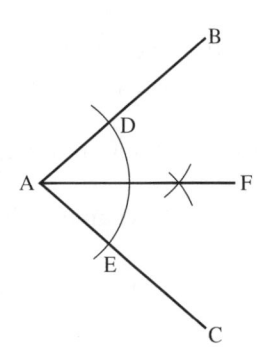

▶ To **bisect a line** using a pair of compasses:

Step 1
With centre A draw an arc with a radius more than half AB.

Step 2
With centre B draw an arc, with the same radius.

Step 3
Draw the bisector. C is the midpoint of AB.

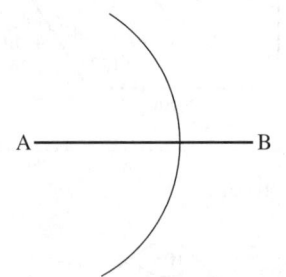

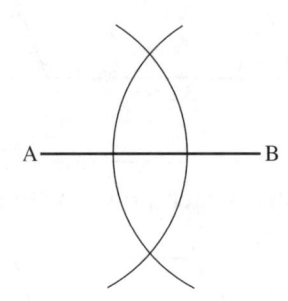

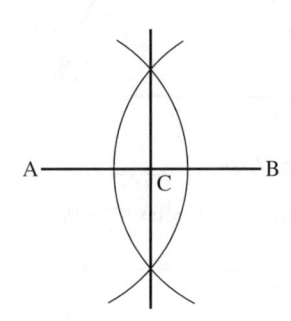

Exercise 7.5A

1 Draw each of these angles, then bisect it using a pair of compasses.
   a 56°   **b** 38°   **c** 70°   **d** 125°   **e** 145°

2 Draw any triangle, then bisect each of the interior angles. What do you notice? Is this true for other triangles?

3 Construct a regular pentagon and bisect each of its interior angles.

4 Draw each of these lines and construct its bisector.
   a 5.8 cm   **b** 7.2 cm   **c** 8.5 cm   **d** 9.5 cm   **e** 10.3 cm

Exercise 7.5B

1 Draw lines with these lengths and bisect each of them.
   a 8.8 cm   **b** 9.7 cm   **c** 10.5 cm   **d** 3.9 cm   **e** 5.5 cm

2 Draw any triangle and bisect each of the sides. What do you notice? Is this true for other triangles?

3 Draw any trapezium and bisect each of the sides.

4 Draw each of these angles then bisect it using a pair of compasses.
   a 88°   **b** 135°   **c** 115°   **d** 45°   **e** 165°

7.6 To construct a perpendicular from a point to a line

Step 1
Draw an arc from X to cut AB twice.

Step 2
Draw equal arcs from the two cut points on the other side of AB.

Step 3
Join X to where the two arcs cross.

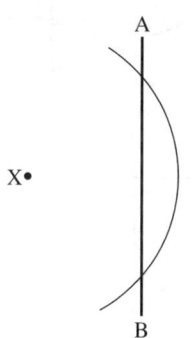

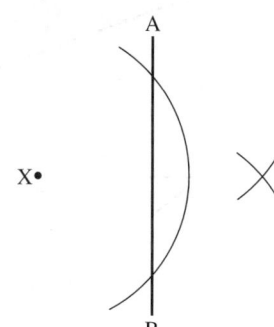

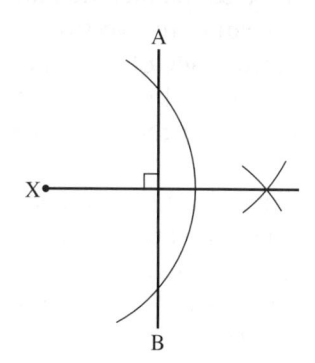

Exercise 7.6A

1 Trace this diagram and draw a perpendicular from P to each side of the triangle.

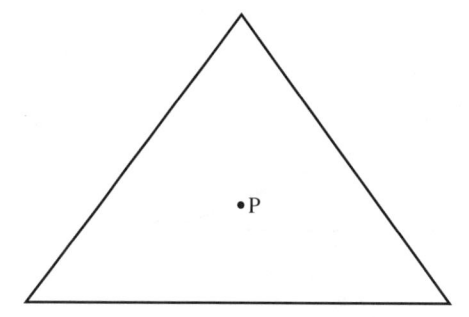

Exercise 7.6B

1 Trace the diagram and draw a perpendicular from P to each side of the triangle.

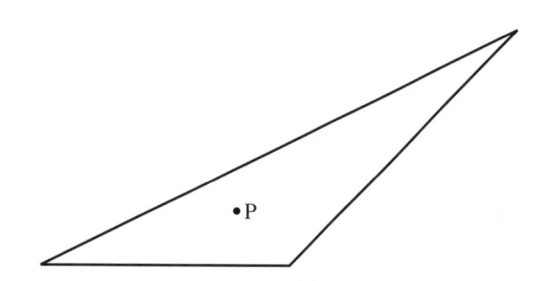

7.7 Congruent triangles*

▶ There are four conditions that show that triangles are congruent.

1 Three sides of one are equal to the three sides of the other. This condition is known as **SSS**.

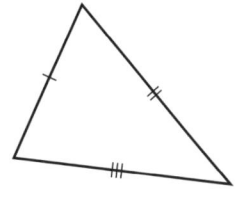

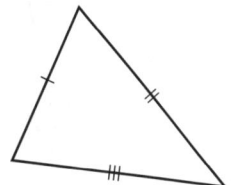

172   Measures and construction

2 Two angles and one side of one are equal to two angles and a corresponding side of the other.
This condition is known as **ASA** or **AAS**.

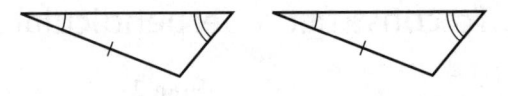

3 Two sides and the included angle of one are equal to two sides and the included angle of the other.
This condition is known as **SAS**
Note: **SAS** is not the same as **SSA**.

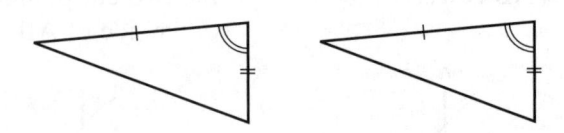

4 Both triangles are right-angled and the hypotenuse and one side of one are equal to the hypotenuse and one side of the other. This condition is known as **RHS**.

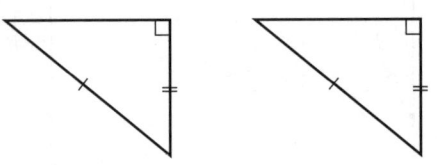

If you state that two triangles are congruent you should be able to give one of the four conditions as a reason for your statement.

Exercise 7.7A

1 In each diagram find a triangle that is congruent to triangle ABC.
You must state the condition you use as a reason.

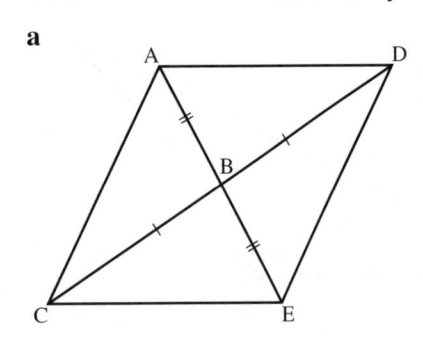

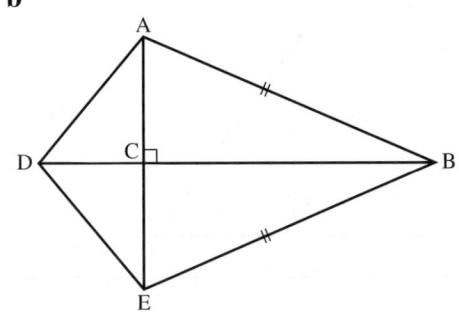

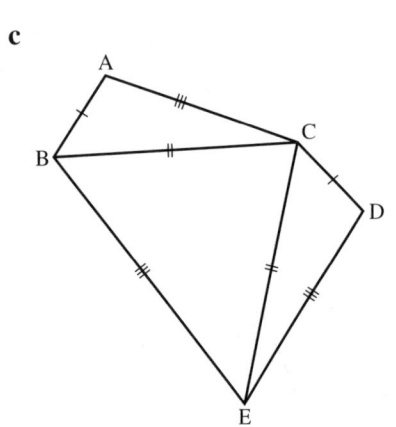

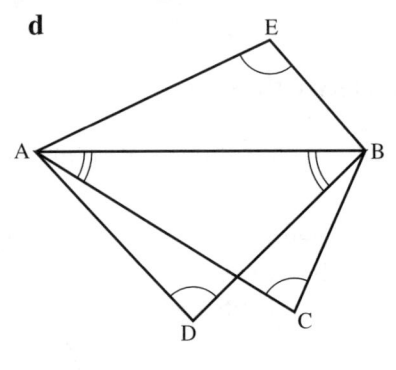

a

b

c

d

Exercise 7.7B

1 In each diagram find pairs of triangles that are congruent.
You must state the condition you use as a reason.

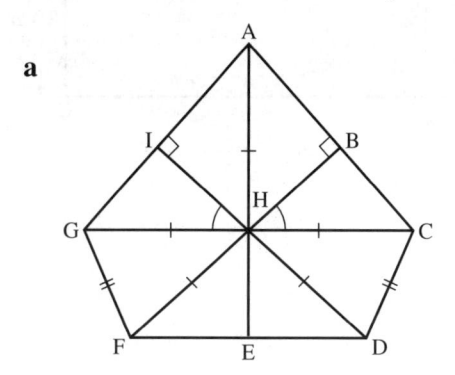

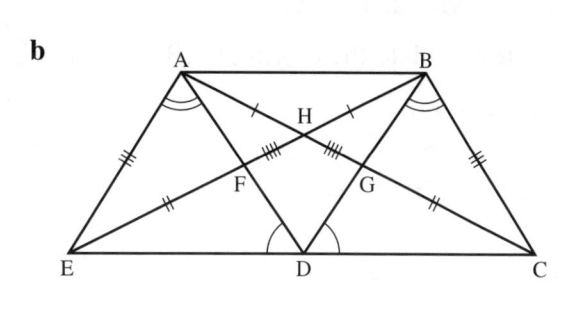

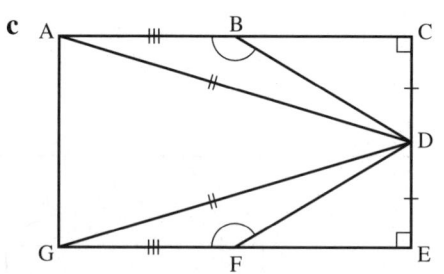

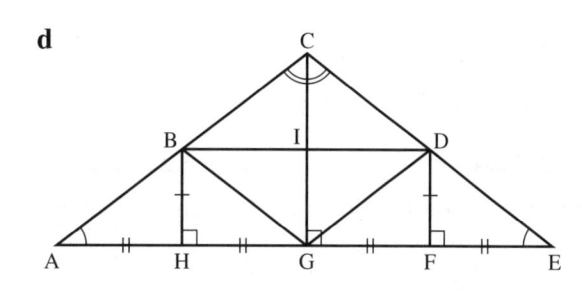

a

b

c

d

2 With a diagram explain why **SSA** is not a reason for congruence.

7.8 The perimeter of 2-D shapes

▶ The perimeter of a 2-D shape is the total distance around its outside edges. The perimeter is given as a single length.

Example 1

Calculate the perimeter of this shape.

The shape has 6 edges.
The perimeter P is given by:
$$P = 6.4 + 4.5 + 2.8 + 5 + 3.6 + 9.5$$
$$= 31.8$$

The perimeter of the shape is 31.8 cm.

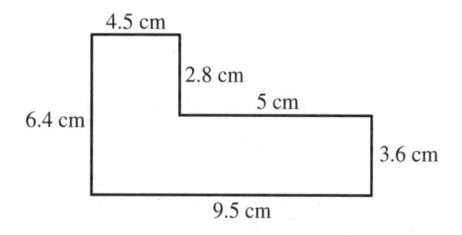

Sometimes you will have to calculate the length of one or more edges before you can calculate the perimeter of the shape.

Example 2

Calculate the perimeter of this shape.

The perimeter P is given by:
$P = 11.8 + AB + 8.4 + 20.7$

You need to calculate the length of AB.

From the diagram:

$AB = EC - ED$
$AB = 20.7 - 6.5$
$ = 14.2$

So, AB is 14.2 cm long.

The perimeter P is given by
$P = 11.8 + 14.2 + 8.4 + 20.7$
$P = 55.1$

The perimeter of the shape is 55.3 cm.

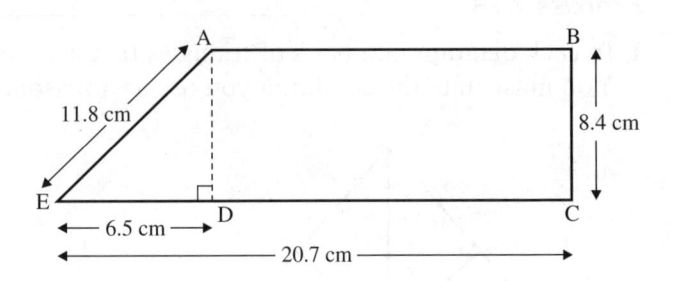

Exercise 7.8A

1 Calculate the perimeter of each of these shapes.

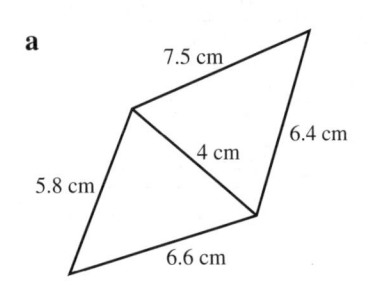

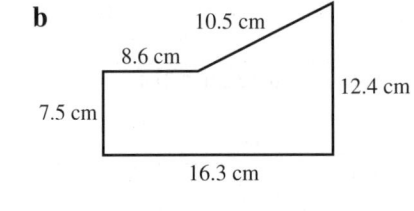

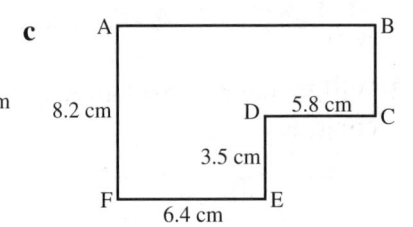

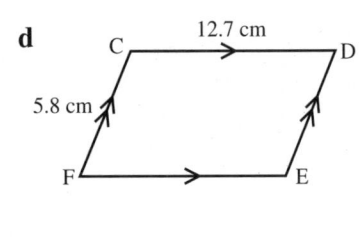

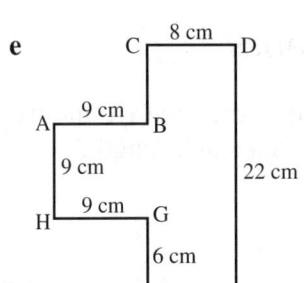

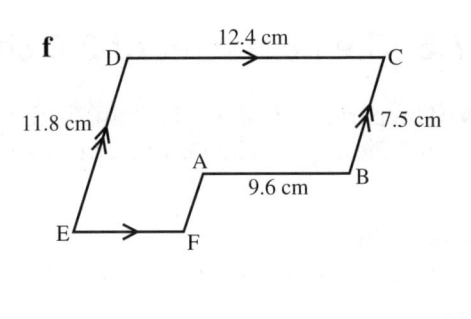

2 An equilateral triangle has a perimeter of 28.5 cm. Calculate the length of one edge of the triangle.

3 One edge of a regular octagon is 23 mm long. Calculate the perimeter of the shape.

4 Calculate the edge length of a square with a perimeter of 10.24 km.

Exercise 7.8B

1 Calculate the perimeter of each of these shapes.

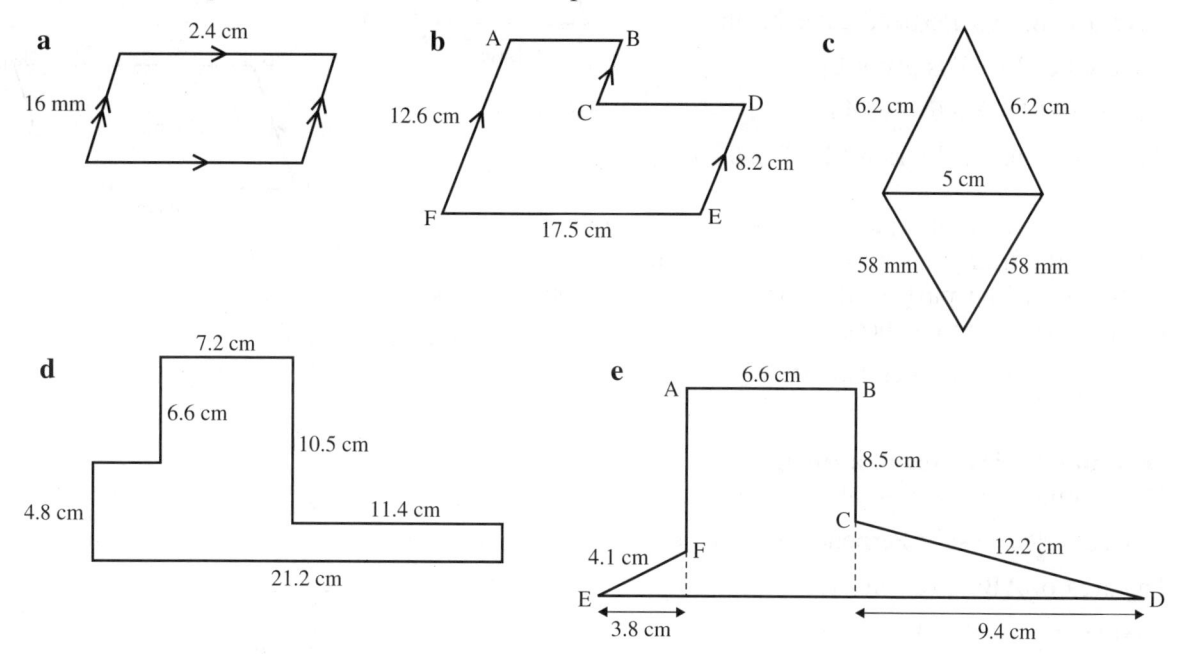

a 2.4 cm, 16 mm

b AB, 12.6 cm, 8.2 cm, 17.5 cm (vertices A, B, C, D, E, F)

c 6.2 cm, 6.2 cm, 5 cm, 58 mm, 58 mm

d 7.2 cm, 6.6 cm, 10.5 cm, 4.8 cm, 11.4 cm, 21.2 cm

e 6.6 cm, 8.5 cm, 4.1 cm, 3.8 cm, 12.2 cm, 9.4 cm (vertices A, B, C, D, E, F)

2 A square and a rectangle have the same perimeter.
The rectangle is 17.5 cm long and 12.5 cm wide.
Calculate the length of one edge of the square.

3 A rectangle and a rhombus have the same perimeter.
One edge of the rhombus is 12.5 cm long and the rectangle is
18 cm long. How wide is the rectangle? Show all your working.

7.9 The area of 2-D shapes

The area of a 2-D shape is a measure of the amount of surface
taken up by the shape.
Area is measured in squared units, for example cm^2, m^2, km^2.

Example 1 The area of a rectangle

The formula for the area of a
rectangle is:

   Area = Length × Width

The area of ABCD is given by:

   Area = 6.5 × 4.8 = 31.2

The area of rectangle ABC is 31.2 cm^2.

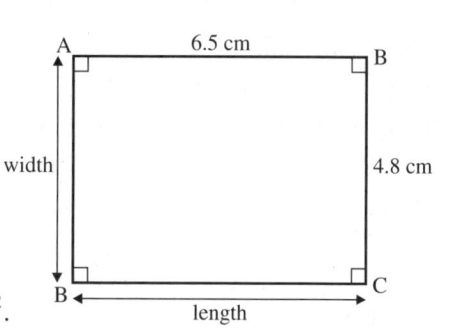

> The width of a rectangle might be called the breadth.

Example 2 The area of a parallelogram
The formula for the area of a parallelogram is:
   Area = Base × Perpendicular height
The area of PRST is given by:
   Area = 12.4 × 5.6 = 69.44
The area of parallelogram PRST is 69.44 cm^2.

Think of the area of a parallelogram in this way:
Remove the triangular part at one end of the shape.
Fit the triangular part to the other end of the shape.
The parallelogram has become a rectangle.
   Area = Base × Perpendicular height

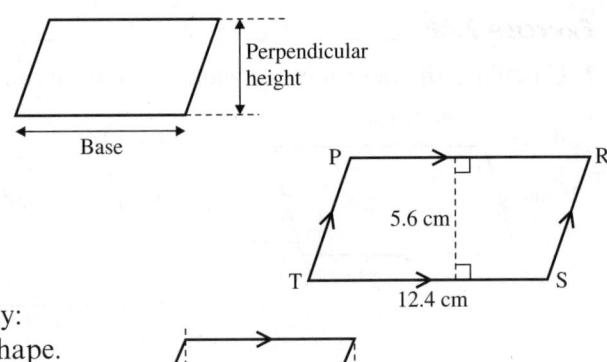

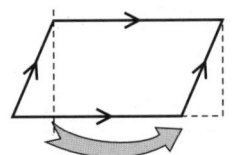

Example 3 The area of a triangle
The formula for the area of a triangle is:
   Area = $\frac{1}{2}$ × Base × Perpendicular height
The area of ABC is given by:
   Area = $\frac{1}{2}$ × 6.4 × 4.8
        = 15.36
The area of triangle ABC is 15.36 cm^2.

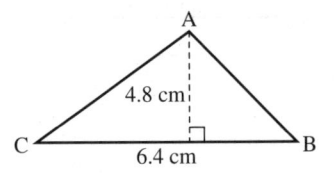

▶ The perpendicular height of a triangle can be:
   inside the triangle, part of the triangle or outside the triangle.

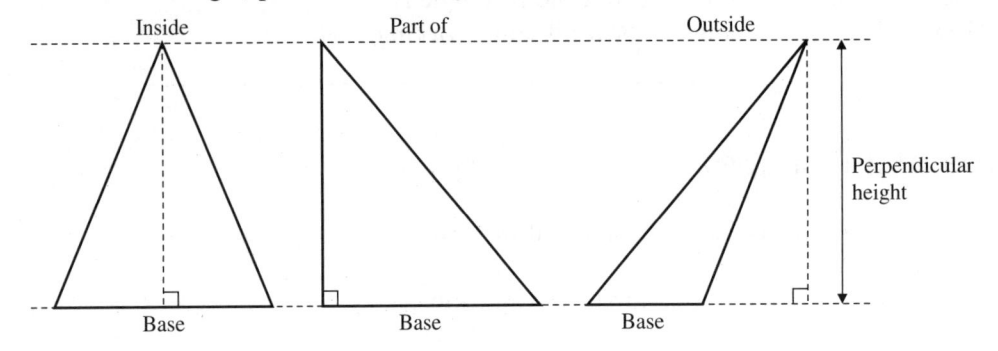

Inside   Part of   Outside

Base   Base   Base

Perpendicular height

Example 4 The area of a trapezium
The formula for the area of a trapezium is:
   Area = $\frac{1}{2}$(the sum of the parallel sides) × perpendicular height
The area of RSTV is given by:
   Area = $\frac{1}{2}$(12.4 + 7.5) × 6.3
        = 62.685
The area of the trapezium RSTV is 62.7 cm^2 (to 1 dp).

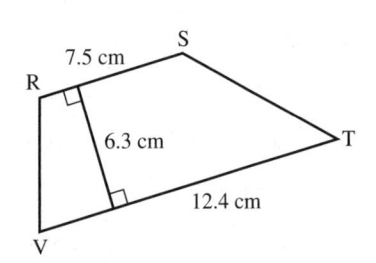

Exercise 7.9A

1 Calculate the area of each of these shapes.

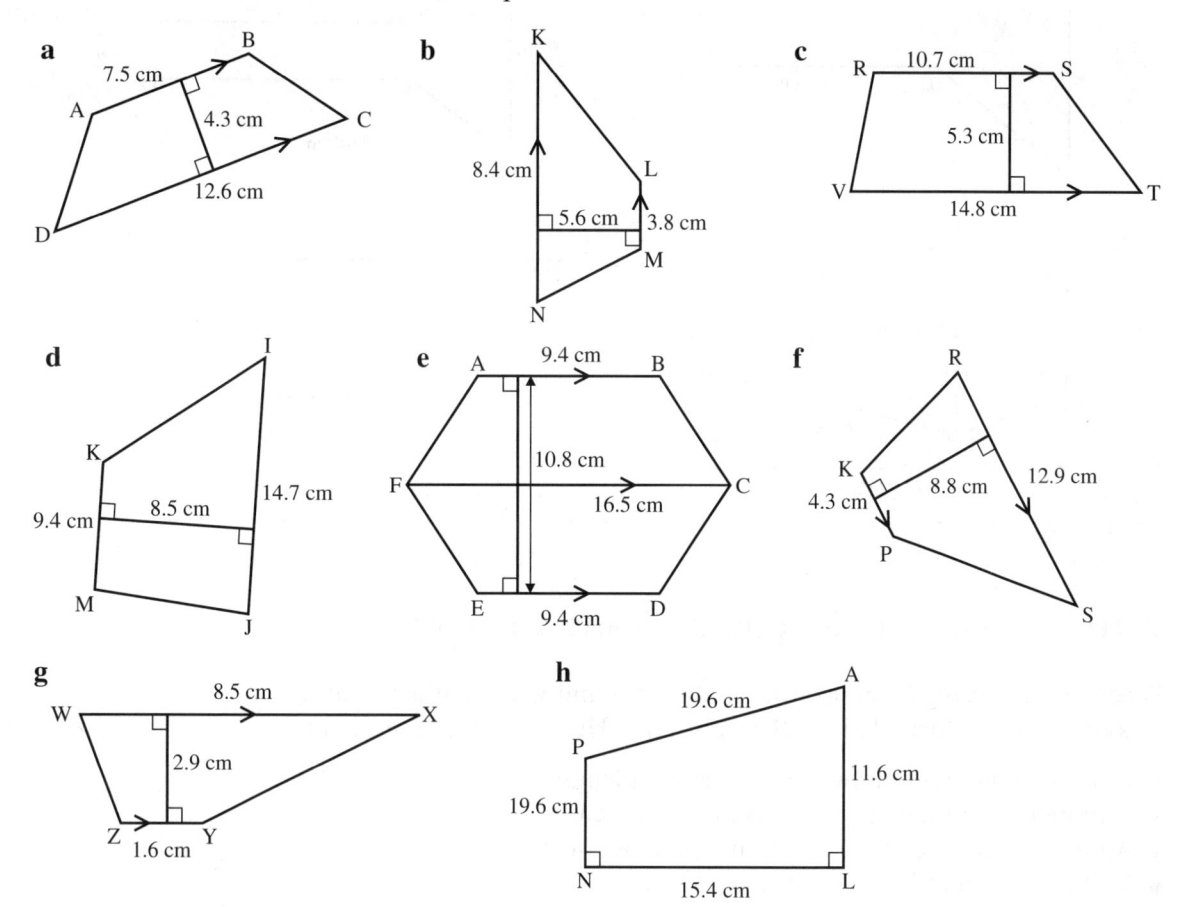

a Parallelogram ABCD with AB = 7.5 cm, height 4.3 cm, DC = 12.6 cm.

b Triangle KMN with K at top, height 8.4 cm to L, NM = 5.6 cm, LM = 3.8 cm.

c Trapezium RSTV with RS = 10.7 cm, height 5.3 cm, VT = 14.8 cm.

d Quadrilateral KIJM with 9.4 cm, 8.5 cm, 14.7 cm.

e Hexagon with AB = 9.4 cm, height 10.8 cm, FC = 16.5 cm, ED = 9.4 cm.

f Triangle RKS with KR = 4.3 cm, altitude 8.8 cm, 12.9 cm, P on KS.

g Trapezium WXYZ with WX = 8.5 cm, height 2.9 cm, ZY = 1.6 cm.

h Quadrilateral PALN with PA = 19.6 cm, AL = 11.6 cm, PN = 19.6 cm, NL = 15.4 cm.

Exercise 7.9B

1 Calculate the area of each of these shapes.

a Trapezium PQRS with PQ = 5.8 cm, height 3.7 cm, SR = 1.4 cm.

b Triangle ABCD with AB = 0.8 cm, 1.7 cm, 5.9 cm.

c Triangle KLM with N on KM, 2.7 cm, 4.3 cm, 6.5 cm.

d Quadrilateral DEFG with DE = 7.2 cm, DG = 5.6 cm, GF = 16.3 cm.

e Hexagon TUVWXY with TU = 17.5 cm, height 10.2 cm, YV = 9.8 cm, XW = 17.5 cm.

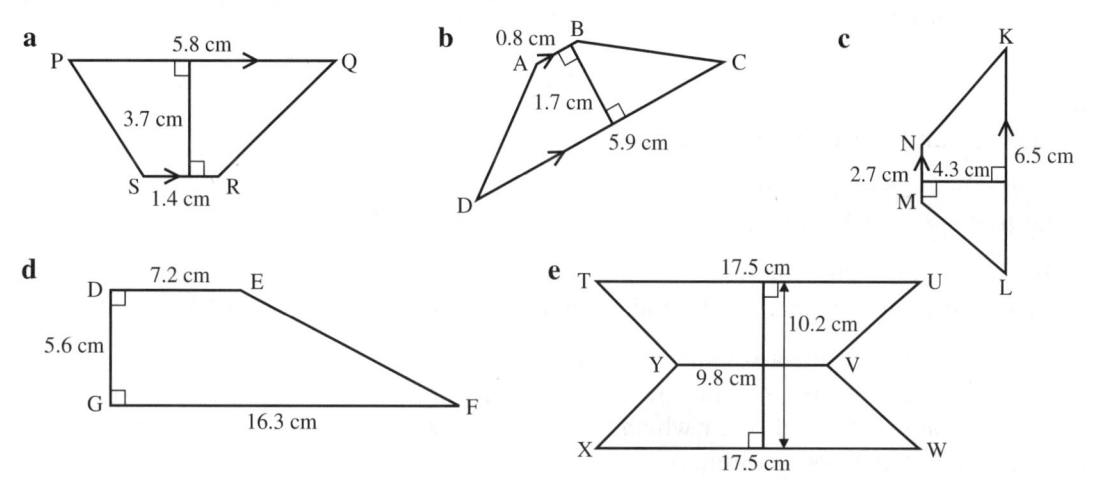

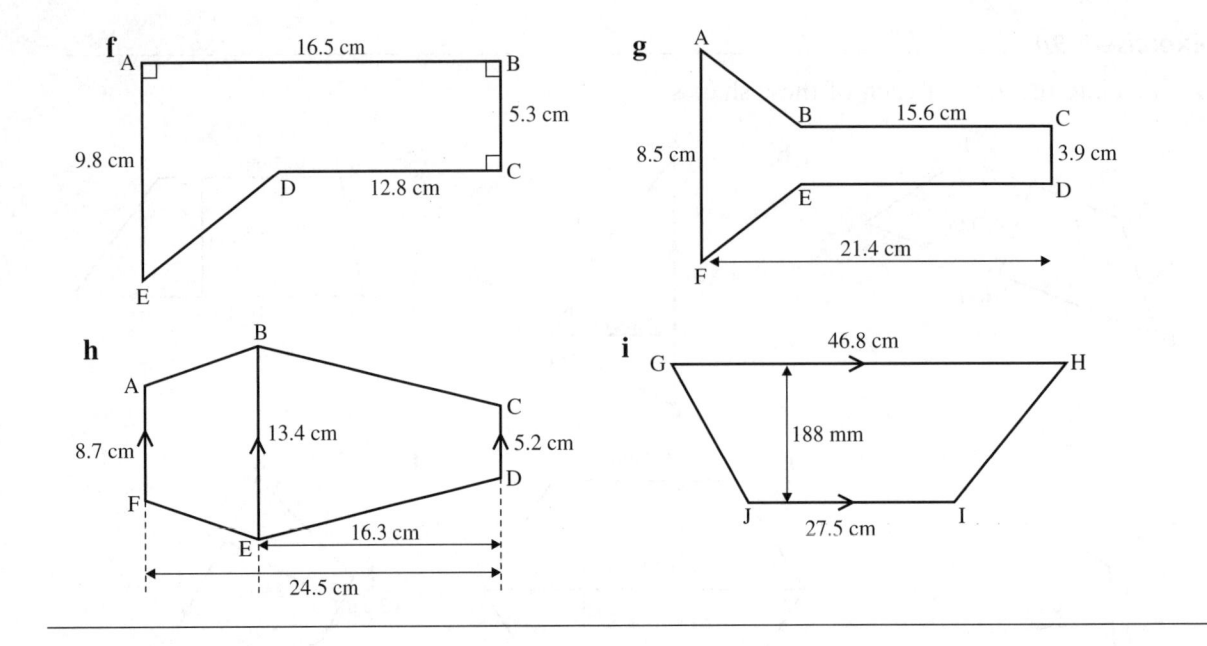

7.10 Formulae for length, area and volume*

When you are using formulae for length, area and volume it is important to know that the formula is of the right type. Here are some useful guides.

- Adding or subtracting two lengths gives a length.
- Adding or subtracting two areas gives an area.
- Adding or subtracting two volumes gives a volume.
- Multiply a length by a length and you get an area.
- Multiply three lengths and you get a volume.
- Square root an area and you get a length.
- Add, subtract, multiply or divide by a constant term and you get whichever of length, area or volume you started with.

Examples of constant terms are numbers such as 2, $\frac{1}{2}$, π, $\sqrt{3}$ etc.

Examples
If the letters y, v and w each represent a length, then:

$4w + y = 2v$ represents a **length**.
(Lengths $4w$, y and $2v$ are added and subtracted to give a length.)

$2y(3w + 5v)$ represents an **area**.
($2y$ is a length, $3w + 5v$ is a length and a length × a length gives an area.)

$3v(2yw + w^2)$ represents a **volume**.
($2yw$ is an area, w^2 is an area, add them and you get an area, this area is then multiplied by $3v$ which is a length, and an area × a length gives a volume.)

Exercise 7.10A

1 In each expression k, y and w each represent a length.
For each expression say if it represents a length, an area or a volume.

- **a** $2(3w + 4k - y)$
- **b** $0.5k(3w + 4y)$
- **c** $3.75(4w - 2k + y)$
- **d** $2.4k(y^2 + 2yw)$
- **e** $4kw - 3.6wy + 3ky$
- **f** $\frac{3}{5}w(k + 2w - 3y)$
- **g** $\frac{2}{3}wy(k - w)$
- **h** $\frac{3}{8}k^2(2w - 3k + y)$

2 The letters y, k and g each represent a length.
Explain why the expression $3(4k + kg - 2gky)$ does not represent a length, an area or a volume.

3 In this expression r and h each represent a length.
Explain why the expression $2\pi(r^2 + rh)$ represents the surface area of a cylinder of radius r and height h and not the volume of the cylinder.

Exercise 7.10B

1 In these expressions w, p and k each represent a length.
For each expression decide if it represents a length, an area or a volume.

- **a** $3w(2k - 5p)$
- **b** $\frac{2}{3}kw(p - k)$
- **c** $0.75k + w + 3.5p$
- **d** $0.2k^2(3p + k - 2.6w)$
- **e** $pw(3k + w + 0.2p)$
- **f** $\frac{1}{4}p^2(2w - k)$
- **g** $\frac{2}{3}k(w + 3p - k)$
- **h** $\frac{5}{8}(3w - 5k + p)$

2 In these expressions a, b and c are lengths.
Which expression represents an area?

$2\pi(3a - b) \quad \pi b^2(3a + 2c) \quad \pi a(3b - c) \quad \pi^2(3a - b + 2c)$

Remember:
π is a constant term.

3 If r and h each represents a length then explain why
$\sqrt{(r^2 + h^2 - 2\pi rh)}$ represents a length.

7.11 Nets of cuboids and similar solids

▶ A net is a group of joined polygons that folds to make a solid.
▶ To draw a net:
  - think about how many faces the solid has
  - think about what faces are joined to each other
  - sketch the net and check that edges that will join are of equal length.

180 Measures and construction

Example
Draw a net for cuboid A.

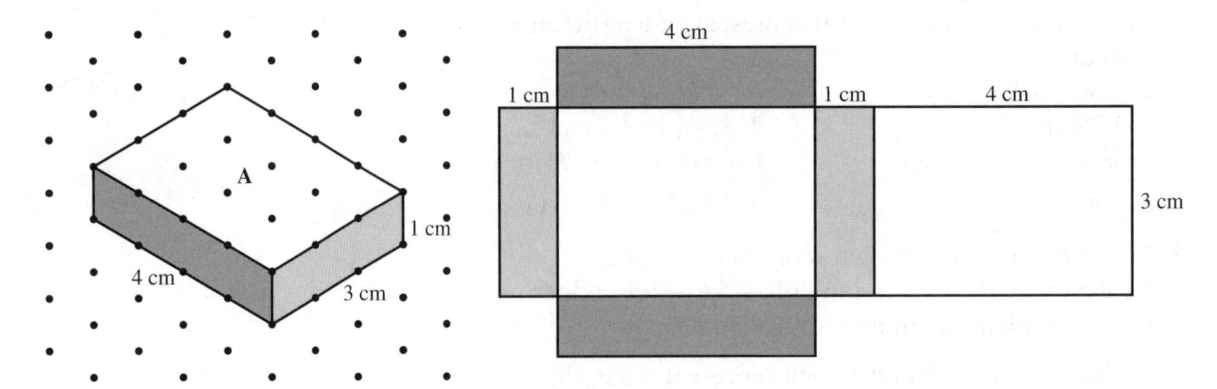

The cuboid has 6 faces so the net must have 6 faces.

Exercise 7.11A

1 Here is one net for a cube with sides of 1 cm. Other nets are possible. Draw as many different nets as you can for the same cube.

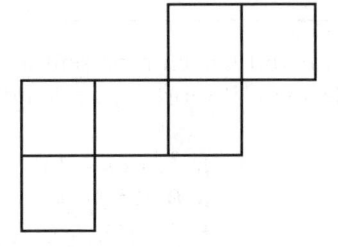

2 One net for cuboid A is shown in the example above.

Draw a different net for the same cuboid.

3 Draw a net for cuboid B.

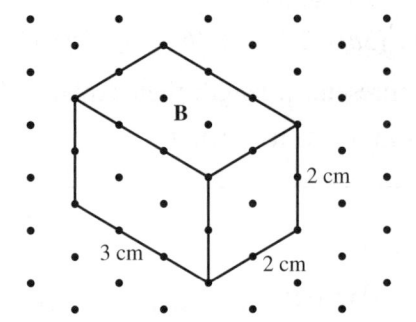

4 A pile of 144 centimetre cubes is to be packed in a cuboidal box.
  a Sketch the box with the smallest possible surface area.
  b Draw a net for this box.

5 Using sketches of nets show that it is impossible to have a cuboid with four square faces and two oblong faces.

Note:
An oblong is a rectangle that is not a square i.e. with unequal sides. A rectangle can be either a square or an oblong.

Exercise 7.11B

1 Draw a net of cuboid A.

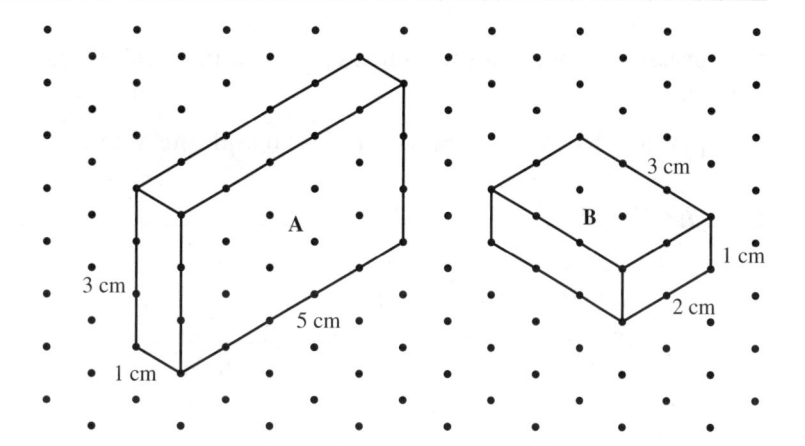

2 Draw a net for cuboid B.

3 Which of these are not true nets of cuboids?
Give reasons for your answers.

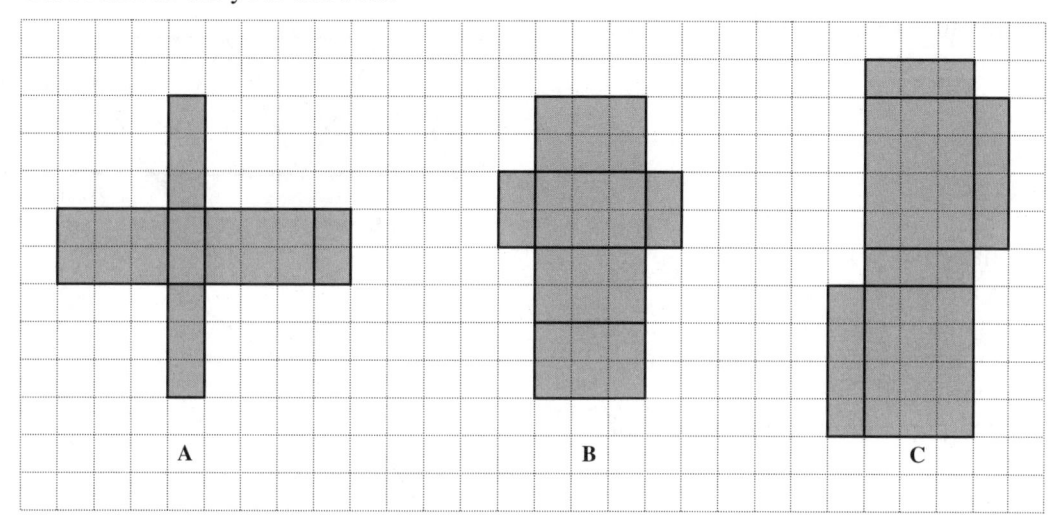

4 These solids are cuboids with steps taken out of them.
Sketch nets for each solid.

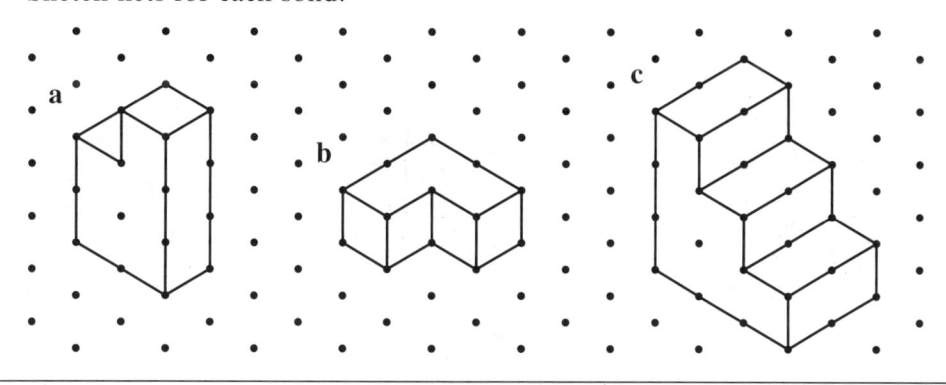

7.12 Nets of prisms and pyramids

▶ A **prism** is a solid with the same cross-section through its length.

▶ A **pyramid** has a base that is a polygon and one apex.

Exercise 7.12A

1 This shows how four equilateral triangles can be used to make the net of a tetrahedron.
   a Copy the diagram onto isometric paper, cut it out and fold to check what a tetrahedron looks like.
   b Draw as many ways as you can of joining four equilateral triangles.
   c Label each one as to whether it is the net of a tetrahedron or not.
   d How many nets can you find?

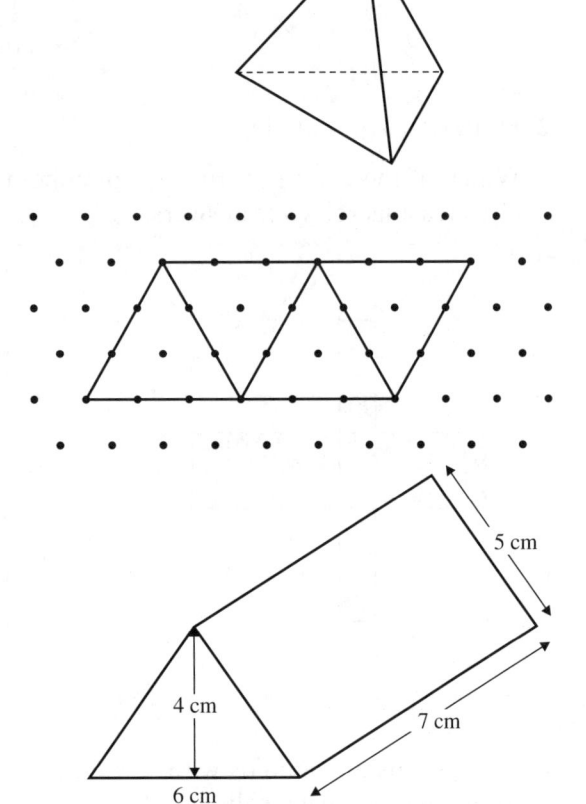

2 Here is a triangular prism.
   Each end is an isosceles triangle.
   a How many faces has the solid?
   b Describe the shapes and dimensions of the different faces.
   c On squared paper draw a full-size net of the prism.

Exercise 7.12B

1 This shows a square-based pyramid.
   The triangle is the true size of a sloping face.
   a By tracing the triangular face, draw a net of the pyramid.
   b Draw a different net for the same pyramid.

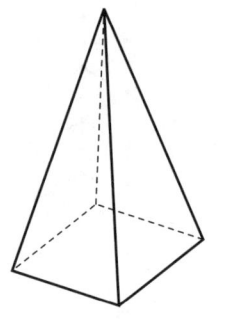

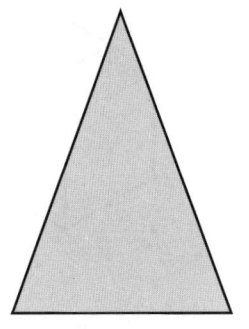

2

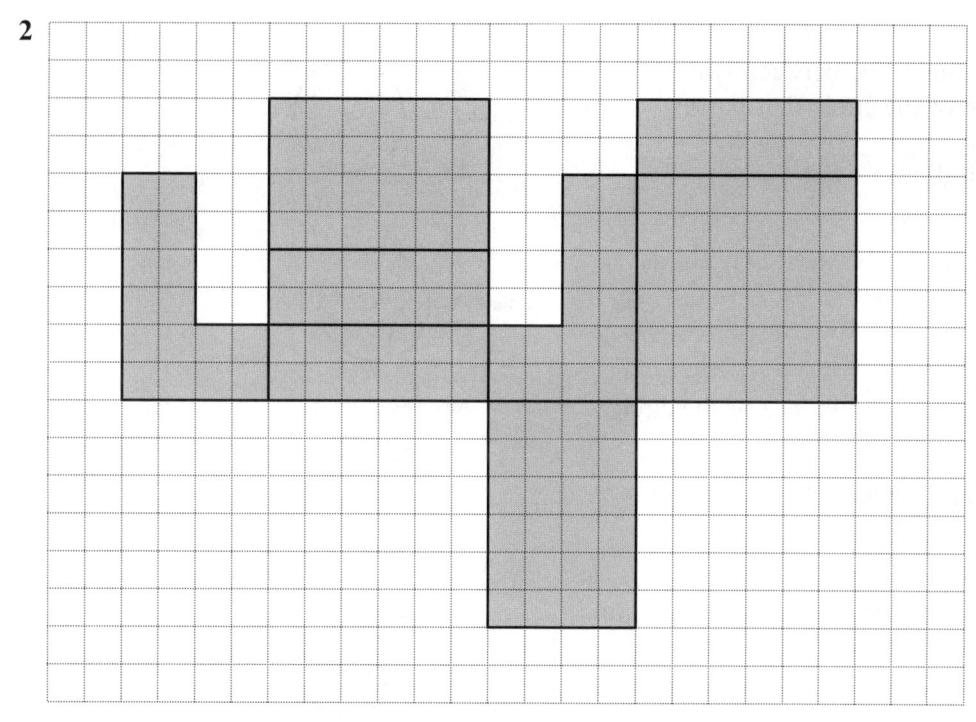

This is a net of a prism.
- **a** Copy the net onto square grid paper.
- **b** Fold to make the solid.
- **c** Describe the shape of the solid.
- **d** Make a different net for the same solid.

7.13 The language of the circle

A circle is a closed curve.
Any point on a circle is an equal distance away from a fixed point, called the centre.
You need to know these terms:

Circumference
The circumference is the distance around the edge of the circle.

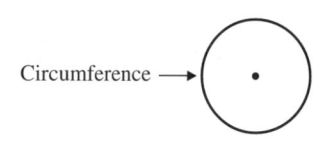

Radius (plural radii)
The radius of a circle is the distance from the centre to the edge in a straight line.

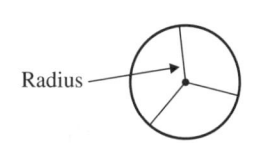

Diameter
A diameter is a straight line between two points on the edge of the circle that passes through the centre.
Diameter = 2 × Radius

Chord
A chord is a straight line between two points on the edge of the circle

Arc
An arc is part of the circumference of the circle.

Sector
A sector is the shape made by two radii and an arc.

Segment
A segment is the shape made by a chord and an arc of the circle.

Semicircle
A semicircle is one half of a circle made by cutting it along a diameter.

Tangent
A tangent is a straight line that touches the circle at one point. AB is a tangent.
At any point on the circumference of a circle, the tangent and radius meet at right angles.

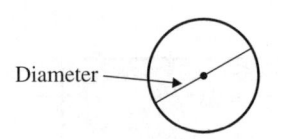

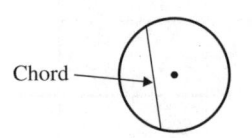

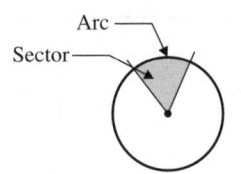

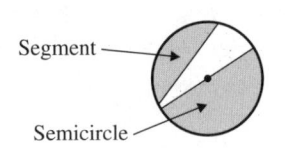

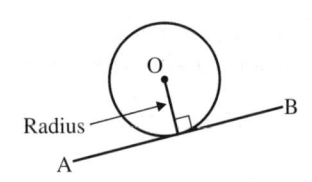

To calculate the circumference of a circle

The formula used to calculate the circumference of a circle is:

Circumference = π × Diameter

For π use either:
π = 3.142
π = $\frac{22}{7}$
or the value of π given by your calculator.

Example
Calculate the circumference of a circle with a diameter of 5.8 cm.

Circumference = π × Diameter
Circumference = π × 5.8
Circumference = 18.2 (to 1 dp)

As π is only approximate give your answer to the same accuracy as the measurements in the question.

The circumference of the circle is 18.2 cm (to 1 dp).

Exercise 7.13A

1 Calculate the circumference of each circle.

a 7.4 cm

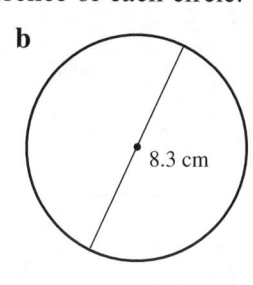

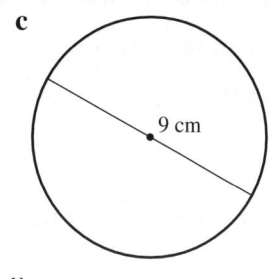

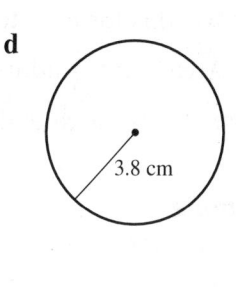

b 8.3 cm

c 9 cm

d 3.8 cm

2 Calculate the circumference of a circle with a diameter of 6.5 cm.

3 A circle has a diameter of 12.7 cm, calculate its circumference.

4 A circle has a radius of 4.6 cm.
   a Calculate the diameter of the circle.
   b Calculate the circumference of the circle.

5 Calculate the circumference of a circle of radius 7.5 cm.

Exercise 7.13B

1 Calculate the circumference of a circle with a diameter of 11.5 cm.

2 A semicircle has a diameter of 0.6 metres, find its perimeter.

3 A circle with a circumference of 12.5 metres has a diameter of about 4 metres. Is this true? Explain your answer.

4 The long hand of a clock is 8.4 cm long.
   a Show this on a diagram.
   b In one hour what shape does the tip of the hand follow?
   c Calculate the distance travelled by the tip of the hand in one hour.
   d Calculate the distance (in km) travelled by the tip in a leap year.

5 A circle has a circumference of 25 metres.
Calculate the diameter of the circle.
Give your answer to 1 dp.

7.14 To calculate the area of a circle

You use this formula to calculate the area of a circle.

$$\text{Area} = \pi \times \text{Radius}^2 \quad \text{or} \quad A = \pi r^2$$

where A is the area and r is the radius.

For π use either:
$\pi = 3.142$
$\pi = \frac{22}{7}$
or the value of π given by your calculator.

Example
Calculate the area of a circle with radius 4.6 cm.

$\text{Area} = \pi \times r^2$
$\text{Area} = \pi \times 21.16$
$\text{Area} = 66.476\ldots$

The area of the circle is 66.5 cm² (to 1 dp).

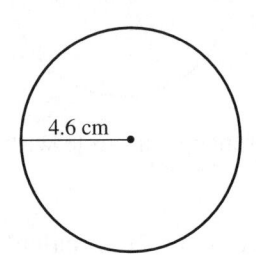

Exercise 7.14A

1 Calculate the area of a circle with radius 5.8 cm.

2 Calculate the area of each circle.

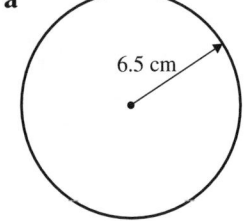

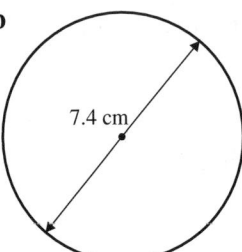

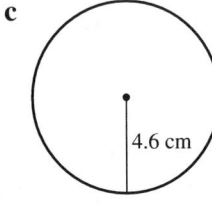

a 6.5 cm   b 7.4 cm   c 4.6 cm

3 Calculate the area of a circle with radius 7 cm. Use $\pi = \frac{22}{7}$ and show all working.

4 A plastic disc is cut from a 10 cm square sheet.
  a Calculate the area of the square sheet.
  b Find the radius of the disc.
  c Calculate the area of the wasted plastic left over.

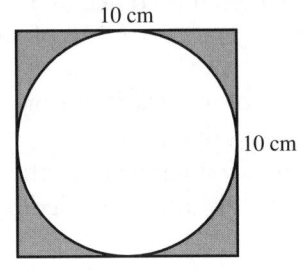

Exercise 7.14B

1 Calculate the area of a circle with:
  a radius 12.4 metres   b diameter 55 metres   c radius 0.62 metres

2 Calculate the area of a circle of radius 14 cm. Use $\pi = \frac{22}{7}$ and show all working.

3 Calculate the area of each shape.

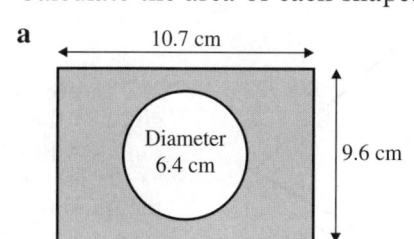

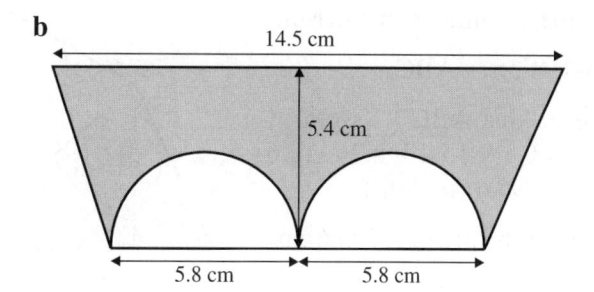

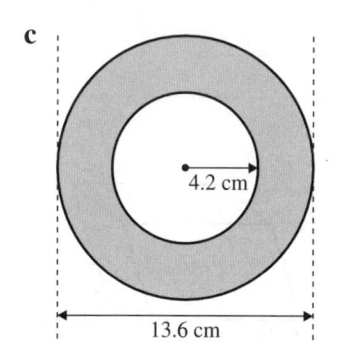

a
10.7 cm
Diameter 6.4 cm
9.6 cm

b
14.5 cm
5.4 cm
5.8 cm   5.8 cm

c
4.2 cm
13.6 cm

4 The diagram shows a strip of aluminium foil.
Discs have been cut from the strip to make tops for milk bottles.

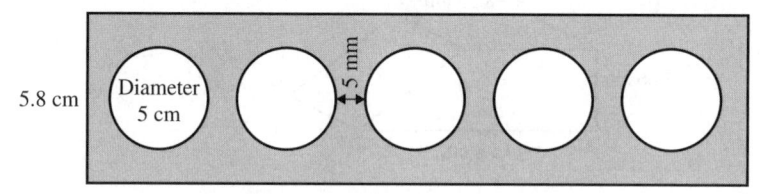

5.8 cm
Diameter 5 cm
5 mm

a Calculate the radius of one of these discs.
b Calculate the area of foil used for a milk bottle top.
c The area of foil wasted after the five discs have been cut out.

7.15 Volume

The volume of a 3-D shape is a measure of how much space is taken up by the shape.
Volume is given in cubed units: cm³, m³, km³.
The formula for the volume of a cuboid is

Volume = length × width × height

or $V = l \times w \times h$

> V stands for volume,
> l stands for length,
> w stands for width,
> h stands for height.

To calculate the volume of a cuboid *or* a prism you can use this formula:

Volume = Area of cross-section × length

Example

Calculate the volume of this prism.

The cross-section is ABC.

Volume = Area ABC × length
Volume = 0.5 × 15.4 × 8.2 × 12.6
Volume = 795.6 (to 1 dp)

The volume of the prism is 795.6 cm³ (to 1 dp).

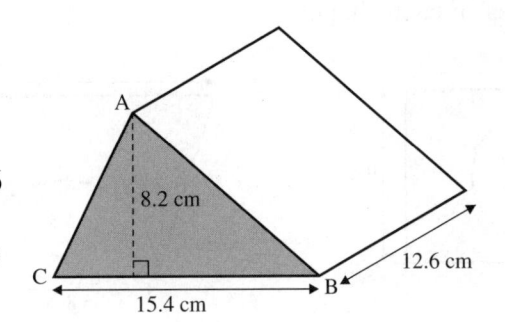

The answer is given to the same accuracy as the data in the question.

Exercise 7.15A

1 Calculate the volume of each prism. Give your answer to 1 dp.

a 8.04 cm, 7.65 cm, 9.61 cm

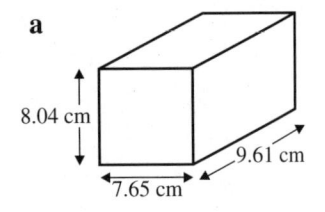

b 6.88 cm, 5.75 cm, 8.16 cm

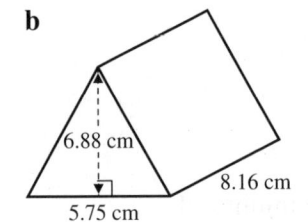

c 9.16 cm, 10.75 cm, 11.67 cm

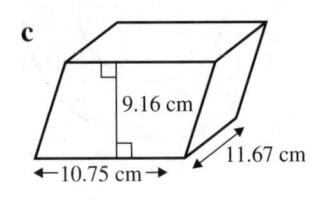

d 16.45 cm, 8.2 cm, 21.7 cm, 12.75 cm

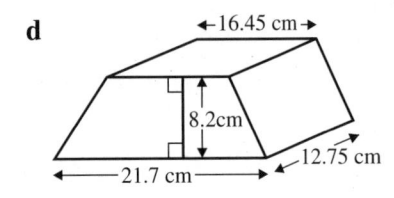

e 8.25 cm, 7.66 cm, 15.8 cm, 4.7 cm

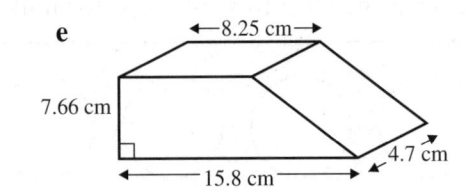

Exercise 7.15B

1 Calculate the volume of each prism. Give your answers to 1 dp.

a 8.18 cm, 9.75 cm, 5.82 cm

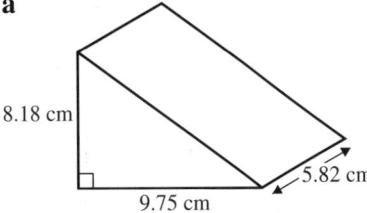

b 14.6 cm, 5.8 cm, 9.72 cm

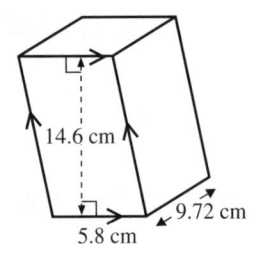

c 5.93 cm, 4.88 cm, 2.54 cm, 3.62 cm

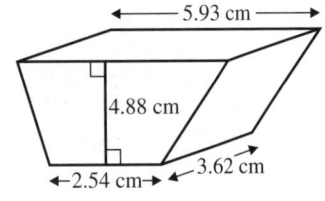

d 76 mm, 16 mm, 54 mm

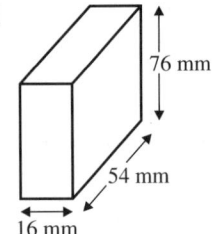

e Diameter 12.4 cm, 6.62 cm

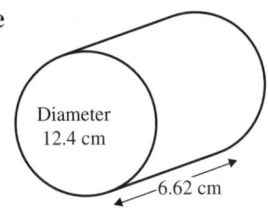

7.16 Surface area

The surface area of a 3-D shape is the total area of all its faces.
When you look at a 3-D shape some of its faces might be the same.

Example 1
Calculate the surface area of this cuboid.

The cuboid has 6 rectangular faces.

2 rectangles measure 7.6 cm × 6.7 cm
The area of these is 7.6 × 6.7 × 2 = 101.84

2 rectangles measure 6.7 cm × 15.4 cm
The area of these is 6.7 × 15.4 × 2 = 206.36

2 rectangles measure 7.6 cm × 15.4 cm
The area of these is 7.6 × 15.4 × 2 = 234.08

The total surface area is 101.84 + 206.36 + 234.08 = 542.28
The total surface is: 542.3 cm^2 (to 1 dp).

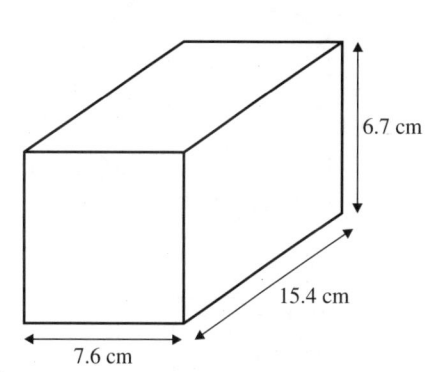

Example 2
Calculate the surface area of this prism.

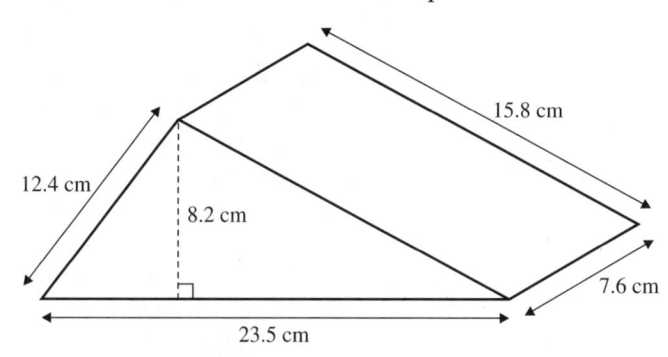

The prism has 5 faces.

2 are triangles each with an area 0.5 cm × 8.2 cm × 23.5 cm
The area of these is: 2 × 0.5 × 8.2 × 23.5 = 192.7

One rectangle measures 7.6 cm × 15.8 cm
The area of this is 7.6 × 15.8 = 120.08

One rectangle measures 7.6 cm × 12.4 cm
The area of this is 7.6 × 12.4 = 94.24

One rectangle measures 7.6 cm × 23.5 cm
The area of this is 7.6 × 23.5 = 178.6

The total surface area is 192.7 + 120.08 + 94.24 + 178.6 = 585.62
The total surface is 585.6 cm^2 (to 1 dp)

Exercise 7.16A

1 Calculate the surface area of each cuboid and prism.

a 30 mm, 50 mm, 40 mm, 82 mm

b 5.94 cm, 12.75 cm, 6.82 cm

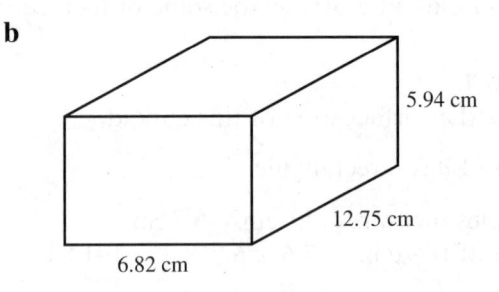

c 7.60 cm, 9.66 cm, 5.38 cm, 4.08 cm, 8.66 cm

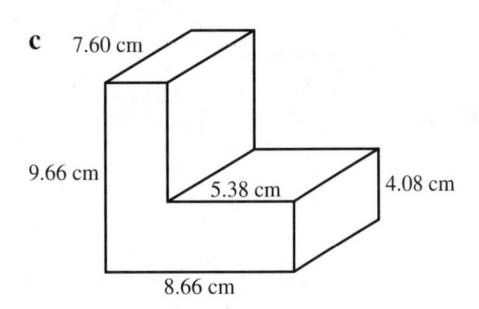

d 13 m, 14 m, 9 m, 12 m, 16.5 cm

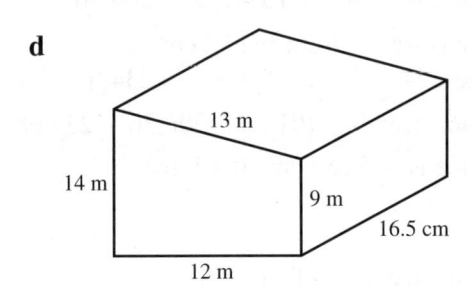

Exercise 7.16B

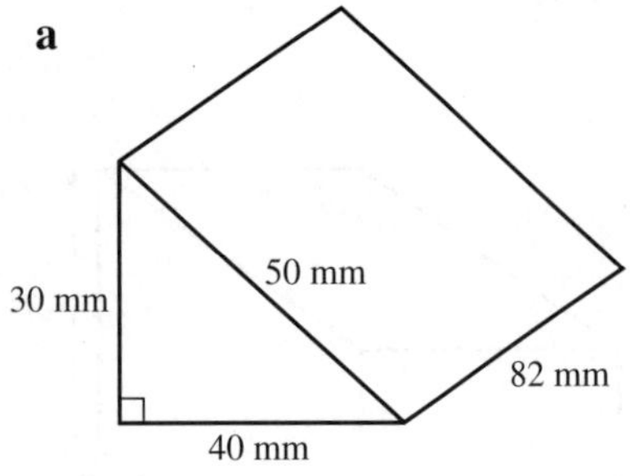

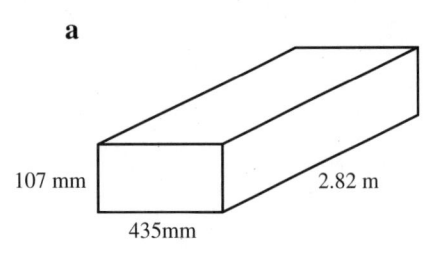

1 Calculate the surface area of each cuboid and prism.

a 107 mm, 435 mm, 2.82 m

b 110.9 mm, 128 mm, 128 mm, 875 mm, 64 mm

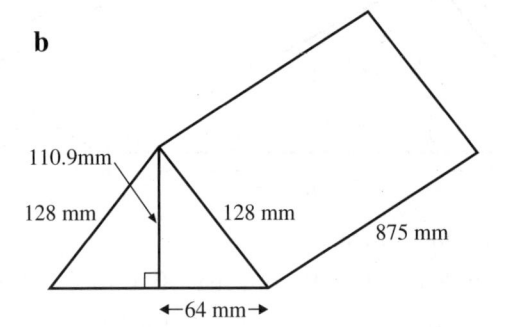

c 2.72 m, 6.16 m, 5.6 m, 6.35 m, 8.65 m, 3.8 m

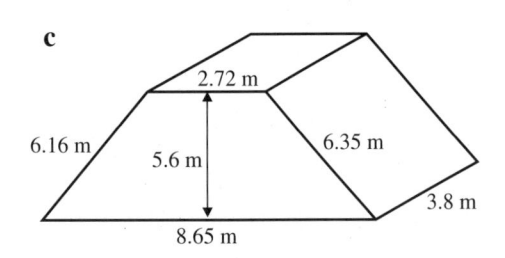

d 4 cm, 29.9 cm, 34.6 cm, 5.85 cm, 11.6 cm, 12.5 cm

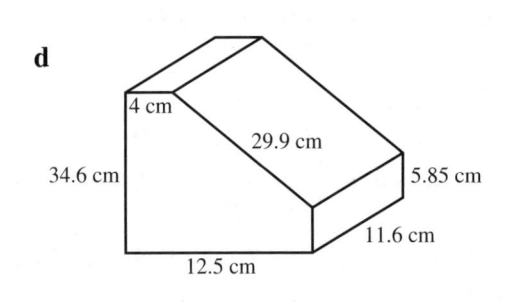

7.17 Loci

▶ A **locus** shows where a set of points satisfies a given condition. For example the locus of points 1 cm from the point A is a circle with radius 1 cm – all points on the circumference are 1 cm from A.

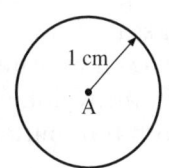

▶ The locus of points 2 cm from the line BC is shaped like this.

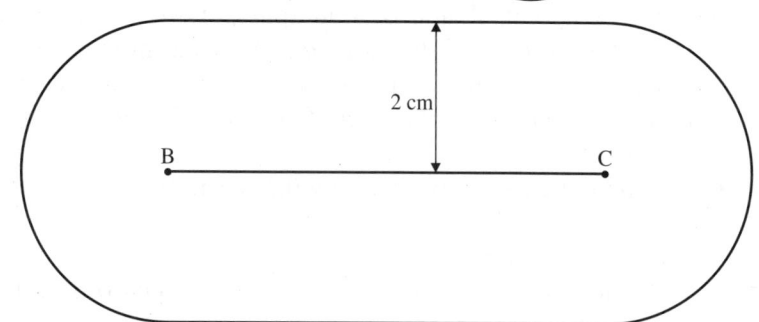

▶ **Loci** can be used to solve some problems. Loci is the plural of locus.

Example
Fierce dog D is tied by a 3 metre chain to point P.
Dog E is on a 2 metre chain but its end can slide along the rail QR.
Show the locus of points each dog can reach and the region where they might fight.
Use a scale of 1 cm = 1 metre.

The shading shows the region where the dogs could meet and might fight.

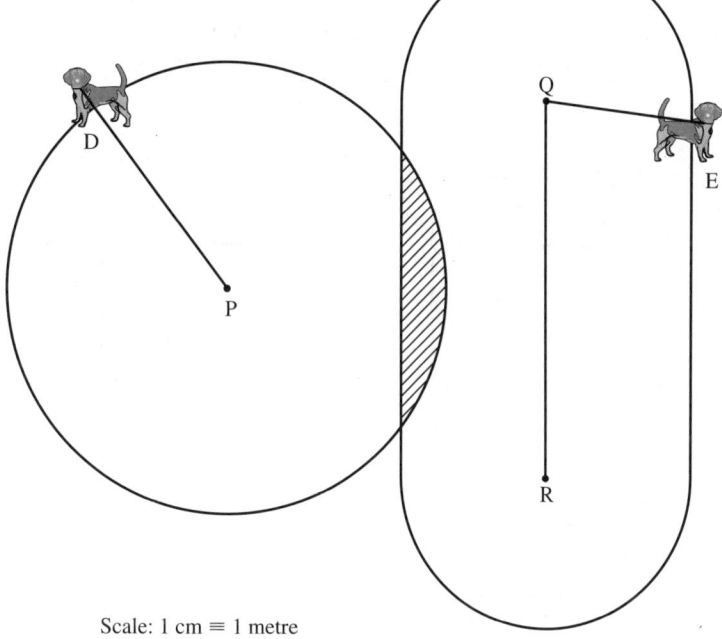

Scale: 1 cm ≡ 1 metre

Exercise 7.17A

1 a Mark a point P. Draw the locus of points 4 cm from P.
  b Mark a point Q on this locus. Now draw the locus of points 3 cm from Q.
  c Shade the region that is less than 4 cm from P and less than 3 cm from Q.

192 Measures and construction

2 Two TV transmitters, T_1 and T_2 are 400 km apart.
T_1 has a range of 250 km and T_2 a range of 300 km.
  a Make a scale drawing of the positions of the transmitters and the area each transmits to. Use a scale of 1 cm = 100 km.
  b Shade in the region where people can receive TV pictures from both transmitters.

3 a Mark two points A and B, 4 cm apart, and join them by a straight line.
  b Draw the locii of points 3 cm from A and 3 cm from B. Mark the two points of intersection of these locii with dots.
  c Draw the locii of points 3.5 cm from A and B and mark similar dots.
  d Continue increasing the radii by 0.5 cm up to 5 cm and mark the dots.
  e Join up all the dots.
  f What do you notice about this line and its relationship to the line AB?

Exercise 7.17B

1 Copy each of these shapes onto squared paper.
Draw the locus of points 1 cm from each shape.

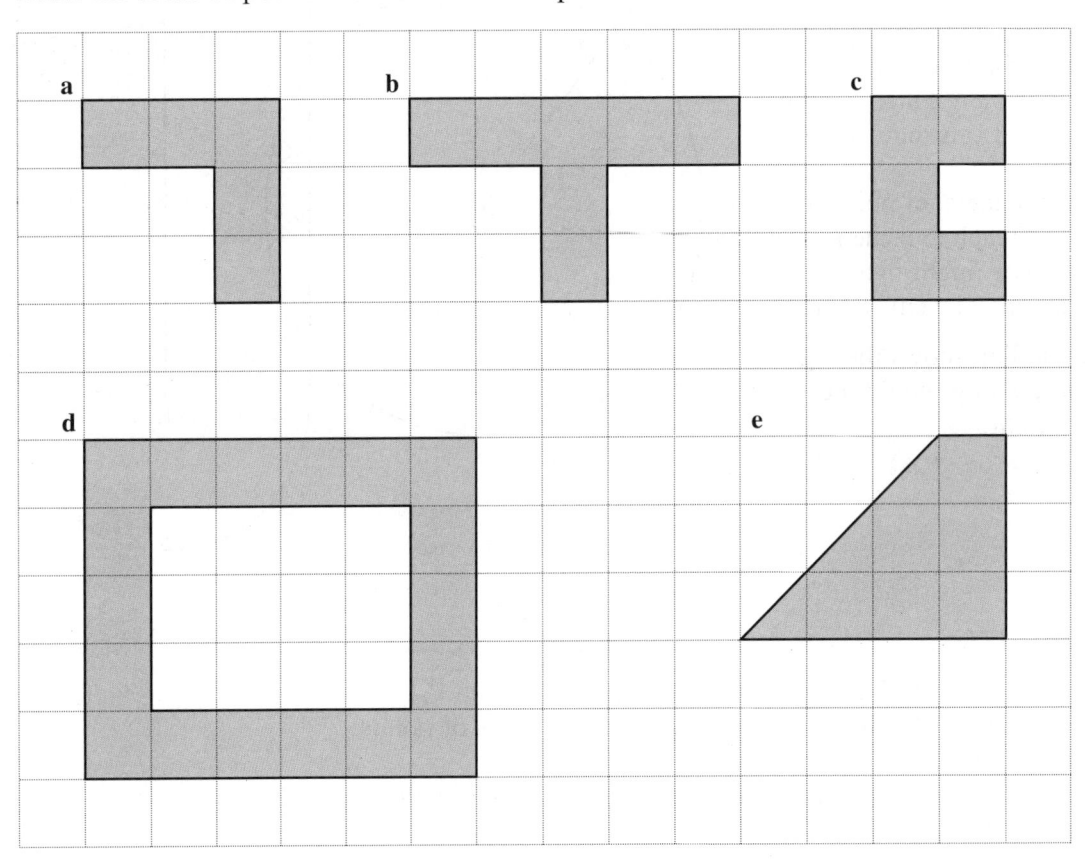

2 A rectangular field is 250 metres by 150 metres. In the centre of the field is a large circular pond of radius 50 metres. A timid horse grazes in the field. It will not graze within 10 metres of a boundary nor within 20 metres of the pond.
  a Make a scale drawing using a scale of your choice and shade the regions in which the horse is prepared to graze.
  b The owner succeeds in making the horse less frightened of ponds. Within what distance must the horse be prepared to graze from the pond for the two grazing regions to just join into one?

3 Four people are making footprints in the sand. Salif and Lisa are walking in straight lines at an angle of 60° to each other.
  a Mark is walking so that he is always an equal distance from Salif and Lisa. Copy the diagram and show the path Mark takes.
  b Sanjit walks so that the distance to Lisa is always twice the distance to Salif. Show and label Sanjit's path on your diagram.

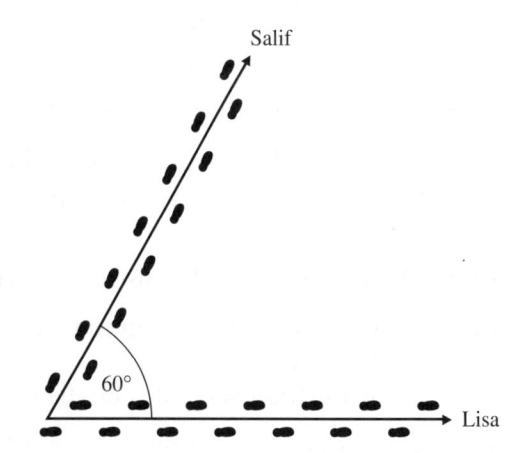

Revision exercise 7   *Review*

1 Give each of these lengths in centimetres.
  a 338 mm   **b** 3.24 m   **c** 4 inches   **d** 2 feet   *Unit 7.1*

2 Give each of these weights in grams.
  a 3.6 kg   **b** 1.22 kg   **c** 0.68 kg   **d** 0.045 kg   *Unit 7.1*

3 A tank holds 25 Imperial gallons.
   Roughly how many litres is this?   *Unit 7.1*

4 The distance between two radio masts is 6.5 miles.
  a How many feet is this?
  b Roughly how many kilometres apart are the masts?
  c What is the distance between the masts to the nearest 1000 yards?   *Unit 7.1*

5 A generator is run for $8\frac{3}{4}$ hours and it uses 3185 litres of fuel.
   How many litres per hour is this?   *Unit 7.2*

6 A vehicle travels 997.5 metres in 15 seconds.
   Calculate the speed of the vehicle in m/s.   *Unit 7.2*

7 A fishing boat uses $5\frac{1}{4}$ gallons of fuel per hour. *Review*
   Roughly how many ml of fuel per second is this? *Unit 7.2*

8 Construct a regular octagon. *Unit 7.3*

9 A triangle has a base of 6.5 cm and base angles of 66° and 54°.
   a Construct the triangle accurately.
   b Measure the lengths of the other two sides.
   c Measure the third angle in the triangle.
      Explain how you can check if your answer is correct. *Unit 7.4*

10 a Draw an angle of 135°.
   b Bisect the angle using a ruler and a pair of compasses. *Unit 7.5*

11 a Draw a line 5.7 cm long.
   b Bisect the line using a ruler and a pair of compasses. *Unit 7.5*

12 a Draw any triangle and label it ABC.
   b From each vertex construct a perpendicular to the
      side opposite. *Unit 7.6*

13 Explain the four conditions for congruent triangles. *Unit 7.7*

14 a Draw a diagram in which there are two triangles that
      are congruent.
   b Shade the triangles and state the reason for their congruence. *Unit 7.7*

15 Explain what is meant by the perimeter of a 2-D shape. *Unit 7.8*

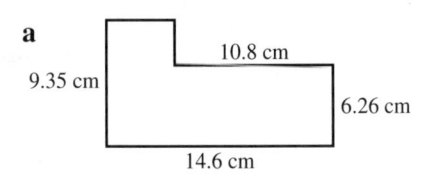

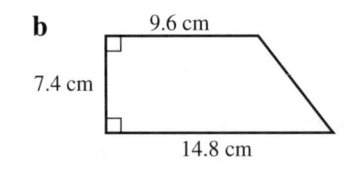

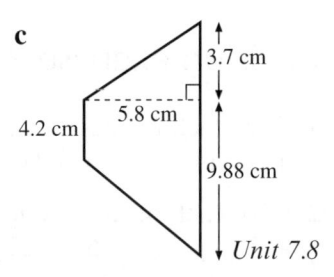

16 Calculate the perimeter of each shape.

   a (shape with 9.35 cm, 10.8 cm, 6.26 cm, 14.6 cm)
   b (shape with 9.6 cm, 7.4 cm, 14.8 cm)
   c (shape with 3.7 cm, 4.2 cm, 5.8 cm, 9.88 cm) *Unit 7.8*

17 Calculate the area of each shape.

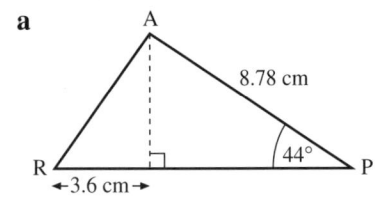

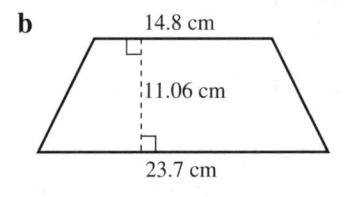

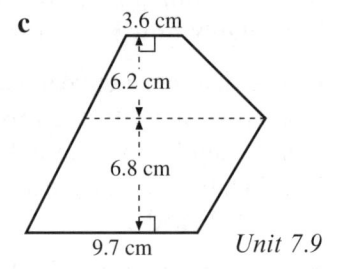

   a Triangle with A, R, P; 8.78 cm, 44°, 3.6 cm
   b Trapezium with 14.8 cm, 11.06 cm, 23.7 cm
   c Shape with 3.6 cm, 6.2 cm, 6.8 cm, 9.7 cm *Unit 7.9*

18 In each expression w, x and y each represent a length.
   For each expression say if it represents a length, an
   area or a volume.
   a $2x(w^2 + 3xy)$ b $2\pi(0.5wx^2 + y^2x)$
   c $2.8(3x + 5y - 4w)$ d $3w^2(4x - y)$ *Unit 7.10*

19 You are asked to make a 1 to 6 dice from a sheet of card.
Draw and label a net you would use for the dice.

Review
Unit 7.11

20 A box in the shape of a cuboid is to be made to hold 36 stock cubes. Each stock cube is a 1 cm cube.
Draw accurately the nets of two possible boxes for the 36 cubes.

Unit 7.11

21 A student drew a net for a cuboid and it was wrongly marked. When the net was cut out it did not fold into a cuboid.
Sketch what this net might have been.

Unit 7.11

22 A triangular prism is 8 cm long and its cross-section is an equilateral triangle of side 5 cm.
Make an accurate drawing of a net for this prism.

Unit 7.12

23 With diagrams, explain the difference between a sector and a segment of a circle.

Unit 7.13

24 Calculate the circumference of a circle of radius 6.8 cm.

Unit 7.13

25 Calculate the area of a circle of diameter 28.5 cm.

Unit 7.14

26 A cuboid has dimensions of 16 cm × 22 cm × 38 mm.
Calculate the volume and surface area of the cuboid.

Unit 7.15

27 Calculate the volume and surface area of a cylinder of diameter 12.4 cm and height 16.5 cm.

Unit 7.16

28 Use an example to explain what the term *locus* means.

Unit 7.17

29 a Mark two points A, B 6 cm apart and join them with a straight line.
  b Draw the locus of points 2.5 cm from A.
  c Draw the locus of points 3 cm from AB.

Unit 7.17

30 a On squared paper draw a rectangle that is 6 cm × 8 cm.
  b Draw the locus of points 4 cm from the edge of the rectangle.
  c Calculate the area inside the locus.

Unit 7.17

Investigation

Aromatic pyramid

Perfume is sold in bottles that are a square-based pyramid.

Each bottle is packed in a box that is a 5 cm cube.

Make a model of the largest bottle that will fit in the box.

Prove your solution by also making the box.

8 Planning and Collecting Data

8.1 Collecting data

Data is information. It often involves counting, or it may involve measuring a length, a weight or a time.

Before you collect data you need to decide what you want to find out.

Then you have to decide how to collect the data.
There are a number of ways to do this.
One way is to design a data collection sheet. It might look like this:

Southway Sports Centre
Western Avenue
Crofton
CR6 9BY

NEW MEMBER

Name _____

Address _____

Post code ☐☐☐☐☐☐   Telephone ☐☐☐☐☐☐☐☐☐☐☐

Please debit my Access/Visa Card by the amount of £ _____

Card number ☐☐☐☐☐☐☐☐☐☐☐☐☐

Expiry date ☐☐/☐☐

Or   I enclose a cheque made payable to SSC for the amount of £ _____

I wish my membership to start on ☐☐☐☐☐ (Date)

Signature

Date ☐☐/☐☐/☐☐

For Centre use only   Membership number ☐☐☐☐☐☐

This data collection form is a quick and easy way to record and hold data.

The important thing is that it collects data on the same things from everyone.

Exercise 8.1A

1 List all different pieces of data collected by this sheet.

2 Which piece of data on the form is not collected from the new member?

3 Design a data collection sheet that could be used to order T-shirts by post.
The sizes are, L and XL, they cost £8.99 each, and they can be red, yellow or blue.

Exercise 8.1B

1 Design a data collection sheet for people booking seats at a cinema by post.
The seats cost £4.75, £5.25 or £6.50.
Showings are at 1600, 1900, 2150 and 0100.

2 Imagine you run a long-stay car park charging £3.85 per day. Design a data collection sheet to send out to customers who want to book a space.

You can design a data collection sheet where questions have to be answered.

The simplest type is where you just answer Yes or No.

> You must think carefully about the questions you will ask.

Customer Choices

1. Are you over 30 years of age?
2. Do you shop everyday?
3. Do you always buy bread when you visit this Supermarket?
4. Do you have a Saver Card?
5. Do you use our delivery service?
6. Do you have children?
7.

Exercise 8.1C

1 Design five more questions that might be on the Customer Choices sheet.

2 Why are these questions no good for the Customer Choices sheet?
   a How often do you eat fish?
   b Do you like fish?

3 Design five Yes/No questions for data collection about how people travel to work.

Exercise 8.1D

1 Why is this not a good Yes/No question on a travel to work data sheet?

   Can you ride a bike?   Yes/No

2 You want to pick out customers in their 20s in your data:
   a Why is 'How old are you?' not a good question?
   b Write a better question. Give reasons why you think it is better.

3 Design five Yes/No questions for data collection about what people watch on TV.

You can use a data collection sheet that has questions and multi-choice lists.

> 5. Which of these TV channels do you watch most?
>
>   Please tick only one box.
>
>   BBC 1   ☐
>
>   BBC 2   ☐
>
>   Channel 4 ☐
>
>   Other   ☐

Exercise 8.1E

1 Design two other multi-choice questions to collect data from TV viewers.

2 Design three multi-choice questions to collect data about travel to school.

Exercise 8.1F

1. Design three multi-choice questions to collect data about home computers.

2. Design five multi-choice questions to collect data on a subject of your choice.

8.2 Frequency tables

The data you collect is often put into a table. This is called a **frequency table**.

> A frequency table shows how frequently some event happened.

Exercise 8.2A

This frequency table gives results from a health survey.

Type of exercise taken

	Gym	Cycling	Walking	Running	Swimming	None
Females	12	8	44	7	17	22
Males	37	4	8	15	11	25

1. How many females exercised by cycling?

2. How many males took no exercise?

3. What was the most popular type of exercise taken:
   a by the females?
   b by the males?

4. Roughly what fraction of the females chose walking or running?

5. Roughly what fraction of all the males took some type of exercise?

6. For females which type of exercise is roughly four times as popular as the gym?

Exercise 8.2B

This frequency table gives data about visits to a supermarket in one week.

Number of visits

	1	2	3	4	More than 4
Females	6	34	25	11	14
Males	14	19	24	8	25

1 Can you compare the data for females and males in the table?
  Explain your answer.

2 From the frequency table showing visits to the supermarket in
  one week:
  a how many females visited the supermarket three times
  b how many males made less than three visits?

3 Roughly what fraction of the males made four visits in the one week?

4 What fraction of the females made two or four visits?

5 The local paper was given the data and they used this headline:

   Twice as many men visit the supermarket more than
   four times a week!

  a Is the headline accurate? Explain your answer.
  b Give reasons why you think more males than females made
    four or more visits in a week.

For widely spread data it can help to group the data.
When you group data into classes, each class should have the
same interval or size.
Classes of 1 to 5 and 6 to 10 are equal class sizes or have equal
class intervals.

> A class interval gives the spread of the class.
> A class of 1 to 5 has an interval of 4.
> A class of 6 to 10 has an interval of 4.

Example
This data gives the ages of people visiting a library.
Make a frequency table for the data using class intervals of:
11 to 20, 21 to 30, 31 to 40, 41 to 50, 51 to 60, 61 to 70, 71 to 80.

Age of people visiting the library

22, 35, 21, 18, 45, 62, 71, 19, 17, 19, 37, 44, 56, 58, 41,
63, 55, 20, 61, 48, 12, 19, 23, 48, 31, 54, 76, 39, 40, 55,
61, 72, 70, 17, 15, 14, 17, 19, 27, 31, 32, 37, 45, 67, 54,
19, 16, 14, 18, 63, 20, 60, 44, 71, 37, 16, 16, 21, 21, 30

Class	Tally	Frequency
11 to 20	⁣𝍩𝍩𝍩 IIII	19
21 to 30	𝍩 II	7
31 to 40	𝍩 IIII	9
41 to 50	𝍩 II	7
51 to 60	𝍩 II	7
61 to 70	𝍩 II	7
71 to 80	IIII	4

> The disadvantage of grouping the data is you cannot tell the frequency of a single piece of data. Here, you cannot say how many 15-year-olds visited the library.

Exercise 8.2C

1 This is data on lottery spending.

> **The amount spent by players on the Lottery in one shop**
>
> £1, £3, £4, £1, £4, £9, £3, £5, £5, £7, £1, £1, £1, £3, £12,
> £10, £4, £5, £1, £2, £2, £4, £7, £2, £5, £8, £10, £2, £1, £1,
> £1, £7, £15, £2, £2, £5, £3, £4, £1, £1, £1, £4, £5, £2, £3,
> £2, £1, £1, £4, £5, £10, £1, £1, £5, £1, £1, £8, £1, £2, £3

  a Make a grouped frequency table for the data.
Use groups of £1 to £4, £5 to £8, £9 to £12, £13 to £16.
  b Which class had the highest frequency?
  c Which class had the lowest frequency?

2 The data shows the number of passengers leaving each bus at the bus station.

    15, 2, 22, 34, 6, 8, 14, 15, 29, 1, 42, 38, 19, 7, 2, 4, 0, 19,
    51, 33, 25, 42, 18, 6, 21, 30, 47, 17, 19, 6, 18, 7, 9, 22, 46,
    20, 15, 7, 9, 54, 24, 16, 8, 3, 0, 9, 3, 35, 2, 17, 5, 6, 0, 0, 2

  a Make a grouped frequency table to show the data.
Use groups of: 0 to 9, 10 to 19, 20 to 29, 30 to 39, 40 to 49, 50 to 59.
  b How many buses had less than 30 passengers leaving at the bus station?
  c Which class had the highest frequency?

3 Use the data for question **2** above.
  a Make a grouped frequency table for the data.
Use groups of: 0 to 14, 15 to 29, 30 to 44, 45 to 59.
  b Which class had the lowest frequency?

4 Students were asked how long, in seconds, they spent cleaning their teeth. Here are the responses:

    16, 22, 25, 31, 40, 42, 12, 15, 26, 22, 34, 28, 19, 48,
    35, 27, 19, 50, 15, 22, 53, 18, 17, 29, 31, 28, 38, 42,
    19, 51, 39, 41, 35, 22, 15, 24, 39, 45, 25, 18, 17, 21,
    16, 29, 46, 52, 17, 35, 42, 8

  a Make a grouped frequency table for the data.
Use groups of: 1 to 10, 11 to 20, 21 to 30, 31 to 40, 51 to 60.
  b The frequency table shows the data for how many students?
  c Which class had the highest frequency?
  d Which class had the lowest frequency?
  e How many students spent less than 30 seconds cleaning their teeth?
  f Does this data give an accurate picture of how long the population of the UK spends cleaning their teeth?
Give reasons for your answer.

Exercise 8.2D

1 This data gives the length in cm after 72 days for beans planted at the same time.

> 8.6, 12.3, 5.8, 14.7, 4.2, 11.5, 17.6, 14.4, 15, 16.3,
> 11.7, 10, 8.2, 14.8, 16.5, 7.6, 15.8, 14.3, 9.8, 18.2,
> 16.3, 14.5, 13.8, 14, 12.6

  a Make a grouped frequency table for the data.
    Use groups of: 0 to 4 cm, 5 cm to 9 cm, 10 cm to 14 cm and 15 cm to 19 cm.
  b Which class had the highest frequency?

2 At a Customer Services desk the time taken in seconds to deal with each customer was recorded. This is the data for one shift:

> 12.5, 16, 23.4, 35.6, 9, 12.5, 44.8, 57.3, 15.5, 56.4, 42,
> 31.5, 38, 57.5, 78.4, 88, 23.5, 19, 12.6, 26.5, 67.2, 74.3, 14,
> 27.8, 35.2, 63, 59, 72, 28.5

  a Make a grouped frequency table for the data.
    Use groups of: 0 to 9 s, 10 s to 19 s, 20 s to 29 s, ..., ..., 80 s to 89 s.
  b Which class had the highest frequency?
  c Which class had a frequency of 3?
  d How many customers were dealt with in less than 40 seconds?
  e Make a different grouped frequency table for the data.
    Use groups 0 to 19 s, 20 s to 39 s, 40 s to 59 s, ..., ..., 80 s to 99 s.
  f Which class has a frequency of 6 in this frequency table?
  g Make a different grouped frequency table for the data.
    This time choose groups of your own.
  h In this frequency table which class has the highest frequency?
  i Does the data give an accurate picture of how long Customer Services take to deal with a customer?
    Give reasons for your answer.

8.3 Questionnaires

A **questionnaire** is a set of questions designed to collect data.

Before you design a questionnaire you must decide:
- the exact purpose of the survey and each question
- the order in which to put the questions.

When you design your questions you should try to control the answers given by people to the questionnaire.

> Planning is important if the data you collect is to be useful. You might want to test your questions before you use them as part of your set.

These are examples of questions and how the answers can be better controlled:

Question   What snacks do you buy?

This is very open-ended and you could get any number of answers.
A better question would be:

Question   Which of these snacks do you buy most often?

    Crisps ☐   Sweets ☐   Nuts ☐

    Fries ☐   Burger ☐   Other ☐

    Please tick one.

Question   When do you buy snacks?

This is also open ended as you may get answers like:
'When I'm hungry'.
A better question would be:

Question   When do you buy most snacks?
    Time
    08.00–10.00   10.00–12.00   12.00–14.00
    14.00–16.00   16.00–18.00   18.00–20.00

    Please tick one.

Exercise 8.3A

1 'Where do you buy your snacks?'
   This is not a good question to ask.
   Write an improved question to collect data on where snacks are bought.

2 One hundred people were asked:
   'How much do you spend in a day on snacks?'
   a Explain why this may not be a good question to ask.
   b Write an improved question to collect data on how much is spent on snacks.

3 a Write a set of six questions for a survey on:
       The TV watching habits of students
   b How many students would you need to ask to give a reasonable picture of TV watching habits?
   Explain your answer.

Exercise 8.3B

1 'Why do you like team games?'
  a Explain why this might not be a good question to ask?
  b Write an improved question to collect this data.

2 a Write a set of questions to be used in a survey of:
    The sporting activity of students
  b How many students would you need to ask to give a reasonable picture of the sporting activity of students?

Revision exercise 8   *Review*

1 Imagine you run a bicycle hire service at a holiday resort. Design a data collection sheet to use with hirers.   *Unit 8.1*

2 Fine Pizzas decide to set up a home delivery service. Design a data collection sheet to be used when a pizza is ordered to be delivered.   *Unit 8.1*

3 Design five Yes/No questions to be used in data collection about how a cinema in a town is used.   *Unit 8.1*

4 Design five multi-choice questions to collect data from passengers using a railway station.   *Unit 8.1*

5 Design five multi-choice questions to collect data from people using a multi-storey car park.   *Unit 8.1*

6 This frequency table gives the results of a survey of potato crisp buyers.

	Flavour				
	Sea salt	Cheese	Spicy tomato	Chive	Bacon
Females	26	12	44	7	11
Males	17	25	18	36	4

  a Which flavour was most popular with females?
  b Which flavour was most popular with males?
  c Use the frequency table to make a statement about these crisp buyers.
  d Can this data let you make a statement about crisp buyers in the UK?   *Unit 8.2*

7 This is data on the time (minutes) taken to dress by a group of students.   *Review*

18, 22, 7, 52, 35, 12, 34, 41, 55, 18, 9, 22, 39, 58, 7, 12, 19
24, 37, 51, 20, 11, 44, 56, 37, 23, 16, 48, 26, 42, 8, 14, 6, 15

  a Make a grouped frequency table for the data.
  b What class size did you choose?
  c Which class had the highest frequency?
  d From your table can you say how many students took less than 20 minutes to dress?
    If your answer is no, draw up a different grouped frequency table that will enable you to answer the question.   *Unit 8.2*

8 a Explain why this might not be a good question on a questionnaire.
'When do you travel by bus?'
  b What might be a better question to ask?   *Unit 8.3*

9 Write six questions for a survey on holidays taken by students.   *Unit 8.3*

10 a Write a set of questions for a questionnaire on leisure activity.
  b Explain how you will decide on the people to take part in the survey.   *Unit 8.3*

Investigation

A private sale

Jade has a hypothesis that second-hand cars are more expensive if you buy them from a garage.

- What sort of data is needed to prove Jade right or wrong?
- Collect and present a set of data that proves or disproves Jade's hypothesis.

You will need to be convincing.

9 Representing and Interpreting Data

9.1 Frequency diagrams

A frequency diagram is a way of showing data with a graph.
There are different types of frequency diagram:

The bar chart
These bar charts show the data from the frequency table.

Frequency table

Shoe size	Frequency
2	2
3	10
4	12
5	15
6	20
7	25
8	18

Bar charts

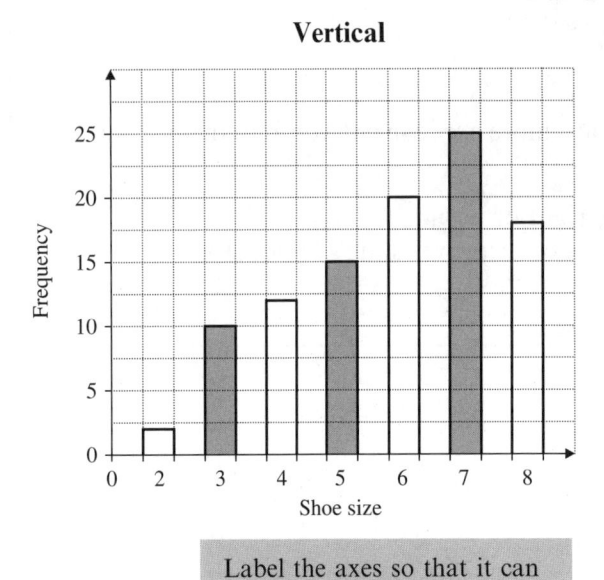

Vertical

Horizontal

Label the axes so that it can be understood by others.

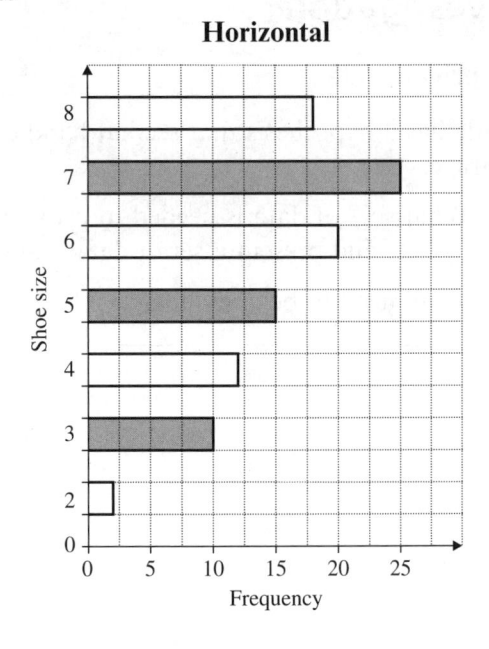

The pictogram

A pictogram uses a symbol to stand for a number of pieces of data and this must be shown:

Frequency table

Size	Frequency
2	4
3	4
4	6
5	8
6	12
7	10

Pictogram

Size	
2	□
3	□
4	□ □
5	□ □
6	□ □ □
7	□ □ □

□ = 4 pairs of shoes

A pictogram must have a key for the symbol.

Remember to show the frequency your symbol stands for.

Exercise 9.1A

1 This data shows the number of cars using a car wash.

Day	Frequency of use
Monday	8
Tuesday	16
Wednesday	12
Thursday	9
Friday	14
Saturday	24
Sunday	28

a Show this data on a bar chart.
b Draw a pictogram for the data.

2 This bar chart shows the data for the number of empty crisp packets in the bin at the end of each day.
   a How many packets were there on Tuesday?
   b What was the frequency for Sunday?
   c Make a frequency table for the bar chart.
   d Show the data with a pictogram.

Graph to show the number of crisp packets in a bin at the end of the day

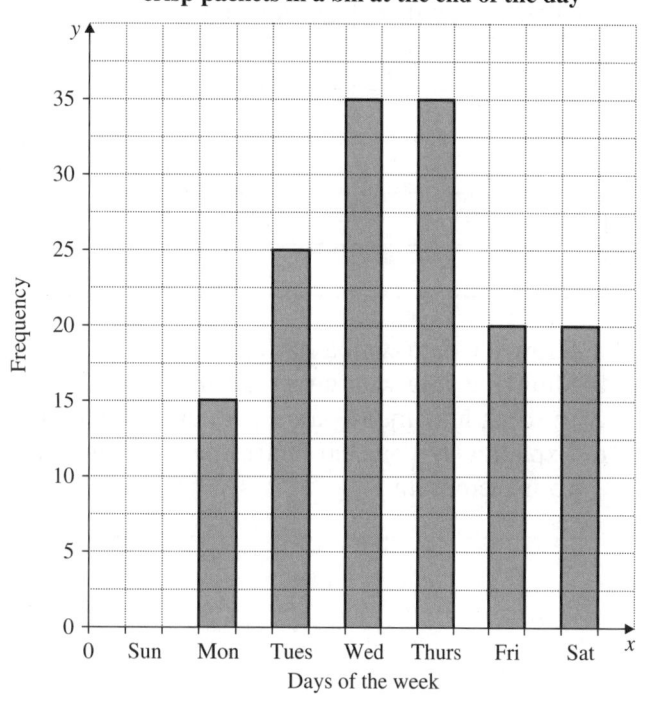

Exercise 9.1B

1 This pictogram shows the data for the number of cars in a car park at noon each day.

Monday	☐☐☐☐
Tuesday	☐☐☐☐▯
Wednesday	☐☐☐☐
Thursday	☐☐☐☐▯
Friday	☐☐☐☐☐
Saturday	☐☐▯
Sunday	☐

☐ = 10 cars

a How many cars were there on Wednesday?
b On which day were there most cars?
c Make a frequency table for the data.
d Draw a bar chart for the data.

2 This data shows the frequency of passengers using a river ferry crossing one day.

Crossing number	Frequency
1	12
2	24
3	32
4	16
5	20

Remember to show the frequency your symbol stands for.

a Show the data with a bar chart.
b Show the data with a pictogram.
c In total, how many passengers used the ferry that day?
d Explain why your bar chart might be more accurate than your pictogram.

9.2 Line graphs

Line graphs can be used to show a set of data.

Bar line graph
This bar line graph shows the data in the table.

Data table

Time	Temperature (°C)
08.00	78
08.30	78.4
09.00	78.2
09.30	78.8
10.00	79
10.30	79.3
11.00	78.5

Bar line graph

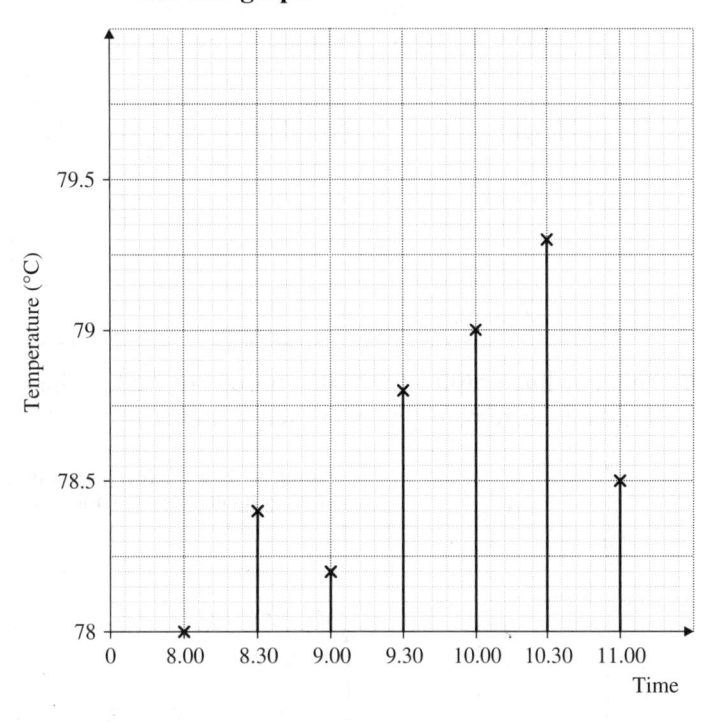

Line graph
This line graph shows the data in the table.

Time	Height (metres)
08.00	3
08.15	3.2
08.30	3.4
08.45	3.6
09.00	3.8
09.15	4.0

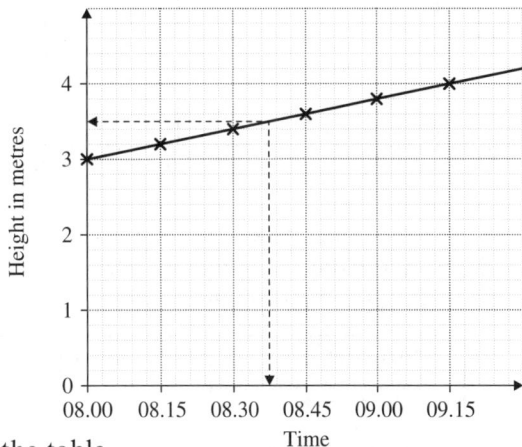

With a line graph you can find more data than is in the table. From the graph you can read off a height for the water at any time between 08.00 and 09.15.
The height of the water at 08.36 was about 3.5 metres.

> Remember when you read data from a graph you only get an estimated value.

Exercise 9.2A

1 A gardener measured a growing sunflower every 5 days. The table gives the data collected.

Number of days	0	5	10	15	20	25	30	35	40	45
Height (cm)	16	19	23.5	27	31.5	36	40	46	52.5	55

  a Draw a bar line graph to show this data.
  b Draw a line graph for the data.
  c From your line graph copy and complete this table with estimates for each ☐.

Height (cm)	Number of days	Height (cm)	Number of days
☐	8	☐	12
☐	22	☐	36
42	☐	25	☐

2 This bar line graph shows the amount of fuel in the tank of a beach cleaner. Readings were recorded every ten minutes.

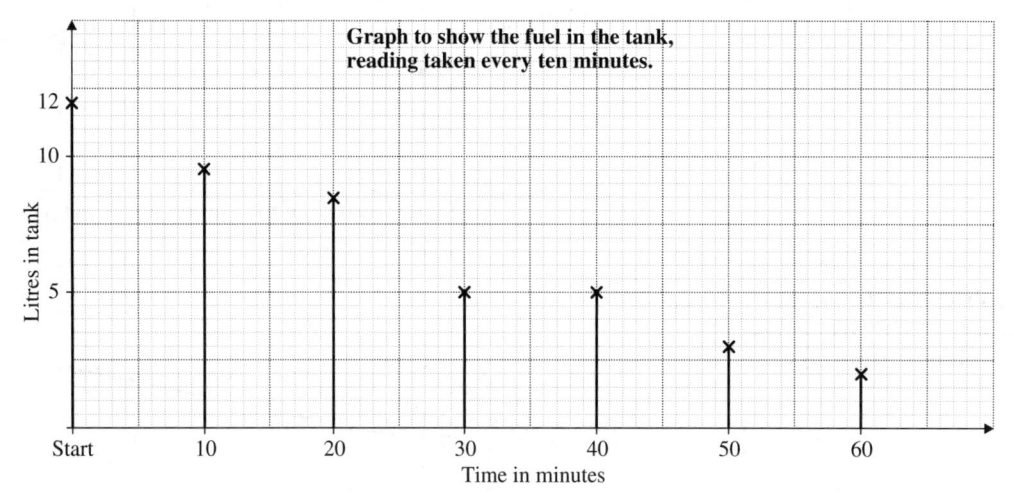

Graph to show the fuel in the tank, reading taken every ten minutes.

  a Put the data shown by the bar line graph in a table.
  b Show the data as a line graph.
  c From your line graph, copy and complete this table with estimates for the fuel.

Fuel (litres)	Minutes	Fuel (litres)	Minutes
☐	6	☐	14
☐	25	☐	32
☐	48	☐	57

Exercise 9.2B

1 The depth of a bore hole is measured every ten minutes:

Time (min)	0	10	20	30	40	50	60	70	80
Depth (m)	0	2.4	3.5	4.2	5.6	7	8.4	9.6	10

   a Draw a bar line graph to show this data.
   b Show the data with a line graph.
   c From your line graph copy and complete this table with an estimate for each ☐.

Time (min)	Depth (m)	Time (min)	Depth (m)
12	☐	25	☐
33	☐	38	☐
☐	6	☐	8

2 This bar line graph shows the length of carpet produced by a weaving machine. The length (m) is measured every 20 minutes.

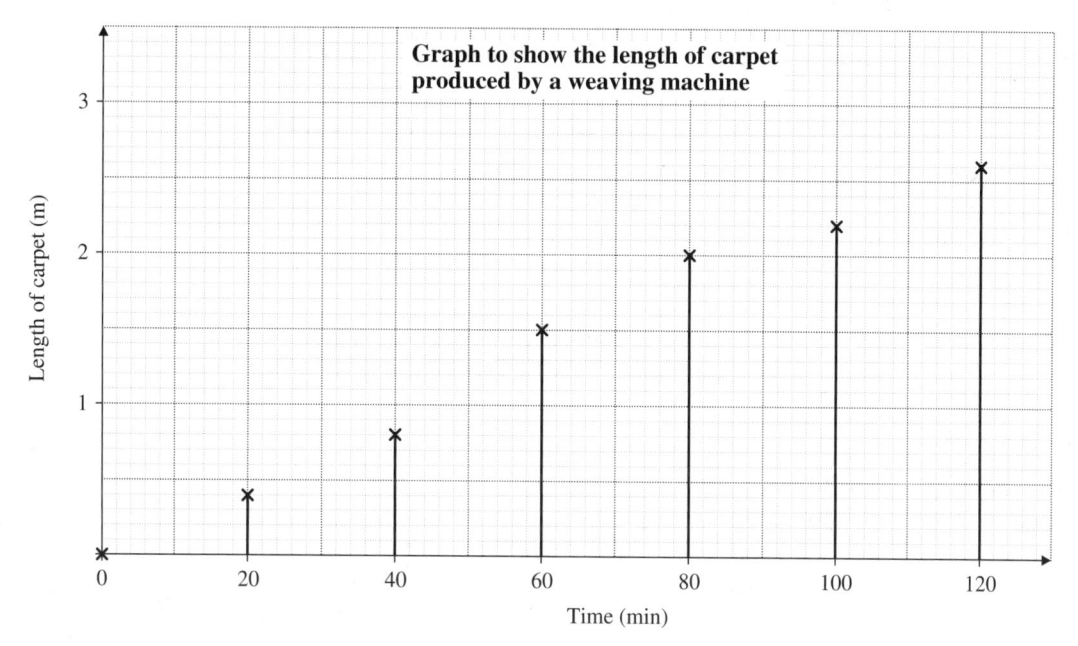

Graph to show the length of carpet produced by a weaving machine

   a Show the data in the bar line graph with a table.
   b Draw a line graph to show the data.
   c From your line graph, copy and complete this table with estimates for each missing value.

Time (min)	Length (m)	Time (min)	Length (m)
10	☐	16	☐
28	☐	45	☐
☐	1	☐	1.4
☐	2	☐	2.4

9.3 Pie charts

A pie chart is a frequency diagram that uses a circle to display data.

The circle is divided into sectors to show the proportions of the total in each class.

Example 1
This data gives the colour of the first twelve cars to enter a car park. Show the data with a pie chart.

Colour	Red	Blue	White	Green	Yellow
Frequency	4	3	2	1	2

The frequencies show a total of $4 + 3 + 2 + 1 + 2 = 12$ cars.

The 360° of the circle must be divided between the 12 cars:

$360 \div 12 = 30°$

Each car is shown by 30° on the pie chart.

Calculate the size of the five sectors:

Each car is shown by 30°, so:

Red cars $\quad 4 \times 30° = 120°$
Blue $\quad\quad\;\; 3 \times 30° = 90°$
White $\quad\;\; 2 \times 30° = 60°$
Green $\quad\;\; 1 \times 30° = 30°$
Yellow $\quad\; 2 \times 30° = 60°$

Pie chart to show the colour of the first ten cars in a car park

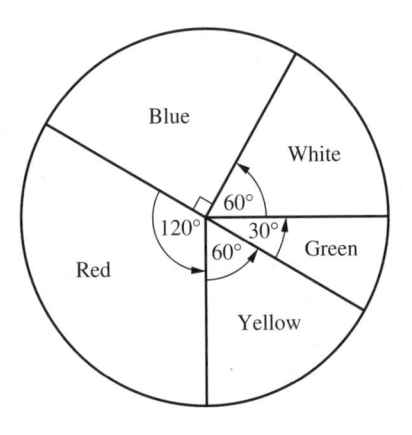

Remember to measure the angles accurately and label each sector with the class it shows.

The circle you draw for your pie chart can be any size.
If you make it too small you will find it:

- difficult to measure the angles accurately
- difficult to fit all the labels in.

You can make your pie chart easier to read by using a different colour for each sector.

Exercise 9.3A

1 Copy and complete this table for the angle used to show each item on a pie chart.

	Total frequency	Angle for each item
	12	30°
a	4	
b	18	
c	20	
d		24°
e		22.5°

For the cars in the car park data the total frequency was 12 and the 360° of the circle was divided into 12 equal parts.
$$360° \div 12 = 30$$

2 This frequency table shows the colour of ski hat worn by students.

Colour	Black	Red	Blue	Purple	Green
Frequency	3	5	9	6	1

a How many students took part in the survey?
b Draw a pie chart to show the data.

3 Students were asked how they travelled to school. The frequency table shows the results for one group.

Method	Walk	Cycle	Bus	Taxi	Car	Other
Frequency	12	7	4	3	1	3

a How many students took part in the survey?
b Show the data with a pie chart.

4 In a health survey people were asked how many times in a week they had chips. The frequency table shows the results.

Chips eaten in a week

Number of times	1	2	3	4	5	6	7	More than 7
Frequency	0	5	4	12	10	3	4	2

    a Calculate the total frequency shown by the table.
    b On a pie chart for this data one sector is 90°.
       What does this sector show?
    c Draw a pie chart to show the data in the frequency table.
    d Does the pie chart show all the data in the table?
       Explain your answer.

5 You want to draw a pie chart. When you find the total frequency it is 32.
    a How many degrees will you allow for each item?
    b Explain why the pie chart might be difficult to draw.

Exercise 9.3B

1 This frequency table shows the shoe size of a group of students.

Shoe size	2	3	4	5	6	7	8	9	10	Over 10
Frequency	4	9	5	7	12	15	10	7	2	1

Draw a pie chart to show the data in the frequency table.

2 This frequency table shows the favourite drink of a group of people in a cafe.

Drink	Tea	Coffee	Milk	Cola	Orange	Other
Frequency	15	18	4	11	7	5

Draw and label a pie chart to show the data in the frequency table.

3 Members of a sports club were asked to name their favourite type of exercise. These are the results of the survey.

Type of exercise	Weights	Circuits	Swim	Cycle	Football	Other
Frequency	8	11	18	5	2	1

Draw a pie chart to show this data.

4 On a pie chart each item is represented by 4°.
    a What is the total frequency shown by this pie chart?
    b One sector of the pie chart had an angle at the centre of the circle of 52°. What frequency did this sector show?
    c What sector angle on the pie chart shows a frequency of 27?

5 On a pie chart printed out by a PC each item was shown by 3.75°.
  a What was the total frequency shown by the pie chart?
  b Explain why this pie chart might be difficult to draw by hand.

The pie chart showed the data in this frequency table.

Bolts to be packed with the Major Chef BBQ Kit

Size of bolt	6 mm	8 mm	12 mm	14 mm	16 mm
Frequency	8	24	32	☐	20

  c How many 14 mm bolts should be packed?
  d Draw a pie chart to show the data in the frequency table.
  e Was the pie chart difficult to draw by hand?
      Explain your answer.

Example 2
This pie chart shows the type of story people like to read.
a Measure the angle used to show each type.

The angles for each sector are:

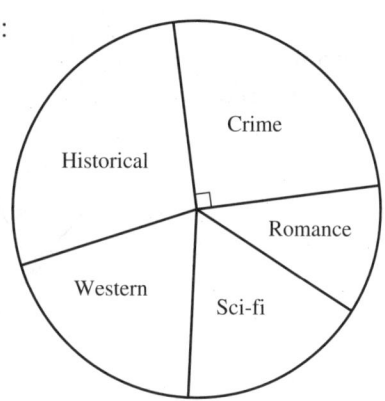

  Crime   90°
  Romance   40°
  Sci-fi   60°
  Western   70°
  Historical 100°

Check each sector with an angle measurer or a protractor.

b The sector for Romance shows a frequency of 4.
  Find the frequency shown by the other sectors.

  For Romance: 40° = a frequency of 4
  Each item is shown by 40° ÷ 4 = 10°

  For the other sectors:

Group	Frequency	
Crime	9	(90 ÷ 10 = 9)
Sci-fi	6	(60 ÷ 10 = 6)
Western	7	(70 ÷ 10 = 7)
Historical	10	(100 ÷ 10 = 10)

This calculation will only be correct if your measurement of the sector angle is accurate.

Exercise 9.3C

1 Estimate the angle for each sector in these pie charts.

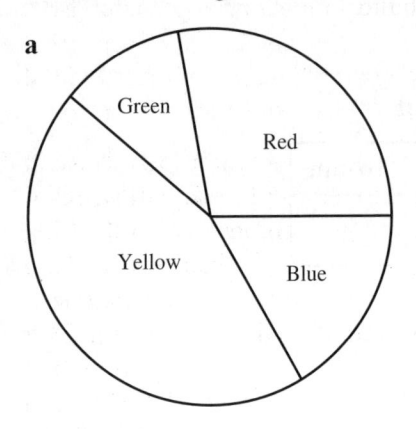

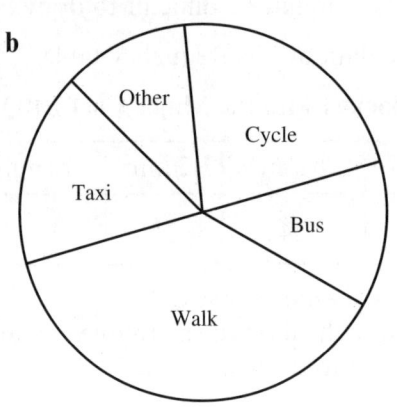

a [Pie chart with sectors: Green, Red, Yellow, Blue]

b [Pie chart with sectors: Other, Cycle, Taxi, Bus, Walk]

2 This pie chart gives the results of a survey of the make of car sold by a dealer in one month.
   a Which two makes had equal sales?
   b Measure the sector angle for Ford.

   There were 12 Ford sales in the month.
   c How many of each other make were sold?

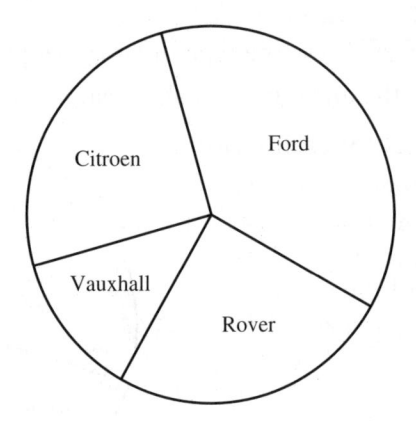

[Pie chart with sectors: Citroen, Ford, Vauxhall, Rover]

3 This pie chart shows the data from a survey on the number of visits to the cinema in a month.
   a Did more people go to the cinema 3 or 4 times?
   b Measure the sector angle size for 2 visits.

   The survey showed that 15 people made two visits to the cinema in the month.
   c Make a frequency table from the pie chart.

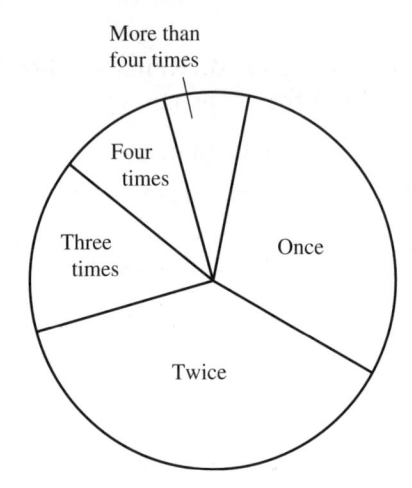

[Pie chart with sectors: More than four times, Four times, Three times, Once, Twice]

Exercise 9.3D

1 The pie chart shows the sun block factor used by people sunbathing on a beach.
  a Did more people use Factor 20 or Total Block? Explain your answer.

The frequency of people using factor 10 was 16.
  b Make a frequency table from the pie chart.

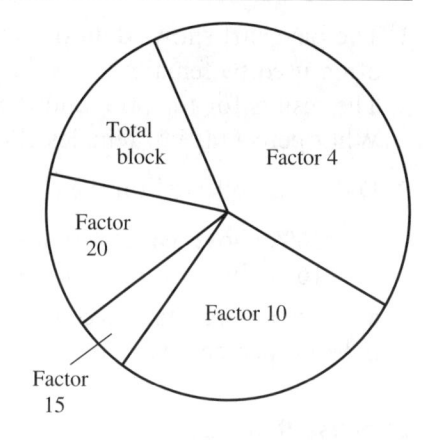

2 The pie chart shows data from a survey of the number of visits made by shoppers to a supermarket in a week.
  a From the pie chart which number of visits have roughly the same frequency?

The frequency for 4 visits was 16.
  b How many people were involved in this survey?
  c Make a frequency table for the data shown by the pie chart.

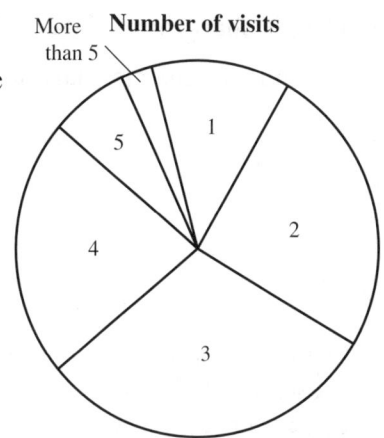

Percentage pie charts

In a percentage pie chart the circle represents 100% of the data displayed.

Example 3

The pie chart shows data on sales of sunscreen. What percentage of sales were Factor 15?

The total for the distribution is 100%

so $\quad$ F4 + F10 + F15 + F25 + F40 = 100%
so $\quad$ 45% + 16% + F15 + 28% + 7% = 100%
so $\quad\quad\quad\quad\quad\quad\quad$ F15 = 4%

So, Factor 15 sales were 4% of the total.

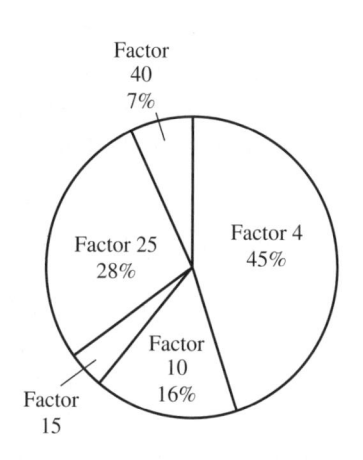

Exercise 9.3E

1 The pie chart shows data on the parts of a sports centre most often used by females.
The results for the pool and the courts were the same.
What percentage of females chose to use the pool?

2 Data was collected on the choice of drink at breakfast.

   36% chose tea, 28% chose coffee,
   16% chose orange juice and the rest chose milk.

   a Draw a percentage pie chart to show this data.
   b What percentage of the group chose milk?

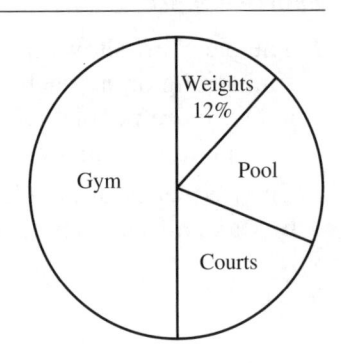

Exercise 9.3F

1 The pie chart shows data on favourite colours.

   Explain why the pie chart has a problem with it.

2 Data was collected on the type of doughnut chosen by students.
The results are shown in this frequency table.

Doughnut	Frequency
Jam	6
Custard	3
Toffee	4
American	7

A percentage pie chart is drawn for the data.
   a Give the percentage used to show each frequency.
   b Draw and label a percentage pie chart to show the data.

3 On a percentage pie chart 18% is shaded to show a frequency of 24.
   a What percentage is used to show a frequency of 12?
   b What frequency is shown by a shading of 45%?
   c What percentage is shaded for a frequency of 20?

9.4 Scatter diagrams

A scatter diagram shows whether two sets of numerical data are related. The relation between two sets of data is called **correlation**.

Example 1
The table shows the marks gained by students in two tests with marks out of 10. The tests were in English and French.

Student	A	B	C	D	E	F	G	H	I	J	K	L	M	N
English	7	8	5	6	9	7	6	3	9	5	7	10	9	4
French	6	8	5	9	3	4	7	5	6	10	5	7	8	5

a Show this data on a scatter diagram.
b Is there any correlation between the two sets of marks?

a For each student you plot:
(mark in English, mark in French)

b For this group of students there seems to be no link between test scores in English and French. So the scatter diagram shows:
no correlation

To look for correlation you need to look at the distribution of the points on the scatter diagram.

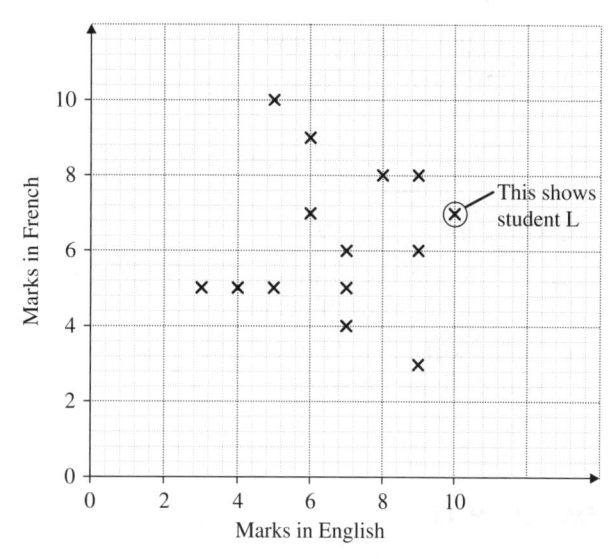

You can identify:

Positive correlation — where an increase in one variable is matched by an increase in the other.

Negative correlation — where an increase in one variable is matched by a decrease in the other.

This shows weak **positive correlation**.

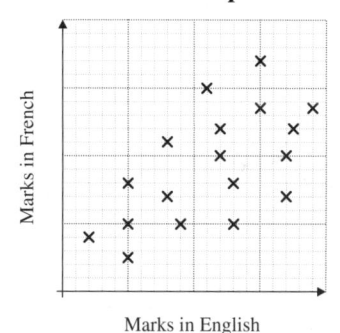

This shows strong **negative correlation**.

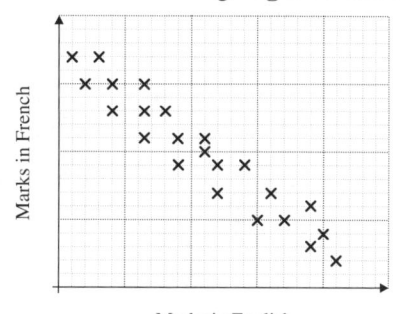

A student with a **high** mark in English would expect a **high** mark in French.

A student with a **high** mark in English would expect a **low** mark in French.

> The words **weak** and **strong** are used here to describe how good the correlation appears to be. Perfect correlation results in a straight line graph.

Exercise 9.4A

1 The table shows the marks, out of 15, for a group of students in English and History.

Student	A	B	C	D	E	F	G	H	I	J	K	L	M	N
English	7	6	5	8	9	10	12	13	11	8	7	9	14	12
French	8	12	11	10	8	8	7	6	9	12	5	6	11	14

a Draw a scatter diagram to show this data.
b Does there appear to be any correlation between the two sets of data?
Explain your answer.

2 This scatter diagram shows data on the number of accidents drivers have and their age.
   a Copy and complete:
   Younger drivers appear to have ... accidents.
   b Copy and complete:
   As the age of drivers increases the number of accidents ...
   c What sort of correlation does this scatter diagram show?

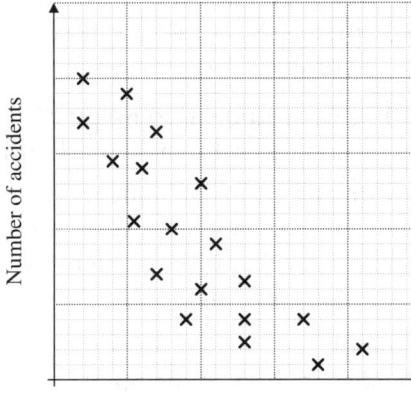

Exercise 9.4B

1 A scatter diagram shows a weak positive correlation between the number of children supermarket shoppers have and the amount of money they spend on food.
Sketch what the scatter diagram might look like.

2 Describe the correlation in each of these scatter diagrams:

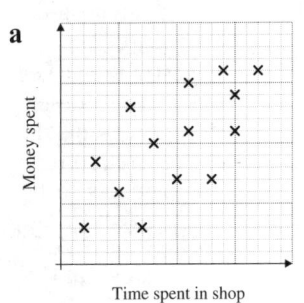

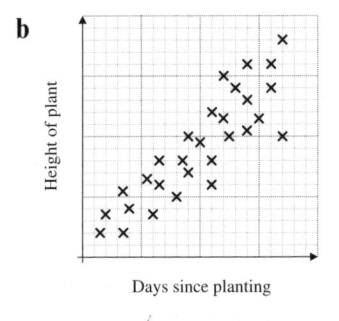

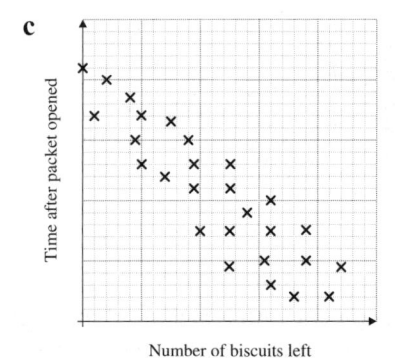

3 A scatter diagram for data on the age of people and the number of visits to the cinema showed a strong negative correlation.
Use this information to copy and complete this statement:

> As the age of people increases the number of visits they make to the cinema ...

Line of best fit

This is a straight line drawn through the middle of the plots on a scatter diagram.

You try to draw a line with the same number of plots on each side.
The stronger the correlation the easier it is to draw the line of best fit.

This line of best fit shows moderate positive correlation. The plots are well scattered either side of the line of best fit.

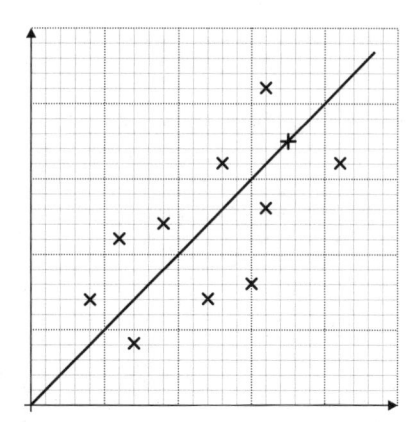

This line of best fit shows strong negative correlation. The points are close to the line of best fit.

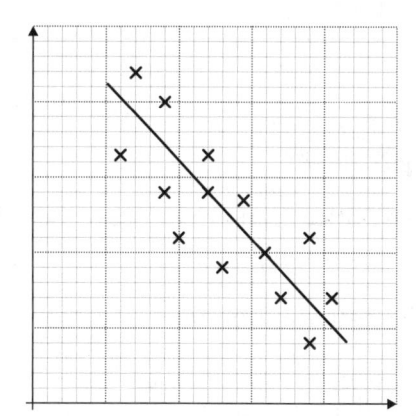

When no correlation is present it is not possible to draw a line of best fit.

You can use the line of best fit to estimate values from a scatter graph.

Example 2
Use the line of best fit to estimate:
a The cost of a house 6.5 miles from the city centre.
b The distance from the city centre of a house costing £80 000.

a 6.5 miles from the city centre the estimated cost of a house is £70 000.

b A house costing £80 000 is estimated to be 5 miles from the city centre.

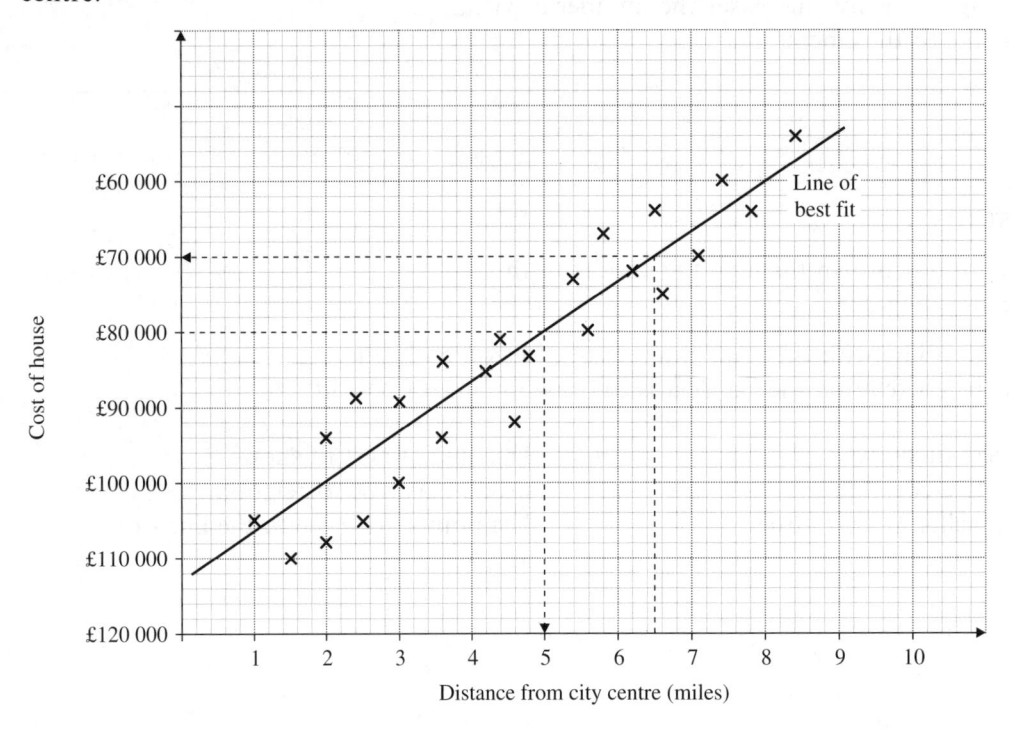

Exercise 9.4C

1 Use the house price graph to estimate the price of a house 2.5 miles from the centre.

2 Estimate the distance from the city centre of a house costing £75 000.

3 This data gives the prices of second-hand Ford Fiestas advertised in a local paper.

Year	Advertised prices (£s)	Year	Advertised prices (£s)
1998	6300, 5750, 6450	1996	4750, 5000, 4800, 5100
1994	3400, 4000, 3500, 3200	1993	2700, 2500, 2750, 2800

a Draw a scatter diagram for the data and draw in a line of best fit.
b Estimate the price of a 1997 Fiesta.
c If you were trying to sell a 1995 Fiesta, estimate what the advertised price might be.

Exercise 9.4D

1 Sketch scatter diagrams with lines of best fit that show:
  a Strong negative correlation
  b Weak positive correlation
  c No correlation
  d Moderate positive correlation

2 This data shows the engine size and petrol consumption of cars.

Engine (litres)	1.6	1.8	2.0	2.2	3.0	2.0	1.4	1.6	1.1	1.8	3.5	4.0
Consumption (mpg)	38	40	34	28	26	35	44	41	52	37	19	22

  a Draw a scatter diagram and draw in a line of best fit.
  b Estimate the petrol consumption of a car with a 3 litre engine.
  c From the data estimate the petrol consumption of a 1.2 litre engine.
  d Describe the correlation shown by the graph.
  e A kit car has a petrol consumption of 20 mpg. Estimate its engine size.

9.5 Cumulative frequency graphs*

The **cumulative frequency** is the total of the frequencies up to any group or piece of data in a data set.
Cumulative frequencies can be shown in a table or on a graph.

Example
Show this data on a cumulative frequency graph.

Marks in a test out of 40

18, 12, 17, 31, 28, 33, 25, 38, 35, 21, 24, 29, 34
25, 16, 7, 36, 27, 33, 35, 31, 23, 30, 14, 22, 19, 21
30, 24, 27, 21, 12, 29, 11, 20, 24, 21

Cumulative frequency table

Marks	1–5	6–10	11–15	16–20	21–25	26–30	31–35	36–40
Frequency	0	1	4	5	11	7	7	2
Cumulative frequency	0	1	5	10	21	28	35	37

Plot the cumulative frequency against the upper class boundaries.

224 Representing and interpreting data

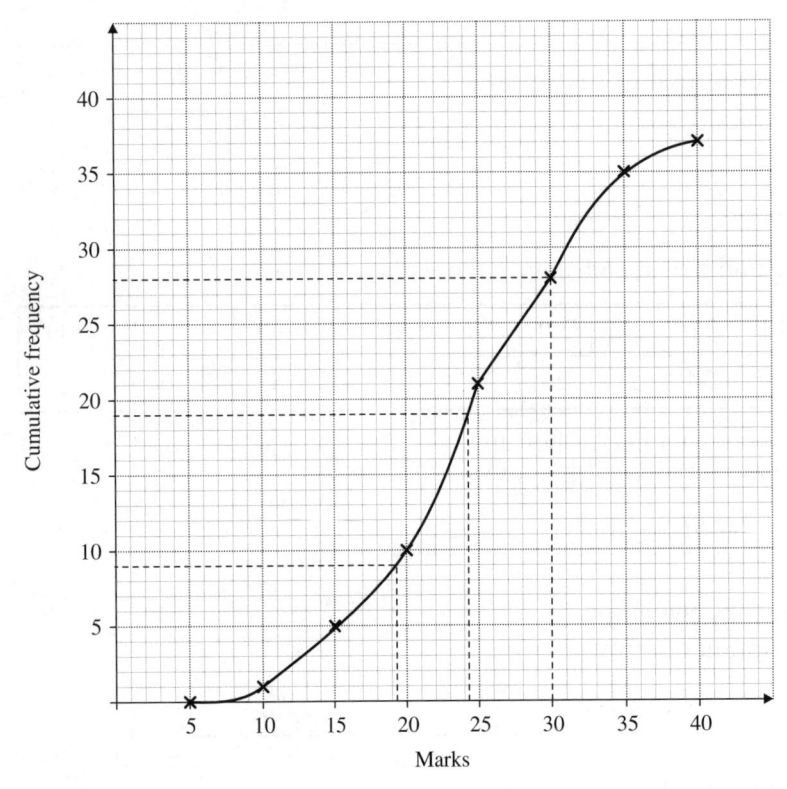

The cumulative frequency curve can be used to find a value for:
- the **median**: the middle value of the data set
- the **upper quartile**: the middle value of the upper half of the data
- the **lower quartile**: the middle value of the lower half of the data
- the **interquartile range**: the upper quartile − the lower quartile.

From the graph:
- the median is the value of the 19th piece of data which is 24
- the upper quartile is the value of the 28th piece which is 30
- the lower quartile is the value of the 9th piece which is   19
- the interquartile range is:
   upper quartile − lower quartile = 30 − 19 which is 11

Exercise 9.5A

1 This data gives the marks out of 50 for a French test.

26, 33, 38, 45, 50, 44, 28, 19, 35, 38, 46, 41, 40, 37, 22,
15, 36, 24, 22, 28, 47, 35, 38, 45, 17, 31, 29, 16, 44, 29,
37, 48, 25, 47, 46, 38, 37, 33, 14, 37, 44, 26, 46, 32, 30

  a Show this data in a cumulative frequency table.
  b Draw a cumulative frequency graph for the data.
  c Use the graph to estimate a value for the median.
  d Give an estimate of the upper quartile, the lower quartile and the interquartile range for the data.

2 The number of calls made by operators in a tele-sales centre in one week are shown by this frequency table.

Number of calls	750–799	800–849	850–899	900–949	950–1000	1000–1049
Frequency	8	13	18	12	9	5

a Draw a cumulative frequency graph for the data.
b Estimate the median number of calls made by operators.
c Calculate an estimate for the interquartile range.
   Explain your calculation.

Exercise 9.5B

1 This data gives the times taken to develop photographic prints.

Time (seconds)	15.5–15.9	16.0–16.4	16.5–16.9	17.0–17.4	17.5–17.9	18.0–18.4
Frequency	3	8	14	29	12	7

a Show the data in a cumulative frequency table.
b Estimate the median value for the time taken to develop a print.
c Estimate the upper quartile value for the data.
d Find the interquartile range for the data.

2 This data shows the age of people shopping at 3 a.m. in a 24-hour supermarket.

Age	16–20	21–25	26–30	31–35	36–40	41–45	46–50
Frequency	2	18	27	25	17	12	7

a Draw a cumulative frequency graph for the data.
b Estimate the median age of this group of shoppers.
c Find a value for the lower quartile.
d Explain how to find the interquartile range.
   What is the value for this data?

9.6 Stem-and-leaf plots

A stem-and-leaf plot is a frequency diagram that shows data in a different way.
It can be used to display numerical data.

> A stem-and-leaf plot may be called a stem plot.

Example
This data shows the number of words in sentences taken from two newspapers. Show the data as a stem-and-leaf plot.

Representing and interpreting data

The Chronicle	The Recorder
37, 44, 21, 18, 34, 25, 30, 19, 22, 31	16, 23, 5, 22, 24, 31, 18, 22, 17, 25
40, 38, 27, 34, 18, 19, 33, 41, 32, 27	28, 24, 29, 31, 19, 25, 30, 8, 21, 19
35, 28, 22, 26, 33, 36, 41, 35, 23, 19	24, 18, 26, 33, 38, 28, 30, 22, 4, 21

Steam-and-leaf plot to show the number of words in a sentence

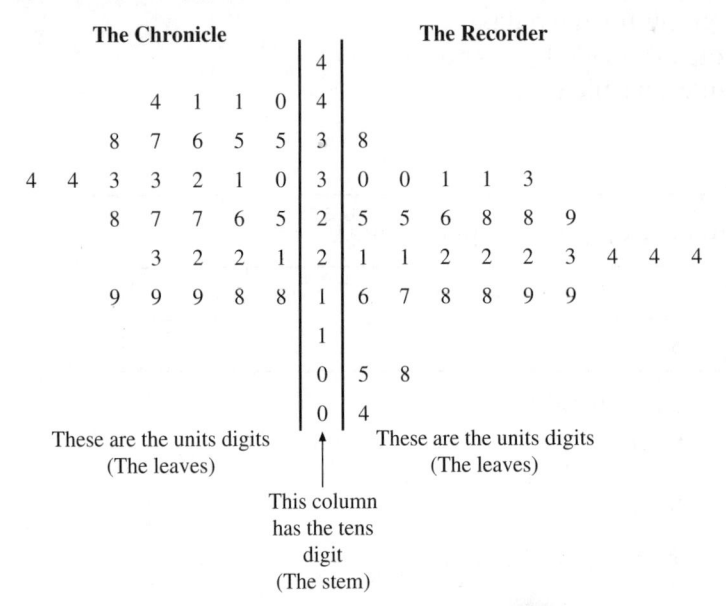

```
        The Chronicle              The Recorder
                              4
              4  1  1  0  | 4 |
           8  7  6  5  5  | 3 | 8
     4  4  3  3  2  1  0  | 3 | 0  0  1  1  3
           8  7  7  6  5  | 2 | 5  5  6  8  8  9
                 3  2  2  1  | 2 | 1  1  2  2  2  3  4  4  4
                    9  9  9  8  8  | 1 | 6  7  8  8  9  9
                              | 1 |
                              | 0 | 5  8
                              | 0 | 4
```

These are the units digits ↑ These are the units digits
(The leaves)   (The leaves)
                This column
                has the tens
                   digit
                 (The stem)

The stem-and-leaf plot gives a picture of the distribution of the data. You may be able to make general statements such as: 'The sentences in the Chronicle have more words than the sentences in the Recorder.'

More details of the median and how it is found on page 228.

Note: As a stem-and-leaf plot shows the data in order of size, it is another way to find the median value for the set of data.

Exercise 9.6A

1 Use the stem-and-leaf plot above to find the median number of words used in a sentence for:
  a The Chronicle
  b The Recorder.

2 This data gives the number of sandwiches sold each day by two shops.

Kwik Bite	Lunch Box
36, 42, 28, 21, 51, 43, 29, 35, 41, 40	55, 39, 44, 48, 42, 39, 38, 32, 47, 56
27, 44, 35, 29, 33, 31, 35, 56, 38, 43	49, 56, 48, 46, 49, 38, 44, 41, 52, 53
26, 37, 46, 38, 29, 28, 29, 41, 37, 33	56, 42, 47, 45, 37, 30, 49, 54, 51, 46

  a Show the two sets of data on a stem-and-leaf plot.
  b For each shop find the median value for the data.
  c Which shop seems to have the better sandwich trade? Explain your answer.

3 This data shows the number of seconds taken for each call made on their mobile phone by two friends.

Claire
18, 22, 19, 38, 34, 16, 7, 56, 11, 9
9, 35, 24, 25, 46, 8, 23, 56, 58, 37
16, 18, 76, 15, 34, 6, 49, 83, 26, 8
24, 14, 7, 56, 40

Liam
8, 12, 6, 34, 55, 67, 39, 7, 34, 22
6, 39, 47, 49, 58, 22, 25, 14, 9, 41
38, 69, 71, 22, 12, 7, 18, 56, 47, 5
55, 30, 6, 7, 17

a Show the data on a steam-and-leaf plot and for each set find the median value.
b 'Females spend longer talking on the phone than males.'
Does the data support this statement? Explain your answer.

Exercise 9.6B

1 The data shows the number of passengers on a ferry route.

Rago to Vesok
56, 84, 57, 67, 88, 94, 26, 45, 54, 40
49, 60, 51, 29, 36, 48, 22, 19, 28, 31
27, 19, 18, 21, 56, 72, 68, 49, 57, 55
34, 56, 47, 49, 44, 21, 17

Vesok to Rago
12, 23, 41, 20, 38, 50, 39, 19, 44, 21
35, 21, 18, 37, 12, 28, 25, 31, 28, 50
38, 29, 31, 24, 48, 47, 17, 31, 47, 50
54, 46, 41, 26, 47, 33, 51

a Show the data on a stem-and-leaf plot and find the median value for each set.
b Which ferry route is used by more travellers? Explain your answer.

2 Two groups of people were asked to estimate a minute. These are the results:

Group A (seconds)
58, 45, 44, 67, 46, 67, 59, 76
71, 49, 50, 41, 38, 49, 62, 75
69, 81, 58, 90, 46, 72, 88, 92

Group B (seconds)
56, 77, 69, 81, 71, 66, 49, 59
63, 61, 68, 88, 59, 79, 78, 66
94, 47, 55, 69, 71, 73, 57, 66

Show the data on a stem-and-leaf plot, find the median value for each group and comment on the results.

9.7 Average values

An **average** is a single value that is typical of a set of data.
There are three types of average:
the **mode**, the **median** and the **mean**.

Mode

▶ The **mode** is the most common value.
  For example:
  The **Mode** for this set of data is shoe size 4.

Shoe size	2	3	4	5	6	7	8	9
Frequency	4	11	15	14	3	2	1	0

> The modal value is the value with the highest frequency.

If two values with the same highest frequency then there will be two modes.

Median

▶ The **median** is the middle value when the data is sorted into size order.

> Most mistakes finding the median are made because people do not put the data in order before they look for the median value.

Example 1
Find the median of each set of data:
  a 5, 7, 1, 2, 8, 5, 8, 3, 4, 9, 5, 8, 4, 10, 7
  b 15, 15, 17, 11, 15, 10, 9, 19, 10, 15, 12, 8, 11, 19, 9, 20

  a Order the data:
      1, 2, 3, 4, 4, 5, 5, 5, 7, 7, 8, 8, 8, 9, 10
                        ↑
              This is the middle value.

> When you put your data set in order you must include each piece of data – even repeated values.

  The median is 5.

  b Order the data:
      8, 9, 9, 10, 10, 11, 11, 12, 15, 15, 15, 15, 17, 19, 19, 20
                                ↑
                    The middle value is
                    between 12 and 15.

> Notice that the median does not have to be one of the values.

  So the median is 13.5.

Exercise 9.7A

1 This data shows the marks for a group in a test.
  Mark: 12, 14, 8, 6, 9, 15, 13, 11, 10, 11, 7, 8, 6, 9, 11, 13, 15
  a What mark is the mode for this data set?
  b Find the median mark.

2 The length of the pod of some beans is measured:
  Length (cm): 11.5, 12.8, 9.7, 12.8, 10.6, 11.5, 13.8, 12.7, 12.2, 11.5, 8.7
  a Find the median length.
  b What is the mode for this data set?

3 The passengers leaving buses at the bus station were counted.
This is the data:

Passengers: 10, 15, 8, 12, 24, 9, 3, 4, 16, 11, 14, 15, 2, 14, 6, 17

   a How many pieces of data are in the set?
   b What number of passengers is the mode?
   c Find the median number of passengers for this data.

4 Find the mode and median for each of these data sets.
   a 6, 12, 4, 5, 8, 19, 20, 16, 15, 8, 6, 4, 8, 12, 14, 8, 20, 9, 6, 11, 13, 8, 19
   b 3.5, 6, 4.2, 7, 4.5, 4.3, 5, 5.6, 6, 7.5, 4.5, 9
   c 25, 33, 45, 55, 43, 24, 38, 35, 36, 46, 51, 45, 19, 66
   d 125, 98, 56, 75, 56, 88, 91, 56, 104, 56, 74, 90

Exercise 9.7B

1 The number of items in baskets at the checkout in a supermarket were recorded. This data shows the results.

   4, 12, 5, 7, 3, 8, 4, 9, 11, 4, 16, 13, 4,
   11, 4, 12, 5, 4, 14, 2, 10, 4, 8, 4, 6, 9

   a Find the median number of items in a basket.
   b What is the mode for this data set?

2 Find the mode and median for each of these data sets.
   a 7, 12, 14, 9, 15, 18, 9, 17, 16, 20, 18, 16, 11, 7, 9, 13, 17, 12
   b 3.4, 4.5, 3.8, 4.2, 4.5, 3.9, 3.7, 4.6, 4.8, 3.1, 5.4, 4, 3.6, 4.5, 5.1,
       4.7, 5, 5.5
   c 0.75, 0.6, 0.4, 0.35, 0.66, 0.25, 0.65, 0.4, 0.54, 0.28, 0.65

3 Explain why the median of a data set with 37 pieces will be the 19th piece of data when the data set is arranged in order.

4 A data set does not have a mode.
What does this tell you about the values in the data set?

Mean

▶ The **mean** for a set of data is:
a numerical value found by adding all the values in the set and dividing this total by the number of values.

> The mean may be called the arithmetic mean.

For example, to find the mean of this data set:

   12, 15, 22, 17, 11, 39, 44, 28, 56, 71, 8, 15, 22, 34, 18

   Add all the values: $12 + 15 + 22 + \ldots + \ldots + 18 = 412$
   The number of values is: 15

The mean is $412 \div 15 = 27.46666\ldots$

The mean of the data set is 27.47 (to 2 dp)

Note: When the term average is used, people take this as being the mean.

Be careful, as you know the mean is just one type of average.

> *The mean is a numerical value. It does not have to be a whole number or a number from the data set.*

Range

▶ The **range** tells you how spread out a data set is.

The range = the greatest value − the smallest value

in a set of data.

Example 2
Calculate the range for this data set.

13, 13, 24, 31, 16, 11, 35, 26, 16, 25, 26, 31, 20, 18, 31

The greatest value: 35   The smallest value: 11

The range = greatest value − smallest value
         = 35 − 11 = 24

The range for the data set is 24.

Exercise 9.7C

1 Calculate the range and mean for this data set.

22, 17, 31, 44, 52, 38, 15, 32, 55,
31, 56, 34, 45, 26, 13, 43, 29

2 Write down five values that have a range of 6.

3 The total of the values in a set of data is 362.
In the set there are 16 values. Calculate the mean for the data set.

4 The mean value for a data set is 17.5.
The data set has 12 pieces of data.
Calculate the total value of the data set.

5 This data shows the number of tickets sold each day for a historic tram ride.

Day	Mon	Tues	Wed	Thur	Fri	Sat	Sun
Tickets	58	76	97	108	48	262	177

  a On which day were most tickets sold?
  b Calculate the range for the data.
  c Calculate the mean number of tickets sold.

6 This data gives the weight of raspberries picked by each person in a group.

Jenny	3.6 kg	Mike	3.4 kg	Ewan	2.7 kg
Cara	4.7 kg	Meg	☐ kg	Kim	3.1 kg
Aysha	3.7 kg	Mikos	2.9 kg	Dan	3.6 kg

Meg forgot the weight of raspberries she picked.
The group picked a mean of 3.5 kg of strawberries each.

a Calculate the total weight of raspberries picked by the group?
b Find the weight of raspberries picked by Meg.

Exercise 9.7D

1 A data set has a range of 16.5. The greatest value in the set is 43. Calculate the smallest value in the set.

2 Calculate the mean for this set of data:
    34.6, 27.2, 18.5, 24.3, 25.8, 18.5, 21.6, 24.3, 7.2

3 A data set has a mean of 16. The total for the data set is 4576. How many values are in the set?

4 Parcels of these weights in kg were sent by a company in one day:
    6.8, 12.45, 8.6, 5.25, 4.08, 2.72, 4.5,
    6.4, 7.25, 8.6, 0.75, 0.65, 1.3

a Calculate the range for this data.
b Calculate the mean weight of the parcels sent.

5 A tram company sells adult tickets, child tickets and saver tickets. This table gives the data for type of tickets sold over a weekend.

Type of ticket

	Adult	Child	Saver
Friday	35	6	27
Saturday	68	39	44
Sunday	76	72	59

a In total how many adult tickets were sold over the three days?
b Calculate the mean number of adult tickets sold each day.
c Calculate the mean number of saver tickets sold each day.
d Find the range for the child ticket data.
e The company said they sold an average of 40 child tickets each day at the weekend.
Is this claim accurate? Explain your answer.

6 A steam railway makes six trips each day.
Last Tuesday the mean number of passengers per trip was 104.
Passengers numbers on the first five trips were:
   127, 55, 116, 92, 88.
Calculate the number of passengers on the last trip of the day.

9.8 Comparing data*

You can compare two sets of data using the average and the range.

Example 1
This data gives the number of chips in a serving given by two dinner ladies.

Jenny: 17, 14, 21, 14, 15, 22, 10, 14, 14, 16, 20, 12, 17
Rita: 17, 14, 17, 15, 18, 15, 16, 12, 16, 19, 17

Who would you choose to serve your chips?
Give reasons for your answer.

Find the mean number of chips per serving for each server.

Jenny: total number of chips 206, number of servings 13
          mean number of chips per serving: $206 \div 13 = 15.85$ (to 2 dp)

Rita: total number of chips 176, number of servings 11
          mean number of chips per serving: $176 \div 11 = 16$

So for Jenny and Rita the mean number of chips per serving is about the same.

Look at the range for the two data sets.

Jenny: Range = greatest value − smallest value
                = 22 − 10
                = 12

Rita: Range = greatest value − smallest value
                = 19 − 12
                = 7

So the data for Rita has a smaller range than the data for Jenny.

Which server to choose?

It is probably best to choose Rita to serve your chips because:
the mean number of chips they serve is about the same but the range for Rita is smaller so these servings are more consistent.

There are three different averages, so which do you choose to compare data?
Most people just choose the mean, but this is not always the best. If the data has a large range it might be better to use the median.

Example 2

This data gives the wages paid to the workers in a small company for one week.

Wages: £175.50, £206.35, £92.65, £105.25, £475, £51, £48, £55.50

The company claims that the average wage is about £145.

Will the workers be happy with this claim? Explain your answer.

The mean for the data is given by:

Total of the values ÷ number of values

Mean = £1029.25 ÷ 8
= £151.16 (to 2 dp)

But the range for the data is large:

Range = £475 − £48 = £427

So the mean is being increased by the one large value in the data set.

To find the median, you arrange the data in size order:

£48, £51, £55.50, £92.65, £105.25, £175.50, £206.35, £475

The median value is mid-way between £92.65 and £105.25 which is £98.95.

So it is better to say that the average wage in the company is £98.95.

> If the data set has a large range the median is a better average to use. So always calculate the range first.

> The easy way to calculate this median value is to find the mean of the two middle values:
> 92.6 + 105.25 = 197.90
> Mean = 197.90 ÷ 2
> = 98.95
> So the median is £98.95

Exercise 9.8A

1 In a fitness final two teams had to do step-ups for one minute. This is the data for the teams.

Team A	1	2	3	4	5	6	7	8	9	10
Step-ups	44	51	63	48	52	62	53	48	50	59

Team B	1	2	3	4	5	6	7	8
Step-ups	48	53	53	57	54	57	45	54

a Calculate the mean for each data set.
b Find the range for each data set.
c Which team do you think is fitter? Give reasons.

2 This data gives the amount spent by a group of customers in a supermarket:

Amount spent: £44.70, £58.62, £75.39, £166.44, £84.70, £16.28, £23.67

The supermarket claims that these customers spent an average of about £67.

a Which average do you think the supermarket used? Explain your answer.

b Do you think this is a fair claim? Explain your answer.

Exercise 9.8B

1 You are a player short in your basketball team.
You have to choose between Al and Joel.
This data shows their recent points scores:

	Points scored
Al:	22, 6, 20, 16, 21, 14, 18, 12, 14, 24, 4, 8, 4, 14, 8, 8
Joel:	12, 14, 12, 16, 12, 14, 20, 18, 14

a Calculate the mean score for each player.
b Calculate the range and median score for each player.
c Who would you choose for your team?
Give reasons for your answer.

2 A solar-powered car was tested on five days.
The distance travelled in three hours was recorded for each day.

Day	1	2	3	4	5
Distance travelled (km)	263	238	24	193	202

A headline in a paper said: 'Solar car does an average of 184 km in 3 hours'. Do you think this headline is fair?
Give reasons for your answer.

9.9 Working with grouped data*

Modal class
The **modal class** is the class with the highest frequency.

Estimating the range and the total of a data set
You can only estimate the range for a set of grouped data as the lowest value could be any value in the first class and the highest value, any value in the last class.

The best estimate of the range is:

the last mid-class value − the first mid-class value

For example, this data shows break scores in snooker:

Score	44–48	49–53	54–58	59–63	64–68	69–73	74–78
Frequency	5	9	15	19	12	7	8

The best estimate of the range is: 30

(76 – 46, difference between last and first mid-class values)

To estimate the total of grouped data you need to:
- estimate the total for each class
- find the total of the estimated class totals.

For example the estimated total of the break scores is given by:

Score	Frequency	Mid-class value	Estimated class total
44–48	5	46	230
49–53	9	51	459
54–58	15	56	840
59–63	19	61	1159
64–68	12	66	792
69–73	7	71	497
74–78	8	76	608
Totals	**75**		**4585**

So, the estimated total of the scores is: 4585.

Estimating the mean

To estimate the mean you calculate:

the estimated total ÷ the frequency

For example to estimate the mean for the break scores data:
The estimated mean is:

4585 ÷ 75 = 61.13 (to 2 dp)

So, the estimated mean is: 61.13 (to 2 dp)

Estimating the median

The median can be estimated from the cumulative frequency graph for the data.

For example the cumulative frequency table for the break scores data is:

Score	44–48	49–53	54–58	59–63	64–68	69–73	74–78
Frequency	5	9	15	19	12	7	8
Cumulative frequency	5	14	29	48	60	67	75

The cumulative frequency graph is:

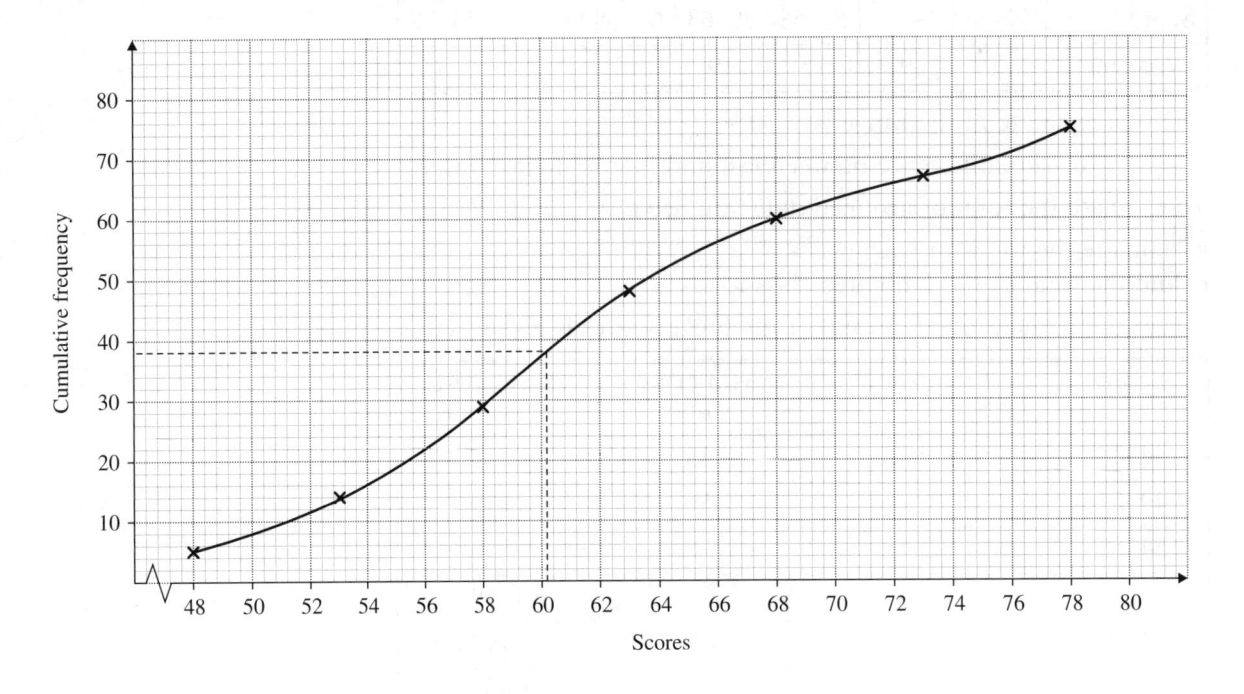

There are 75 scores so the median value will be the 38th score.
From the graph the 38th score is about 60.

So an estimate of the median score is 60.

Using frequency polygons to compare distributions
A **frequency polygon** is made from the straight lines joining the midpoint at the top of each bar of a histogram.

This data shows the scores of the first 60 breaks in two snooker matches.

Match A

Score	44–48	49–53	54–58	59–63	64–68
Frequency	5	9	15	19	12

Match B

Score	44–48	49–53	54–58	59–63	64–68
Frequency	8	14	18	12	8

The frequency polygons are:

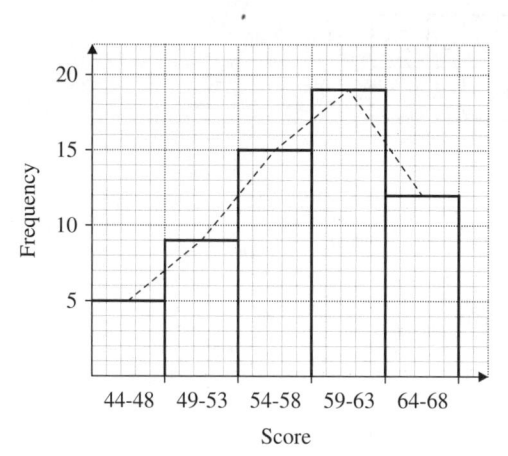

Match A

Match B

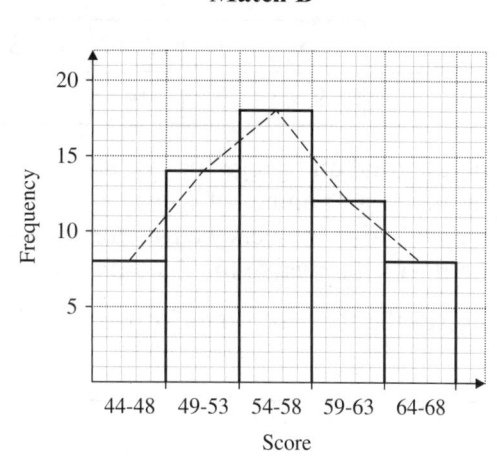

You can compare by plotting both polygons on the same diagram.

You plot the frequencies against the mid-class values.

Comparing the graphs, the players in Match A were probably better than the players in Match B, as the break scores in general were higher in Match A.

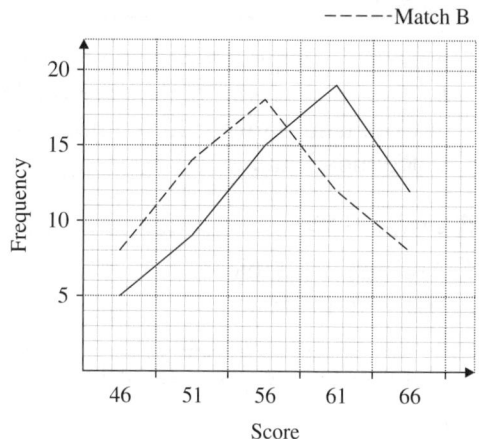

Exercise 9.9A

1 This data shows the number of items in supermarket trolleys at the checkout.

Number of items	1–10	11–20	21–30	31–40	41–50
Frequency	7	17	22	15	8

  a Estimate the range for this set of data.
  b Estimate the total for the data set.
  c Estimate the mean number of items in each trolley.
  d Draw a cumulative frequency for the data.
  e Use the cumulative frequency curve to estimate the median value.

2 A group was asked to count the number of coins they had on them. This is the data:

Number of coins	0–5	6–11	12–17	18–23	24–29	30–35
Frequency	9	23	14	8	4	1

a Estimate the total and range for this data set.
b Estimate the mean number of coins.
c Draw a cumulative frequency curve for the data.
d Estimate the median value for the data set.

3 This data gives the times of riders in two rounds of a time trial.

Time (seconds)	44–48	49–53	54–58	59–63	64–68	69–73
Round 1	2	5	14	22	17	5
Round 2	0	3	8	34	11	9

a Draw a frequency polygon for each data set.
b Draw a diagram to compare the frequency polygons. Comment on what the comparison shows you about times in Rounds 1 and 2.

Exercise 9.9B

1 A group of people was asked to estimate one minute. Here are the results:

Estimate (seconds)	45–49	50–54	55–59	60–64	65–69	70–74
Frequency	5	11	24	17	21	7

a Estimate the range for the data set.
b Calculate an estimate of the total for the data set.
c Estimate a value for the mean.
d Show the data with a cumulative frequency curve.
e Estimate the median value for the data.

2 A group was asked to estimate one metre. Here are the results.

Estimate (cm)	80–85	86–91	92–97	98–103	104–109	110–115
Frequency	8	17	23	15	25	12

a Estimate the range for the data.
b Find an estimate of the mean value for the data.
c Estimate the median value of the data.

3 Students were allowed to study a group of 20 items for 20 seconds. After one minute they were asked to write down as many as they could remember.
The students then did the experiment again with a different set of 20 items. Here are the results:

Number remembered	1–4	5–8	9–12	13–16	17–20
Experiment 1	2	9	28	15	6
Experiment 2	1	7	16	26	10

a Draw a frequency polygon for each experiment.
b By comparing frequency polygons comment on the results of the two experiments.

Revision exercise 9 *Review*

1 This data shows the number of letters delivered to one address over one week.

Mon	Tues	Wed	Thurs	Fri	Sat	Sun
12	8	10	16	22	14	0

a Show the data with a bar chart.
b Show the data with a pictogram.
c Show the data with bar line graph. *Unit 9.1*

2 This data gives the height of a growing sunflower every five days.

Number of days	0	5	10	15	20	25	30	35	40	45
Height (cm)	11	24	29	38	46	52	60	66	71	79

a Draw a bar line graph for the data.
b Draw a line graph for the data.
c Estimate the height after 28 days.
d Estimate after how many days the height was 40 cm. *Unit 9.2*

3 This data gives the colour of the first twenty cans of paint sold by a DIY store one Friday.

Colour	White	Cream	Lavender	Peach	Teracotta
Frequency	9	2	3	1	5

Show the data with a pie chart. *Unit 9.3*

4 On a pie chart a frequency of 7 is shown by a sector of 56°.
What total frequency is shown by the pie chart?

Review
Unit 9.3

5 Data was collected on the team supported by a group of fans.
16 supported Rovers, 12 supported City, 4 supported Royals,
2 supported Hoppers and 6 supported United.
Draw and label a percentage pie chart for the data.

Unit 9.3

6 Sketch scatter graphs that show:
  a strong positive correlation
  b weak negative correlation
  c no correlation.

Unit 9.4

7 This data gives the marks for a group of students in two tests out of 20.

Student	A	B	C	D	E	F	G	H	I	J	K	L	M	N
French	14	12	6	11	18	15	9	17	16	20	14	8	18	13
History	16	10	6	14	12	14	10	18	12	18	10	5	14	8

  a Draw a scatter graph for the data.
  b Describe any correlation shown by the graph.
  c Draw a line of best fit on your graph.
  d A student scored 19 in French but was absent for the History test.
  Use the line of best fit to estimate a score for this student in History.

Unit 9.4

8 a Show the data for the scores in French on a cumulative frequency graph.
  b Use your graph to estimate the median score in French.
  c Give an estimate of the upper quartile score, the lower quartile score and the interquartile range.

Unit 9.5

9 a Show the data for the French and History tests on a stem-and-leaf plot.
  b On the stem-and-leaf plot show the median score in History.

Unit 9.6

10 This data shows the marks for a group in a test.
   14, 16, 11, 8, 20, 15, 17, 9, 11, 13, 12, 19, 18, 14, 15, 17, 13
   10, 17, 14, 8, 14, 20, 14, 16, 13, 14, 17, 14, 9, 7, 14
   a What is the mode and range for the data?
   b Calculate the mean for the set of data.
   c Find the median value for the data.
   d What is the interquartile range for the data?

Unit 9.7

11 A data set has a range of 38.62. The greatest value in the set is 141.08. Calculate the smallest value in the set.

Unit 9.7

12 A data set has a mean of 83.42. The total for the set is 172 846.24.
How many pieces of data are in the set?

Review

Unit 9.7

13 You are a player short on your darts team.
You have to choose between Ravi and Jade with this data.

	Recent points scored
Jade	52, 63, 44, 38, 76, 90, 120, 46, 58, 87, 100, 82
Ravi	56, 34, 58, 48, 65, 72, 81, 78, 80, 64, 65, 59

Which player would you choose and why?

Unit 9.8

14 These are estimates of one minute by students.

Time (s)	40–44	45–49	50–54	55–59	60–64	65–69
Frequency	7	12	14	16	18	15

a Estimate the range and mean for the data.
b Estimate the median for the data.
c Draw a cumulative frequency graph for the data.
d Draw a frequency polygon for the data.

Unit 9.9

10 Experiments and Probability

10.1 Simple probability

▶ Any probability can be shown in a scale 0 to 1:

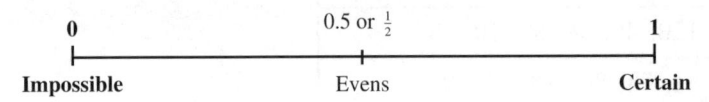

```
0                0.5 or 1/2              1
|───────────────────┼───────────────────|
Impossible         Evens              Certain
```

▶ An event with an **evens** chance of happening is just as likely to happen as not happen.

An event can have different **outcomes**.

For example.

There are six possible outcomes from the roll of a dice.

   1, 2, 3, 4, 5 or 6.

> Rolling the dice is an **event**.
> The number on the dice is an **outcome**.

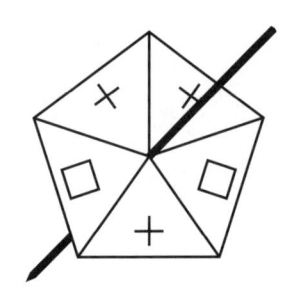

▶ Some outcomes are **equally likely**.
For example, getting a 6 or getting a 4 are equally likely outcomes.

▶ Other outcomes are **not equally likely.**
For example, getting an even number has 3 chances (2, 4 or 6) but getting a number less than 3 has only 2 chances (1 or 2).

▶ Taking something **at random** means picking so that every item has an equal chance of being picked.

▶ When outcomes are equally likely you can calculate probabilities.

Example This five-sided spinner has sides of equal length. Calculate the probability that it will land on a cross.

There are 5 sides and each side is equally likely.
(They are all of equal lengths).

The probability of the spinner landing on any one side is '1 out of 5' or $\frac{1}{5}$

But there are 3 crosses.
So the probability of the spinner landing on a cross is $\frac{3}{5}$.

▶ The total of all the probabilities in an event is 1 (providing the outcomes do not affect each other).
For example, for the spinner above the probability of a cross is $\frac{3}{5}$ and the probability of a square is $\frac{2}{5}$ so $\frac{3}{5} + \frac{2}{5} = 1$.
Similarly, the probability of **not** landing on a cross is $1 - \frac{3}{5} = \frac{2}{5}$.

Exercise 10.1A

1 Give examples of real events with a probability of:
   a less than an 0.5   **b** zero   **c** about evens

2 Give a probability of 0.2, 0.4, 0.6 or 0.8 to each of these.
   Explain your reasons.
   a The next person you meet will be left-handed.
   b A man over 60 will be balding.
   c A computer will crash when you are using it.
   d A letter will be sent by First Class mail.
   e It will rain tomorrow.
   f A maths text book will be less than 1 cm thick.

3 Alison throws a dart at a dartboard.
   Some of the outcomes are that she scores 20, 4, 50 or 60.
   Are these outcomes equally likely? Explain your answer.

4 Which of these is picking at random?
   If you think it is not explain why not.
   a Spinning a coin to decide who goes first in a game.
   b Picking who washes up from the colour of people's shoes.
   c You need a painter. You use a pin in the painter's section of Yellow Pages.
   d You need to pick a letter of the alphabet at random.
   You open a book and stick a pin in the page.
   You choose the letter it lands on.

5 Mike says that the wind could either blow from the North, the West, the East or the South. He says that the probability of it blowing from the North is therefore $\frac{1}{4}$. Why is he wrong?

6 A box has six identical shaped blocks in it.
   Three blocks are red, two are green and one is yellow.
   A block is picked out at random.
   Calculate the probability, as a fraction in its lowest terms, that it is:
   a red   **b** yellow   **c** green
   d blue   **e** not red   **f** a colour

7 This shows the shapes in a bag. A shape is picked at random.
   Give the probability that it is:
   a a square   **b** a circle
   c a triangle   **d** not a square
   e an equilateral triangle
   f a right-angled triangle

Exercise 10.1B

1 Sasha says that the probability of him being ill this winter is 0 because he is never ill. Why is this not true?

2 Give an estimate (as a decimal) of the probability that:
   a A person picked at random will cycle to work.
   b A ship will hit an iceberg on its maiden voyage.
   c A pupil will eat in the canteen today.
   d A teacher picked at random in your school will be female.
   e A vegetarian will eat beef today.
   f A cat will be sleeping when it is next seen.

3 A 1 to 10 dice is spun. Are these outcomes equally likely:
   a a 6 or a 9
   b a prime number or an odd number
   c a square number or a multiple of 3?

4 Three runners, Chris, Dave and Afzal, run a race. Why are the probabilities: Chris wins, Dave wins, Afzal wins, not equally likely to be $\frac{1}{3}$?

5 There are six cars in a showroom: 1 red, 3 blue and 2 white.
   Why is the probability that Sally buys a red car not $\frac{1}{6}$?

6 This diagram shows the socks in a drawer.

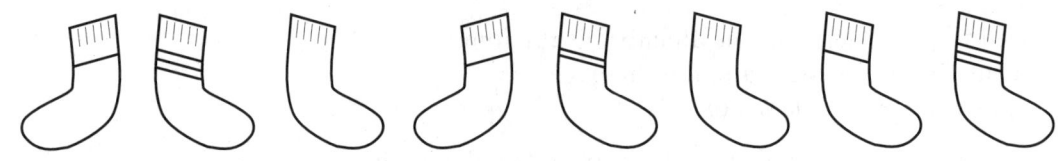

   A sock is pulled from the drawer at random.
   What is the probability that:
   a it has one stripe
   b it has two stripes
   c it has no stripes
   d it has stripes
   e it is a sock
   f there is a similar sock still in the drawer?

7 This 1 to 6 dice is rolled.
   What is the probability of getting:
   a a six
   b an even number
   c an eight
   d a number less than 5
   e a factor of 3
   f a multiple of 2
   g a number greater than 4
   h a number that is not greater than 4
   i a pattern of dots with 4 lines of symmetry.

8 Calculate the probability that a major earthquake in the year 2017 will fall:
   a on a Friday
   b on a weekday
   c on 25 December
   d in January.

10.2 Experimental probability

▶ When outcomes are not equally likely you cannot calculate a theoretical probability. You must do an experiment to estimate the probability. This is called **experimental probability**.

Example The table shows the results when this odd-shaped dice was rolled 240 times. Estimate the probability of getting C.

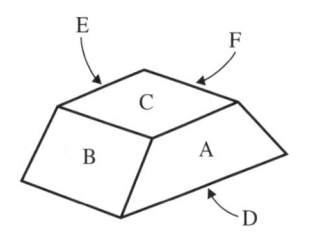

Result	Tally	Frequency
A	卌 卌 卌 卌 卌 IIII	29
B	卌	5
C	卌 卌 卌 卌 卌 卌 卌 卌 卌 卌 卌 IIII	59
D	卌 卌 卌 卌 卌 卌 卌 卌 卌 卌 卌 卌 卌 卌 卌 卌 卌 卌 卌 I	96
E	卌 卌 卌 卌 卌 卌 卌 I	36
F	卌 卌 卌	15

The experimental probability of C is $\frac{59}{240} = 0.24583$
So an estimate of the probability of C is 0.25 (to 2 dp).

> Experimental probability is usually written as a decimal fraction.

Exercise 10.2A

1 For the experiment above estimate the probability of:
   a getting E   b getting D
   c getting A   d not getting B
   Give each answer as a decimal (to 2 dp).

> See page 20 for rounding to 2 dp

2 If you rolled the die 50 times, roughly how many times would you expect to get C? Explain your answer.

3 If you were to roll the same die 180 times estimate how many times D would come up.

4 A bag has an unknown number of beads in it.
These are the results of an experiment when Mandy pulls a bead out of the bag at random then replaces it.

Colour	Red	Blue	Green	Yellow
Frequency	120	45	75	80

Estimate the probability that in her next draw from the bag Mandy will pull out:

a a red bead   **b** a green bead   **c** a blue bead
d a yellow bead   **e** a bead that is not yellow.

Exercise 10.2B

Choose one of the experiments to do.

Experiment 1
Roll an empty match box 100 times.
a Which type of face do you predict it will land on least often? Predict the probability of this happening.
b Roll the box 100 times and record the type of face that it lands on uppermost.
c From your results give an estimate of the probability of landing on each type of face.
d If you did the experiment 1 000 000 times what effect do you think this would have on your results?

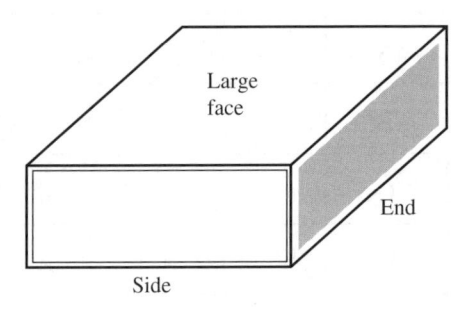

Experiment 2
Test a biased coin by spinning it on a book.

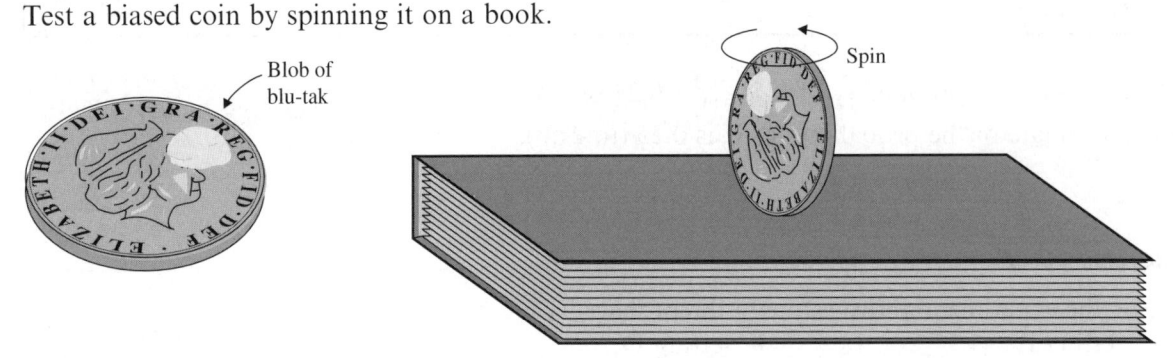

a Make a biased coin by fixing a blob of blu-tak or plasticine on the heads side.
b Which side do you predict will come up most often?
c Decide how you will record your results and how many times you will spin the coin.
d Do the experiment and record your results.
e Give estimates of the probabilities of getting a head or a tail.

10.3 Relative frequency

▶ In cases where outcomes are not equally likely **relative frequency** may be used as an estimate of probability. For example, when finding the probability that a train will arrive on time.

▶ Relative frequency uses data from what has happened before and is usually written as a decimal.

Example This table shows the punctuality of trains arriving at Reading station on one day.
a Estimate the probability that a train will be on time.
b Estimate how many trains out of an annual total of 138 000 will arrive on time.

Punctuality	Number
On time	452
< 5 mins late	185
5–15 mins late	86
> 15 mins late	17

a There were 740 trains in total and 452 were on time so the probability of a train being on time is $\frac{452}{740} = 0.61$ (to 2 dp).
b In a year $138\,000 \times 0.61 \approx 84\,000$ (to 2 sf) trains will arrive on time.

Exercise 10.3A

1 In the train example above, estimate:
   a the probability that a train will be 5 or more minutes late
   b the number of trains per year that will be 5 or more minutes late.

2 Fernando plays 64 tennis matches and wins only 25 of them.
   a What is the relative frequency that he wins?
   b Give the relative frequency that he loses.

3 The police calculated that, out of a survey of 900 cars, the relative frequency of a car breaking the speed limit was about 0.234.
   a Estimate the probability that a car will **not** be breaking the limit.
   b Roughly how many cars in the survey were speeding?

Exercise 10.3B

1 Gregor Mendel crossed plants with short stems with plants with long stems and got 787 plants with long stems and 277 with short stems. What is the relative frequency of getting a plant with a short stem?

Note that the answer is not 0.35.

2 The relative frequency of a sunny day in October is about 0.226. How many days in October would you expect to be sunny?

3 A survey asked people to choose from a list the breakfast they had eaten. 128 said they had a cooked breakfast, 264 had cereal only, and 13 said they had eaten nothing.
Give the relative frequency of each category on the list.

10.4 Sample space diagrams

▶ You can list combined outcomes on a **sample space diagram**.

Example
a Show the outcomes from rolling a dice and spinning a coin on a sample space diagram.
b Find the probability of getting a head and an even number.

a
	H	H,1	H,2	H,3	H,4	H,5	H,6
Outcomes of coin	T	T,1	T,2	T,3	T,4	T,5	T,6
		1	2	3	4	5	6

Outcomes of dice

A sample space diagram is a clear and organised way to set out the combined outcomes.

b This shows that there are 12 possible combined outcomes. 3 of these outcomes give a head and an even number (H2, H4 and H6). So the probability of scoring a head and an even number is $\frac{3}{12} = \frac{1}{4}$.

Exercise 10.4A

1 a Copy and complete the sample space diagram for spinning the spinner twice.

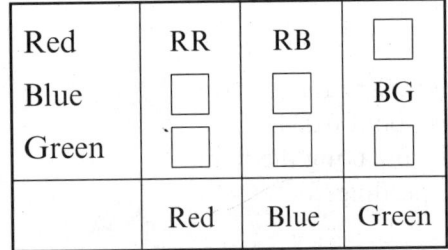

Colour on 1st spin	Red	RR	RB	
	Blue			BG
	Green			
		Red	Blue	Green

Colour on 2nd spin

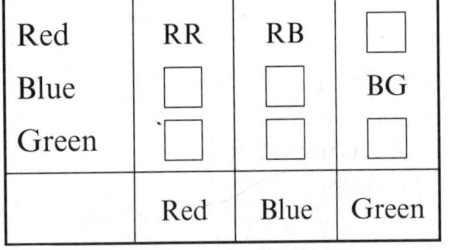

b How many outcomes are there?
c What is the probability of getting the same colour on both spins?
d Give the probability that the colours will be different.

Suppose the spinner had 12 different sections.
e How many outcomes would there be now?
f What would be the probability now of getting the same colour on both spins?

Now imagine that the spinner has n different sections.
g What is the probability now of getting the same colour on both spins?
h What is the probability that the colours will be different?

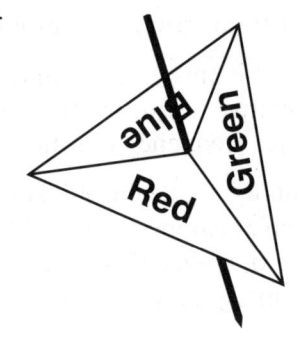

2 a Draw a sample space diagram to show the outcomes of spinning these two spinners.

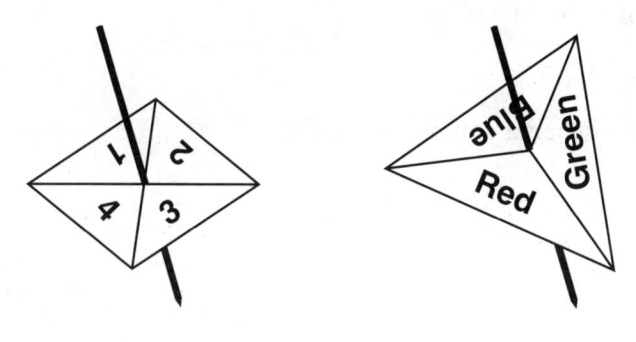

Spinner A

Spinner B

b Calculate the probability of getting:
  i blue and a factor of 6
  ii a colour and a 4
  iii a colour that is not blue and a number that is not a multiple of 2.

Exercise 10.4B

1 a Draw a sample space diagram to show the outcomes when you roll a red 1 to 6 dice and a blue 1 to 6 dice.
  b Ring each outcome that gives a total score of 9.
  c How many outcomes give a total score of 9?
  d Calculate the probability of scoring a total of 9 in one roll of the two dice.

2 A five-faced spinner has the numbers 2, 3, 4, 6 and 8 on its faces. The spinner is spun twice.
  a Draw a sample space diagram to show the combined outcomes.
  b Ring those pairs with a product of 24.
  c What is the probability of getting a product of 24 when you spin the spinner twice?
  d What is the probability that of getting a total of 6 when you spin the spinner twice?

3 Why is a sample space diagram not helpful for showing three dice being rolled?

4 A dice has two red faces, two blue faces and two yellow faces. It is rolled twice.
Using a sample space diagram to help find the probability that in the two rolls it will show:
  a two red faces
  b two faces of the same colour
  c two faces of different colours
  d a red and a yellow face
  e a blue face and a face that is not red
  f at least one red face
  g at most one blue face.

10.5 Tree diagrams

▶ Another way to show outcomes is using a **tree diagram**.

Example
Use a tree diagram to show the outcomes when a coin is spun twice.

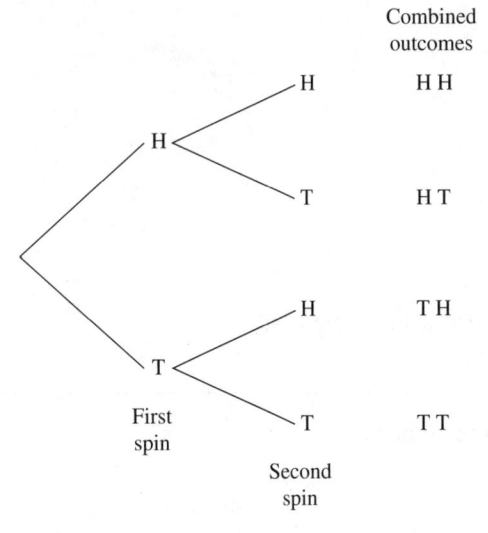

```
                         Combined
                         outcomes
              H          H H
         H <
              T          H T

              H          T H
         T <
              T          T T
    First    Second
    spin     spin
```

Each branch shows one outcome.
You follow a route to find the combined outcomes.

Exercise 10.5A

1 a In the tree diagram above how many combined outcomes are there?
  b How many combined outcomes show different faces?
  c What is the probability of getting different faces in two spins of a coin?

2 Copy and complete this tree diagram for two spins of this spinner.

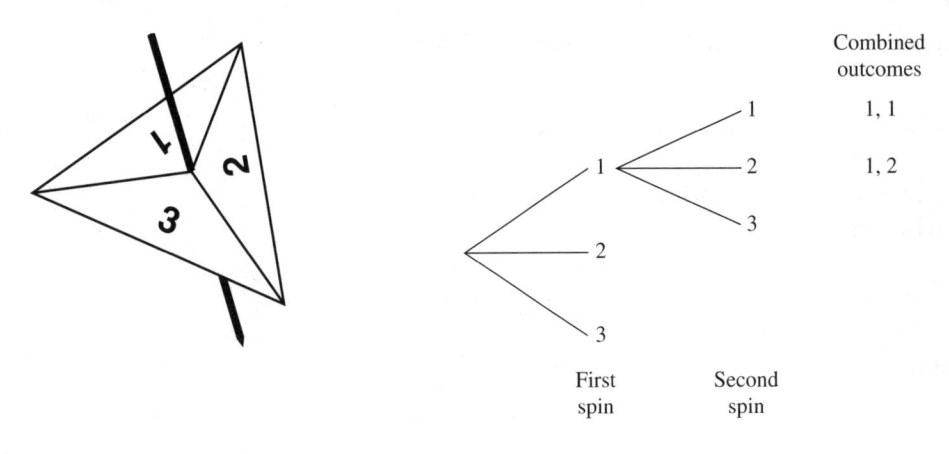

```
                              Combined
                              outcomes
                    1         1, 1
              1 <   2         1, 2
                    3
         <    2
              3
        First    Second
        spin     spin
```

Exercise 10.5B

1. A four-sided dice (numbered 1 to 4) is rolled and a coin is spun. Draw a tree diagram to show the combined outcomes.

2. Why would a tree diagram not be a good way to show the results from rolling a 1 to 6 dice twice?

3. On her way to work Simone either has a coffee or a tea. On her way home she either has a coffee, a cola or a beer. Use a tree diagram to show Simone's choices of drinks over the day.

4. A bus can either arrive early, late or on time.
   a Are these three outcomes equally likely?
   b Draw a tree diagram to show the arrival of a red bus and a blue bus.

10.6 Probabilities from two events*

▶ To calculate the probability of an outcome after two events the probabilities of each separate event are multiplied.

Two spinners. A has four equal sections with ■ ■ ▲ ◆

B has five equal sections with ■ ▲ ▲ ✢ ✢

Example

The two spinners A and B are spun. Draw a tree diagram to show the outcomes and give the probability of getting:

a two ▲'s   **b** two of the same symbol.

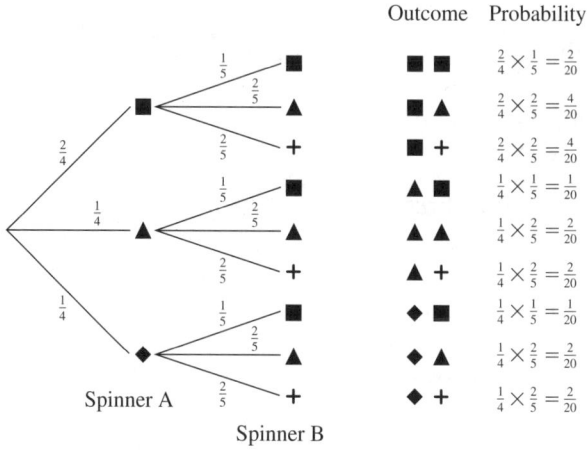

a The probability of two ▲'s is $\frac{1}{4} \times \frac{2}{5} = \frac{2}{20} = \frac{1}{10}$.

b The outcomes that give two the same are:

■ ■: probability $\frac{2}{20}$ and ▲ ▲: probability $\frac{2}{20}$

so the total probability is $\frac{2}{20} + \frac{2}{20} = \frac{4}{20} = \frac{1}{5}$.

Each branch of the tree diagram shows a probability. For any route along the branches the probabilities are multiplied. Do not simplify the fractions until the end.

Exercise 10.6A

1. For the example on page 251 what is the probability of:
   a at least one ✢
   b at least one ▲
   c an outcome that does not include a ■?

2. A fair coin is spun, then spun again.
   a Complete the tree diagram to show the outcomes and probabilities.
   b Calculate the probability of getting:
      i two heads
      ii two faces that are different.

3. There are three shirts in a drawer, two red and one blue. In a wardrobe are five ties, three blue and two red. A shirt is picked at random from the drawer and a tie from the wardrobe.
   a Draw a tree diagram to show the colour outcomes and probabilities.
   b Use your diagram to calculate the probability of picking:
      i a red shirt and a red tie
      ii a blue shirt and a blue tie
      iii a red shirt and a blue tie
      iv a shirt and tie of different colours.

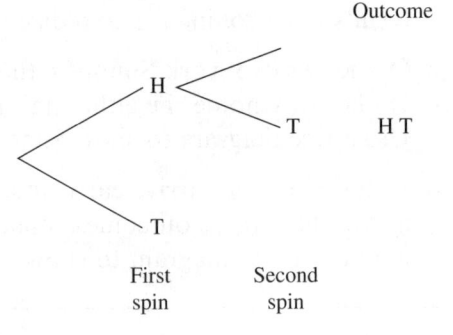

Exercise 10.6B

1. Spinner A has three equal sections with the numbers 4, 5, 6 on each one.
   Spinner B also has three equal sections with the numbers 1, 2, 3.
   a Complete the tree diagram to show the outcomes and probabilities.
   b Calculate the probability of getting a total score of:
      i 5   ii 6   iii 7   iv 8   v 9

2. A fair dice has two red faces, one blue face and three green faces. It is rolled twice and the outcomes in terms of colour are recorded.
   a Draw a tree diagram to show the colour outcomes from the two throws. Show the probabilities on each branch.
   b Calculate the probability of getting in the two rolls:
      i two red faces
      ii two blue faces
      iii two green faces
      iv a red then a green face
      v a red and a green face in any order
      vi two faces of the same colour
      vii at least one green face.

3 At station A, a train is late 12% of the time. At the return station B, a train is late 15% of the time.
Alex leaves for work at station A and returns home from station B.
  a Draw a tree diagram to show the probabilities that his trains leave on time or are late.
  b Calculate the probability that at least one of Alex's trains is late.

10.7 Dependent and independent events*

▶ A **dependent event** depends on what has happened before. For example if an item is picked from a bag and not replaced before another one is picked then the second pick depends on what happened first time.

Example A bag contains 2 bronze coins and 3 silver coins. Draw a tree diagram to show the effect of picking twice from the bag when:
a the first coin is replaced   **b** the first coin is not replaced.

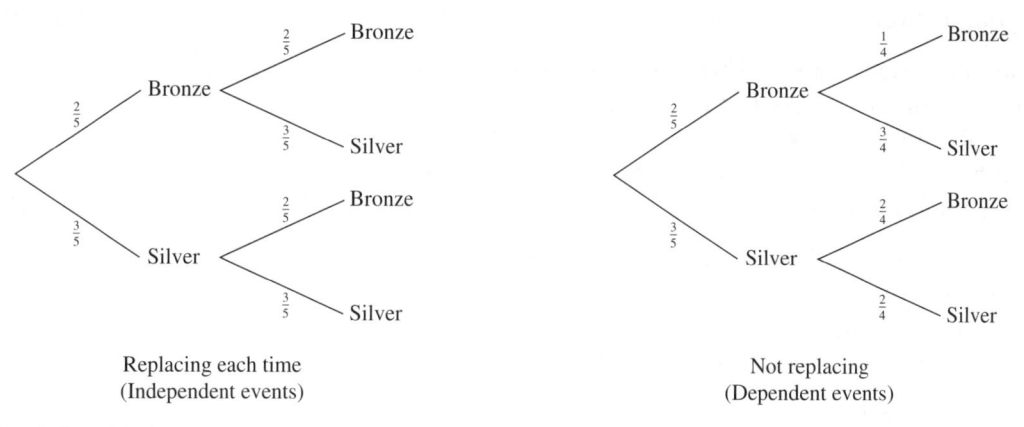

Replacing each time
(Independent events)

Not replacing
(Dependent events)

Exercise 10.7A

1 Calculate the probability of picking two bronze coins when the first coin is:
  a replaced   **b** not replaced.

2 When the coins above are not replaced calculate the probability of picking two coins of different metals.

3 A bag contains 3 lime sweets, 4 tangerine and 1 cherry.
Amy takes a sweet at random, pops it in her mouth, then offers the bag to Kate who takes one sweet.
  a Draw a tree diagram to show the probabilities and outcomes.
  b Calculate the probability that they pick a sweet of the same colour.

Exercise 10.7B

1 A bowl contains 4 apples, a pear and 2 bananas.
  Mustapha takes one fruit at random then Aiden takes one.
  a Draw a tree diagram to show the probabilities and outcomes.
  b Calculate the probability that both men take:
    i a banana   **ii** an apple   **iii** either a pear or an apple or both.

2 There are 8 red straws, 6 green, 3 blue and 5 yellow straws in a pot. A straw is picked, not replaced and a second is picked at random. Calculate the probability that:
  a both straws are green   **b** neither straw is red
  c the straws are of the same colour
  d at least one straw is blue.

Revision exercise 10   *Review*

1 Give an example of a real event with a probability of less than 0.5.   *Unit 10.1*

2 Are both players in a tennis match equally likely to win?
  Explain your answer.   *Unit 10.1*

3 A bag contains nine counters. Three are blue, four red and two white. A counter is picked at random.
  Give the probability of picking:
  a a red counter   **b** a white counter
  c a counter that is not red.   *Unit 10.1*

4 Give an estimate (decimal) of the probability that:
  a A cat will fly a plane tomorrow.
  b A student will eat chips today.
  c A person picked at random will wear a digital watch.   *Unit 10.2*

5 A 0 to 9 dice is rolled.
  What is the probability of rolling:
  a an even number   **b** a prime number   **c** a multiple of 4
  d a perfect number   **e** less than 5   **f** more than 7.   *Unit 10.2*

6 A biased dice is rolled 200 times.
  This data gives the results.

Score	1	2	3	4	5	6
Frequency	28	31	27	58	33	23

  For this experiment estimate the probability of:
  a scoring 2   **b** scoring 4
  c scoring less than 3   **d** scoring more than 4   *Unit 10.2*

Review

7 If this same dice were rolled 500 times how many times would you expect to score:
  a a 4
  b less than 4
  c an even number
  d more than 2.

Unit 10.2

8 This data is for buses arriving at the terminus one day.

Minutes late	0	< 5	5–15	> 15
Frequency	36	122	54	38

Estimate the probability that a bus will be:
  a on time
  b between 5 and 15 minutes late.
  Each year 77 480 buses arrive at the terminus.
  c Estimate how many buses in a year will be on time.
  d Estimate how many buses in a year will be less than fifteen minutes late. Explain your answer.

Unit 10.3

9 A 0 to 6 dice and a four-sided spinner are used together.
  The spinner has sides of red, blue, yellow and green.
  Both the dice and the spinner are fair.
  a Make a sample space diagram to show all possible outcomes.
  Give the probability of getting:
  b a red and a 5
  c blue and more than 2
  d yellow and an odd number
  e 5 and not red
  f blue and no more than 4
  g 2 or 3 and not blue

Unit 10.4

10 A fair coin and spinner are used together.
  The spinner has sides of white, black, red, blue, and green.
  The coin is spun first.
  a Draw a tree diagram to show all possible outcomes.
  b What is the probability of a tail and white?
  c Find the probability of a head and not blue.

Unit 10.5

11 Two fair spinners are spun.
  Spinner A has sides of: $+, +, \div, \times, \times, \times$
  Spinner B has sides of: A, B, C
  a Draw a tree diagram to show the outcomes.
  b Mark the probabilities on the tree diagram.
  Give the probability of getting:
  c $\div$ and C
  d $+$ and B.

Unit 10.5

12 Explain the difference between dependent and independent events.
  You might need a diagram or to use an example.

13 A bag contains 12 dice: 3 red, 4 blue and 5 yellow.
Give the probability of picking a yellow and blue dice if:
a the first dice is replaced
b the first dice is not replaced.
Give the probability of picking two red dice if:
c the first dice is replaced
d the first dice is not replaced.
Connor picked blue followed by blue.
He did not replace a dice.
e Find the probability that he would not get blue and blue.
Rina picked red followed by yellow without replacing.
f Calculate the probability of doing this.

Review

Unit 10.6

14 A lottery machine contains 50 balls:
10 red, 10 white, 10 green, 10 yellow and 10 blue.
Balls are not replaced after being picked.
Calculate the probability of getting 5 balls in this order.
a Red, blue, green, red and blue.
b White, green, blue, blue and blue.
c Red, red, red, blue and blue.
d Green, yellow, green, red and yellow.
e Five balls all the same colour.

Unit 10.7

Investigation

Dicey money

Your group has to run a stall to make money for the school.

Invent a dice game where you will be sure to make money.
But the player must think that they have a reasonable chance to win.

How much will you charge?
Predict how much your stall might make from 300 players.

Explain your game and your expected profits using probability.

Test your game and write a report of your findings.

After the test, explain any changes you decide to make to the game.

SATS Paper 1 – Non Calculator – Time 1 hour

1. | 6 | 0.6 | −3 | 4 | −6 | 0.4 | 3 | −4 | $\frac{1}{3}$ |

   Using only numbers from these cards copy and complete.

   a □ × □ = −1.2
   b □ + □ + □ = 4
   c (□ ÷ □) + □ = 7
   d (6 + □)(2 − □) = 12
   e $8^□ = 2$ (5 marks)

2. For a garden trellis, rods are welded into triangles which are then fixed together horizontally with bolts.

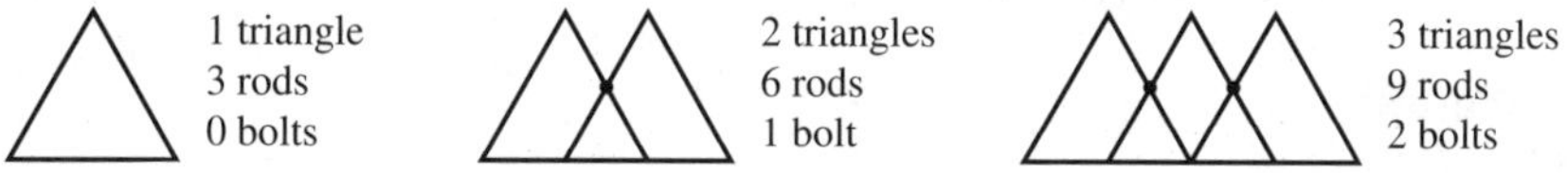

   1 triangle, 3 rods, 0 bolts
   2 triangles, 6 rods, 1 bolt
   3 triangles, 9 rods, 2 bolts

   a When 10 bolts are used in a trellis how many rods are used?   (1 mark)
   b A trellis has *n* triangles. How many bolts are used?   (1 mark)
   c A trellis uses *r* rods. Write an expression for the number of bolts. (1 mark)
   d When 45 rods are used *b* bolts are needed.
      Write an expression in *b* for the number of rods, and solve it to find *b*. (2 marks)
   e Stephen feels the trellis needs bolts at the bottom as well.
      The sequence of bolts he uses is 1, 3, 5, 7, ...
      Write an expression for the number of bolts he uses for *n* triangles. (2 marks)

3. Mike buys square tiles of side 25 cm and regular octagons of width 60 cm to tile a floor.

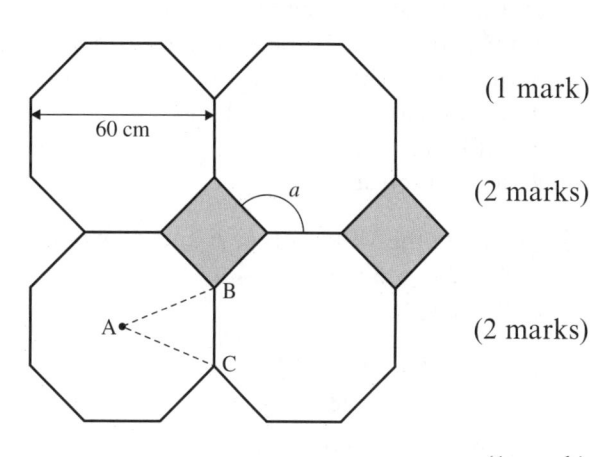

   a Calculate the size of angle *a*.   (1 mark)
   b Point A is at the centre of the octagon.
      By finding the area of triangle ABC, calculate the area of an octagon. (2 marks)
   c Mike uses this tile pattern, without cutting, to cover a floor 3 metres square.
      What area of floor can he not cover by tiles?   (2 marks)
   d Sadie buys similar regular octagon tiles but they are 30 cm wide. How does the area of one of these tiles compare with the area of Mikes octagon tiles? (1 mark)

4 These shapes are made with bars of different lengths.

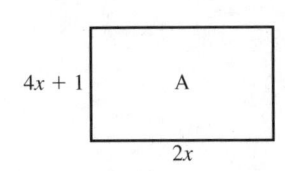

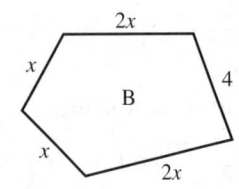

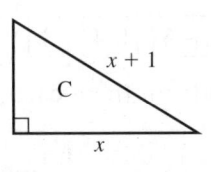

a Write an expression for the perimeter of rectangle A. (1 mark)
b Write an expression for the area of rectangle A. (1 mark)
c The perimeter of pentagon B is 22 units.
 Write an equation using x and simplify it.
 Solve the equation and find the value of x. (1 mark)
d Use Pythagoras' Rule to help you write an expression for
 the length of the missing side of Triangle C.
 Simplify your expression as much as you can. (2 marks)

5 This diagram shows the graphs of
$y = 3x + 4$ and $y = 32 - 4x$. 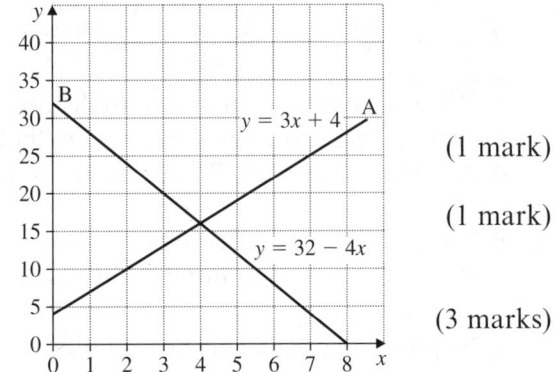
 a Another equation gives a graph that is
  parallel to Graph A but 5 units lower.
  What is this equation? (1 mark)
 b Explain how the graph of $y - 2x = 4$
  differs from graph A. (1 mark)
 c Solve this pair of simultaneous equations.
  $y = 32 - 4x$
  $y = 3x + 4$ (3 marks)
 d What point on the graph corresponds to
  this solution? (1 mark)

6 There are 3 red sweets, 4 blue sweets and
 5 green sweets in a bag.
 A sweet is picked at random, replaced
 and then a second sweet is picked.
 Choose one of the labels for the probability that:
 a the first sweet is either blue or green (1 mark)
 b the second sweet is not blue (1 mark)
 c both sweets are red (1 mark)
 d both sweets are not red. (1 mark)

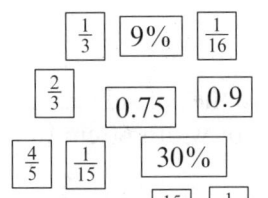

Labels: $\frac{1}{3}$, 9%, $\frac{1}{16}$, $\frac{2}{3}$, 0.75, 0.9, $\frac{4}{5}$, $\frac{1}{15}$, 30%, 25%, $\frac{15}{16}$, $\frac{1}{9}$

7 Calculate the values of A, B and C when $g = {^-}4$
 a $A = 2g^2 - 60$ (1 mark)
 b $B = 2g(g^2 + 3)$ (1 mark)
 c $C = \dfrac{g(g+5)(g-6)}{(2-5g)}$ (1 mark)
 d Simplify this expression $\dfrac{12a^2b^3}{6a^2b}$ (1 mark)

8 This table gives the amount per hour earned by six people.

Alison	Barry	Clare	Dave	Ellen	Fred
£12		£23	£14	£16	£99

The mean wage is £31 per hour.
   a How much does Barry earn per hour? (1 mark)
   b Explain why the mean is a poor measure of average to use in this situation. (1 mark)
   c What is the median rate per hour? (1 mark)
   d Suppose wage rates for all six people are increased by £5.76 an hour. What effect does this have on the mean? (1 mark)
   e If wage rates were all multiplied by 1.6 what effect would this have on the median? (1 mark)

9 Steve draws this shape where lines AG and BH are parallel, AB = 4 cm, AE = 1.2 cm, EF = 1.3 cm and BC = 3.5 cm.
   a Calculate the size of angle BEF. (1 mark)
   b Calculate angle DFG. (1 mark)
   c Calculate the sum of the interior angles of the trapezium ABCF. (1 mark)
   d Calculate the area of trapezium ABCF. (1 mark)

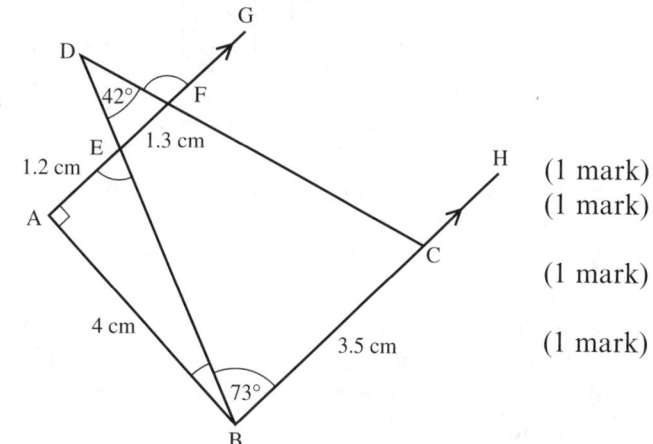

10 This cuboid has an unknown height h.
   a Express the area of Face A in terms of h. (1 mark)
   b Write and simplify an expression in h for the total surface area of the cuboid (1 mark)
   c The cuboid has a surface area of 148 cm². Calculate its height, h. (1 mark)
   d A similarly shaped larger cuboid has a volume 8 times as large. Give the dimensions of the larger cuboid. (1 mark)

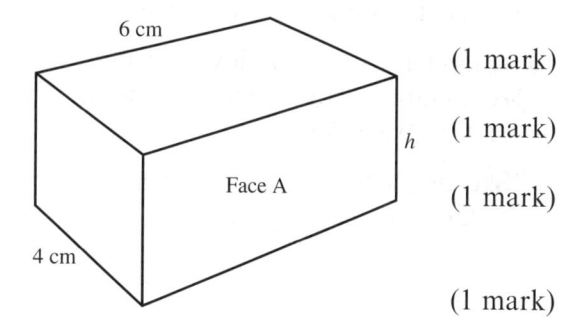

11 Using only this set of numbers:

   65×10^5 6500×10^{-1} 6.5×10^3 650×10^{-2}
   0.065×10^2 650×10^2 65×10^1 0.065×10^7

   a Which number is written in standard form? (1 mark)
   b Which is the smallest number? (1 mark)
   c Which is the largest number? (1 mark)
   d Which two numbers are of equal value? (1 mark)
   e Write the number 0.065×10^7 in standard form. (1 mark)

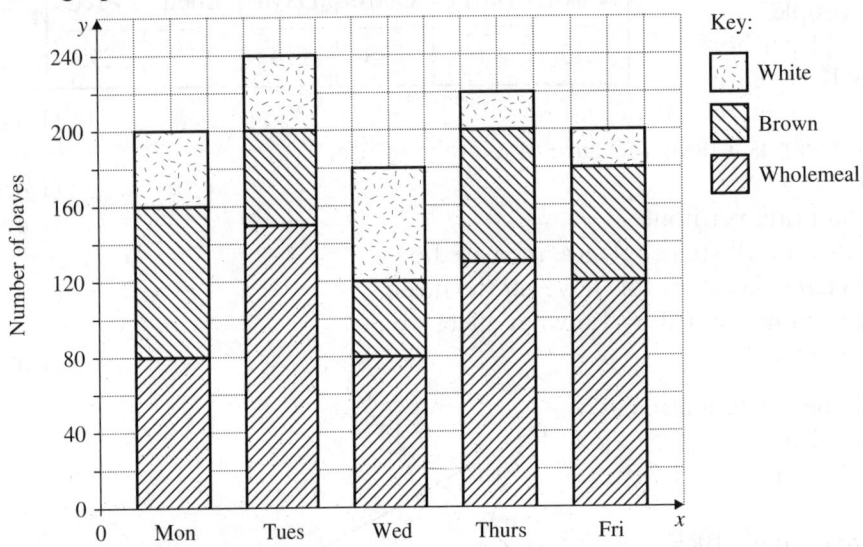

12 This graph shows sales of three types of bread over a week.

[Bar chart showing stacked sales of White, Brown, and Wholemeal bread from Monday to Friday. Key: White, Brown, Wholemeal. Y-axis: Number of loaves (0 to 240).]

Approximate values from the graph:
- Mon: Wholemeal 0–80, Brown 80–160, White 160–200
- Tues: Wholemeal 0–150, Brown 150–200, White 200–240
- Wed: Wholemeal 0–80, Brown 80–120, White 120–180
- Thurs: Wholemeal 0–130, Brown 130–200, White 200–220
- Fri: Wholemeal 0–120, Brown 120–180, White 180–200

a In its simplest form, what fraction of those loaves sold on Monday were brown bread? (1 mark)

b In its simplest form, give the ratio white : brown : wholemeal for Friday. (1 mark)

c What percentage of the loaves sold in total over Tuesday, Wednesday and Thursday were brown bread? (1 mark)

d The shop owner decides to draw a pie chart of the sales of bread on Tuesday.
What angle should she use to represent wholemeal bread? (1 mark)

13 A tap has a constant flow of water coming from it.
A container with a circular cross-section is held under the tap and the water level is recorded against time to give this graph.

Sketch what you think the profile of the container looks like. (3 marks)

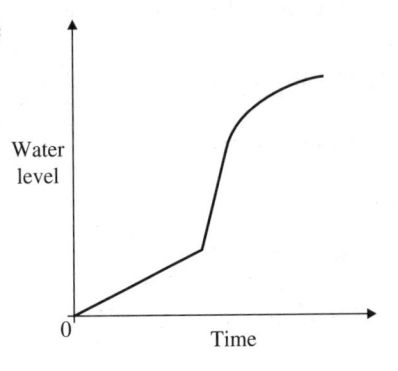

[Graph of Water level vs Time: curve rises gradually, then has a short steep section, then rises gradually again and levels off.]

(Total 62 marks)

SATS Paper 2 – Calculator allowed – Time 1 hour

1. When Simon makes a fruit punch he mixes grape juice, orange juice and apple juice in the ratio 4 : 6 : 12.
   a. For the school dance Simon buys 18 litres of orange juice.
      How many litres of punch does he make altogether? (1 mark)
   b. For Alison's party he makes 44 litres of punch.
      How many litres of grape juice does he use? (1 mark)
   c. If Simon were to use 27 litres of Apple juice, how many litres of grape juice and orange juice would he use? (1 mark)
   d. What percentage of Simon's mix is grape juice?
      Give your answer correct to 1 dp. (1 mark)

2. The commands in LOGO for drawing this pentagon from point C anticlockwise are:

   FD 40, LT 90, FD 38, LT 45, FD 28, LT 90, FD 28, LT 45, FD 38, LT 90

   where FD means Forward and LT means Left.
   a. Give the LOGO commands to draw a rectangle with sides of 5.8 cm and 3 cm. (1 mark)
   b. These commands draw a shape:

   FD 40, RT 130, FD 31, RT 100, FD 31, RT 130

   Give a detailed description of the shape. (1 mark)
   c. The commands for drawing a regular hexagon of side 8 cm can be written as:

   REPEAT6(FD 80, LT60)

   Write the commands for drawing a regular pentagon of side 6 cm. (2 marks)

3. The numbers on each edge of a square are the sum of the numbers at each of its ends.
   Copy each square and write in the missing numbers. (4 marks)

   a.
   -3 — ? — 5
   7 — — -1
   ? — ? — -6

   b.
   2.6 — 5.7 — 3.1
   ? — — ?
   ? — -2 — 4.8

   c.
   $\frac{3}{4}$ — ? — $\frac{7}{8}$
   $-\frac{1}{4}$ — — ?
   $\frac{1}{2}$ — ? — $\frac{5}{8}$

   d.
   a — ? — $2(a+b)$
   $\frac{a+ab}{b}$ — — ?
   ? — $\frac{b^2+a}{b}$ — b

4 Mike calculates the diameter of a tree by measuring its girth
(the distance all round it).
He finds an oak with a girth of 1.41 metres.
  a Calculate the diameter of the oak tree in centimetres. (1 mark)
  b Mike saws horizontally through the trunk.
  What circular area of wood is exposed on the stump? (1 mark)
  c The trunk is 4.3 metres high and approximates to a cylinder.
  What volume of wood is in the tree? (1 mark)

Mike's friend uses this formula in his forestry work.

$$J = \frac{3f^2 + 2d^2}{h}$$ where f, d and h are lengths.

  d Is J in this formula a length, an area or a volume? (2 marks)

5 Clare spins this 5-sided spinner.
  a Calculate the probability that the
  spinner will land on a prime number. (1 mark)

Clare spins the spinner twice and
records the totals in this table.
  b Copy and complete the table. (1 mark)
  c Give the probability that the
  total will be 14 or more. (1 mark)

On a different occasion Clare
spins the spinner twice
and subtracts the second spin
from the first.
  d What is the probability that
  this score will be negative? (2 marks)

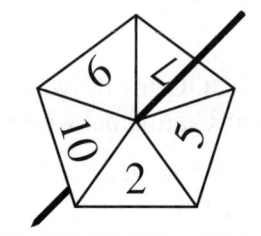

Second spin 10	12		17		
9					
7		12			
5					
2				9	
	2	5	7	9	10
		First spin			

6 At the time of writing 1 Euro € is worth 61 pence.
The French franc is fixed to the Euro at 1 Franc = 0.15€
The Finnish Markka is valued at 1€ = 5.98 Markka
  a What is £6.20 worth in Euros? (1 mark)
  b What is £1 worth in Finnish Markka? (2 marks)
  c What is 400 French francs worth in Finnish Markka? (2 marks)

7 This is a sequence of patterns that have white and black dots.

Pattern 1   Pattern 2   Pattern 3

  a How many black dots will there be in pattern 20? (1 mark)
  b Which pattern will have 31 black dots? (1 mark)
  c Which pattern will have a total of 74 dots? (1 mark)
  d How many white dots are in Pattern n? (1 mark)
  e How many black dots are in Pattern n? (1 mark)
  f Write an expression for the total number of dots in Pattern n. (1 mark)

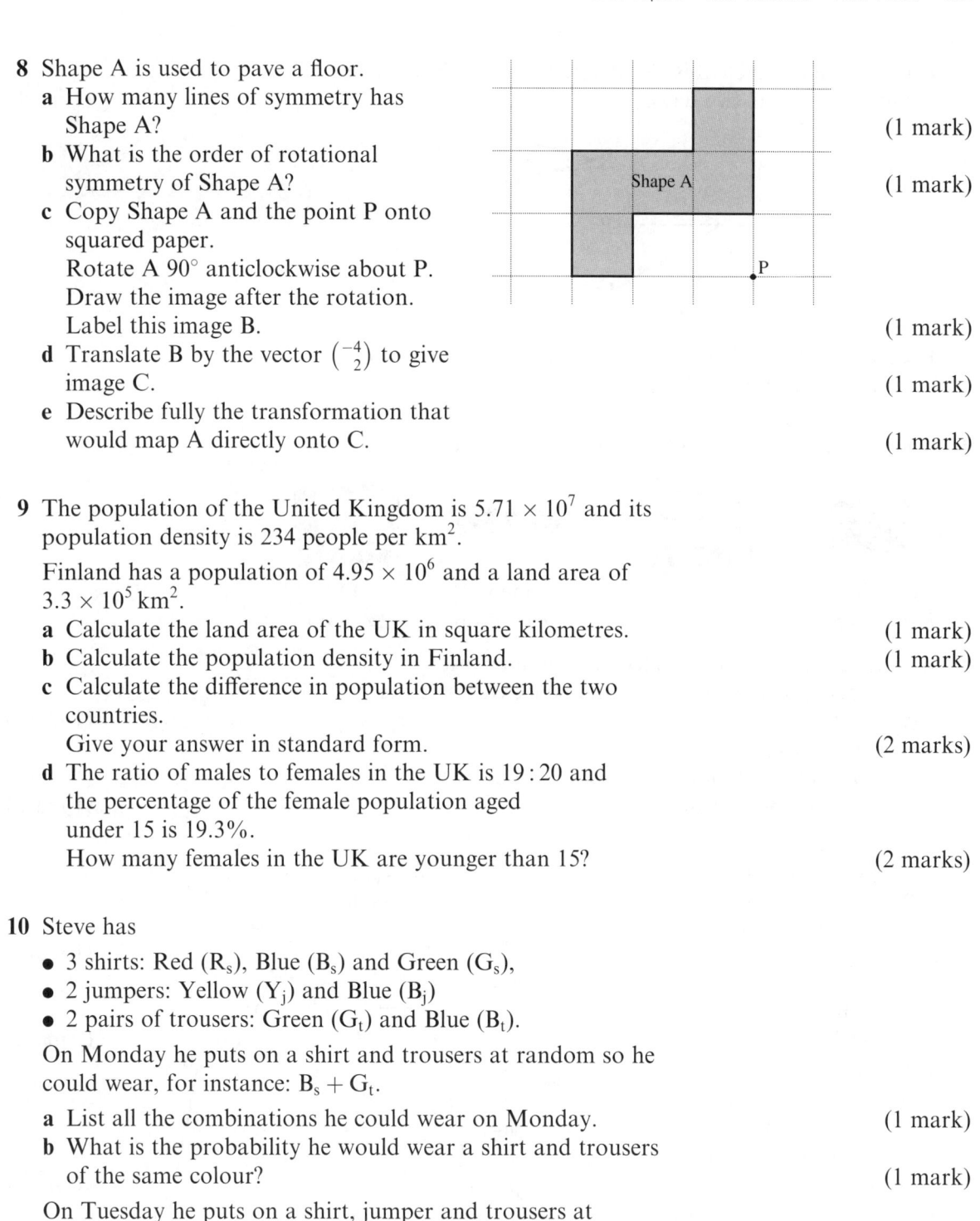

8 Shape A is used to pave a floor.
  a How many lines of symmetry has Shape A? (1 mark)
  b What is the order of rotational symmetry of Shape A? (1 mark)
  c Copy Shape A and the point P onto squared paper.
  Rotate A 90° anticlockwise about P.
  Draw the image after the rotation.
  Label this image B. (1 mark)
  d Translate B by the vector $\begin{pmatrix} -4 \\ 2 \end{pmatrix}$ to give image C. (1 mark)
  e Describe fully the transformation that would map A directly onto C. (1 mark)

9 The population of the United Kingdom is 5.71×10^7 and its population density is 234 people per km^2.

Finland has a population of 4.95×10^6 and a land area of 3.3×10^5 km^2.
  a Calculate the land area of the UK in square kilometres. (1 mark)
  b Calculate the population density in Finland. (1 mark)
  c Calculate the difference in population between the two countries.
  Give your answer in standard form. (2 marks)
  d The ratio of males to females in the UK is 19:20 and the percentage of the female population aged under 15 is 19.3%.
  How many females in the UK are younger than 15? (2 marks)

10 Steve has
  - 3 shirts: Red (R_s), Blue (B_s) and Green (G_s),
  - 2 jumpers: Yellow (Y_j) and Blue (B_j)
  - 2 pairs of trousers: Green (G_t) and Blue (B_t).

On Monday he puts on a shirt and trousers at random so he could wear, for instance: $B_s + G_t$.
  a List all the combinations he could wear on Monday. (1 mark)
  b What is the probability he would wear a shirt and trousers of the same colour? (1 mark)

On Tuesday he puts on a shirt, jumper and trousers at random.
  c List all the combinations he could wear on Tuesday. (1 mark)
  d What is the probability that Steve would wear no two items of the same colour? (2 marks)

e Copy and complete this tree diagram for the shirts Steve puts on over the two days. (1 mark)

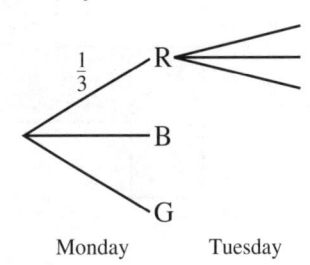

```
        1/3   R <
              
         <    B
              
              G
       Monday  Tuesday
```

f Calculate the probability that Steve puts on shirts of the same colour on both days. (2 marks)

11 These are the prices in £ of several items in a store.

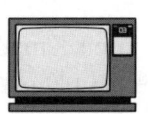

Camera	CD player	Video	TV
$b(a^3 - 205)$	$3a + 2b$	$2(a+b) + 6$	$2b^2 - 4a$

a The CD player and the video are the same price. Use this to form an equation and hence calculate the value of a. (1 mark)

b The TV costs £254. Use this information to calculate the value of b. (1 mark)

c How much does a camera cost? (1 mark)

12 This graph shows journeys that Siobhan and Mark made.

a At what time did Siobhan set off? (1 mark)

b At what speed was Siobhan travelling between A and B? (1 mark)

c Describe Siobhan's journey as fully as you can. (3 marks)

d Between which two points was Siobhan travelling most quickly? (1 mark)

e What do the points where the two graphs cross indicate? (1 mark)

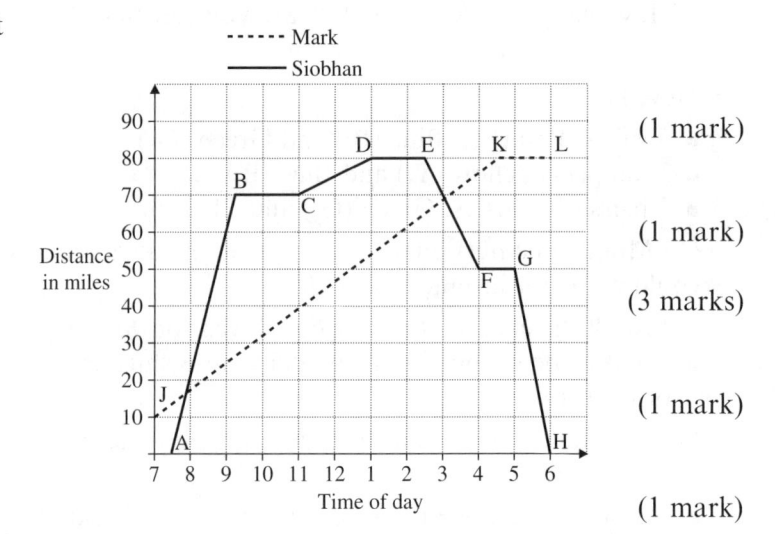

(Total 62 marks)

Index

acute angles 110
acute-angled triangles 117
addition
    decimals 53–5
    fractions 38–9
algebra, brackets in 62–4
alternate angles 110
angles 110–12
    bisecting 169–70
    in polygons 123–4
    in triangles 116–17, 119–20, 152–4
arcs 184
area
    circles 186–7
    formulae 178–79
    surface 189–90
    two-dimensional shapes 175–8
average speed 101
averages 227–32

bar charts 206
bar line graphs 209–12
bearings 113–16
BODMAS rule 34–5
brackets
    in algebra 62–4
    in equations 70
    and operations 33–5

chords 184
circles 183–7
circumference 183, 184–5
common factors 10–12
compound interest 50
compound units 163–4
congruent triangles 119, 171–3
constructions 161–95
coordinates 90–1
correlations 219
corresponding angles 110
cosine ratio 152
cube numbers 12–13
cube roots 13–14
cubic equations 71–2
cuboids, nets 179–81
cumulative frequency graphs 223–5

data
    collecting 196–9
    comparing 232–4
    grouped 234–7
    interpreting 206–41
    representing 206–41
decimals 16–18

addition 53–5
division 55–8
and fractions 18–20
multiplication 55–8
rounding 20–1
subtraction 53–5
dependent events 253–4
dependent variables 97
diameter 184
direct proportion 24–5
directed numbers 4–5
    operations 5–6
distance–time graphs 98–101
division
    decimals 55–8
    fractions 41–2
    indices 7
    integers 1–3, 30–1

edges 126–7
elevations 130–1
enlargements 144–8
equations 61–83
    with brackets 70
    with fractions 68–9
    solving 66–72
    trial and improvement method 71
equilateral triangles 117
equivalent fractions 15
equivalent ratios 23
estimations 234–6
Euler, Leonhard (1707–83) 127
events 251–4
experimental probability 245–6

faces 126–7
factorising, simple 64–6
factors 10–12
formulae 61–83, 178–9
    constructing 74–6
    subject of 76–8
    substitution 72–4
fractions 37–8
    addition 38–9
    of amounts 36–7
    comparing 16
    and decimals 18–20
    division 41–2
    in equations 68–9
    multiplication 40–1
    ordering 16
    and percentages 45
    simplifying 14–15
    subtraction 39–40

frequency diagrams 206–8
frequency graphs, cumulative 223–5
frequency polygons 236–7
frequency tables 199–202
    cumulative 223
functions 84–110

geometry 110–34
gradient 94
graphs 84–110
    distance–time 98–101
    frequency 223–5
    from sequences 88–9
    line 91–2
    linear 92–8
    of vessels 102–3
grouped data 234–39

highest common factor 10

identities 61–83
imperial units 161–3
independent events 253–4
indices
    division 7
    multiplication 7
inequalities 103–6
integers
    division 1–3, 30–1
    multiplication 1–3, 29–30
    operations 31–3
intercept 94
interquartile range 224
isometric drawings 127–9
isosceles triangles 117

kites 122

length, formulae 178–9
like terms, collecting 61–2
line of best fit 221–2
line graphs 91–2, 209–12
line symmetry 135–6
linear graphs 92–8
lines, bisecting 169–70
loci 191–3
lower quartiles 224
lowest common multiple 10

mathematical operators 31
mean 227, 229–30
    estimating 235
measures 161–95
median 224, 227, 228–9
    estimating 235–6

metric units 161–3
modal class 234
mode 227, 228
multiples 10–12
multiplication
    decimals 55–8
    fractions 40–1
    indices 7
    integers 1–3, 29–30

negative correlations 219
nets 179–183
number lines 4
numbers 1–28
    calculations 29–60

obtuse angles 110
obtuse-angled triangles 117
operations, and brackets 33–5
order of rotational symmetry (ORS) 137
outcomes 242

parallelograms 121
    area 176
patterns, sequences from 84–5
percentages
    of amounts 42–4
    decrease 47
    and fractions 45
    increase 46
    pie charts 217–18
    problems 48
perimeters, two-dimensional shapes 173–5
perpendiculars, constructing 171
pictograms 207–8
pie charts 212–18
    percentages 217–18
plane symmetry 138–9
plans 130–1
polygons
    angles 123–4
    constructing 164–5
polyhedra 126
positive correlations 219
powers *see* indices
prime factors 10–12
prime numbers 10–12
prisms, nets 182–3
probability 242–56
pyramids, nets 182–3
Pythagoras' theorem 124–6

quadratic equations 71–2
quadratic sequences 87–8
quadrilaterals 121–3
    constructing 165–9
quartiles 224–5
questionnaires 202–4

radius 183
range 230
    estimating 234–5
ratios 21–3, 51–3
    trigonometric 152–3
rectangles 121
    area 175
recurring decimals 18
reflections 139–41
reflex angles 110
relative frequency 247
rhombuses 121
right-angled triangles 118, 152–6
rotational symmetry 137
rotations 141–2
rounding 3–4
    decimals 20–1

sample space diagrams 248–9
scale drawings 148–50
scalene triangles 118
scales 148–50
scatter diagrams 219–23
second differences 87
sectors 184
segments 184
semicircles 184
sequences 84–110
    continuing 85–6
    from patterns 84–5
    graphs from 88–9
    quadratic 87–8
    rules for 86–7
shapes
    similar 150–2
    three-dimensional 126–31, 187–90
    two-dimensional 173–8
similar shapes 150–2
simple interest 49
simultaneous equations 78–80
sine ratio 152
speed 98–101
square numbers 12–13
square roots 13–14
squares 121

standard form 8–9
stem-and-leaf plots 225–7
straight line graphs 92–8
substitution, in formulae 72–4
subtraction
    decimals 53–5
    fractions 39–40
surface area, three-dimensional shapes 189–90
surveys 202
symmetry 135–9

tangent ratio 152
tangents 184
terms 84
three-dimensional shapes 126–31
    surface area 189–90
    volume 187–8
transformations 135–60
translations 143–4
trapeziums 121
    area 176
tree diagrams 250–1
trial and improvement method 71
triangles
    angles 116–17, 119–20
    area 176
    congruent 119, 171–3
    constructing 165–9
    right-angled 118, 152–6
    sides 155–6
    types of 117–19
trigonometric ratios 152–3
trigonometry 152–6
two-dimensional shapes
    area 175–8
    perimeters 173–5

units
    compound 163–4
    imperial 161–3
    metric 161–3
upper quartiles 224

variables, dependent 97
vertically opposite angles 110
vertices 126–7
vessels, graphs of 102–3
volume
    formulae 178–9
    three-dimensional shapes 187–8